Canadian
Immigration

Economic Evidence for a
Dynamic Policy Environment

Canadian Immigration

Economic Evidence for a Dynamic Policy Environment

**Ted McDonald, Elizabeth Ruddick,
Arthur Sweetman, and Christopher Worswick,** Editors

Queen's Policy Studies Series
School of Policy Studies, Queen's University
McGill-Queen's University Press
Montreal & Kingston • London • Ithaca

SCHOOL OF
Policy Studies

Publications Unit
Robert Sutherland Hall
138 Union Street
Kingston, ON, Canada
K7L 3N6
www.queensu.ca/sps/

The preferred citation for this book is:
McDonald, T., E. Ruddick, A. Sweetman, and C. Worswick, eds. 2010. *Canadian Immigration: Economic Evidence for a Dynamic Policy Environment*. Montreal and Kingston: Queen's Policy Studies Series, McGill-Queen's University Press.

Library and Archives Canada Cataloguing in Publication

Canadian immigration : economic evidence for a dynamic policy environment / edited by Ted McDonald ... [et al.].

(Queen's policy studies series)
Co-published by School of Policy Studies, Queen's University.
Includes bibliographical references.
Abstracts in English and French.
ISBN 978-1-55339-282-8 (bound).—ISBN 978-1-55339-281-1 (pbk.)

1. Immigrants—Canada—Economic conditions. 2. Immigrants—Canada—Social conditions. 3. Canada—Emigration and immigration—Economic aspects. 4. Canada—Emigration and immigration—Social aspects. 5. Canada—Emigration and immigration—Government policy. I. McDonald, James Ted II. Queen's University (Kingston, Ont.). School of Policy Studies

JV7220.C34 2010   325.71   C2010-900615-1

CONTENTS

ACKNOWLEDGEMENTS

We believe that good policy emerges from a solid foundation of evidence, and we hope that this volume of research essays provides insight that is helpful in the policy-making process. The idea for the series of books of which this is one grew out of the Metropolis Project (http://www.canada.metropolis.net/), and we are grateful to many who have been involved in it, including John Biles, Meyer Burstein, and Howard Duncan. We also thank the Metropolis Project for funding the production of this volume. Metropolis is an international network for comparative research and public policy development on migration, diversity, and immigrant integration in cities in Canada and around the world. Metropolis's third five-year funding phase (1 April 2007 to 31 March 2012) is marked by an increased focus on knowledge transfer. We hope this focus will make an important contribution to how issues surrounding immigration and diversity are approached, leading to a better Canada.

The chapters in this volume have benefited enormously from the work of many referees, translators, and others. Our thanks go to Jean Bernard, Colleen Dempsey, David Gray, Martha Justus, Stan Kustec, Christine Laporte, Jessie-Lynn MacDonald, Louis-Philippe Morin, Andrejs Skaburskis, Frances Woolley, and other anonymous referees.

For their many efforts in keeping us on track, and for much helpful guidance, we would like to thank Mark Howes and Valerie Jarus at the Queen's University School of Policy Studies Publication Unit, and copy editor Maureen Garvie.

Many of the statistical analyses in the papers in this volume were produced from Statistics Canada microdata. Thanks, therefore, go to that organization for providing the data and the research data centres where many authors accessed the data. The interpretation and opinions expressed are those of the authors and do not represent those of Statistics Canada.

Ted McDonald
Professor
Department of Economics
University of New Brunswick, Fredericton

Elizabeth Ruddick
Director General
Research and Evaluation
Citizenship and Immigration Canada

Arthur Sweetman
Professor
School of Policy Studies
Queen's University

Christopher Worswick
Associate Professor
Department of Economics
Carleton University

1

INTRODUCTION TO CURRENT CANADIAN ISSUES IN THE ECONOMICS OF IMMIGRATION

TED McDONALD, ELIZABETH RUDDICK, ARTHUR SWEETMAN, AND CHRISTOPHER WORSWICK

Les aspects économiques et sociaux de l'immigration sont au premier plan de l'actualité en matières de politiques publiques au Canada. Dans ce contexte, de nouvelles données scientifiques crédibles constituent donc un élément important. Étant donné d'une part le déclin marqué de la situation économique des immigrants au cours des dernières décennies, et d'autre part les changements importants entourant les politiques dans ce domaine, il est essentiel d'accroître nos connaissances pour créer et mettre en place de nouvelles politiques en matière d'immigration et d'intégration. Dans cette introduction, nous faisons un survol des différents articles de cet ouvrage; ils rendent comptent d'études empiriques qui permettent de mettre à jour et d'approfondir notre compréhension de différents facteurs économiques aux implications sociales certaines en matière d'immigration. Les sujets traités sont les suivants : l'intégration des immigrants au marché du travail, considérée sous divers aspects, dont l'origine ethnique et le genre; l'incidence de l'éducation chez les immigrants; le travail et le travail indépendant; le programme des travailleurs qualifiés; les travailleurs étrangers temporaires; le logement; une comparaison internationale des résultats scolaires des enfants immigrants; la fécondité; et la santé.

Economic and social issues regarding immigration are at the forefront of the Canadian policy agenda, and credible evidence is an important input into good policy-making. Given the marked decline in immigrant economic outcomes over the past few decades, and the important changes in the policy environment, expanding the evidence base for new immigration and integration policy is crucial. This introduction surveys the essays in this volume, most of which have an economics orientation. Extending and updating our understanding of selected economic and closely related social factors regarding

Canadian Immigration: Economic Evidence for a Dynamic Policy Environment, ed. T. McDonald, E. Ruddick, A. Sweetman, and C. Worswick. Montreal and Kingston: Queen's Policy Studies Series, McGill-Queen's University Press.
© 2010 The School of Policy Studies, Queen's University at Kingston. All rights reserved.

immigration, each chapter is an empirical investigation with topics addressing labour market integration, including ethnic and gender aspects; immigrant economic returns to schooling; employment and self-employment; the skilled worker program; temporary foreign workers; housing; an international comparison of immigrant children's success in school; fertility; and health.

Immigration in Canada has evolved beyond being an important economic and social policy to become a part of our national identity. This has occurred, and perhaps accelerated, over the past 40 years in an economic environment that has seen it become more difficult for new labour market entrants – both the foreign born and in many cases the Canadian born as well – to establish themselves. Public support for immigration has remained strong despite significant restructuring in the post-FTA and post-NAFTA Canadian economy and in the post-911 world. Support for immigration has also remained strong, despite numerous research studies showing deteriorating labour market performance for new immigrants to Canada since the 1970s.

The evolving response of immigration policy in light of this combination of strong public support and deteriorating economic outcomes has been aimed at facilitating the successful integration of new immigrants into the Canadian economy. Examples of policy innovations that have occurred over this period include the introduction of the business and investor categories in the late 1970s, the expansion of the share of immigrants admitted under the economic categories in the 1980s and 1990s, the points system's increased emphasis on university education in the 1990s and on official language ability in 2002 for skilled worker admission, and, more recently, new emphasis on Canadian education and work experience through the introduction of the Canadian Experience Class. Increased investments in settlement services were also made across these decades. In addition, the past 20 years have seen a growing role for provincial governments in the selection of immigrants arriving with the intention of settling in a specific province, first with the Canada-Quebec Accord, and then later with the introduction of the Provincial Nominee Program. The past 10 years have also witnessed a significant expansion of the number of foreign workers entering Canada through Temporary Foreign Worker (TFW) programs, introducing an additional supply of foreign born labour to the Canadian economy.

Within this dynamic context of deteriorating labour market outcomes of recent immigrants and extensive policy development, there is an ever-increasing need for Canadian evidence to inform Canadian policy. The timing could not be better for a collection of analytical studies on immigration integration from a primarily economic perspective. The chapters, all by leading researchers in their fields, examine a wide range of economic and social aspects of immigration. In a single volume of this kind, it is not possible to cover all the relevant topics regarding the way in which immigrants participate in the Canadian economy, and the selection of topics is somewhat eclectic, reflecting diverse policy priorities. However, we feel that there is strong coverage of the key topics of interest. The papers presented should not be thought of as the final word on any specific topic, but each paper provides important insights that we hope will form a foundation for evidence-informed policy-making.

In the first chapter, Li Xue presents a detailed overview of the labour market outcomes of different groups of immigrants using the Longitudinal Survey of Immigrants to Canada (LSIC). A cohort of immigrants – those who landed between October 2000 and September 2001 – are tracked in the LSIC through their first four years in Canada. The richness of the LSIC data enables Xue to present average labour market outcomes separately for those who entered as: 1) family class immigrants, 2) principal applicants in the skilled worker class, 3) spouses and dependants entering through the skilled worker class, 4) other economic class immigrants, and 5) refugees. Xue finds significant progress at gaining employment over the four years of the survey by LSIC immigrants in each of these categories. The evidence indicates that immigrants gravitated over time toward more highly skilled occupations appropriate for their training. The author also finds that the immigrants were generally satisfied with their jobs and that a majority of them felt their skills were adequately utilized. The chapter's analysis provides a detailed description of different aspects of the immigrant selection program but also gives a sense of how immigrants entering through different streams of the program fare more generally in the Canadian labour market over the first four years. Ideally, a future project would expand this analysis to study more cohorts of immigrants. Later chapters in the book using Census data and Longitudinal Immigration Database (IMDB) data serve in part to provide some of the cross-cohort comparisons that shed light on how changes in the selection systems over time may have affected the earnings outcomes of immigrants from different arrival cohorts.

The issue of the recognition of educational credentials is addressed directly in an innovative chapter by Barry Chiswick and Paul Miller. Using data from the 2001 Census of Canada, they propose and test the hypothesis that lower payoff to schooling for immigrants in Canada is due to the different effects that both over-education and under-education have on earnings. Under-education is interpreted as arising from the immigrant selection process; individuals with relatively low levels of education may still be employed in jobs normally requiring higher education, since the immigrants have been selected based on other attributes. Over-education is interpreted as a case of an immigrant's credentials not being recognized by Canadian employers. The effects on earnings of under-education are found to be twice as large as the effects of over-education. However, the authors conclude that favourable selection, in the sense of immigrants finding jobs with educational requirements that exceed their actual education levels, is less important in Canada than in the United States.

The chapter by David Green and Christopher Worswick extends their earlier study (Green and Worswick 2002) using more recent data taken from the IMDB, the Survey of Consumer Finances (SCF) and the Survey of Labour and Income Dynamics (SLID) of Statistics Canada. The additional survey years allow their analysis to be extended to cover the period 1981 through 2003, a time of deteriorating labour market performance of recent immigrants in Canada. The authors carry out an analysis of the earnings of different immigrant arrival cohorts of men based on both age at arrival and source country region. Data on Canadian born men are taken from the SCF and SLID samples and organized into labour market entry cohorts, while data on immigrant men (age 25-44 at the time of landing) are taken from the IMDB and organized into labour market entry cohorts based on the year of landing. Organizing the data for both groups in this way allows the earnings of immigrants who arrived in a particular period (three or four year intervals) to be compared with the earnings of Canadian born men who entered the Canadian labour market during the same time. The authors are then able to decompose the cross-cohort deterioration of immigrant entry earnings. Thus 74 percent of the decline in entry earnings between the 1980-82 and the 2000-02 immigrant cohorts can be explained by a combination of 1) general new entrant effects (39 percent), 2) shifts in the source country composition (16 percent), and 3) a residual flattening of the foreign experience profile – and / or a reduction in the returns to age-at-migration (24 percent). In addition, the increase in the 1990s in the points allocated to principal applicants with a university degree actually worked in the opposite direction; in the absence of the shift toward skilled immigrants having a university degree, immigrant entry earnings would have been even lower.

While the literature on the earnings of immigrants in Canada is extensive, relatively little research has compared the earnings of immigrants to the earnings of Canadian born members of the same visible minority groups. The chapter by McDonald and Worswick contributes to our understanding of the intersection of immigrant status and visible minority status in the Canadian labour market. The authors carry out what is probably the first analysis for Canada that compares the experience/ earnings profiles of labour market entry cohorts by visible minority group for both immigrants and the Canadian born. Using data from the 20 percent master files of the Canadian Census for the years 1991, 1996, 2001, and 2006, they estimate earnings profiles by gender and education groups separately for each of the four largest racial groups in Canada: whites, blacks, Chinese, and South Asians. The analysis illustrates the importance of age, education, cohort, and immigrant status in terms of understanding the evolution of differences in earnings across visible minority groups in Canada. For recent labour market entry cohorts of the Canadian born, differences in earnings across visible minority groups are found to be small. In contrast, pronounced declines are found in the entry earnings for the more recent arrivals from certain visible minority groups. However, there are also strong returns to Canadian work experience for the more recent immigrant arrival cohorts in each of the visible minority categories, indicating that the large initial disadvantages upon entry into the Canadian labour market may not be permanent. Of course, this paper does not address how these relationships are manifested for immigrants who arrive at older ages or as children; the patterns in these cases are likely to be substantially different.

The propensity of Canadian immigrants to pursue self-employment is relatively under-researched, and yet with rates of self-employment over 15 percent, self-employment represents an important way for immigrants to support themselves and their families. Moreover, there are substantial benefits to understanding this process in the international context. The chapter by Herbert Schuetze involves a cross-country comparison using the 1971 through 2001 public use Canadian Census files and the 1970 through 2000 US Census files. Schuetze estimates the incidence of self-employment and finds that wage employment is an important part of the transition to self-employment for immigrants in both Canada and the United States. In the Canadian case, Schuetze identifies a shift in the immigrant assimilation profiles that coincides with the introduction of the Canadian points system. The cross-country comparison indicates that the introduction of the business class may have also increased the incidence of self-employment among immigrants in Canada.

Arthur Sweetman and Casey Warman explore indirect effects of Canada's skilled worker "immigration points" system. Their chapter asks how well the Canadian system, which is intended to select skilled worker principal applicants (SWPAs) with superior labour market outcomes, selects spouses – who immigrate simultaneously with those principal applicants – for labour market success. As a comparison group, they also look at spousal couples who immigrate together in the family class. Clearly, the points system selects SWPAs with better labour market outcomes than either SWPA spouses or family class couples. However, among SWPAs there is no statistically distinguishable difference in labour market outcomes between males and females. Spouses of SWPAs, and the relevant family class comparison group, are imputed points to compare to those of the SWPAs. Spouses are found to have on average slightly, but not dramatically, lower points than their partners. However, the outcomes of spouses do not appear to be quite as good as might be expected, based on their characteristics as measured by the points system. This gap does not appear to be based on the economic rate of return to immigration points. Rather, the intercept is very large and negative, suggesting that spouses, and especially female spouses, with low points have relatively poor labour market outcomes. Family class immigrants who immigrate as couples have much lower imputed points and lower labour market outcomes than SWPA spouses.

The number of temporary foreign workers in Canada has grown dramatically over the past 10 years to the point where the total number of temporary foreign workers currently living in Canada is roughly equal to the number of immigrants landing in Canada each year. This expansion has occurred with relatively little public debate or analysis of its implications for the Canadian economy. Casey Warman is one of the first economists to study the economic performance of those working on a temporary (non-permanent) basis in Canada. Using Canadian Census data, he finds that TFWs do not face the same difficulties in having their foreign education recognized by Canadian employers as do recent cohorts of landed immigrants. In addition, TFWs have high returns to their foreign work experience, unlike what is typically found for immigrants. One reason for these outcomes might be the screening that takes place before a TFW is admitted into Canada; the potential employer will only sponsor someone to come to Canada if that person is believed to have the necessary education and work experience to be successful in the job. This role of the employer is small in the overall selection system for immigrants to Canada. Warman's findings raise the question of whether better outcomes in terms of returns to education and returns to foreign work experience would occur if employers were given a greater role in the sponsorship and ultimate selection of immigrants to Canada.

A key part of immigrants' successful integration into Canadian society is their securing adequate housing to meet their families' needs. The capacity to purchase a dwelling is linked to the success that adult members have in the labour market but also relies on their capacity to accumulate wealth for a down payment and to access mortgage credit. Michael Haan's chapter makes an important contribution to the growing literature on immigrant housing outcomes. Using data from all three waves of the LSIC, Haan tests between the assimilation theory and the stratification theory of immigrant housing integration. He is able to track the housing outcomes of the cohort of immigrants who arrived in Canada between October 2000 and September 2001 through the first four years after arrival in Canada. The focus of his analysis is on seven groups of immigrants based on ethnicity. Three ethnic groups of immigrants (Arabs, blacks, and Chinese) have significantly lower home ownership rates than do white immigrants, and these differences are not accounted for by a range of socio-economic and demographic characteristics. While Haan finds entry wealth and credit constraints to be important determinants of home ownership among immigrants, they are not a major explanatory factor. Given that nearly half of Canada's immigrant groups experience unexplained gaps in their access to home ownership, it may be time for Canadian policy-makers to develop a national housing strategy to address issues like those Haan identifies.

An immigration program can be evaluated not only through the labour market performance of first generation adult immigrants but also through the subsequent labour market performance of their children. A key part of the integration and adaptation of children of immigrants relates to the level of success that they experience in the schools of the receiving country. Arthur Sweetman's study, employing data on test scores from the Third International Math and Science Survey (TIMSS), is among the first to look at the school performance of immigrant children. One of the strengths of the TIMSS is that it was carried out in many different countries. Sweetman uses data from three important immigrant receiving countries: Canada, the United States, and Australia. He finds that immigrants have test scores that are typically below those of domestic born children, with the gaps larger in science (relative to math), in Canada and the United States; however, immigrant children in Australia have scores that are similar to those of Australian born children. He finds evidence in the test scores consistent with assimilation toward the domestic born average levels in North America in that the immigrants' scores are much closer to those of the domestic born at age 13 relative to age 9. Sweetman does not find that time in the school system has a significant impact on performance but does find that school level characteristics are correlated with student test scores in each of the three countries. Once controls for self-reported language used at home and the average language skill in the students' school are introduced, the immigrant/domestic born gaps in the Canadian data and the American data are no longer present. The results indicate that there are commonalities across immigrant receiving countries in terms of the success of immigrant children in the school systems, but also important differences.

Immigration is often identified as having an important role to play in the maintenance of a future workforce that is large enough to create the tax revenue needed to provide health care and other government programs to the aging baby boom cohorts. Given that fertility rates among the Canadian born are below replacement levels, it is important to understand not only how immigration affects the growth of the Canadian population but also to understand the follow-on effect in terms of fertility rates of immigrant women after arrival in Canada. The chapter by Alicia Adsera and Ana Ferrer is among the first Canadian studies to analyze fertility rates for immigrant women. They employ the 20 percent samples of the confidential Canadian Census master files for the years 1991, 1996, 2001, and 2006. An important relationship between fertility and age-at-migration is found, with immigrant women arriving in Canada in their late teens having the highest fertility rates among immigrant women. They also analyze the fertility rates of second generation Canadians using the information on parental place of birth available in the 2001 and 2006 Census files and find that second generation Canadians have similar fertility rates to other Canadian born women. However, second generation women whose parents were born in Asia have especially low fertility rates.

Poor health has a strong negative impact on individuals, their family members, and friends, but it also imposes costs on the broader society, given the nature of universal health care in Canada. When we think about immigration, we typically do not consider the negative externality that may result from immigrants arriving in Canada with either pre-existing conditions or new conditions such as depression that may arise as part of the settlement process. Any comprehensive analysis of the costs and benefits of immigration needs to take into account immigrant health outcomes. Zhao, Xue, and Gilkinson contribute to a small but growing literature on the health outcomes of immigrants in Canada by using the LSIC data to analyze those outcomes. They track the health status of a cohort of recent immigrants in Canada over the first four years after arrival. Using a network-based approach, the authors incorporate social capital into their analysis in order to estimate the relationship between social capital and health status for recent immigrants. The authors find support for the "healthy immigrant effect," wherein immigrants are a selected group (both by the decision to apply for immigration into Canada and by the decision to be admitted into Canada), resulting in better health on average than otherwise similar Canadian born. However, this effect is found to diminish over time. The authors also find evidence that health status varies systematically across different groups. Principal applicants under the skilled workers program are found to be more likely to be healthy, while refugees are less likely to be healthy. Friendship networks are associated with better health outcomes for immigrants.

While the chapters in this volume each stand alone as an important contribution to the relevant research area, we also believe they stand well together and provide an important collection of research on the broader topic of immigrants and their involvement in the Canadian economy. Not all current policy issues related to immigration are covered here, but a great number are. The authors of several chapters in this book have contributed to our understanding of the earnings of recent immigrants (Xue; Green and Worswick; McDonald and Worswick; Sweetman and Warman), the determinants of the returns to education for immigrants (Chiswick and Miller), and their self-employment propensities (Schuetze). Each of these chapters sheds light on the effectiveness of the immigrant admission system at selecting immigrants who are likely to succeed in the Canadian labour market. Xue's chapter uses the visa category information in the LSIC to explicitly compare the labour market outcomes of different immigrant groups. The chapters by Green and Worswick, and by McDonald and Worswick, employ a cohort approach to estimation, allowing comparisons to be made across periods of arrival when different characteristics of the immigrant admission system were in place. The chapter by Schuetze uses variations across time in the Canadian Census data, as well as differences between the self-employment propensities of Canadian immigrants and American immigrants in the US Census, to explore the impact of the introduction of the business stream of immigrant admission in the late 1970s. Sweetman and Warman explore the operation of the points system, looking at indirect effects on spouses of skilled worker principal applicants. The chapter by Warman extends the focus of the economic outcomes of immigrants to the case of temporary foreign workers, a large and growing group of foreign born workers in Canada. His finding of relatively high returns to foreign education and work experience for temporary foreign workers relative to what is found for immigrants has important implications for the effectiveness of temporary foreign worker programs at supplying labour services to the Canadian economy.

Moving beyond the evaluation of the labour market outcomes of the foreign born, Haan's chapter extends our understanding of the challenges that some immigrants face in terms of purchasing a home. These findings are relevant not only for immigrant selection and settlement policy but also for public policy toward housing. Sweetman's chapter provides insights into the school performance of immigrant children in Canada, the United States, and Australia. Once again, the performance of immigrant children can be thought of as an extension of the immigrant settlement process, and these findings shed light not only on the effectiveness of immigration policy but also on the effectiveness of the education system. In addition, Adsera and Ferrer's chapter on fertility rates of immigrant women extends our understanding of the demographic impact of immigration. The chapter on the health of immigrants by Zhao, Xue, and Gilkinson provides evidence on the overall health of immigrants and the extent to which they are likely to rely on Canada's health care systems in years to come. Taken together, this collection pushes forward the frontier of knowledge on the immigrant experience in Canada while also revealing a number of important avenues for future research.

NOTE

All chapters mentioned in this introduction are from the collected volume: McDonald, T., E. Ruddick, A. Sweetman, and C. Worswick, eds. 2010. *Canadian Immigration: Economic Evidence for a Dynamic Policy Environment*. Montreal and Kingston: Queen's Policy Studies Series, McGill-Queen's University Press.

REFERENCE

Green, D.A., and C. Worswick. 2002. "Earnings of Immigrant Men in Canada: The Roles of Labour Market Entry Effects and Returns to Foreign Experience." Paper presented at 2002 CERF Conference on Immigration, Calgary (June).

2

A COMPREHENSIVE LOOK AT THE EMPLOYMENT EXPERIENCE OF RECENT IMMIGRANTS DURING THEIR FIRST FOUR YEARS IN CANADA

LI XUE

À partir des données de l'Enquête longitudinale auprès des immigrants du Canada (ELIC), cet article étudie les premières expériences du marché du travail qu'ont vécues les immigrants arrivés au pays en 2000-2001. Une importance particulière est accordée aux transitions sur le marché du travail au cours des quatre premières années suivant l'arrivée, ainsi qu'aux disparités dans les résultats d'emploi entre les différentes catégories d'immigration (regroupement familial, travailleurs qualifiés, conjoints et personnes à charge des travailleurs qualifiés, autres catégories économiques et réfugiés). Les résultats suggèrent que, malgré le fait que ces immigrants soient arrivés au cours d'une période de ralentissement économique, ils ont fait des progrès importants sur le marché du travail, peu importe la catégorie d'immigration : les ratios emploi/ population et les salaires hebdomadaires ont augmenté de façon continue durant les quatre premières années après l'installation au pays. L'on observe aussi une tendance à occuper des emplois plus spécialisés et des postes mieux adaptés à leur niveau d'éducation/formation. La majorité des immigrants affirment par ailleurs qu'ils ont bien utilisé leurs qualifications et leur spécialisation sur le marché du travail après quatre ans au Canada. Enfin, le degré de satisfaction face au travail a augmenté avec les années.

Drawing upon the Longitudinal Survey of Immigrants to Canada (LSIC), this paper looks at the initial employment experience of immigrants who landed in Canada during 2000-01. Particular emphasis is placed on transitions in the labour market over the first four years in Canada and on disparities between employment outcomes among different immigration categories, namely family class, skilled worker principal applicants, skilled worker spouses and dependants, other economic class immigrants, and refugees. Results suggest that despite the "unlucky" timing of landing at a time of economic slowdown,

Canadian Immigration: Economic Evidence for a Dynamic Policy Environment, ed. T. McDonald, E. Ruddick, A. Sweetman, and C. Worswick. Montreal and Kingston: Queen's Policy Studies Series, McGill-Queen's University Press.
© 2010 The School of Policy Studies, Queen's University at Kingston. All rights reserved.

LSIC immigrants from all categories made significant progress in the Canadian labour market. For all immigrants, employment to population ratios and weekly wages continuously increased throughout the first four years in Canada. Immigrants also demonstrated movement toward higher skilled occupations and occupations that were commensurate with their education/training. The majority of employed immigrants felt that their specialization and skills were adequately used in their work four years after landing. Overall job satisfaction increased over time.

INTRODUCTION

Employment is not only a critical step for most immigrants integrating into a host society but is also a key indicator of their settlement and integration success. Research has shown that the economic outcomes of recent immigrants deteriorated since 2000; recent arrivals are experiencing more difficulties finding employment than earlier cohorts, and relative earnings and incomes of recent immigrants are declining, despite their above average educational attainment and skill levels (e.g., Aydemir and Skuterud 2005; Picot and Sweetman 2005; Picot, Hou, and Coulombe 2007). Results from the Labour Force Survey (LFS) further show that while established immigrants who landed more than 10 years ago have labour market outcomes comparable to the Canadian born population in terms of employment rates, very recent immigrants who had been in Canada for less than five years recorded the poorest outcomes in the Canadian labour market (Zietsma 2007). This finding points to the need to better understand the early labour market experience of recent immigrants.

The completion of the Longitudinal Survey of Immigrants to Canada (LSIC) provides a unique opportunity to capture the initial settlement and integration experiences of immigrants who landed in Canada from October 2000 to September 2001. The longitudinal nature of the LSIC enables researchers to examine the dynamics of the entire adaptation process of newcomers over their first four years in Canada.

LONGITUDINAL SURVEY OF IMMIGRANTS TO CANADA

The LSIC is designed to study how immigrants adapt to living in Canada during their early settlement and integration process. It contains rich information that expands upon datasets already available to assess integration experiences, such as the Census and the Longitudinal Immigration Database (IMDB), by providing longitudinal information, identifying immigration category, and capturing information that moves beyond economic aspects to include the social and cultural aspects of integration – information critical to understanding the determinants of immigrant integration outcomes.

The target population of the survey consists of immigrants who landed in Canada from abroad in October 2000 to September 2001 and were 15 years of age or older at the time of landing. Immigrants who applied and landed from within Canada are excluded from the survey.[1]

The survey has a longitudinal design, interviewing the same selected immigrants in the target population at three points in time: approximately six months (wave 1), two years (wave 2), and four years (Wave 3) after landing. About 12,000 individuals took part in the wave 1 interview; 9,300 of them participated in the wave 2 interview; and 7,700 took the wave 3 interview. The percentages of observations remaining at each of the subsequent two waves of 77.5 percent and 82.8 percent make the final response rate 64.2 percent of the original wave 1 survey sample size. The final sample represents the 157,600 immigrants from the above-mentioned target population, who are the final wave 3 population of interest: those immigrants in the target population still residing in Canada at the time of the wave 3 interview.[2] This paper focuses on the 7,700 immigrants who participated in all three waves. The estimates presented are all weighted estimates, using the final weights designed to reduce attrition effects.[3]

The results from the first two waves of the LSIC showed that, as time went on, LSIC immigrants made considerable progress in the Canadian labour market.[4] This analysis takes a comprehensive look at the employment outcomes of these immigrants during their first four years in Canada, with a focus on transitions in the labour market over time and on immigrants' perceptions. Particular emphasis is placed on disparities between employment outcomes among different immigration categories, namely family class, skilled worker principal applicants, skilled worker spouses and dependants, other economic class immigrants, and refugees.

Highlights include:

1. Nearly seven in 10 (68 percent) immigrants were employed at four years after landing, an increase of 23 percentage points compared to six months after landing.
2. The employment to population ratios and weekly wages for all immigration categories increased with time spent in Canada. Skilled worker principal applicants had the highest employment rate throughout the first four years. Refugees and skilled worker spouses and dependants made the greatest gains in terms of employment acquisition.
3. The proportion of immigrants who reported encountering problems finding work decreased with time. Lack of Canadian experience, problems with recognition of foreign qualifications or work experience, and language barriers were the top difficulties barring labour market entry during the first four years.

4.   Employment outcomes varied with demographic characteristics. Male newcomers and those of prime working age fared best. Immigrants who came from the Philippines and Romania made the greatest gains in terms of finding a job. Knowledge of official languages, especially English, was associated with better labour market outcomes. Immigrants who settled in the Prairies outperformed those residing in other provinces.

5.   On average, it took about six months for immigrants to get their first job. About eight in 10 employed immigrants worked full time four years after landing.

6.   The occupational distribution shifted toward professional work and higher skill level jobs over the four years. The proportion of newcomers working in their intended occupations exhibited little change.

7.   Four years after landing, about half (48 percent) of employed immigrants worked in a field related to their education. Nearly six in 10 (58 percent) reported using their skills or specializations adequately.

8.   Overall job satisfaction increased with time. As compared to their pre-landing situation, 45 percent reported feeling better about their general employment situation four years after landing, and 26 percent felt the same. Compared to two years after landing, the majority (55 percent) of LSIC immigrants reported that at four years after arrival their employment situation was better with respect to salary and benefits, work environment, match with specialization or training, opportunities for advancement or development, and job security.

CHARACTERISTICS OF LSIC IMMIGRANTS

From October 2000 to September 2001, an estimated 164,200 immigrants aged 15 and over landed in Canada from abroad. About four years after landing, around 157,600 of them still resided in Canada.

Of these 157,600 immigrants, 66 percent entered Canada under the economic category, including skilled worker principal applicants (35 percent), skilled worker spouses and dependants (25 percent), and other economic immigrants (6 percent). Family class immigrants constituted 27 percent of the LSIC population, while refugees made up the remaining 6 percent. Of the 54,527 skilled worker principal applicants, the vast majority (81 percent) were in the prime working age group of 25 to 44 years at four years after landing. This proportion was much higher than those for other immigration categories: skilled worker spouses and dependants (71 percent), other economic immigrants (36 percent), family class (48 percent), and refugees (56 percent) (see Table 1).

A large proportion of other economic immigrants (38 percent) were in the older working age group of 45 to 64 years four years after landing. This was a much higher share in comparison to immigrants in other

Note to readers

The LSIC was not designed to allow proper measurement of unemployment and labour force participation rates. It was deemed impossible to differentiate, from the pool of respondents who did not work, between those who were in the labour force and those who were not, because respondents were not asked if they were looking for a job during every jobless spell. This being said, the current study only looks at employment to population ratios for the LSIC population.

Definitions of terms

Employment to Population Ratio: The number of currently employed LSIC immigrants over the total number of the LSIC immigrants aged 15 and over (i.e., the overall LSIC population) at the time of an interview. This ratio differs from the standard employment rate, as the reference period is not strictly comparable.

Immigration categories

Family class: Permanent residents sponsored by a Canadian citizen or a permanent resident living in Canada who is 18 years of age or over. Family class immigrants include spouses and partners (i.e., spouses, common-law partners, or conjugal partners); parents and grandparents; and other eligible relatives. The LSIC excludes those family class immigrants who landed from within Canada.

Economic class: Permanent residents selected for their skills and ability to contribute to Canada's economy. The *economic immigrant* category includes skilled workers, business immigrants, provincial or territorial nominees, and live-in caregivers.

> *Skilled workers*: Economic immigrants selected for their ability to participate in the labour market and to establish themselves economically in Canada. Skilled workers are assessed on the basis of selection criteria that stress education, language ability, and skilled work experience. This category consists of two sub-categories: *skilled worker principal applicants* and *skilled worker spouse and dependants*. Only the principal applicants are assessed on the basis of selection criteria in place at the time of the application. Spouses and dependants of skilled worker principal applicants are admitted without an evaluation of their skills.

> *Other economic*: Economic immigrants other than those in the skilled worker category, including business immigrants, provincial/territorial nominees, and live-in caregivers. The spouse or common-law partner and the dependent children of these economic immigrants are also included in this category. The LSIC excludes live-in caregivers, as they usually land from within Canada.

Refugees: Permanent residents in the refugee category include government-assisted refugees, privately sponsored refugees, refugees who landed in Canada, and refugee dependants (i.e., dependants of refugees landed in Canada, including spouses and partners living abroad or in Canada). The LSIC only includes government-assisted refugees, privately sponsored refugees, and refugee dependants who landed from abroad.

TABLE 1
Age Group and Gender Makeup, by Immigration Category, Wave 3

| | Immigration Category | | | | | |
	Family	Skilled Workers (PA)	Skilled Workers (S&D)	Other Economic	Refugees	All Immigrants[a]
All immigrants	42,615	54,527	40,016	9,835	9,741	157,615
(% of all immigrants)	27%	35%	25%	6%	6%	100%
Age group						
15-24	13%	F	X	X	X	10%
25-44	48%	81%	71%	36%	56%	65%
45-64	22%	18%	14%	38%	21%	20%
65+	16%	F	F	F	F	5%
Gender						
Male	37%	77%	25%	47%	50%	49%
Female	63%	23%	75%	53%	50%	51%

Notes: [a] All immigrants includes a small number of immigrants who landed in categories not listed in the table.
F: Too unreliable to be released.
X: Suppressed for confidentiality.
Source: Longitudinal Survey of Immigrants to Canada (2005).

categories, such as family class immigrants (22 percent), skilled worker principal applicants (18 percent), skilled worker spouse and dependants (14 percent), and refugees (21 percent).

Young immigrants, aged 15 to 24, were over-represented among refugees and skilled worker spouses and dependants at the time of the wave 3 interview, compared to 10 percent for all immigration categories. In contrast, immigrant seniors aged 65 and over accounted for 16 percent of family class immigrants four years after landing, much higher than the proportions of seniors among all other categories.

The gender makeup of LSIC immigrants was balanced: 49.5 percent male and 50.5 percent female. Skilled worker principal applicants were more likely to be men (77 percent), while skilled worker spouse and dependants were more likely to be women (75 percent). Family class immigrants also had an over-representation of women (63 percent).

China and India were the top two source countries of LSIC immigrants, representing 19 percent and 16 percent, respectively.

Over half of LSIC immigrants had a bachelor's degree at landing (54 percent). Among all immigration categories, skilled worker principal applicants had the highest proportion with a bachelor's degree or above (87 percent), followed by skilled worker spouses and dependants (54 percent), other economic class immigrants (30 percent), family class immigrants (29 percent), and refugees (12 percent).

LOOKING FOR EMPLOYMENT AND DIFFICULTIES IN FINDING EMPLOYMENT

During the 24 months between two and four years after landing, nearly half (49 percent) of LSIC immigrants looked for work (Table 2). Compared to the proportions of 71 percent during the first six months in Canada and 58 percent two years after landing, this large decline was accompanied by increases in employment and job satisfaction levels.[5] The declining trend of immigrants looking for jobs suggests improved employment status over time. As more immigrants secured jobs and were satisfied with their current jobs, fewer continued to look for work. The employment to population ratio for all LSIC immigrants increased from 45 percent at six months after landing to 59 percent at two years and 68 percent at four years after arrival.

All immigration classes except refugees had decreasing proportions of immigrants who reported finding work as time went on. Compared to immigrants in other categories, family class and other economic immigrants were less likely to look for jobs during wave 3 (38 percent and 34 percent, respectively). Refugees were the only group that did not experience a

TABLE 2
Looked for Employment, by Immigration Category, Waves 1, 2, and 3

	Immigration Category					
	Family	Skilled Workers (PA)	Skilled Workers (S&D)	Other Economic	Refugees	All Immigrants[a]
All immigrants	42,615	54,527	40,016	9,835	9,741	157,615
Proportion of immigrants who looked for employment						
Wave 1	62%	92%	65%	49%	46%	71%
Wave 2	47%	69%	58%	42%	59%	58%
Wave 3	38%	57%	52%	34%	52%	49%
Employment to population ratio						
Wave 1	41%	62%	36%	29%	22%	45%
Wave 2	50%	74%	53%	51%	45%	59%
Wave 3	55%	84%	65%	62%	56%	68%
Job satisfaction rate						
Wave 1	78%	73%	69%	75%	77%	74%
Wave 2	88%	83%	83%	90%	83%	84%
Wave 3	89%	85%	86%	85%	86%	86%

Note: [a] All immigrants includes a small number of immigrants who landed in the categories not listed in the table.
Source: Longitudinal Survey of Immigrants to Canada (2005).

continual decline in job search over time. After peaking at 59 percent during the 18 month period between six months to two years after landing, job hunting for refugees declined to 52 percent during the period from two years to four years after landing. Compared to 46 percent during the first six months, the proportion of refugees who looked for jobs increased substantially after the initial months, reflecting the active participation of refugees in the labour market following their active participation in the classroom during the first six months in Canada.[6]

While a large number of immigrants reported that they had difficulties finding employment, the proportion decreased with time (Table 3). Six months after landing, 70 percent of newcomers who tried to find work reported having problems. Two years after landing, this proportion dropped slightly to 68 percent and further decreased to 59 percent four years after landing.

TABLE 3
Had Problems Finding Employment, by Immigration Category, Waves 1, 2, and 3

	Immigration Category					
	Family	Skilled Workers (PA)	Skilled Workers (S&D)	Other Economic	Refugees	All Immigrants[a]
Wave 1						
Immigrants who looked for employment	26,461	49,909	26,111	4,823	4,505	112,652
Immigrants who had problems finding employment	55%	76%	76%	56%	68%	70%
Wave 2						
Immigrants who looked for employment	20,091	37,512	23,346	4,128	5,736	91,414
Immigrants who had problems finding employment	58%	73%	72%	57%	69%	68%
Wave 3						
Immigrants who looked for employment	16,328	31,137	20,920	3,320	5,081	77,328
Immigrants who had problems finding employment	50%	64%	60%	52%	60%	59%

Note: [a] All immigrants includes a small number of immigrants who landed in the categories not listed in the table.
Source: Longitudinal Survey of Immigrants to Canada (2005).

Among all immigration categories, skilled worker principal applicants reported the most problems finding employment at all three interviews during the first four years. Four years after landing, 64 percent of skilled worker principal applicants who had looked for work reported encountering problems, closely followed by skilled worker spouses and dependants (60 percent), refugees (60 percent), and family class immigrants (50 percent). This result complements the research finding that by the early 2000s, skilled worker immigrants were more likely to encounter deteriorating economic outcomes than their family class counterparts (Picot, Hou, and Coulombe 2007). The downturn in the IT sector after 2000 may be a partial explanation, as more than half of skilled workers were seeking IT and related occupations.[7]

Although skilled workers, both principal applicants and spouses and dependants, had the highest proportions reporting difficulties finding work, there was a declining trend as time went on. For immigrants who landed in other categories, the proportion who reported encountering employment barriers increased slightly two years after landing compared to at six months in Canada, and then dropped substantially four years after landing. The results show that LSIC immigrants overcame some labour market barriers as time went on, even though the initial period presented challenges for most of them.

Looking at the most serious problems for LSIC immigrants in finding employment over time reveals some patterns (Figure 1). Lack of job experience in Canada was the most cited serious problem for newcomers when looking for jobs during their first four years in Canada. A lack of

FIGURE 1
The Most Serious Problems Finding Employment, Waves 1, 2, and 3

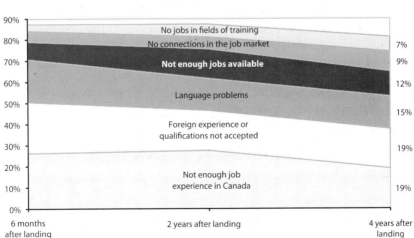

Source: Longitudinal Survey of Immigrants to Canada (2005).

foreign work experience or qualifications recognition was reported by immigrants as the second most serious problem in finding work while language problems remained a key problem even four years after landing. Lack of job opportunities, connections, and jobs in their fields of study were also barriers commonly cited by newcomers trying to enter the labour market.

Foreign credential recognition problems were particularly pertinent for skilled worker principal applicants. Four years after arrival, 23 percent of this group cited difficulties getting foreign experience or qualifications recognized as the most serious problem entering the Canadian labour market. Family class immigrants and skilled worker spouses and dependants faced similar employment barriers. A higher proportion of skilled worker spouses and dependants reported lack of recognition of foreign qualifications and experience as a serious problem four years after landing.

The share of immigrants reporting language problems as the most serious barrier in entering the labour market decreased over time for almost all immigration categories. However, for refugees and other economic immigrants, language problems were more common. For example, four years after landing, the proportion of refugees reporting language barriers as the most serious problem in finding employment, though down significantly from 43 percent at six months after landing, was still high at 25 percent for this group.

CONSTANT INCREASE IN EMPLOYMENT TO POPULATION RATIO AND WEEKLY WAGES

Despite a number of barriers entering the Canadian labour market, LSIC immigrants made great gains in terms of employment growth over time. Figure 2 shows the weekly employment to population ratio for LSIC immigrants by category during their first four years after arrival. For all immigrants, the employment to population ratio increased constantly from 45 percent at six months after landing to 59 percent at two years and 68 percent at four years after arrival. This rate caught up with and surpassed the Canadian average employment rate of 62.7 percent in 2005.[8]

Skilled worker principal applicants were the main drivers behind the employment increase. During the first four years in Canada, this group had a higher than average employment to population ratio: 62 percent at six months, 74 percent at 24 months, and 84 percent at 48 months after landing.

Despite the initial sub-par performance compared to family class and other economic immigrants, skilled worker spouses and dependants managed to increase their employment to population ratio steadily, and surpassed the rate of family class immigrants two years after landing and

FIGURE 2
Employment to Population Ratio by Weeks after Landing, by Immigration Category

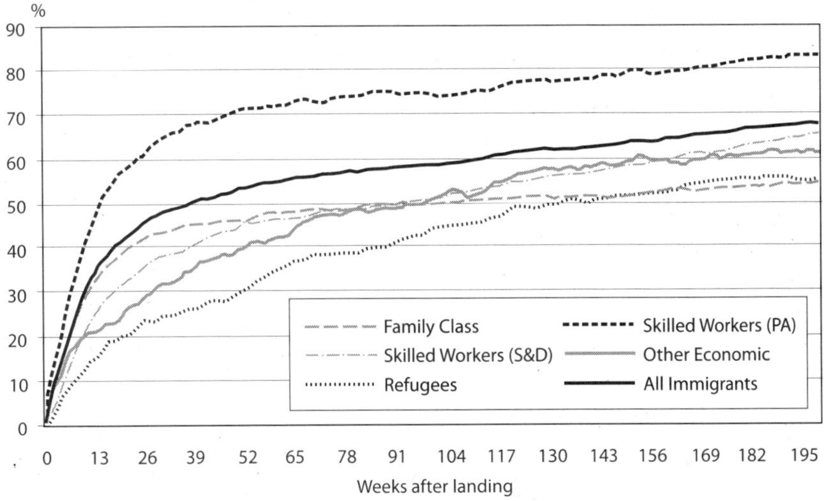

Source: Longitudinal Survey of Immigrants to Canada (2005).

that of other economic immigrants three years after landing. After four years in Canada, the employment to population ratio of skilled worker spouses and dependants reached 65 percent, close to the average rate for all LSIC immigrants (68 percent).

In spite of a lower employment to population ratio compared to most other categories, refugees experienced the biggest gain in the labour market as time passed. As shown in Figure 2, the strongest upward trend was found in the employment dynamic for refugees. Three years after landing, refugees outperformed family class immigrants when looking at employment ratios. In contrast, family class immigrants noted minimal gains in their employment to population ratio after large increases in the initial months in Canada.

During the first four years in Canada, average weekly wages for employed immigrants increased with the time in Canada.[9] Six months after landing, the average weekly wage for all LSIC immigrants was $494 ($565 for male immigrants and $384 for female immigrants). Two years after landing, this number increased by $137 or 28 percent. Four years after landing, the average weekly wage for all LSIC immigrants showed an increase of $103 or 16 percent compared to two years after landing.

Figures 3 and 4 show the mean weekly wages (in 2005 dollars) of employed immigrants at six months, two years, and four years after landing for male and female immigrants. Skilled worker principal applicants reported the highest weekly wages at the time of all three interviews during the first four years in Canada. Refugees reported the lowest wages among all immigration categories. However, the increase in average weekly wages over time is evident for both genders and for all major immigrant categories, including family class, skilled workers, other economic, and refugees.

FIGURE 3
Mean Weekly Wages of Male Employed Immigrants, by Immigration Category, Waves 1, 2, and 3

(2005$)

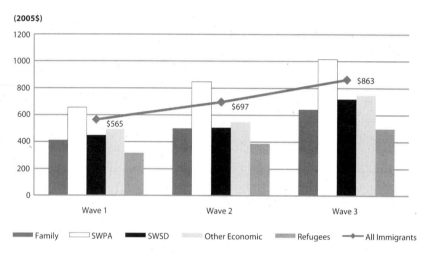

Source: Longitudinal Survey of Immigrants to Canada (2005).

FIGURE 4
Mean Weekly Wages of Female Employed Immigrants, by Immigration Category, Waves 1, 2, and 3

(2005$)

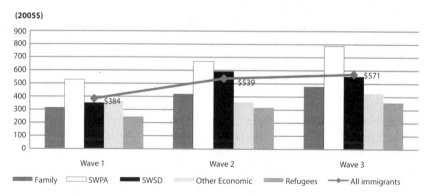

Source: Longitudinal Survey of Immigrants to Canada (2005).

For male immigrants, average weekly wages four years after landing for family class reached $642, representing an increase of $230 or 56 percent compared to six months after landing. Refugees recorded an increase of $180, or 57 percent, and the growth was equally strong for economic immigrants: increases of 55 percent, 61 percent, and 51 percent for skilled worker principal applicants, skilled worker spouse and dependants, and other economic immigrants, respectively. Average weekly wages for female immigrants displayed a similar pattern over time.

DEMOGRAPHIC DISPARITIES IN EMPLOYMENT OUTCOMES

Employment to population ratios differed among age groups and between genders (Table 4). Compared to male immigrants, female newcomers were less likely to obtain employment, and this was reflected in lower employment ratios across all three waves. Besides the gender disparity in attitudes and preferences toward labour market participation, this difference is also explained by the gender distribution differences across immigration categories. As most skilled worker principal applicants were male (77 percent), while female newcomers prevailed in family class (63 percent) and skilled worker spouses and dependants (75 percent), male immigrants were more likely to succeed in the labour market, given the education and labour market qualifications required of skilled worker principal applicants.

There are also distinctions in employment to population ratios by age group. Immigrants in the prime working age group of 25 to 44 years had the highest ratios at all three interviews during the initial four years. Three in four in this group were employed four years after landing, compared

TABLE 4
Employment to Population Ratio by Gender and Age Group, Waves 1, 2, and 3

	Wave 1 (%)	Wave 2 (%)	Wave 3 (%)
Gender			
Male	56	70	78
Female	35	48	58
Age group			
15 to 24 years	36	50	60
25 to 44 years	51	64	75
45 to 64 years	38	56	65
65 years and older	11^{E}	11^{E}	12

Note: ^{E} Use with caution.
Source: Longitudinal Survey of Immigrants to Canada (2005).

to 60 percent and 65 percent for immigrants aged 15 to 24 and 45 to 64, respectively. Given their relatively low participation in the labour market, only 12 percent of immigrants of retirement age (65 and over) were employed four years after landing.

While immigrants from all world areas made significant progress in the labour market in terms of higher employment ratios over time, some variation existed across region of origin (Table 5).

TABLE 5
Employment to Population Ratio by Major Source Areas, Waves 1, 2, and 3

World Region	Number of Immigrants	Wave 1 (%)	Wave 2 (%)	Wave 3 (%)
North America	1,768	58	68	65
Europe	24,038	50	68	76
Asia	100,619	46	58	67
Middle East	6,141	29	44	54
Africa	14,547	37	53	66
Caribbean and Guyana	4,847	53	66	73
South and Central America	4,703	41	63	73
Oceania and Australia	835	63	86	85

Source: Longitudinal Survey of Immigrants to Canada (2005).

Through their first four years after arrival, immigrants from Oceania and Australia, Europe, and North America continued to fare well, which was shown by relatively higher employment to population ratios. Newcomers from South and Central America and the Caribbean made significant gains in the Canadian labour market by four years after landing. For example, the employment to population ratio for immigrants from South and Central America increased from 41 percent six months after landing to 73 percent four years after landing. In contrast, immigrants from the Middle East had relatively weaker outcomes than other groups: four years after landing, immigrants from the Middle East had an employment to population ratio of 54 percent, 14 percent lower than the rate for all LSIC immigrants. Similarly, immigrants from Asia and Africa also had lower than average employment to population ratios.

Employment outcomes also varied by country of origin. Figure 5 shows employment to population ratios by main source countries over the three waves.

While immigrants from India, Philippines, and Romania had better employment ratios throughout the three waves, those from Romania, South Korea, Iran, and Morocco exhibited the strongest employment growth

FIGURE 5
Employment to Population Ratio, by Main Source Countries, Waves 1, 2, and 3

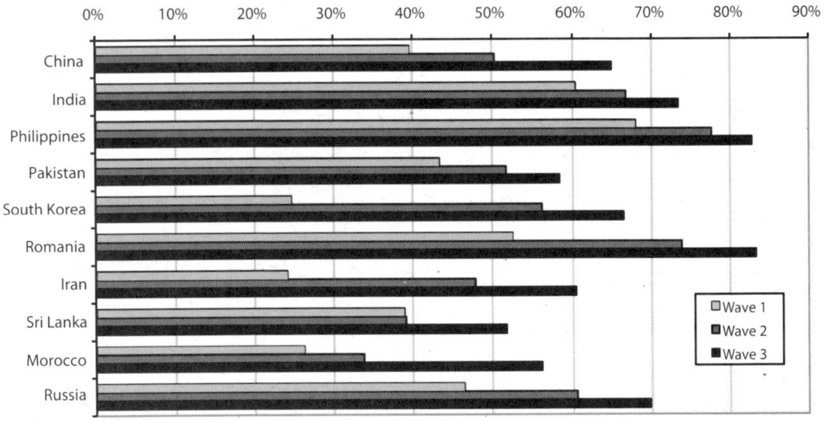

Source: Longitudinal Survey of Immigrants to Canada (2005).

in the first four years in Canada. Newcomers from Morocco outpaced other immigrants in employment growth, increasing their employment ratio from 26 percent six months after landing to 56 percent four years after arrival.

Although the employment to population ratio improved for immigrants from all major source countries, newcomers from Iran, Sri Lanka, and Morocco had relatively poorer outcomes in comparison with immigrants from other main source countries. Immigrants from the leading source countries – China and India – fared differently in the labour market. Throughout the first four years, Indian immigrants had higher than average employment to population ratios, while Chinese immigrants had lower than average ones.

A number of factors could explain the differential outcomes by source country, including differences in official language knowledge, recognition of credentials, category of admission, and age and gender disparities.

Employment to population ratios also varied with knowledge of official languages (Figure 6). Immigrants who could converse in English had the strongest employment outcomes, exhibiting higher employment ratios throughout the three waves as compared to those who could not converse in English. Bilingual newcomers also fared well in the Canadian labour market four years after landing.

The biggest gain was found for those who spoke French only. Four years after landing, immigrants who could only converse in French had an employment to population ratio of 54 percent, rising substantially from 29 percent at six months after landing.

FIGURE 6

Employment to Population Ratio, by Knowledge of Official Languages, Waves 1, 2, and 3

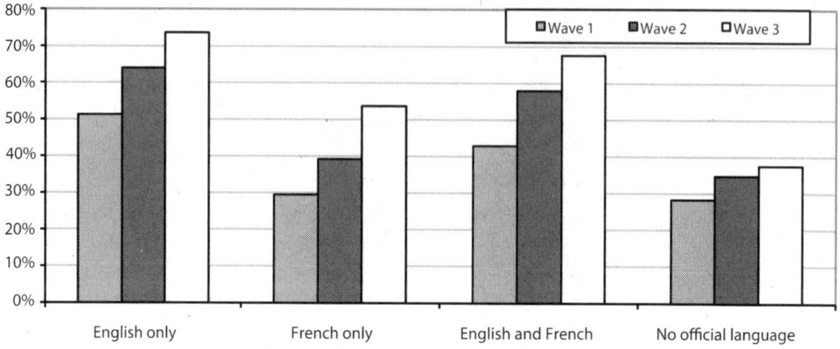

Source: Longitudinal Survey of Immigrants to Canada (2005).

Variances in Employment Outcomes by Areas of Residence

The geographic patterns of employment success exhibited by LSIC immigrants (Table 6) were consistent with results from the Labour Force Survey (LFS) (Zietsma 2007).

Immigrants living in the Prairies (Alberta, Manitoba, and Saskatchewan) benefited from strong local economies and had some of the best labour market outcomes among all immigrants. Continuing the pattern exhibited in wave 2 results, the Prairies showed continued improvement in employment outcomes in wave 3. For example, four years after landing, 77 percent of immigrants who lived in Alberta were employed, a much higher rate than in any non-Prairie province.

In contrast, immigrants living in Quebec faced tougher labour market conditions. After four years in Canada, immigrants who chose to live in Quebec had an employment to population ratio of 59 percent, well below that for all LSIC immigrants (68 percent) and lower than in any other province.

Employment to population ratios recorded in major CMAs (Census Metropolitan Areas) confirmed the provincial patterns. Among the five big CMAs,[10] newcomers who lived in Montreal had the lowest employment to population ratio four years after landing, while immigrants residing in Calgary reported the best performance.

Residing in a big city does not necessarily afford an advantage to immigrants. On the contrary, newcomers residing in areas other than the largest five CMAs achieved a higher employment ratio four years after arrival, compared to those living in the largest CMAs, excluding Calgary.

TABLE 6
Employment to Population Ratio by Province of Residence and Selected CMAs,
Waves 1, 2, and 3

	Wave 1 (%)	Wave 2 (%)	Wave 3 (%)
Canada	45	59	68
Province of residence[a]			
Atlantic provinces[b]	47	59	73
Quebec	33	46	59
Ontario	48	62	70
Manitoba	59	72	80
Saskatchewan	55[E]	63[E]	81[E]
Alberta	58	66	77
BC	40	57	66
Census Metropolitan Area (CMA)			
Toronto	50	62	70
Montreal	32	45	58
Vancouver	38	57	66
Calgary	56	65	75
Ottawa-Gatineau	41	56	67
Other areas	49	62	72

Notes:
[a] The Territories are not listed in the table due to the extremely small number of immigrants living there.
[b] Atlantic provinces refers to Nova Scotia, New Brunswick, Prince Edward Island, and Newfoundland and Labrador.
[E] Use with caution.
Source: Longitudinal Survey of Immigrants to Canada (2005).

NUMBER AND TYPE OF EMPLOYMENT

During their first four years in Canada, 84 percent of LSIC immigrants had a job or ran a business. Among them, about one in three (34 percent) had only one job throughout that period. A similar (32 percent) proportion of immigrants held two jobs since landing. Nearly one in five (19 percent) worked at three jobs since coming to Canada. Only 15 percent of immigrants held four or more jobs during their initial four years in the country. About 25,000 (or 16 percent) immigrants were not employed during their initial four years in Canada. (See Table 7.)

As shown in Table 8, the distribution between full time and part time work status did not change much over time for LSIC immigrants. About eight in 10 immigrants who were employed at the time of an interview worked full time (80 percent, 80 percent, and 82 percent during wave 1, wave 2, and wave 3 interviews, respectively). However, disparities exist among different immigration categories. Skilled worker principal applicants were most likely to work full time (87 percent, 88 percent, and 91 percent at six months, two years, and four years after landing). Refugees

TABLE 7
Number of Jobs Held Since Landing, by Immigration Category, Wave 3

	Immigration Category					
	Family	Skilled Workers (PA)	Skilled Workers (S&D)	Other Economic	Refugees	All Immigrants[a]
All immigrants	42,615	54,527	40,016	9,835	9,741	157,615
Immigrants who had a job or business since landing	30,751	52,278	33,843	7,611	7,261	132,624
(% of all immigrants)	72%	96%	85%	77%	75%	84%
Number of jobs held since landing						
1	34%	30%	35%	54%	42%	34%
2	32%	33%	31%	27%	30%	32%
3	19%	21%	19%	10%	17%	19%
4 or more	15%	16%	14%	9%[E]	11%	15%

Notes:

[a] All immigrants includes a small number of immigrants who landed in the categories not listed in the table.

[E] Use with caution.

Source: Longitudinal Survey of Immigrants to Canada (2005).

and other economic immigrants were less likely to be employed full time. In terms of changes over time, refugees made gains in increasing the proportion in full time work from 63 percent at two years after landing to 71 percent at four years after landing. These results are consistent with the fact that refugees were largely involved in educational courses during their initial years and may have chosen to work part time to accommodate these activities.

On average, it took about six months for an LSIC immigrant to obtain a first Canadian job (Figure 7). It is not surprising to see that skilled worker principal applicants secured jobs first (3.7 months) among all immigration categories. Probably benefiting from the availability of a family network, family class immigrants had faster access to employment (5.3 months) compared to other immigrants: it took about nine months for skilled worker spouses and dependants, 11.5 months for other economic immigrants, and 14.9 months for refugees to find their first job in Canada.

OCCUPATIONAL OUTCOMES

Table 9 lists the occupational distribution of pre-and-post migration jobs over time for LSIC immigrants.

TABLE 8
Full Time / Part Time Work Status of Current Main Job, by Immigration Category,
Waves 1, 2, and 3

| | Immigration Category | | | | | |
	Family	Skilled Workers (PA)	Skilled Workers (S&D)	Other Economic	Refugees	All Immigrants[a]
Wave 1: Six months after landing						
Immigrants currently employed	**17,474**	**34,072**	**14,444**	**2,829**	**2,155**	**71,693**
Full time[b]	77%	87%	70%	74%	69%	80%
Part time[c]	23%	13%	30%	26%	31%	20%
Wave 2: Two years after landing						
Immigrants currently employed	**21,254**	**40,512**	**21,105**	**5,007**	**4,398**	**93,077**
Full time	79%	88%	68%	69%	63%	80%
Part time	20%	11%	31%	30%	36%	20%
Wave 3: Four years after landing						
Immigrants currently employed	**23,640**	**45,562**	**26,108**	**6,098**	**5,488**	**107,662**
Full time	81%	91%	73%	69%	71%	82%
Part time	19%	8%	26%	30%	28%	17%

Notes:
[a] All immigrants includes a small number of immigrants who landed in the categories not listed in the table.
[b] Refers to the immigrants working 30 hours or more per week as a proportion of all employed immigrants at the time of the interview.
[c] Refers to the immigrants working less than 30 hours per week as a proportion of all employed immigrants at the time of the interview.
Source: Longitudinal Survey of Immigrants to Canada (2005).

Before landing, of the 121,200 immigrants who worked, 27 percent worked in natural and applied sciences and related occupations, 16 percent in business, finance, and administrative categories, and 13 percent in occupations in social science, education, government, and religion services. These occupations are characterized as professional and high skilled jobs.

Six months after landing, the occupational distribution shifted to be more concentrated in sales and services occupations (29 percent) and occupations unique to processing, manufacturing, and utilities (22 percent), which are classified as lower skilled and require lower levels of educational attainment. It appears that in the initial settlement process, new immigrants accepted lower skilled occupations to start their employment pathway in Canada.

FIGURE 7

Number of Months between Landing Date and the Date When First Job Was Attained, by Immigration Category

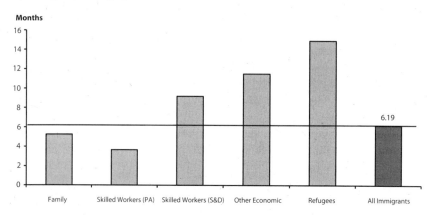

Source: Longitudinal Survey of Immigrants to Canada (2005).

TABLE 9

Occupational Distribution of Pre-Migration Jobs, Post-Migration Jobs[a]

	Before Landing	Six Months after Landing	Two Years after Landing	Four Years after Landing
All immigrants employed at the time of the interview[b]	**121,200**	**71,214**	**82,269**	**107,000**
Occupation group				
Management occupations	11%	3%	6%	7%
Business, finance, and administrative occupations	16%	12%	14%	16%
Natural and applied sciences and related occupations	27%	14%	16%	17%
Health occupations	6%	3%	4%	5%
Occupations in social science, education, government service, and religion	13%	6%	6%	6%
Occupations in art, culture, recreation and sport	3%	1%	1%	2%
Sales and service occupations	11%	29%	26%	23%
Trades, transport and equipment operators, and related occupations	6%	7%	8%	9%
Occupations unique to primary industry	2%	2%	2%	1%
Occupations unique to processing, manufacturing, and utilities	4%	22%	16%	14%

Notes:

[a] Post-migration jobs refers to the current main jobs at the time of the interviews only.

[b] Immigrants who were employed exclude those for whom the occupation was not reported or could not be coded.

Source: Longitudinal Survey of Immigrants to Canada (2005).

With increased time in Canada, more immigrants found jobs in management occupations, business, finance, and administrative occupations, natural and applied sciences and related occupations, and health occupations, all of which are higher skilled. The proportions of immigrants working in professional jobs became more consistent with the pre-migration distribution. For instance, four years after landing, 16 percent of employed immigrants worked in business, finance, and administrative occupations, up from 12 percent at six months after landing and equivalent to the pre-migration level.

The distribution of the skill levels of pre-migration and post-migration jobs further points to progress toward higher skilled occupations of LSIC immigrants (Table 10).[11] Before landing, most immigrants (81 percent) worked in skilled occupations usually requiring university education, college education or apprenticeship training (skill levels O, A, B). Six months after landing, four in 10 employed immigrants worked in skilled jobs. The proportion increased to 50 percent two years after landing and reached 54 percent four years after landing. Although there was still a distance between the pre-migration level and the proportion four years after landing, the upward trend over time indicated progress with respect to high-skilled employment.

The biggest gap between pre-migration and-post migration jobs was found in skill level A, which generally requires university education. Compared to 48 percent of all immigrants employed in occupations with skill level A before landing, only 23 percent were employed in such occupations four years after landing.

TABLE 10
Skill Level of Pre-Migration Jobs and Post-Migration Jobs[a]

	Before Landing	Six Months after Landing	Two Years after Landing	Four Years after Landing
All immigrants employed at the time of the interview[b]	121,200	71,214	80,859	107,000
Skill level				
O	11%	3%	6%	7%
A	48%	19%	22%	23%
B	22%	18%	22%	24%
C	16%	35%	32%	32%
D	2%	25%	17%	14%
Skilled jobs (O, A, B levels)	81%	40%	50%	54%

Notes:
[a] Post-migration jobs refers to the current main jobs at the time of the interviews only.
[b] Immigrants who were employed exclude those for whom the occupation was not reported or could not be coded.
Source: Longitudinal Survey of Immigrants to Canada (2005).

After four years in Canada, 35 percent of skilled worker principal applicants who were employed found jobs in their intended occupations. This proportion was similar during all three interviews of the LSIC.[12] (See Table 11.)

Among the top intended occupations, about half (49 percent) of skilled worker principal applicants who intended to work as teachers and professors were employed in this occupational group. Compared with the high share (75 percent) of immigrants who found jobs in this intended occupational field six months after landing, the drop in this occupation warrants additional research. This occupational group includes teaching assistants (TA) and research assistants (RA), and further breakdown revealed that the biggest drop happened for this subgroup. Six months after landing, 29 percent of skilled worker principal applicants intending to work as teachers and professors actually worked as TAs or RAs. This proportion declined to 18 percent two years after landing and to 12 percent four years after arrival. Considering the temporary nature of this occupation and the connection with educational participation, the decrease in the proportion may imply that while a considerable number of skilled worker principal applicants worked as TAs or RAs during their studies in the initial settlement period, more newcomers left this occupation over time as a result of completing their schooling and/or finding other employment.

TABLE 11
Worked in an Intended Occupation by Selected Intended Occupations, Skilled Worker Principal Applicants, Wave 3

	Selected Intended Occupations					
	Professional Occupations in Business and Finance	Clerical Occupations	Professional Occupations in Natural and Applied Sciences	Technical Occupations Related to Natural and Applied Sciences	Teachers and Professors	All Intended Occupations
Skilled worker principal applicants employed at the time of the Wave 3 interview[a]	2,820	1,574	17,865	1,946	1,987	36,351
Employed in a different than intended occupation	63%	75%	60%	84%	51%	65%
Employed in intended occupation	37%	25%[E]	40%	16%[E]	49%	35%

Notes:
[a] Excludes skilled worker principal applicants for whom the intended occupation was not reported or could not be coded.
[E] Use with caution.
Source: Longitudinal Survey of Immigrants to Canada (2005).

Four in 10 employed skilled worker principal applicants who intended to work in professional occupations in natural and applied sciences actually worked in this field in Canada. This share remained constant throughout all three waves of the LSIC. The proportion of immigrants working in professional occupations in business and finance was 37 percent four years after landing, improving slightly from 34 percent two years after landing.

HOW EDUCATION AND SKILLS WERE USED IN THE EMPLOYMENT

Employment in professional and higher-skilled occupations rose steadily over time, as more immigrants found employment related to their education/training. Four years after landing, nearly half (48 percent) of LSIC immigrants had worked in a job related to their studies. Compared to 40 percent two years after landing, this result reflects a progression toward education-matched employment for these newcomers (Figure 8).

While skilled worker principal applicants were most likely to work in occupations related to their training, the biggest gain was found for skilled worker spouses and dependants: from 35 percent employed in education-matched jobs two years after landing to 47 percent four years after arrival. In spite of lower proportions of employment in the fields related to education or training, refugees made the most gains in terms of increases in the proportion working in education-related fields over time (19 percent four years after landing compared to 12 percent two years after landing).

FIGURE 8
Had Job Related to Education, by Immigration Category, Wave 2 vs. Wave 3

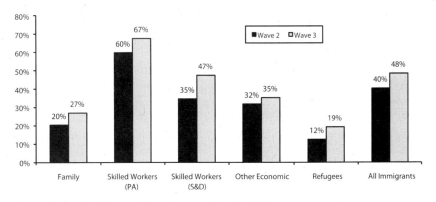

Source: Longitudinal Survey of Immigrants to Canada (2005).

When asked about how qualifications and skills were used in current jobs four years after landing, most employed immigrants (58 percent) reported that their skills were adequately used (Table 12). Among all immigration categories, family class immigrants were most likely to report skills adequately being used (64 percent), while skilled workers had the lowest proportions of immigrants reporting that qualifications and skills were satisfactorily being used (58 percent for skilled worker principal applicants and 52 percent for skilled worker spouses and dependants).

TABLE 12
How Qualifications and Skills Were Used in the Current Job, by Immigration Category, Wave 3

	Immigration Category					
	Family	Skilled Workers (PA)	Skilled Workers (S&D)	Other Economic	Refugees	All Immigrants[a]
Immigrants currently employed[b]	**23,349**	**45,339**	**26,042**	**6,068**	**5,433**	**106,977**
How qualifications and skills were used in the job						
Adequately used	64%	58%	52%	60%	60%	58%
Under-used	36%	42%	48%	40%	40%	42%

Notes:
[a] All immigrants includes a small number of immigrants who landed in the categories not listed in the table.
[b] Excludes those immigrants who did not respond to the question.
Source: Longitudinal Survey of Immigrants to Canada (2005).

Job Satisfaction

Despite a large number of immigrants working in lower skilled or different than intended occupations, most immigrants were quite content with their current jobs. While the majority of LSIC immigrants were either satisfied or very satisfied with their jobs throughout the first four years, the proportion of immigrants who reported job satisfaction increased with time (74 percent at six months after landing, 84 percent at two years after landing, and 86 percent at four years after landing).

A further breakdown by category (Table 13) shows that family class immigrants had the highest level of job satisfaction (88 percent), followed closely by refugees (85 percent) and the economic class (skilled worker principal applicants at 84 percent, skilled worker spouses and dependants at 85 percent, and other economic at 85 percent). Among all immigration categories, skilled worker principal applicants had the highest proportion reporting that they were very satisfied with their jobs (26 percent).

TABLE 13
Current Job Satisfaction, by Immigration Category, Wave 3

	Immigration Category					
	Family	*Skilled Workers (PA)*	*Skilled Workers (S&D)*	*Other Economic*	*Refugees*	*All Immigrants[a]*
Immigrants currently employed[b]	**23,802**	**45,562**	**26,178**	**6,108**	**5,521**	**107,964**
Job satisfaction						
Very satisfied	25%	26%	23%	25%	21%	25%
Satisfied	63%	58%	62%	60%	65%	61%
Dissatisfied	10%	13%	13%	12%	12%	12%
Very dissatisfied	F	2%	1%[E]	F	F	1%

Notes:
[a] All immigrants includes a small number of immigrants who landed in the categories not listed in the table.
[b] Includes a small number of immigrants who did not respond to the question.
[E] Use with caution.
[F] Too unreliable to be released.
Source: Longitudinal Survey of Immigrants to Canada (2005).

Compared to the employment situation two years after landing, the majority of immigrants (55 percent) felt that their employment situation had improved by wave 3 (Table 14). Four in 10 felt that there was no change in their employment situation, while only one in 20 reported that their situation was worse than at wave 2. Among all immigration categories, skilled worker spouses and dependants had the highest proportion reporting an improved employment situation (61 percent) and the lowest proportion reporting a worse employment situation (4 percent) compared to the previous wave. Other economic immigrants had the lowest share reporting better employment (39 percent) and the highest declaring a worse situation (7 percent).

Immigrants who reported better employment situations were further asked about aspects of their improved employment (Table 15). The most cited factor was better salary and benefits (70 percent), followed by work environment (27 percent), better match with specialization or training (22 percent), opportunities for advancement or development (22 percent), and job security (19 percent). Differences were noted, however, across immigration categories, with skilled worker principal applicants more likely to value the match with specialization (29 percent) and opportunities for development (28 percent) as reasons for better employment circumstances.

Despite many immigrants working in lower-skilled occupations compared to their pre-migration jobs, a large number of immigrants (45 percent) believed that their employment situation four years after land-

TABLE 14
Employment Situation Compared to Last Wave, by Immigration Category, Wave 3

| | Immigration Category | | | | | |
	Family	Skilled Workers (PA)	Skilled Workers (S&D)	Other Economic	Refugees	All Immigrants[a]
Immigrants currently employed[b]	17,877	36,651	17,760	4,363	3,549	80,951
Employment situation						
Better	55%	55%	61%	39%	51%	55%
The same	39%	40%	35%	55%	43%	40%
Worse	6%	5%	4%	7%E	5%E	5%

Notes:
[a] All immigrants includes a small number of immigrants who landed in the categories not listed in the table.
[b] Refers to immigrants who were currently employed at the time of the wave 3 interview and had employed at the time of the wave 2 interview too. Those immigrants who did not respond to the question are excluded.
[E] Use with caution.
Source: Longitudinal Survey of Immigrants to Canada (2005).

TABLE 15
Aspects of Employment Situation Which Are Better Compared to Last Wave, by Immigration Category, Wave 3

| | Immigration Category | | | | | |
	Family	Skilled Workers (PA)	Skilled Workers (S&D)	Other Economic	Refugees	All Immigrants[a]
Immigrants reported better employment situation[b]	9,829	19,975	10,782	1,672	1,812	44,486
Better aspects of current employment						
Salary and benefits	75%	71%	67%	47%	72%	70%
Work environment	27%	25%	29%	30%	22%	27%
Better match with specialization or training	14%	29%	20%	20%	9%E	22%
Opportunities for advancement or development	14%	28%	21%	17%	17%	22%
Job security	14%	21%	20%	23%	20%	19%

Notes: As multiple responses were allowed, the total of the percentages may exceed 100 percent.
[a] All immigrants includes a small number of immigrants who landed in the categories not listed in the table.
[b] Refers to immigrants who were currently employed at the times of the wave 3 and the wave 2 interviews, and reported a better employment situation compared to last wave. Those immigrants who did not respond to the question are excluded.
[E] Use with caution.
Source: Longitudinal Survey of Immigrants to Canada (2005).

ing was better than before landing. About three in 10 (29 percent) of LSIC immigrants felt their employment situation had worsened (Table 16).

Family class immigrants and refugees were most likely to report an improved situation compared to pre-landing (55 percent and 60 percent respectively), while skilled workers were more likely to view their employment situation as worse than pre-migration (32 percent and 33 percent for skilled worker principal applicants and skilled worker spouses and dependants, respectively).

TABLE 16
Employment Situation Compared to before Landing, by Immigration Category, Wave 3

| | Immigration Category | | | | | |
	Family	Skilled Workers (PA)	Skilled Workers (S&D)	Other Economic	Refugees	All Immigrants[a]
Immigrants currently employed[b]	15,808	43,909	20,760	4,639	3,579	89,329
Employment situation						
Better	55%	41%	43%	39%	60%	45%
The same	25%	27%	24%	35%	19%	26%
Worse	20%	32%	33%	25%	20%	29%

Notes:
[a] All immigrants includes a small number of immigrants who landed in the categories not listed in the table.
[b] Refers to immigrants who were currently employed at the time of the wave 3 interview and had also employed before landing. Those immigrants who did not respond to the question are excluded.
Source: Longitudinal Survey of Immigrants to Canada (2005).

CONCLUSIONS

LSIC immigrants entered Canada during October 2000 and September 2001, a period coinciding with the final stages of the IT boom and the subsequent slowdown in the economy. Research indicates that macro conditions at the time of entry to the labour market have adverse impacts on employment assimilation of immigrants (e.g., McDonald and Worswick 1997; Aydemir 2003). However, despite the "unlucky" timing, four years after landing these newly arrived LSIC immigrants had made great efforts to settle, adapt, and integrate into the Canadian labour market. Among various settlement tasks, securing employment was one of the most critical steps for these newcomers.

LSIC immigrants faced barriers and challenges to participating in the labour market. Language problems, lack of Canadian work experience, and foreign credential recognition problems were the main hurdles. As time went on, some of the difficulties diminished (e.g., language problems) while some persisted (e.g., foreign credential recognition). Nevertheless, after four years in Canada, immigrants had made significant progress in the labour market. Most had found employment and also demonstrated movement toward higher skilled occupations and occupations that were commensurate with their education/training.

Employment to population ratios continuously increased throughout the first four years in Canada for all immigrants. Four years after landing, 68 percent of all LSIC immigrants were employed. This employment to population ratio caught up with and surpassed the Canadian average employment rate of 62.7 percent in 2005.

While immigrants from all categories made great progress in their initial Canadian labour market experience, skilled worker principal applicants were the most successful in the labour market, and skilled worker spouses and dependants and refugees made the biggest gains in terms of employment growth.

Four years after landing, the majority of employed immigrants felt that their specialization and skills were adequately used in their work. Compared to their pre-landing employment situation and that of two years after landing, the majority of immigrants felt that, four years after landing, their employment situation was the same or better. Overall job satisfaction rose over time, with 86 percent of employed immigrants satisfied or very satisfied with their current jobs after 48 months in Canada.

This report provides a comprehensive picture of the early labour market experience of recent immigrants to Canada. As a starting point, it also highlights the need for further research to explore and better understand the results. A closer look at the socio-economic determinants of labour market outcomes will inform these research questions.

NOTES

Sincere thanks go to Martha Justus, Stan Kustec, Jessie-Lynn MacDonald, and Colleen Dempsey for their support and review. Thanks as well to Arthur Sweetman and Chris Worswick for their helpful comments. All errors are solely the responsibility of the author.

1. Immigrants who applied and landed from within Canada include Family Class – Spouse or Common-Law Partner in Canada, Live-In Caregivers, Protected Persons, and Convention Refugees in Canada.
2. For more information on the LSIC sample design, use of weights, non-response adjustments, and imputation, please refer to "Microdata User Guide" (2007).
3. Tests are done to compare the immigration categories and demographic characteristics for the first and third waves' populations of interest. The characteristics are very similar.

4. Research papers based on the previous two waves of the LSIC are available through Citizenship and Immigration Canada: see S. Kustec (2005) and L. Xue (2006).

5. The employment to population ratios and job satisfaction over time will be discussed in detail in the later sections of the chapter.

6. During the first wave period, 73 percent of refugees took part in educational courses or language training, whereas 46 percent of all the LSIC immigrants participated in education or language training.

7. Data from CIC's landing records show that among the 2001 landing cohort, the lion's share of skilled worker principal applicants (52.6 percent) stated intentions to work in NOC21 (mainly engineering and computer and information systems professionals), and an additional 7.2 percent intended to work in NOC22 (mainly technical occupations to support engineering and computer and information systems occupations).

4. Source: Statistics Canada, CANSIM, tables 282-0002 and 282-0022, and Catalogue no. 71F0004XCB.

5. The mean weekly wages are calculated for those who reported being "currently" employed at the time of the interviews and who reported positive (non-zero) wages, All wage numbers have been adjusted to 2005 constant dollars using the Consumer Price Index.

6. The largest five CMAs refer to Toronto, Montreal, Vancouver, Ottawa-Gatineau and Calgary.

7. Skill level was decided according to the National Occupational Classification (NOC) 2001. In the context of the NOC, skill level corresponds to the type and/or amount of training or education typically required to work in an occupation. The NOC consists of four skill levels identified A through D. Occupations with skill level A usually require university education. Skill level B usually requires college education or apprenticeship training. Occupations with skill level C usually require secondary school and/or occupation-specific training, while those with skill level D have no formal education requirements. Management occupations are represented by skill level O, considered as skilled occupations in the current paper.

8. The proportion of skilled worker principal applicants who worked in intended occupations was 41 percent and 38 percent at six months and two years after landing, respectively. Although the proportion declined slightly over time, this should not be viewed as a negative employment outcome. The intended occupation was asked during wave 1, and the intended occupation measurement here cannot capture the possible changes of occupational intentions over time. Thus the comparison across time should be interpreted with caution.

REFERENCES

Aydemir, A. 2003. "Effects of Business Cycles on the Labour Market Assimilation of Immigrants." *Analytical Studies Research Paper Series*, No. 203, Statistics Canada.

Aydemir, A., and M. Skuterud. 2005. "Explaining the Deteriorating Entry Earnings of Canada's Immigrant Cohorts, 1966-2000." *Canadian Journal of Economics* 38 (2): 641-72.

Kustec, S. 2005. "Overview of the Employment Situation of New Immigrants: Evidence from the First Wave of the Longitudinal Survey of Immigrants to Canada (LSIC) – Six Months after Arrival." Ottawa: Citizenship and Immigration Canada.

"Longitudinal Survey of Immigrants to Canada, Wave 3 – User Guide." 2007. Ottawa: Statistics Canada.

McDonald, J.T., and C. Worswick. 1997. "Unemployment Incidence of Immigrant Men in Canada." *Canadian Public Policy* 23 (4): 353-73.

"Microdata User Guide, Longitudinal Survey of Immigrants to Canada, Wave 3." 2007. Statistics Canada.

Picot, G., F. Hou, and S. Coulombe. 2007. "Chronic Low-Income and Low-Income Dynamics among Recent Immigrants." *Analytical Studies Research Paper Series*, No. 294, Statistics Canada.

Picot, G., and A. Sweetman. 2005. "The Deteriorating Economic Welfare of Immigrants and Possible Causes." *Analytical Studies Research Paper Series*, No. 262, Statistics Canada.

Xue, L. 2006. "The Labour Market Progression of the LSIC Immigrants: A Perspective from the Second Wave of the Longitudinal Survey of Immigrants to Canada (LSIC) – Two Years after Landing." Ottawa: Citizenship and Immigration Canada.

Zietsma, D. 2007. "The Canadian Immigrant Labour Market in 2006: First Results from Canada's Labour Force Survey." The Immigrant Labour Force Analysis Series. Ottawa: Statistics Canada.

3

AN EXPLANATION FOR THE LOWER PAYOFF TO SCHOOLING FOR IMMIGRANTS IN THE CANADIAN LABOUR MARKET

BARRY R. CHISWICK AND PAUL W. MILLER

Cet article analyse, à l'aide des données du Recensement de 2001, l'incidence de la scolarité entre les immigrants et les personnes nées au Canada. Nous observons la situation des hommes et des femmes, et nous comparons les données canadiennes avec des données semblables pour les États-Unis. Nous utilisons le concept « suréducation/scolarité exigée/ sous-éducation » (Hartog 2000), ainsi qu'une décomposition développée par Chiswick et Miller (2008) qui lie la suréducation au caractère moins que parfait de la transférabilité du capital humain des immigrants, et la sous-éducation à la sélection favorable en immigration. Les résultats montrent que l'incidence de la scolarité est plus faible chez les immigrants que chez les personnes nées au Canada, à cause des effets différents de la sous-éducation et de la suréducation sur leurs revenus. Les effets de la sous-éducation (ou de la sélection favorable en immigration) sont cependant plus importants que les effets de la suréducation (ou du caractère limité de la transférabilité internationale du capital humain). La sélection favorable en immigration semble toutefois moins importante au Canada qu'aux États-Unis, où elle est très présente chez les nombreux immigrants très peu scolarisés quand on les compare aux personnes nées aux États-Unis.

This paper examines the difference between the payoffs to schooling for immigrants to Canada and the Canadian born, using 2001 Census data. Analyses are presented for males and females and offer comparisons with findings for the United States. The paper uses the "over-education/required education/under-education" framework (Hartog 2000) and a decomposition developed by Chiswick and Miller (2008) that links over-education to the less than perfect international transferability of immigrants' human capital, and under-education to favourable selection in immigration. The results show that immigrants

Canadian Immigration: Economic Evidence for a Dynamic Policy Environment, ed. T. McDonald, E. Ruddick, A. Sweetman, and C. Worswick. Montreal and Kingston: Queen's Policy Studies Series, McGill-Queen's University Press.

have a lower payoff to schooling than the Canadian born because of the different effects of under-education and over-education on their earnings. The effects of under-education, or selection in immigration, are larger than the effects of over-education or limited international transferability of human capital. Favourable selection in immigration appears, however, to be less important in Canada than in the United States, where it predominates among the much larger proportion of immigrants with very little schooling compared to the domestic born.

INTRODUCTION

Studies of immigrant earnings in Canada have established a number of robust findings (Abbott and Beach 1993; Baker and Benjamin 1994; Ferrer and Riddell 2008). Recently arrived immigrants earn less than comparable Canadian born workers, though this earnings gap diminishes with duration of residence in Canada. There is a positive relationship between the growth in post-arrival earnings and the earnings disadvantage in the immediate post-arrival period. And the returns to education among the foreign born are less than the returns to education for the Canadian born, as measured by the coefficient of the years of educational attainment variable in a human capital earnings function. This latter empirical regularity is the focus of the current study.

A cursory review of the literature shows that the gap in the returns to education (referred to as the payoff to schooling) for immigrants and the Canadian born is substantial. Baker and Benjamin (1994), for example, reported that the partial effect of years of schooling on earnings was 7.3 percent for Canadian born males and 4.8 percent for male immigrants in 1971; 6.6 percent and 4.4 percent, respectively, for these groups in 1981; and 7.6 percent and 4.9 percent, respectively, for the two groups in 1986.[1] More recently, Ferrer and Riddell (2008), using data from the 1981, 1986, 1991, 1996, and 2001 Censuses, reported a payoff to schooling of 5.3 percent for Canadian born males, 4.6 percent for their foreign born counterparts who arrived in Canada before turning 20 years of age, and 3.8 percent for foreign born males who arrived at age 20 or later. Ferrer and Riddell's analyses for females revealed a similar pattern, although the payoff to schooling for Canadian born females, at 8.2 percent, was much higher than that for Canadian born males (5.3 percent), and the absolute difference between the payoff to education for female immigrants and their Canadian born counterparts was greater than in the analyses for males.

Two major factors have been the focus in the discussion of these earnings and schooling payoff differentials between immigrants and the domestic born. These factors are the less than perfect international transferability of human capital acquired before immigration, and the selection processes, either by immigration authorities or by the immigrants themselves (i.e., self-selection), that might result in immigrants having a different set of unobservable characteristics than those of the domestic born (Chiswick 1978).

At first glance, it would seem that of these two issues, the one that will be of most importance when considering the relatively low payoff to schooling among the foreign born is the less than perfect international transferability of skills acquired abroad. Years of schooling acquired in a foreign country, where the curriculum may differ from that in Canadian schools, where the instruction may be in a language other than English or French, and where the school culture may differ from that in Canadian schools, may simply not be equivalent to years of schooling acquired in Canada, in terms of actual labour market productivity or employer perceptions. As a result, foreign schooling attracts a lower return in Canada than schooling acquired domestically.

In Chiswick and Miller (2008) we developed a method to assess the contributions of the less than perfect international transferability of human capital and selection in migration to the lower payoff to schooling for the foreign born. This method involves the estimation of Hartog's (2000) over-education/required education/under-education (ORU) earnings equation for the foreign born and the domestic born, and the use of the estimates to predict earnings for the foreign born at each level of schooling. The predictions are obtained under alternatives that involve the replacement of estimates and values of regressors for the foreign born sample with corresponding values from the domestic born sample. By applying the method to data from the 2000 US Census, we showed that the greater part of the much lower payoff to schooling in the United States for the foreign born (payoff of 5.3 percent) than for the domestic born (payoff of 10.6 percent) was due to factors that appear to be associated with favourable self-selection in immigration, the issue of skill transferability playing a lesser role. This, of course, may reflect the much larger share of very low-skilled immigrants in the immigrant pool in the United States. The pattern we reported (2008) is consistent with the less than perfect international transferability of human capital impacting more on the highly educated, and self-selection in immigration being more intense among the less well educated (see Chiswick 1999).[2]

This paper applies our decomposition to data from the 2001 Census of Canada. This application will indicate whether there are similarities in the way that immigrant schooling is rewarded in Canada and the United States. The analyses also provide an opportunity to examine whether there is path dependence in the decomposition. Path dependence may arise in this decomposition if the findings are sensitive to the order in which the substitution of coefficients and regressors of the Canadian born for coefficients and regressors of immigrants is undertaken. The decompositions are also undertaken for various age-at-arrival groups to

reflect the concerns of Schaafsma and Sweetman (2001) and Ferrer and
Riddell (2008), among others, that the outcomes of immigrants who arrive
as children and hence undertake some or all of their education in Canada
will differ from the outcomes of immigrants who moved to Canada during
their adult years. We also conduct separate investigations for a number
of birthplace regions, and for Quebec and the other provinces of Canada.
Finally, we conduct the decomposition for females, and this should be
an important addition to the literature, given Ferrer and Riddell's (2008)
findings of a larger gap between the payoffs to schooling for immigrants
and the Canadian born among females than among males.[3]

The paper is structured as follows. We begin with a brief overview of
the over-education/under-education (ORU) methodology and of our
decomposition (Chiswick and Miller 2008). The next section introduces
the Canadian data and discusses the sample exclusions. The regression
and decomposition results for Canada are then presented, followed by
comparisons with findings for the United States. The final section contains
a summary and conclusion.

THE CHISWICK-MILLER DECOMPOSITION

The starting point for our approach outlined in Chiswick and Miller
(2008) is the ORU specification of the earnings equation (Hartog 2000).
In this model the dependent variable is the natural logarithm of earnings
(ln Y_i) and the variable for actual years of education that is used in the
conventional human capital earnings equation is decomposed into three
terms: a term for years of over- or surplus education, a term for years of
required education, and a term for years of under-education.[4] The terms
for years of over- and under-education are measured relative to the central
tendency for education in the respondent's occupation. For simplicity,
occupation is treated as exogenous. Specifically,

$$\ln Y_i = \alpha_0 + \alpha_1 \text{Over\_Educ}_i + \alpha_2 \text{Req\_Educ}_i + \alpha_3 \text{Under\_Educ}_i + ... + u_i \quad (1)$$

where   Over_Educ = years of surplus or over-education,

              Req_Educ = the usual or reference years of education,

              Under_Educ = years of deficit or under-education,

and the actual years of education equals Over_Educ + Req_Educ – Under_
Educ. Note that for each individual, "Over_Educ" and "Under_Educ"
cannot both be positive.[5] Either one or both must be zero. Equation (1)
will also contain other variables generally included in earnings functions, such as years of potential labour market experience, marital status,

official language skills, location, and, among the foreign born, duration of residence in Canada.

We use estimates of equation (1) for the foreign born to predict earnings for each immigrant at a particular level of schooling. Hence:

$$\ln Y = \alpha_0^{FB} + \alpha_1^{FB} \text{Over\_Educ}^{FB} + \alpha_2^{FB} \text{Req\_Educ}^{FB} + \alpha_3^{FB} \text{Under\_Educ}^{FB} + ... \forall$$

immigrants at level of schooling level "j," j = 1, ..., J, \hfill (2)

where J is the number of schooling categories.

The predictions obtained for each level of schooling were then averaged, and these averages were regressed on the level of schooling. In this supplementary simple regression, each observation was weighted by the number of immigrants with the particular level of schooling (w_j). That is:

$$\ln Y_j w_j = \beta_0 w_j + \beta_1 \text{EDUC}_j w_j + v_j w_j, \text{ where } w_j \text{ are the weights.} \hfill (3)$$

β_1 in this weighted simple regression is an estimate of the payoff to schooling for the foreign born, formed from the means of the predictions of earnings, *ceteris paribus*, for each schooling category and the associated years of schooling.

In the second step, the estimated earnings effects from the ORU variables for the Canadian born were used to predict earnings for the foreign born. Specifically, the predictions are:

$$\ln Y = \alpha_0^{FB} + \alpha_1^{NB} \text{Over\_Educ}^{FB} + \alpha_2^{NB} \text{Req\_Educ}^{FB} + \alpha_3^{NB} \text{Under\_Educ}^{FB} + ... \forall$$

immigrants at level of schooling level "j," j = 1, ..., J. \hfill (4)

The predictions obtained from (4) were then related to the years of schooling in the weighted simple regression outlined in equation (3). β_1 in this second supplementary regression is the payoff to schooling for the foreign born under the assumption that the payoffs to over-education, required education, and under-education are the same for immigrants and the Canadian born. Comparison of this payoff with that obtained using the predictions of equation (2) shows the contribution of the differences in the estimated effects of the ORU variables for the two birthplace groups to the conventional estimate of the payoff to schooling. The predictions in equation (4) can also be obtained replacing one estimated coefficient at a time, in order to identify the estimated coefficients that have the greater impacts.

In the third step, the ORU variables for the foreign born were replaced using the sample averages, conditional upon the particular level of schooling "j," for the Canadian born. That is,

$$\ln Y = \alpha_0^{FB} + \alpha_1^{NB} \overline{\text{Over\_Educ}}^{NB} + \alpha_2^{NB} \overline{\text{Req\_Educ}}^{NB} + \alpha_3^{NB} \overline{\text{Under\_Educ}}^{NB} + ... \forall$$

immigrants at level of schooling level "j," j = 1, ..., J. \hfill (5)

Again, the averages of the predictions at each level of schooling are regressed on the years of schooling via the weighted simple regression in equation (3). β_1 in this third supplementary regression is the estimate of the payoff to schooling for the foreign born under the twin assumptions that the payoffs to the ORU variables for immigrants are the same as for the Canadian born and that the mean values of these variables for immigrants are the same as for the Canadian born. This simulated payoff to schooling can be compared to that obtained in the previous step to show the incremental contribution of differences in values of the ORU variables for immigrants and the Canadian born to the payoff to schooling obtained by immigrants. Similar to the procedure followed in relation to the predictions obtained from equation (4), the predictions in equation (5) can be obtained replacing the values of the regressors for one ORU variable at a time to identify the relative contributions that these make.

The final step in our procedure involves using the number of the Canadian born at each level of schooling for the weighting variable in the supplementary weighted simple regression depicted in equation (3). Following this change, the β_1 obtained from the simple regression will be an estimate of the payoff to schooling for the Canadian born.

Thus, the sequence of substitutions outlined above progressively moves us from the payoff to schooling for the foreign born to the payoff to schooling for the Canadian born. The order in which the substitutions are undertaken (i.e., whether those in equation (5) are undertaken prior to those in equation (4)) can be changed to assess the importance of path dependence. Similarly, the complete set of substitutions for the over-education, required education, and under-education components of schooling may be undertaken sequentially, so that only the coefficients and means for over-education (or required education or under-education) are replaced first, and then this is followed by the replacement of the coefficients and means for a further variable in the ORU specification of the earnings equation.

Table 1 illustrates the approach using one of the sets of our findings.

In Table 1 the payoff to schooling for domestic born males in the United States in the 2000 US Census data computed using the weighted simple regression outlined in equation (3) is 10.5 percent, and that for foreign born males is 5.3 percent. Thus there is a gap in the payoffs to schooling for domestic born and foreign born males of 5.2 percentage points. Standardization for the earnings effects of the ORU variables closes this gap by 3.2 percentage points (8.5-5.3). Standardization for the mean values of the ORU variables closes the gap by only 0.1 percentage point (8.6-8.5). Finally, standardization for the distribution of the birthplace groups across schooling categories accounts for the remaining 1.9 percentage points. This latter standardization is important because the foreign born in the United States, particularly immigrants from Mexico, are disproportionately represented in low-schooling categories where under-education has

TABLE 1
Implied Payoffs to Schooling, Adjusting for Over-Education, Required Education, and Under-Education, United States, 2000

	% Payoff
Domestic born males	10.5
Foreign born males	5.3
No adjustment	
(a) Assuming same earnings effects to the ORU variables as for domestic born males	8.5
(b) As for (a) but also same levels of ORU variables within each schooling category as for domestic born males	8.6
(c) As for (b) but also assuming same distribution across schooling categories for foreign born males as for domestic born males	10.5

Source: Chiswick and Miller (2008, Table 6).

the effect of reducing the conventionally estimated payoff to schooling because of the favourable selectivity in migration.

We repeated these analyses focusing only on the effects of under-education. The findings were broadly in line with those reported in Table 1, suggesting that under-education is a more important phenomenon than is over-education when considering the lower payoff to schooling for immigrants.[6] Thus, we concluded (2008, 1331):

> It is quite clear, therefore, that almost all the gap between the payoff to schooling for the foreign born and the domestic born is due to the earnings effects associated with under-education, and the different distributions of the two birthplace groups across the schooling categories that leads to the foreign born being disproportionately represented among the under-educated categories. In other words, the lower payoff to schooling for the foreign born appears to be driven largely by the consequences of the positive selection in immigration, in particular among immigrants with low levels of schooling.

We also conducted separate analyses for the major foreign birthplace groups in the United States and found that the gap in the payoff to schooling between immigrants and the domestic born varied with the stage of development of the immigrant's country of origin, being minimal for advanced Western countries and large for less developed countries. In each instance of a sizeable gap in the payoff to schooling, however, the general pattern in the decomposition was the same as that which characterizes Table 1.[7]

This paper explores whether these findings carry over to the Canadian labour market and whether they hold for females, as well as whether they are sensitive to different assumptions concerning the order in which the adjustments are implemented (i.e., whether the results exhibit path dependence). We explore regional differences through the separate analyses for Quebec and the rest of Canada.

Data

The data for this analysis are from the 2001 Census of Canada, 3 percent (technically 2.7 percent) Public Use Microdata File (PUMF). This dataset contains comprehensive information on all the standard labour market and demographic measures.[8] In determining the sample to use, our statistical analyses follow the philosophy behind the sample exclusions used by Baker and Benjamin (1994) and Ferrer and Riddell (2008). Thus the data are restricted to full-time, full-year male and female workers aged 25-64 years in order to minimize conflating wage and labour supply issues.[9] There is also a focus on those employed in the week prior to census enumeration, to be consistent with both Baker and Benjamin (1994) and Ferrer and Riddell (2008). The analyses are further restricted to wage and salary earners, to enable a sharper focus on the returns to human capital that are central to the paper. Self-employment income will include returns on financial/physical capital as well as a return on human capital.[10] Self-employment income also appears to be subject to greater reporting errors than wage and salary income. Residents of the Atlantic provinces are excluded from the analysis because of the limited detail provided in the census microdata file on many variables for residents of these provinces.

The study covers all immigrants meeting these restrictions, which gives samples of 24,690 male immigrants and 18,807 female immigrants. Similarly sized comparison groups of the Canadian born (22,852 males and 19,291 females) are obtained by using a 30 percent random sample from the Census PUMF.[11, 12]

These sample restrictions do not match exactly those of any previous study. However, like Ferrer and Riddell (2008), who report that variations of their sample restrictions have little effect on the statistical results, we find that similar changes in the cut-offs have little effect on the material findings.

The variables used in this study are defined in Appendix A. Four variables – earnings, years of schooling, the required or usual level of schooling in each occupation, and the occupation of employment – are central to the analysis, and some comment on these is in order. Earnings are the sum of wage and salary earnings in the year 2000.[13] The years of schooling variable is based on Ferrer and Riddell (2008) and is defined as the sum of years of schooling completed in primary and secondary school, in university, and in post-secondary institutions other than universities. We experimented with alternative definitions formed using years of schooling equivalents for the highest level of schooling completed and found that this was of little consequence for the analysis.

The required or usual level of schooling is derived using a "realized matches" procedure. It is given as the mean level of schooling of all workers, male or female, full-time or part-time, in each occupation. Previous analyses (e.g., Hartog 2000; Chiswick and Miller 2008; Chiswick and Miller 2009a) have demonstrated that the material findings from application of the ORU specification of the earnings function are not sensitive to the measurement of the reference or usual level of schooling in the respondent's occupation. There are two occupation variables in the Census PUMF, one termed "Employment Equity Designations" and another based on the 2001 National Occupational Classification for Statistics. The latter is used as it contains more (25) categories than the former (14).

Finally, the analyses focus only on workers meeting the restrictions for inclusion in the sample set out above. There is no attempt to account for selectivity in labour force activity in 2000, which will affect both males and females, though it is generally argued to be of greater importance for females. It is not obvious, however, that any sample selectivity bias to the estimates of the payoffs to schooling or to the ORU variables would differ between the domestic born and immigrants.

STATISTICAL ANALYSIS

The empirical investigation is organized into six sub-sections. First, we establish the extent of the mismatch between workers' educational attainments and the levels of schooling that are usual in their occupations. Then we present findings from regression analyses of the determinants of earnings for all the Canadian born and foreign born, followed by decompositions of the gap in the payoff to schooling in the aggregate-level analyses for the foreign born and Canadian born and by analyses (regression and decomposition) by age at migration and by birthplace region. Finally, we conduct analyses separately for Quebec and the other provinces of Canada.

The Extent of Mismatch

Tables 2 and 3 provide information on the mean years of schooling and the extent of educational mismatch in the Canadian labour market. These data are presented for the Canadian born, all the foreign born, and the foreign born disaggregated by region of birth. In compiling these data, we follow the convention of measuring a correct match as an actual level of schooling within one standard deviation of the usual level of schooling (given by the occupational mean) for the worker's occupation (Hartog 2000).

TABLE 2
Mean Schooling and Incidence of Over-Education and Under-Education by Country of Birth, Males 25-64, Canada, 2001 Census

	Mean Schooling (years)	% Correctly Matched	% Over-Educated	% Under-Educated
Canadian born	14.018	69.15	18.35	12.49
Foreign born	14.404	59.62	27.07	13.31
Region of birth				
United States of America	15.854	65.72	28.16	6.13
United Kingdom	15.164	68.24	24.87	6.89
Europe	13.604	57.88	21.78	20.34
Asia	14.584	57.45	31.15	11.40
Other countries	14.517	59.73	28.55	11.72

Source: 2001 Census of Canada PUMF.

Table 2 shows that the mean level of schooling of foreign born males (14.4 years) is slightly higher than that of Canadian born males (14.0 years). Among Canadian born males, 69 percent are correctly matched, and this is 10 percentage points more than the level of correct matches among foreign born males. Of the Canadian born, 19 percent are over-educated, and 12 percent are under-educated. Among the foreign born, the extent of under-education is similar to that for the Canadian born, but the extent of over-education, at 27 percent, is considerably greater than is the case for the Canadian born. Immigrants from the United States and Asia are shown to have a relatively high incidence of over-education, whereas male immigrants from Europe have a relatively high incidence of under-education.

Similar patterns emerge from study of the Table 3 data for females, even though the mean level of schooling for foreign born females is slightly lower than that for Canadian born females.

TABLE 3
Mean Schooling and Incidence of Over-Education and Under-Education by Country of Birth, Females 25-64, Canada, 2001 Census

	Mean Schooling (years)	% Correctly Matched	% Over-Educated	% Under-Educated
Canadian born	14.326	73.35	13.94	12.71
Foreign born	14.230	65.64	19.77	14.59
Region of birth				
United States of America	15.767	70.32	23.81	5.87
United Kingdom	14.616	76.10	14.58	9.32
Europe	13.636	60.29	18.08	21.62
Asia	14.295	63.54	23.23	13.23
Other countries	14.322	69.33	17.89	12.78

Source: 2001 Census of Canada PUMF.

These data therefore establish that educational mismatch is an important phenomenon in the Canadian labour market. The next section explores the consequences of this mismatch for earnings.

Aggregate-Level Regression Analyses

Table 4 lists selected estimates of the conventional (column i) and ORU (column ii) versions of the earnings equations for males. It also includes the mean and standard deviation of the selected regressors. The estimates on the left-hand side are for the Canadian born, and those on the right-hand side are for the foreign born. Differences between the coefficients estimated for the Canadian born and foreign born that are statistically significant are denoted by an asterisk against the estimate for the foreign born.[14] Table 5, which has a structure identical to that of Table 4, is for females. The full sets of results are presented in Appendix B, Tables B.1 and B.2.[15]

TABLE 4
Selected Estimates of Conventional and ORU Earnings Equations, Adult Males in Paid Employment, Canada, 2001 Census[a]

Variable	Canadian Born			Foreign Born		
	(i)	(ii)	Mean/(SD)	(iv)	(v)	Mean/(SD)
Actual education	0.077	(c)	14.018	0.061*	(c)	14.404
	(35.12)		(3.09)	(27.38)		(3.57)
Usual education [b]	(c)	0.123	13.867	(c)	0.145*	13.925
		(34.07)	(1.63)		(34.85)	(1.66)
Over-education	(c)	0.055	1.112	(c)	0.035*	1.446
		(13.66)	(1.55)		(8.05)	(1.77)
Under-education	(c)	-0.061	0.961	(c)	-0.031*	0.966
		(11.06)	(1.55)		(6.05)	(1.83)
Other control variables included [d]	yes	yes	–	yes	yes	–
$\overline{R}^2$	0.102	0.111	–	0.109	0.129	–
Sample size	25,852	25,852	25,852	24,690	24,690	24,690

Notes: (a) Heteroscedasticity consistent 't' statistics in parentheses; (b) computed using the realized matches procedure as the reference level of schooling; (c) variable not entered into specification; (d) other control variables are years of potential labour market experience and its square, weeks worked, married, resident of Census Metropolitan Area, fluent in English or French, province of residence, and for the foreign born, duration of residence in Canada and its square and citizenship status; * = estimated coefficient for the foreign born is significantly different from that for the Canadian born. Dependent variable: natural logarithm of earnings in 2000.

Source: 2001 Census of Canada PUMF.

According to Table 4, column i, the return to an additional year of schooling for the Canadian born is 7.7 percent. The comparable return for the foreign born is 1.6 percentage points lower, at 6.1 percent. This magnitude of difference in payoffs to schooling between the Canadian born and immigrants for males is consistent with studies by Baker and Benjamin (1994) and Ferrer and Riddell (2008). Among females (Table 5, column i), the payoff to schooling is 10.2 percent for the Canadian born and 6.9 percent for the foreign born. The wider gap in the payoffs to schooling between the Canadian born and foreign born for females (3.3 percentage points) than for males (1.6 percentage points) is consistent with the findings reported by Ferrer and Riddell (2008).

Among males, the return to the usual or reference years of education for the Canadian born is 12.3 percent (see Table 4, column ii), which is almost 5 percentage points higher than the return to actual years of schooling. It is higher because the return captures two factors: the possession of an additional year of schooling within one's occupation and mobility to an occupation where the additional year of schooling can be used effectively.

TABLE 5
Selected Estimates of Conventional and ORU Earnings Equations, Adult Females in Paid Employment, Canada, 2001 Census[a]

Variable	Canadian Born			Foreign Born		
	(i)	*(ii)*	*Mean/(SD)*	*(iv)*	*(v)*	*Mean/(SD)*
Actual education	0.102	(c)	14.326	0.069*	(c)	14.230
	(37.23)		(2.90)	(25.42)		(3.45)
Usual education[b]	(c)	0.174	14.481	(c)	0.160*	14.136
		(39.39)	(1.54)		(32.66)	(1.59)
Over-education	(c)	0.074	0.936	(c)	0.038*	1.224
		(12.57)	(1.37)		(6.97)	(1.60)
Under-education	(c)	-0.068	1.091	(c)	-0.040*	1.130
		(9.67)	(1.46)		(6.94)	(1.86)
Other control variables included[d]	yes	yes	-	yes	yes	-
$\bar{R}^2$	0.116	0.135	-	0.102	0.126	-
Sample size	19,291	19,291	19,291	18,807	18,807	18,807

Notes: See Table 4.
Source: 2001 Census of Canada PUMF.

The return to the reference years of education for foreign born males is 14.5 percent. The difference between the returns to the actual years of schooling and required schooling is greater among the foreign born (8.4 percentage points) than the Canadian born (4.6 percentage points). This implies that labour market matching is more important to earnings determination for the foreign born than it is for the Canadian born. This pattern is also a feature of the US labour market (Chiswick and Miller 2008).

The return to reference years of schooling is higher for females than for males, for both the Canadian born (17.4 percent for females compared to 12.3 percent for males) and foreign born (16.0 percent for females compared to 14.5 percent for males). The increments in earnings associated with correctly matched schooling were greater for females than for males in many of the studies summarized by Hartog (2000).

An additional year of surplus schooling is associated with 5.5 percent higher earnings for Canadian born males and 3.5 percent higher earnings for foreign born males. Thus, the returns associated with over-education are only 25 percent (foreign born) to 45 percent (Canadian born) of the returns associated with correctly matched schooling. Among females, the payoff to surplus schooling for the Canadian born, at 7.4 percent, is 43 percent of the payoff to correctly matched schooling (17.4 percent). The payoff to surplus schooling for foreign born females, at 3.8 percent, is 24 percent of the payoff to correctly matched schooling (16.0 percent). These relativities are broadly the same as for the male labour market. Moreover, the fact that years of surplus schooling attract a relatively low return for the foreign born mirrors findings for the US labour market. This feature of the returns to surplus education is likely to reflect the less than perfect international transferability of schooling acquired abroad. It could also, however, reflect unmeasured quality differences in schooling acquired in Canada and in other countries.

Years of under-education are associated with lower earnings, compared to workers in the same occupation who have the usual level of schooling for that occupation. The earnings penalty for under-education is 6.1 percent for Canadian born males and 3.1 percent for foreign born males. It is 6.8 percent for Canadian born females and 4.0 percent for foreign born females. The smaller (in absolute value) earnings penalty associated with years of under-education for the foreign born than for the Canadian born is similar to the way that earnings are structured in the US labour market. We have argued (2008) that this is likely to be a reflection of the foreign born at lower levels of schooling possessing greater levels of unobservables that are positively associated with earnings, and that this can be linked to immigrant self-selection.

Thus, the Canadian and US labour markets exhibit similar reward/penalty systems in terms of payoffs to correctly matched and mismatched educational attainment. While the magnitude of the payoffs varies between the two countries, as indeed is also the case for the return to actual years of schooling, there is no conflict in terms of the overall patterns in the empirical findings.

Aggregate-Level Decompositions

Tables 6 (males) and 7 (females) report the results of the decomposition of the gap in the returns to education between Canadian born and foreign born workers.

The payoff to education for Canadian born males computed from the means of the predicted earnings at each level of schooling is 7.6 percent. For foreign born males the implied payoff to schooling is 6.0 percent.

TABLE 6
Implied Payoffs to Schooling, Adjusting for Effects of ORU Variables, Canada, Males

	% Payoff
Canadian born males	7.6
Foreign born males	6.0
No adjustment	
(a) Assuming same earnings effects to reference education, under-education and over-education as Canadian born males	7.4
(b) As for (a) but also same levels of reference education, under-education and over-education within each schooling category as Canadian born males	7.5
(c) As for (b) but also assuming same distribution across schooling categories for foreign born males as for Canadian born males	7.6

Source: Authors' calculations.

TABLE 7
Implied Payoffs to Schooling, Adjusting for Effects of ORU Variables, Canada, Females

	% Payoff
Canadian born females	7.6
Foreign born females	6.0
No adjustment	
(a) Assuming same earnings effects to reference education, under-education and over-education as Canadian born females	7.4
(b) As for (a) but also same levels of reference education, under-education and over-education within each schooling category as Canadian born females	7.5
(c) As for (b) but also assuming same distribution across schooling categories for foreign born females as for Canadian born females	7.6

Source: Authors' calculations.

If it is assumed that the effects on earnings of the ORU variables are the same for the foreign born as they are for the Canadian born, then the payoff to schooling for the foreign born would increase by 1.4 percentage points to 7.4 percent among males, and it would increase by 2.7 percentage points to 9.5 percent among females. These changes represent 88 percent of the gap in the payoff to schooling for the two birthplace groups in the case of males, and 84 percent of the gap in the case of females. For males in the US labour market, our (2008) calculations show that this adjustment accounts for 62 percent of the much greater gap in the payoffs to schooling for the domestic born and immigrants.

The further adjustment for the mean levels of the ORU variables (i.e., equation (5)) results in only a minor upward change of 0.1 percentage point in the payoff to schooling for both foreign born males and foreign born females in the Canadian labour market. This mirrors the minor 0.1 percentage point change we reported (2008) for the US labour market, and it follows from the broad similarity in the distributions of the domestic born and the foreign born across the educational match/mismatch categories at each level of schooling.

Finally, the adjustment for the different distributions of the foreign born and Canadian born across schooling categories results in a further very small increase in the payoff to schooling for foreign born men (by 0.1 of a percentage point) and a somewhat larger, though still small, increase (by 0.4 of a percentage point) for females. These changes contrast with the 1.9 percentage points effect associated with this adjustment in the United States (see Table 1). Unlike the United States, Canada does not have a high representation of very low-educated immigrants, and this absence accounts for the difference.[16]

These analyses suggest, therefore, that it is the earnings effects associated with the ORU variables that have the greatest impact on the differences between the payoffs to actual years of schooling received by immigrants and the domestic born. Given this, the calculations were repeated changing the three earnings effects (to reference levels of education, years of under-education, and years of over-education) one at a time. These adjustments showed slightly different patterns for men and women, owing to the return to reference years of schooling being higher for foreign born men than for Canadian born men, and lower for foreign born women than for Canadian born women. Thus, adjustment for the payoffs to reference years of schooling is actually associated with a widening of the gap in the payoffs to actual years of schooling by 0.5 of a percentage point for males, and a narrowing of this gap by 0.3 of a percentage point for females (see Chiswick and Miller (2009b) Appendix B, Tables B.3 and B.4). Adjustment for the earnings effects of under-education was associated with a narrowing of the gap in the payoffs to schooling by 1.2 percentage points for males and by 1.3 percentage points for females. Adjustment for the earnings effects of over-education was associated with a narrowing of the gap in the returns to schooling by 0.7 of a percentage point for males and by 1.1 percentage points for females. Hence, both the earnings effects of over-education and under-education contribute to the differential in the payoffs to schooling for immigrants and the domestic born in Canada, although under-education is slightly more important in this regard. This contrasts with the situation in the United States, where the under-education phenomenon was much more important (Chiswick and Miller 2008).

The potential impact of path dependence was examined by repeating the calculations in Tables 6 and 7 by first standardizing for the mean values of the ORU variables (i.e., the adjustment outlined in equation 5) and then standardizing for the coefficients of the ORU model (i.e., the adjustment outlined in equation 4). This sensitivity test revealed that path dependence is not an issue.

A second test of path dependence involves changing the order in which the ORU coefficients are used to examine their relative importance. In the examination discussed above, the order of replacement was R, U, and then O. Reversing this order has little material impact on the findings. Detailed calculations are presented in Chiswick and Miller (2009b) Appendix B, Tables B.5 and B.6.[17]

We (Chiswick and Miller 2008) associate the smaller payoff to over-education for immigrants than for the domestic born with the less than perfect international transferability of schooling acquired abroad. We associate the smaller (in absolute value) earnings effect of under-education for immigrants than for the domestic born to favourable selection in migration that results in immigrants with low levels of schooling obtaining jobs for which their paper qualifications suggest they are under-qualified. This self-selection in migration will be more intense among the less well educated (where under-education is a more important characteristic) where there are fixed costs of migration (Chiswick 1999). Thus, within this framework, the decomposition results reported in Tables 6 and 7 suggest that both the less than perfect international transferability of human capital and self-selection in migration contribute to the relatively low payoff to schooling for the foreign born in the Canadian labour market. This is the case for both males and females.

Analyses by Age at Migration

The variables on date of birth and year of migration in the 2001 Census of Canada, together with an estimated month of migration, permit the computation of the age at migration. In the PUMF sample, age at migration is provided in broad bands: 0-4 years, 5-12 years, and 13-19 years, and then five-year bands to age 55-59. The upper category is 60 years and over.

Immigrants who arrived as children and hence completed all or some of their schooling in Canada, and those who arrived as adults and hence would not usually have undertaken any of their schooling in Canada, can be categorized in various ways using this information. For example, child immigrants might be categorized as those who arrived before they turned 12. Adult immigrants might be those who arrived at age 20 or more. Ferrer and Riddell (2008) used arrival in Canada before age 20 to define a "youth" sample, and arrival at or after age 20 and after age 34 as alternative definitions of adult samples. They note that these separations "imperfectly control for Canadian acquired education" (2008, 196).

The current analysis also employs alternative definitions of "adult" and "youth" immigrants.[18] "Adult" is defined using age 20 or more, 25 or more, 30 or more, and 35 or more as the lower threshold age at migration. Youth or child at migration is defined using age 19 or younger and age 12 or younger as the upper threshold, respectively. Selected results from the ORU and conventional models of earnings determination using these alternatives are presented in Table 8 for males and in Table 9 for females. These tables also include, for comparison purposes, the earlier results (Tables 4 and 5) for the Canadian born and total foreign born in the final two rows.

The first column of results for males and females in Tables 8 and 9, respectively, is for years of actual education. It is seen that the payoff to actual years of education falls with an older age at migration. That is, as one moves down the column, from the foreign born who are highly likely

TABLE 8
Selected Estimates of Conventional and ORU Models of Earnings by Age at Arrival, Canada, Males, 2001 Census[a]

Age at Arrival	Years of Actual Education	Years of Over- Education	Years of Reference Education[b]	Years of Under- Education	R^2	Sample Size
Child immigrants						
≤ Age 12	0.068	0.038	0.129	-0.044	0.109	5,182
	(11.62)	(3.79)	(15.52)	(4.08)		
≤ Age 19	0.065*	0.035*	0.137	-0.042*	0.124	8,533
	(15.69)	(4.63)	(20.88)	(5.15)		
Adult immigrants						
≥ Age 20	0.057*	0.032*	0.147*	-0.025*	0.132	15,862
	(19.23)	(5.84)	(26.65)	(3.73)		
≥ Age 25	0.055 *	0.032*	0.152*	-0.018*	0.133	11,784
	(15.06)	(4.84)	(22.70)	(2.27)		
≥ Age 30	0.048*	0.028*	0.159*	-0.004*	0.125	7,282
	(9.64)	(3.34)	(17.35)	(0.41)		
≥ Age 35	0.042*	0.019*	0.158*	-0.009*	0.117	4,006
	(5.47)	(1.62)	(11.57)	(0.61)		
Total foreign born	0.061*	0.035*	0.145*	-0.031*	0.129	24,690
	(27.38)	(8.05)	(34.85)	(6.05)		
Canadian born	0.077	0.055	0.123	-0.061	0.111	25,852
	(35.12)	(13.66)	(34.07)	(11.06)		

Notes: R^2 is for the ORU model. See notes to Table 4.
Source: 2001 Census of Canada PUMF.

to have undertaken all or most of their schooling in Canada to samples that also include some foreign born who may have undertaken all or most of their schooling abroad, to samples that largely comprise the foreign born who completed all their schooling abroad, the coefficient on actual years of schooling falls. Thus, when the sample is restricted to immigrants who arrived in Canada before they turned 13 years of age, the payoff to years of schooling is 6.8 percent among males and 8.4 percent among females. These payoffs compare with the payoffs of 7.7 percent (males) and 10.2 percent (females) for the Canadian born sample, and 6.1 percent (males) and 6.9 percent (females) for the total foreign born sample. When the sample is restricted to immigrants who arrived in Canada after age 34, however, the payoff to actual years of schooling is much lower, 4.2 percent for males and 4.5 percent for females. Clearly, age at migration matters to the payoff to schooling, and the impact is in the expected direction (see Friedberg 2000), with child immigrants having a payoff to schooling that is much more like that of the Canadian born than is the case for adult immigrants.[19]

TABLE 9
Selected Estimates of Conventional and ORU Models of Earnings by Age at Arrival, Canada, Females, 2001 Census[a]

Age at Arrival	Years of Actual Education	Years of Over-Education	Years of Reference Education[b]	Years of Under-Education	R^2	Sample Size
Child immigrants						
≤ Age 12	0.084* (12.06)	0.040* (3.05)	0.174 (16.54)	-0.063 (3.97)	0.122	3,975
≤ Age 19	0.080* (16.51)	0.055 (6.02)	0.167 (20.23)	-0.050 (4.90)	0.120	6,709
Adult immigrants						
≥ Age 20	0.064* (18.16)	0.032* (4.61)	0.156* (24.66)	-0.036* (5.11)	0.123	11,896
≥ Age 25	0.062* (13.40)	0.031* (3.75)	0.152* (18.80)	-0.038* (4.11)	0.117	8,245
≥ Age 30	0.056* (8.94)	0.033* (2.95)	0.143* (13.02)	-0.029* (2.34)	0.113	4,923
≥ Age 35	0.045* (4.88)	0.022* (1.48)	0.131* (7.97)	-0.027* (1.54)	0.112	2,641
Total foreign born	0.069* (25.42)	0.038* (6.97)	0.160* (32.66)	-0.040* (6.94)	0.126	18,807
Canadian born	0.102 (37.23)	0.074 (12.57)	0.174 (39.39)	-0.068 (9.67)	0.135	19,291

Notes: R^2 is for the ORU model. See notes to Table 4.
Source: 2001 Census of Canada PUMF.

The next three columns in Tables 8 and 9 are from the ORU specification of the earnings equation. The general conclusion that can be drawn from these results mirrors that established for the years of actual education variable: the payoffs to the ORU variables for child immigrants are closer to those for the Canadian born than are the respective estimates for adult immigrants. For example, among males, when the sample is restricted to immigrants who arrived in Canada before they turned 13 years of age, the payoff to usual years of schooling is 12.9 percent, which is similar to the 12.3 percent payoff for the Canadian born. Among females, the payoff to usual years of schooling for this group of child immigrants is 17.4 percent, which is the same as for the Canadian born.

However, two features of the estimates of the effects on earnings of over-education and under-education should be noted. First, among both males and females, the payoff to years of over-education is negligible among the group of adult immigrants with the highest threshold age at migration. Thus, the group assumed to have the greatest component of their schooling acquired abroad has the smallest payoff to surplus schooling. This adds to the suggestion that the smaller payoff to years of over-education for the foreign born than for the Canadian born is due to the less than perfect international transferability of schooling acquired abroad.

Second, the negative earnings effect of years of under-education is more pronounced among child immigrants than it is among adult immigrants. Indeed, among immigrants who were at least 35 years of age when they arrived in Canada, the effect on earnings of years of under-education is negligible. This means that these immigrants have about the same earnings as their better-educated counterparts who work in the same occupation. As such, it is presumed that they have relatively higher endowments of unobservables that are favourable to earnings determination in Canada. According to our model (2008), this implies that adult immigrants to Canada are more intensely favourably selected for immigration than child immigrants – who presumably were tied movers.

We now turn to the decomposition of the difference between the payoffs to schooling for adult and child immigrants and the Canadian born. Results of the decompositions are displayed in Table 10 (males) and Table 11 (females).

For each age-at-arrival group, it is quite clear that essentially all of the difference in the payoffs to schooling for that group and the Canadian born is due to the different estimated earnings effects associated with the ORU variables (column v). The effects of the adjustment for the means of the ORU variables (column vi) are inconsequential in each case, including the decomposition undertaken for adult immigrants. There is, therefore, no evidence that, controlling for duration in Canada, child immigrants have a better "match" in the labour market, at least from the perspective of the impact on earnings. It is surprising that child immigrants do not have a better match compared to adult immigrants, given that more or all of their schooling was received in Canada.

When the analyses are repeated replacing the estimated coefficients on the ORU variables for the foreign born age-at-arrival groups one at a time, three patterns emerge.

TABLE 10

Decomposition of Immigrant/Canadian Born Difference in Payoff to Education by Immigrant's Age at Arrival, Canada, Males

Age at Arrival	Payoff: Canadian Born	Payoff: Foreign Born	Payoff: Foreign Born Adjusting for Estimated R Effect	Payoff: Foreign Born Adjusting for Estimated RU Effects	Payoff: Foreign Born Adjusting for Estimated ORU Effects	Payoff: Foreign Born Adjusting for Means of ORU Variables	Payoff: Foreign Born Adjusting for Weights
	(i)	(ii)	(iii)	(iv)	(v)	(vi)	(vii)
Child immigrants							
≤ Age 12	7.6	6.6	6.4	7.0	7.6	7.6	7.6
≤ Age 19	7.6	6.5	6.1	6.9	7.6	7.5	7.6
Adult immigrants							
≥ Age 20	7.6	5.6	5.0	6.5	7.4	7.4	7.6
≥ Age 25	7.6	5.5	4.8	6.6	7.4	7.5	7.6
≥ Age 30	7.6	4.9	4.1	6.4	7.3	7.5	7.6
≥ Age 35	7.6	4.5	3.7	5.9	7.2	7.5	7.6
Total foreign born	7.6	6.0	5.5	6.7	7.4	7.5	7.6

Source: Authors' calculations.

TABLE 11

Decomposition of Immigrant/Canadian Born Difference in Payoff to Education by Immigrant's Age at Arrival, Canada, Females

Age at Arrival	Payoff: Canadian Born	Payoff: Foreign Born	Payoff: Foreign Born Adjusting for Estimated R Effect	Payoff: Foreign Born Adjusting for Estimated RU Effects	Payoff: Foreign Born Adjusting for Estimated ORU Effects	Payoff: Foreign Born Adjusting for Means of ORU Variables	Payoff: Foreign Born Adjusting for Weights
	(i)	(ii)	(iii)	(iv)	(v)	(vi)	(vii)
Child immigrants							
≤ Age 12	10.0	8.2	8.2	8.4	9.6	9.9	10.0
≤ Age 19	10.0	8.1	8.2	9.0	9.6	9.7	10.0
Adult immigrants							
≥ Age 20	10.0	6.3	6.7	8.1	9.5	9.5	10.0
≥ Age 25	10.0	6.2	6.7	8.0	9.4	9.5	10.0
≥ Age 30	10.0	5.6	6.2	8.0	9.3	9.4	10.0
≥ Age 35	10.0	4.6	5.4	7.4	9.1	9.4	10.0
Total foreign born	10.0	6.8	7.1	8.4	9.5	9.6	10.0

Source: Authors' calculations.

First, adjustment for the earnings effects associated with the reference levels of schooling (R, see column iii) results is a modest decline in the implied payoff to schooling for all groups of foreign born males and a modest increase in the implied payoff to schooling for all groups of foreign born females. These changes are in line with the aggregate-level results.

Second, the effects of the additional adjustment for the earnings effects of under-education (U, see column iv) are more pronounced among adult immigrants than they are among child immigrants. As argued above, child immigrants will comprise tied movers, among whom the effects of favourable selection should be less intense.

Third, the effect of the further adjustment for over-education (O, see column v) is also more pronounced among adult immigrants than among child immigrants. As adult immigrants will have acquired more of their schooling abroad than child immigrants, and hence the effects of limitations on the international transferability of human capital should be more intense for adult than for child immigrants, this pattern of effects is intuitively reasonable.

Analyses by Country of Origin

The major immigrant groups that can be distinguished using the 2001 Census of Canada PUMF are: (a) US; (b) UK; (c) Other Europe; (d) Asia; and (e) Other countries.[20] The conventional and ORU models of earnings determination were estimated for each of these groups, and the decomposition was undertaken of the difference between the return to schooling for each birthplace group and the domestic born. Selected regression estimates are presented in Table 12 (males) and Table 13 (females).

The results for each of the major birthplace groups largely mirror the findings for the total foreign born sample. Thus, the payoff to actual years of schooling for the foreign born in each country group is less than that for the Canadian born. For each country group other than Asia, the payoff to actual schooling for females exceeds the payoff for males.

The results of the decompositions of the difference between the payoff to schooling for each of these major birthplace groups and the Canadian born are presented in Table 14 for males and Table 15 for females.

Among males, for each birthplace group, the effects on earnings of years of over-education, years of usual schooling, and years of under-education have the same relativities to the respective estimates for the domestic born as were established in the aggregate-level analysis. With one exception, the same situation is observed in the analyses for females. The exception is the impact of years of under-education among female immigrants from the United States. For this group, the estimated effect of years of under-education is -0.087, which compares with values of -0.040 for the total foreign born, and -0.068 for the domestic born. This

TABLE 12
Selected Estimates of Conventional and ORU Models of Earnings by Country of Origin, Canada, Males, 2001 Census[a]

Birthplace	Years of Actual Education	Years of Over- Education	Years of Reference Education[b]	Years of Under- Education	R^2	Sample Size
US	0.060	0.030	0.129	-0.008	0.079	898
	(4.69)	(1.15)	(6.05)	(0.23)		
UK	0.057*	0.026*	0.135	-0.038	0.123	2,963
	(10.05)	(2.66)	(14.04)	(2.72)		
Other Europe	0.050*	0.024*	0.125	-0.033*	0.083	7,127
	(12.31)	(2.93)	(15.52)	(4.24)		
Asia	0.060*	0.044	0.142*	-0.025*	0.138	8,879
	(15.97)	(6.09)	(18.85)	(3.28)		
Other countries	0.067	0.035	0.165*	-0.036	0.126	4,823
	(13.25)	(3.74)	(17.06)	(3.25)		
Total foreign born	0.061*	0.035*	0.145*	-0.031*	0.129	24,690
	(27.38)	(8.05)	(34.85)	(6.05)		
Domestic born	0.077	0.055	0.123	-0.061	0.111	25,852
	(35.12)	(13.66)	(34.07)	(11.06)		

Notes: R^2 is for the ORU model. See notes to Table 4.
Source: 2001 Census of Canada PUMF.

TABLE 13
Selected Estimates of Conventional and ORU Models of Earnings by Country of Origin, Canada, Females, 2001 Census(a)

Birthplace	Years of Actual Education	Years of Over- Education	Years of Reference Education[b]	Years of Under- Education	R^2	Sample Size
US	0.088	0.036	0.151	-0.087	0.105	886
	(7.25)	(1.46)	(7.62)	(2.45)		
UK	0.073*	0.036*	0.167	-0.046	0.124	2,147
	(9.83)	(2.36)	(13.07)	(2.79)		
Other Europe	0.063*	0.038*	0.156	-0.033*	0.110	5,034
	(12.69)	(3.47)	(16.23)	(3.68)		
Asia	0.056*	0.033*	0.145*	-0.030*	0.135	6,804
	(14.19)	(4.16)	(18.34)	(3.83)		
Other countries	0.083*	0.044*	0.172	-0.061	0.116	3,936
	(13.13)	(3.36)	(14.72)	(4.84)		
Total foreign born	0.069*	0.038*	0.160*	-0.040*	0.126	18,807
	(25.42)	(6.97)	(32.66)	(6.94)		
Domestic born	0.102	0.074	0.174	-0.068	0.135	19,291
	(37.23)	(12.57)	(39.39)	(9.67)		

Notes: R^2 is for the ORU model. See notes to Table 4.
Source: 2001 Census of Canada PUMF.

means that this group of under-educated (and presumably low-educated) female immigrants do not do as well as otherwise comparable domestic born workers with whom they have an occupation in common. From the perspective of the selectivity in migration hypothesis, this suggests that low-educated females from neighbouring United States are less intensely selected for immigration than the typical immigrant and, indeed, possess fewer unobserved skills than the typical domestic born person. In other words, low-educated female immigrants from the United States are characterized by less positive or negative selection in immigration. This could arise where they have a disproportionately high propensity to be tied movers.[21]

TABLE 14
Decomposition of Immigrant/Domestic Born Difference in Payoff to Education by Immigrant's Country of Origin, Canada, Males

Birthplace	Payoff: Domestic Born	Payoff: Foreign Born	Payoff: Foreign Born Adjusting for Estimated ORU Effects	Payoff: Foreign Born Adjusting for Means of ORU Variables	Payoff: Foreign Born Adjusting for Weights
US	7.6	6.1	8.2	7.8	7.6
UK	7.6	5.7	7.4	7.8	7.6
Other Europe	7.6	5.1	7.3	7.4	7.6
Asia	7.6	6.1	7.4	7.5	7.6
Other countries	7.6	6.8	7.4	7.5	7.6
Total foreign born	7.6	6.0	7.4	7.5	7.6

Source: Authors' calculations.

TABLE 15
Decomposition of Immigrant/Domestic Born Difference in Payoff to Education by Immigrant's Country of Origin, Canada, Females

Birthplace	Payoff: Domestic Born	Payoff: Foreign Born	Payoff: Foreign Born Adjusting for Estimated ORU Effects	Payoff: Foreign Born Adjusting for Means of ORU Variables	Payoff: Foreign Born Adjusting for Weights
US	10.0	8.7	10.0	10.0	10.0
UK	10.0	7.3	9.7	10.0	10.0
Other Europe	10.0	6.2	9.4	9.4	10.0
Asia	10.0	5.7	9.4	9.5	10.0
Other countries	10.0	8.3	9.6	9.7	10.0
Total foreign born	10.0	6.8	9.5	9.6	10.0

Source: Authors' calculations.

The decompositions disaggregated by birthplace have the same general features as the aggregate-level decompositions. Thus, most of the difference in the payoffs to schooling for immigrants from a particular birthplace and the domestic born is linked to differences in the payoffs of the ORU variables. Indeed, standardizing for these effects results in an over-adjustment in the case of male immigrants from the United States.[22] This is offset by a downward effect of the adjustment for the means of the ORU variables, implying that male immigrants from the United States are less likely to be incorrectly matched to the educational requirements of their jobs at a given level of schooling. Presumably this arises because the United States and Canada are so similar in terms of institutions and incomes.[23] This overall impression of similarity, in the face of minimal variation in the payoff to schooling across the birthplace groups, suggests that the results of the decomposition analysis are robust.

Quebec versus Anglophone Canada

Analyses were undertaken on separate samples of workers in Quebec and the other provinces of Canada (here termed "anglophone Canada").[24] In conducting these analyses, the reference years of schooling were compiled separately for the two regions, to take account of possible provincial differences in the schooling systems. As well, the 0.3 random sample of the Canadian born was stratified by Quebec/anglophone Canada. Selected regression results are presented in Table 16 for males and in Table 17 for females.

The findings for males in anglophone Canada mirror the aggregate-level analyses. The findings for males in Quebec, however, have several distinctive, and apparently related, features. Thus, the payoff to schooling for males is higher in Quebec than in anglophone Canada, and the estimate for the foreign born (8.7 percent) is not significantly different from that for the Canadian born (8.8 percent). While the foreign born in Quebec have a lower return (6.7 percent) on surplus schooling than do the Canadian born (7.2 percent), these two payoffs also are not significantly different. Similarly, the earnings effect associated with years of under-education for foreign born males in Quebec (-0.039) is not significantly different from that for the Canadian born (-0.064). However, the payoff to correctly matched years of schooling for the foreign born in Quebec, at 17.3 percent, is fully 4 percentage points higher than the payoff to correctly matched years of schooling for the Canadian born in Quebec (13.0 percent). This difference is statistically significant. The comparable difference in payoffs in anglophone Canada is just 2 percentage points.

There are also differences in the ways that earnings are determined among females in Quebec compared to the rest of Canada. In anglophone Canada, the pattern is similar to that described above for the aggregate-level analysis. In Quebec, however, the payoff to schooling for foreign

TABLE 16
Selected Estimates of Conventional and ORU Earnings Equations, Adult Males in Paid Employment, Living in Quebec and Anglophone Canada, 2001 Census[a]

Variable	Canadian Born			Foreign Born		
	(i)	*(ii)*	*Mean/(SD)*	*(iv)*	*(v)*	*Mean/(SD)*
Quebec						
Actual education	0.088	(c)	13.825	0.087	(c)	14.361
	(20.94)		(3.43)	(12.90)		(3.94)
Reference education[b]	(c)	0.130	13.656	(c)	0.173*	13.890
		(20.52)	(1.88)		(14.58)	(1.95)
Over-education	(c)	0.072	1.212	(c)	0.067	1.560
		(9.42)	(1.63)		(5.11)	(1.84)
Under-education	(c)	-0.064	1.043	(c)	-0.039	1.089
		(6.56)	(1.71)		(2.46)	(1.99)
$\overline{R}^2$	0.097	0.105	-	0.106	0.126	-
Sample size	7,728	7,728	7,728	3,007	3,007	3,007
Anglophone Canada						
Actual education	0.073	(c)	14.087	0.057*	(c)	14.410
	(28.41)		(2.95)	(24.17)		(3.52)
Reference education[b]	(c)	0.121	13.934	(c)	0.144*	13.971
		(28.05)	(1.55)		(31.52)	(1.58)
Over-education	(c)	0.047	1.069	(c)	0.030*	1.409
		(9.48)	(1.50)		(6.56)	(1.74)
Under-education	(c)	-0.063	0.916	(c)	-0.028*	0.971
		(9.24)	(1.41)		(5.26)	(1.82)
$\overline{R}^2$	0.100	0.110	-	0.104	0.124	-
Sample size	18,260	18,260	18,260	21,683	21,683	21,683

Notes: See notes to Table 4.
Source: 2001 Canadian Census PUMS.

born females is only 1.1 percentage points less than that for Canadian born females, and this difference is not statistically significant. Moreover, in contrast to the findings for anglophone Canada, the earnings effects of years of under-education for foreign born females in Quebec do not differ from the earnings effects for their Canadian born counterparts (both estimates are -0.053). This implies that female immigrants in Quebec with relatively low levels of schooling are less favourably selected for immigration than is the case of female immigrants in anglophone Canada with relatively low levels of schooling.

The payoff to years of correctly matched schooling for female immigrants in Quebec, at 20.1 percent, exceeds the payoff to correctly matched schooling for their Canadian born counterparts (17.8 percent), although

66   *Barry R. Chiswick and Paul W. Miller*

the 2 percentage points difference is not statistically significant. This relativity is similar to that for males, but contrasts with the lower payoff to correctly matched schooling for foreign born females compared with Canadian born females in anglophone Canada. Thus, the only earnings effect associated with an education variable that is statistically different for foreign born females and Canadian born females in Quebec is that for over-education, where the payoff is 8.6 percent for the Canadian born and only 4.5 percent for the foreign born.

It is not immediately obvious why the patterns of earnings determination for the foreign born in Quebec are so different from those in the rest of Canada. It could be that the immigrants are from predominately francophone countries, and the similarity of their mother tongue with that

TABLE 17
Selected Estimates of Conventional and ORU Earnings Equations, Adult Females in Paid Employment, Living in Quebec and Anglophone Canada, 2001 Census [a]

	Canadian Born			Foreign Born		
Variable	(i)	(ii)	Mean/(SD)	(iv)	(v)	Mean/(SD)
Quebec						
Actual education	0.103	(c)	14.333	0.092	(c)	13.952
	(20.68)		(3.16)	(11.21)		(4.05)
Reference education [b]	(c)	0.178	14.398	(c)	0.201	13.951
		(22.97)	(1.68)		(14.18)	(1.92)
Over-education	(c)	0.086	1.045	(c)	0.045*	1.330
		(8.64)	(1.45)		(2.52)	(1.72)
Under-education	(c)	-0.053	1.110	(c)	-0.053	1.329
		(4.53)	(1.60)		(3.17)	(2.13)
$\bar{R}^2$	0.108	0.131	-	0.110	0.146	-
Sample size	5,789	5,789	5,789	2,076	2,076	2,076
Anglophone Canada						
Actual education	0.101	(c)	14.325	0.065*	(c)	14.265
	(30.15)		(2.77)	(22.74)		(3.36)
Reference education [b]	(c)	0.176	14.522	(c)	0.155*	14.182
		(33.21)	(1.48)		(29.20)	(1.52)
Over-education	(c)	0.059	0.890	(c)	0.038*	1.201
		(8.34)	(1.33)		(6.52)	(1.57)
Under-education	(c)	-0.078	1.087	(c)	-0.037*	1.118
		(8.92)	(1.38)		(6.06)	(1.83)
$\bar{R}^2$	0.114	0.136	-	0.097	0.119	-
Sample size	13,418	13,418	13,418	16,731	16,731	16,731

Notes: See notes to Table 4.
Source: 2001 Canadian Census PUMS.

of the Canadian born in Quebec leads to greater homogeneity in labour market outcomes. This matter warrants investigation in future research.

The decomposition was undertaken using the results of the ORU models estimated separately for Quebec and anglophone Canada. As the findings for anglophone Canada follow the pattern reported above for all of Canada, only the results for Quebec are presented and discussed here. The decompositions for male workers in Quebec are presented in Table 18 and the companion results for female workers in Quebec are presented in Table 19.

TABLE 18

Implied Payoffs to Schooling, Adjusting for Over-Education, Required Education, and Under-Education, Adult Males in Paid Employment, Living in Quebec, Canada Census, 2001

	% Payoff
Canadian born males	8.7
Foreign born males	8.5
No adjustment	
(a) Assuming same earnings effects to the ORU variables as for Canadian born males	8.5
(b) As for (a) but also same levels of ORU variables within each schooling category as for Canadian born males	8.6
(c) As for (b) but also assuming same distribution across schooling categories for foreign born males as for Canadian born males	8.7

Source: Authors' calculations.

TABLE 19

Implied Payoffs to Schooling, Adjusting for Over-Education, Required Education, and Under-Education, Adult Females in Paid Employment, Living in Quebec, Canada Census, 2001

	% Payoff
Canadian born females	10.0
Foreign born females	9.2
No adjustment	
(a) Assuming same earnings effects to the ORU variables as for Canadian born females	9.7
(b) As for (a) but also same levels of ORU variables within each schooling category as for Canadian born females	9.3
(c) As for (b) but also assuming same distribution across schooling categories for foreign born females as for Canadian born females	10.0

Source: Authors' calculations.

Table 18 shows that the implied payoffs to schooling for Canadian born and foreign born males in Quebec are similar. Adjustment for the earnings effects associated with the ORU variables, or for the mean values of these variables, has a negligible impact on the implied payoff to schooling for the foreign born. This contrasts with the aggregate-level findings in Table 6 (and similar findings for anglophone Canada, not reported here), which indicate that differences in the earnings effects for the foreign born and Canadian born associated with the ORU variables are largely responsible for a lower payoff to schooling for foreign born males in anglophone Canada.

Among females in Quebec there is also far greater similarity in the payoffs to schooling for the foreign born and Canadian born (a differential of only around 1 percentage point) than is the case in anglophone Canada (a differential of almost 4 percentage points). The Table 19 results reveal that the differences between the earnings effects associated with the ORU variables contribute to a modest 0.5 percentage point difference in the payoff to schooling for immigrants and the Canadian born. This is an attenuated version of the changes observed for the aggregate-level analyses for females in Table 7. Differences between foreign born females and their Canadian born counterparts in Quebec in the mean values of the ORU variables at each level of schooling are associated with a slight lowering of the payoff to schooling for the foreign born. Thus, the results in Tables 18 and 19 show that where there are only minor differences in the payoffs to schooling for birthplace groups, the decomposition methodology (Chiswick and Miller 2008) has little explanatory power.

US-Canada Comparisons

Finally, it is useful to draw explicit comparisons between the US and Canadian labour markets. These comparisons are restricted to males (owing to the focus in the comparison literature) and limited to the incidence of correctly matched and mismatched education and to findings from application of the decomposition methodology that is the novel contribution of this study. Table 20 lists information on the distribution of male workers across the correctly matched, over-educated, and under-educated categories in Canada and the United States.

The Table 20 data reveal that domestic born men in Canada are less likely to be correctly matched to the educational norms of their occupation than are domestic born men in the United States. They are, correspondingly, more likely to be either over-educated or under-educated than their counterparts in the United States. In contrast, while the foreign born in Canada and the United States have similar representation in the "correctly matched" category, the foreign born in Canada are more likely to be over-educated and less likely to be under-educated than the foreign born in

TABLE 20
Mean Schooling and Incidence of Correctly Matched, Over- and Under-Education by Country of Birth, Males 25-64, Canada and the United States

	Mean Schooling (years)	% Correctly Matched	% Over-Educated	% Under-Educated
Canada:				
Domestic born	14.018	69.15	18.35	12.49
Foreign born	14.404	59.62	27.07	13.31
United States:				
Domestic born	13.665	80.23	12.17	7.60
Foreign born	11.874	61.87	14.07	24.05

Source: 2001 Census of Canada PUMF; 2000 US Census PUMS.

the United States. The extent to which these differences in the incidence of correctly matched education, over-education and under-education impacts comparisons of earnings determination is explored in Table 21, which lists results of the decompositions undertaken for the two countries.

TABLE 21
Cross-Country Comparison of Decomposition of Immigrant/Domestic Born Difference in Payoff to Education, Canada and the United States, Males

Country	Payoff: Domestic Born	Payoff: Foreign Born	Payoff: Foreign Born Adjusting for Estimated ORU Effects	Payoff: Foreign Born Adjusting for Means of ORU Variables	Payoff: Foreign Born Adjusting for Weights
Canada	7.6	6.0	7.4	7.5	7.6
Canada-Developed	7.6	5.7	7.4	7.5	7.6
Canada-LDC	7.6	6.3	7.4	7.5	7.6
US	10.5	5.3	8.5	8.6	10.5
US-Developed	10.5	7.1	9.7	9.9	10.5
US-LDC	10.5	4.7	8.3	8.5	10.5

Note: Developed in Canada covers the US, UK, Netherlands, Germany, and Other Europe.
LDC = Less Developed Countries.
Source: Table 4 of this paper and Tables 6 and 8 of Chiswick and Miller (2008).

The first feature of Table 21 is that schooling is associated with a higher payoff for the domestic born in the United States (10.5 percent) than for the domestic born in Canada (7.6 percent). In contrast, the payoff to schooling for the foreign born in the United States, at 5.3 percent, is less than the payoff for the foreign born in Canada (6.0 percent). However, if the focus in the analyses for the United States is restricted to immigrants from the developed countries – to make allowance for the Hispanic effect (see Antecol et al. 2003) – the foreign born have a higher payoff to schooling in the United States than in Canada.

For both the United States and Canada, adjustment for differences in means of the ORU variables at each level of actual schooling has little effect on the implied payoff to schooling. Hence, the first main difference in the results of the decomposition is associated with the fact that in the United States, but not in Canada, adjustment for the different distributions of immigrants and the domestic born across the education categories matters. Consequently, whereas in Canada virtually all of the difference in the payoff to schooling for immigrants and the domestic born is linked to differences in the estimated effects of the ORU variables, in the United States only 62 percent of the gap in the payoffs to schooling is due to this source. In the case of developed countries, in the United States, the figure is 76 percent: for less developed countries it is 62 percent.

The second main difference arises when the effects on earnings of the ORU variables are considered one at a time. As noted in the previous section, adjustment for the earnings effects of under-education in Canada is associated with a narrowing of the gap in the payoffs to schooling by 1.2 percentage points for males, and adjustment for the earnings effects of over-education is associated with a narrowing of the male gap in the returns to schooling by 0.7 percentage points (a ratio of effects of 1.7, showing that under-education is more important in this regard). In the United States, the under-education phenomenon was much more important, accounting for 2.0 percentage points of the total coefficients effect compared to the 0.2 percentage point effect for over-education (a ratio of effects of 10) (Chiswick and Miller 2008). The implication is that the US labour market is characterized by a more intense favourable selection among the large number of low-skilled immigrants compared to Canada, which has few very low-skilled immigrants.

Conclusion

This paper has examined the reasons for the lower payoff to schooling for the foreign born than for the domestic born in the Canadian labour market among both males and females. It applies the decomposition developed by Chiswick and Miller (2008) to assess the determinants of the relative contributions to this low payoff of over-education among the foreign born (which is linked to less than perfect international transferability of human capital) and under-education among this group (which is linked to favourable selection in immigration). The results show that while both over-education and under-education contribute to the lower payoff to schooling for the foreign born, it is the latter labour market phenomenon that is more important. However, under-education in the labour market in Canada is far less important than it is in the United States.

The low payoff to immigrants' schooling should not necessarily be seen as a matter of concern. The framework used here suggests that only part of this apparent immigrant disadvantage is related to a potential labour market problem. This is the part linked to over-education, the less than perfect international transferability of human capital, or the non-recognition of foreign educational credentials. The part that is associated with under-education is in fact linked to immigrants doing better than what might be expected, given their level of schooling. As such, rather than being linked to disadvantage, this component of the lower payoff to schooling for immigrants is linked to superior labour market outcomes, particularly among the less well educated.

The role of over-education needs further investigation. The investigation needs to ascertain whether over-education is simply the result of the less than perfect international transferability of immigrants' human capital that was emphasized in the early writings of Chiswick (1978; 1979) or is due to quality differences in schooling undertaken in Canada and schooling undertaken abroad.[25] It might also result from barriers to the full recognition of foreign educational credentials due to occupational licensing, cultural differences, employer discrimination, or other factors. Policy interventions, including retraining or retooling programs, as well as efforts to increase information about foreign credentials and combating discrimination, might be fruitful activities.

Notes

We thank Derby Voon for research assistance, and Ted McDonald and an anonymous referee for helpful comments. Paul Miller acknowledges financial assistance from the Australian Research Council.

1. Abbott and Beach (1993) report a 20 percent lower payoff to schooling for immigrants than for the domestic born in their study of males based on the 1973 Job Mobility Survey, though this difference was not statistically significant.

2. To simplify the argument, the issue of the transferability of skills is minimal for those with few skills, while the ratio of out-of-pocket costs of migration to foregone earnings is higher for the less educated, thereby encouraging a higher propensity for favourable selectivity.

3. We also take the opportunity in passing to offer comments on the reason for the higher payoff to schooling for females than for males within each birthplace group (see Ferrer and Riddell 2008).

4. In the immigration literature, over-education or surplus education is often referred to as the non-recognition of foreign educational credentials. The central tendency of the educational attainment in an occupation is variously referred to in the ORU literature as the "usual," "reference," or "required" level of

education. As there is no standard terminology in the ORU literature, these terms are used interchangeably here as well. In the empirical application, studies differ in their use of the mean or the modal educational attainment to represent the "required" level.

5. The standard equation, $\ln Y_i = \beta_0 + \beta_1 \text{Actual Educ}_i + ... + \upsilon_i$, forces $\alpha_1 = \alpha_2 = |\alpha_3|$. As this condition does not hold, the ORU specification results in a higher R-squared and $\alpha_2 > \beta_1$.

6. An issue that was not explored was whether there was path dependence in the methodology, that is, whether the relative importance of under-education to the gap in the payoff to schooling between immigrants and the domestic born would change if adjustments were first made for differences in over-education and required education.

7. Chiswick and Miller (2008) focus on males only. The analyses below are done separately for males and females in Canada.

8. See Appendix A for the definitions of the dependent and explanatory variables.

9. Baker and Benjamin (1994) defined full-year using a threshold of 40 weeks worked in 2000, whereas Ferrer and Riddell (2008) use 52 weeks worked. The 40-week cut-off is used here, though a weeks worked variable is included in the analyses. Full-time refers to usually working 30 hours or more per week. Baker and Benjamin (1994) covered both part-time and full-time workers, though they included a number of hours-of-work dummy variables in their estimating equation. Ferrer and Riddell (2008) focus on 16-64 year olds, as do Baker and Benjamin (1994). The 25 years of age lower threshold used here will reduce the potential impact of selectivity issues associated with schooling and job training commitments among young adults.

10. Ferrer and Riddell (2008) include only wage and salary income. Baker and Benjamin (1994), however, include all those with positive earnings, defined as the sum of wage and salary and self-employment earnings.

11. Ferrer and Riddell (2008) use a 0.25 sampling fraction. Baker and Benjamin (1994) use a 1 in 6 random sample for the domestic born other than for blacks (for whom all records were used).

12. The purged sample of the foreign born represents 50 percent (males) and 36 percent (females) of the population aged 25-64 years of age. The more important sample exclusions involve the restriction to wage and salary earners (around one-half of the excluded observations, depending on the order of the exclusions), full-time workers (around 10 percent of exclusions for males and 20 percent for females), weeks worked of 40 or more (about 15 percent of exclusions for both males and females), and worked in the reference week (around 15 percent of exclusions for both males and females).

13. Self-employment earnings are included for those who worked mainly as wage and salary earners. Self-employment earnings, however, account for only 1 percent of total earnings in the sample under study.

14. Statistical significance is assessed through estimation of an earnings equation on data pooled across the domestic born and foreign born, with a full set of foreign-born interaction terms.

15. Appendix B can be obtained from the authors or from Chiswick and Miller (2009b).

16. When making comparisons between the United States and Canada, Antecol, Cobb-Clark, and Trejo (2003) have drawn attention to the importance in the United States of Latin American immigrants, especially those from Mexico, with very low levels of schooling.

17. When the gender difference in the payoffs to schooling is examined using this decomposition, the results are as follows. Among the domestic born, of the 2.4 percentage point gap in the payoffs, fully 96 percent is linked to differences in estimated coefficients, and of this amount, 61 percent is due to differences in the payoffs to reference levels of schooling, 13 percent to differences in the payoffs to under-education and 26 percent due to differences in the payoffs to over-education. In the case of the foreign born, all of the 0.8 percentage point gap in the payoffs to schooling is due to differences in estimated coefficients, with the reference and under-education variables making approximately equal contributions in this regard.

18. The information in the PUMF on age and year of arrival could be used to construct an alternative age at arrival variable that has more categories. We use the Census-provided derived variable to assist replication by other researchers of the results presented in this section.

19. Similar findings are reported by Schaafsma and Sweetman (2001, 1093) when they focus on the returns of schooling by age-at-arrival category.

20. The Census birthplace variable has categories for only the following foreign birthplaces: (i) US; (ii) UK; (iii) Germany; (iv) Netherlands; (v) Other European countries; (vi) Asia; and (vii) Other countries and regions.

21. Of the married female immigrants to Canada born in the United States, the spouse's country of birth was 74 percent in Canada, 13 percent in the United States, 8 percent in Europe, 2 percent in Asia, and 3 percent all other places.

22. Tests were conducted to determine whether US born men living in Canada in 2001 who immigrated at ages 18 to 26 years during the Vietnam War era had earnings significantly different from those of other male immigrants from the United States. The tests were inconclusive, perhaps because of the small sample size of those young men who came from the United States at this time and remained in Canada.

23. Study of male immigrants from Canada in the United States shows that the only adjustment that matters is a slight 0.6 percentage point effect for the distribution across schooling categories (Chiswick and Miller 2008).

24. Because of the data restrictions in the Census micro data file noted previously, those living in the Atlantic provinces are excluded.

25. One approach would be to relate the estimates from the ORU model for various birthplace groups to characteristics of the immigrants' countries of origin, such as the internationally standardized scores from the Programme for International Student Assessment (PISA). The limited detail on birthplace among the foreign born prevents pursuing this with the 2001 Census data, but it would be possible with 2000 US Census data. We are grateful to Charles Beach for this suggestion.

REFERENCES

Abbott, M.G., and C.M. Beach. 1993. "Immigrant Earnings Differentials and Birth-Year Effects for Men in Canada: Post-War–1972." *Canadian Journal of Economics* 26 (3): 505-24.

Antecol, H., D.A. Cobb-Clark, and S.J. Trejo. 2003. "Immigrant Policy and the Skills of Immigrants to Australia, Canada and the United States." *Journal of Human Resources* 28 (1): 192-218.

Baker, M., and D. Benjamin. 1994. "The Performance of Immigrants in the Canadian Labor Market." *Journal of Labor Economics* 12 (3): 369-405.

Chiswick, B.R. 1978. "The Effect of Americanization on the Earnings of Foreign Born Men." *Journal of Political Economy* 86 (5): 897-921.

– 1979. "The Economic Progress of Immigrants: Some Apparently Universal Patterns." In *Contemporary Economic Problems 1979*, edited by W. Fellner, 357-99. Washington, DC: American Enterprise Institute for Public Policy Research.

– 1999. "Are Immigrants Favorably Self-Selected?" *American Economic Review* 89 (2): 181-5.

Chiswick, B.R., and P.W. Miller. 2008. "Why Is the Payoff to Schooling Smaller for Immigrants?" *Labour Economics* 15 (6): 1317-40.

– 2009a. "Does the Choice of Reference Levels of Education Matter in the ORU Earnings Equation?" Discussion Paper No. 4382 (August). Bonn: Institute for the Study of Labor (IZA).

– 2009b. "An Explanation for the Lower Payoff to Schooling for Immigrants in the Canadian Labour Market." Discussion Paper No. 4448 (September). Bonn: Institute for the Study of Labor (IZA).

Ferrer, A., and W.C. Riddell. 2008. "Education, Credentials, and Immigrant Earnings." *Canadian Journal of Economics* 41 (1): 186-216.

Friedberg, R.M. 2000. "You Can't Take It with You? Immigrant Assimilation and the Portability of Human Capital." *Journal of Labor Economics* 18 (2): 221-51.

Hartog, J. 2000. "Over-Education and Earnings: Where Are We, Where Should We Go?" *Economics of Education Review* 19 (2): 131-47.

Schaafsma, J., and A. Sweetman. 2001. "Immigrant Earnings: Age at Immigration Matters." *Canadian Journal of Economics* 34 (4): 1066-99.

APPENDIX A
DEFINITIONS OF VARIABLES

The variables used in the statistical analyses are defined below.

Data source: 2001 Census of Canada, Public Use Microdata Sample, 2.7 percent sample of the foreign born, and 0.3 random sample of this microdata file for the domestic born.

Definition of population: Domestic born and foreign born men and women aged 25 to 64 who are classified as being in full-time, full-year paid employment, excluding the Maritime or Atlantic provinces and those full-time who are self-employed.

Dependent Variables

Income in 2000	Natural logarithm of earnings in 2000, where earnings are defined as gross earnings from wages/salaries and self-employment income.

Explanatory Variables

Years of education	This variable records the total years of full-time equivalent education. It has been constructed from the Census data on the total years of schooling completed in primary and secondary school, in university, and in post-secondary institutions other than universities. Experimentation with alternative definitions, formed using years of schooling equivalents for the highest level of schooling completed, did not result in any major changes to the findings.
Usual level of education	This variable records the required years of education. It is the mean level of education in the worker's occupation, based on the "realized matches" procedure.
Years of under-education	The under-education variable equals the difference between the years of education that are usual in persons' occupation and their actual years of education where this computation is positive. Otherwise, it is set equal to zero.
Years of over-education	The over-education variable equals the difference between persons' actual years of education and the years of education that are usual in their occupation where this computation is positive. Otherwise, it is set equal to zero.
Weeks worked in 2000	This is a continuous variable for the numbers of weeks the individual worked in 2000.
Experience	Age minus years of education minus 6.
Metropolitan area	The location variable records residence in a metropolitan area.
Province	Four dichotomous variables have been constructed to record different provinces and territories: Quebec, Ontario, Prairie, and British Columbia (the benchmark). Residents of the Atlantic provinces are excluded.
Marital status	This is a binary variable that distinguishes individuals who are married (equal to 1) from all other marital states.
Official language proficiency	This is a dichotomous variable used to record whether the individual is fluent in English or French.
Years since migration	This is computed from the year the foreign born person arrived in Canada.
Citizenship	This is a dichotomous variable set equal to 1 for foreign born who hold Canadian citizenship.

4

ENTRY EARNINGS OF IMMIGRANT MEN IN CANADA: THE ROLES OF LABOUR MARKET ENTRY EFFECTS AND RETURNS TO FOREIGN EXPERIENCE

DAVID A. GREEN AND CHRISTOPHER WORSWICK

Dans cet article, nous analysons les causes de la baisse des gains initiaux des immigrants au cours des années 1980 et 1990 et au début des années 2000. Nous observons tout d'abord que cette baisse ne touche pas que les immigrants; les nouveaux arrivants sur le marché du travail nées au Canada ont également subit des baisses de gains initiaux. En faisant la différence entre les gains initiaux des immigrants et ceux des Canadiens de naissance qui entrent sur le marché du travail au même moment, nous éliminons les effets des changements dans l'économie canadienne qui ne sont pas propres aux immigrants. Subséquemment, nos résultats montrent que le recul du rendement de l'expérience de travail acquise à l'étranger joue un rôle important dans la baisse des gains initiaux des immigrants des différentes cohortes étudiées; et que le recul de ce rendement est fortement liée au changement que l'on observe dans la composition des pays d'origine des immigrants. Ainsi, nous expliquons 74 pourcent de la baisse des gains initiaux entre les immigrants de la cohorte 1980-1982 et les immigrants de la cohorte 2000-2002 par une combinaison de différents facteurs : des effets communs à tous les nouveaux arrivants (39 pourcent), des changements dans la composition des pays d'origine (16 pourcent), et l'aplatissement du profil d'expérience acquise à l'étranger (24 pourcent). L'augmentation, durant les années 1990, du nombre de points alloués aux candidats à l'immigration ayant une scolarité de niveau universitaire a en fait influencé la tendance dans la direction opposée, c'est-à-dire que les gains initiaux des immigrants auraient connu une baisse encore plus importante (d'environ 5 %) sans cette mesure, qui a occasionné une modification de la composition de l'immigration en matière de niveau de scolarité.

Canadian Immigration: Economic Evidence for a Dynamic Policy Environment, ed. T. McDonald, E. Ruddick, A. Sweetman, and C. Worswick. Montreal and Kingston: Queen's Policy Studies Series, McGill-Queen's University Press.
© 2010 The School of Policy Studies, Queen's University at Kingston. All rights reserved.

*Investigating the sources of declines in entry earnings for Canadian immigrants in the
1980s, 1990s, and early 2000s, we find that these declines are not unique to immigrants:
Canadian born new entrants to the labour market also faced declines in entry earnings.
Differencing immigrant entry earnings relative to those of domestic born workers entering the labour market at the same time provides a means of removing the effects of
changes in the Canadian economy that are not specific to immigrants. After doing this,
we find that substantial declines in returns to foreign experience play an important role
in declines in entry earnings across immigrant cohorts. The declining return to foreign
experience is strongly related to shifts in the source country composition of immigration.
In the end, we can account for 74 percent of the decline in entry earnings between the
1980-82 and the 2000-02 immigrant cohort with a combination of general new entrant
effects (39 percent), shifts in the source country composition (16 percent), and flattening
of the foreign experience profile (24 percent). The substantial increase in the 1990s in the
points allocated to immigrant applicants with university education actually worked in the
opposite direction, meaning that immigrant entry earnings would have been even lower
in the absence of the resulting shift in educational composition (equivalent to 5 percent
of the decline in entry earnings).*

Introduction

Policy concern has once again become concentrated on issues relating
to immigrant adaptation to Canadian society. Recent research indicates
that all of the increase in Canada's low income rate over the last 20 years
can be accounted for by increases in poverty among immigrants (Picot
and Hou 2003). This raises issues relating to the impact of immigrants
on the public purse but, perhaps more importantly, points to increasing
difficulties for immigrants in finding a place in Canadian society. Those
difficulties, as measured by the low income rate, are particularly acute
just after immigrants arrive in Canada. Not surprisingly, very similar
patterns are observed in immigrant earnings. Extensive research shows
that average immigrant earnings in the first year after arrival fell by over
20 percent in the 1980s (Baker and Benjamin 1994; Bloom, Grenier, and
Gunderson 1995; Grant 1999; Reitz 2001). But as large as those declines
were, the drops in entry earnings in the 1990s were even larger (Li 2003;
Aydemir and Skuterud 2005; Sweetman and Warman 2008). Our goal in
this paper is to investigate the source of the declines in immigrant entry
earnings in the 1980s, 1990s, and early 2000s in Canada. While the earnings
patterns for Canadian immigrants in the 1980s are well documented, we
know little about why the outcomes worsened in the 1990s and became
worse still in the 2000s. Moreover, data limitations in earlier papers mean
that there is more to be learned about the 1980s declines.

One key possible explanation for the fall in immigrant entry earnings in the 1980s and 1990s is that it is not unique to the immigrant experience but reflects declines in labour market outcomes among all new entrants to the labour market. Beaudry and Green (2000) show substantial declines in weekly earnings for more recent cohorts of all labour market entrants (the Canadian born and immigrants). The poor immigrant performance may just reflect the same forces underlying the poor outcomes for young Canadian born workers. In order to evaluate this possibility, we adopt an approach in which we compare cohorts of immigrants to Canadian born workers entering the labour market at the same time. To do this, we use both a unique dataset that links immigrant landing and tax records (the Immigrant Database, or IMDB, for the years 1981 through 2003) to get immigrant data, and a series of representative surveys to get Canadian born data (the Surveys of Consumer Finance, or SCFs, for the years 1981 through 1997 and the Survey of Labour and Income Dynamics, or SLID, for the years 1996 through 2003). We carry out our entire investigation for males broken down by broad educational class.

Our findings indicate that the Canadian born do experience substantial declines in entry earnings across entry cohorts. However, the cross-cohort declines for immigrants are substantially larger. Thus we need to look for explanations beyond problems faced by any worker (immigrant or non-immigrant) in gaining entrance to the Canadian labour market. We find that a key feature of earnings patterns for immigrants is the evaporation of earnings differentials by years of foreign experience between the early 1980s and through the 1990s and early 2000s. For the 1980-82 entry cohort, immigrants in all education groups have earnings patterns reflecting substantial "returns" to foreign experience; by the 1990-92 entry cohort, however, there is no evidence of any differential in entry earnings by years of foreign experience. The finding of a flat foreign experience profile fits with Friedberg's (2000) results for Israel, but in Canada's case the pattern represents a dramatic shift from earlier periods. The shift is largely (though not completely) explained by shifts in the source country composition of immigration toward countries from which one would expect that it is more difficult to transfer human capital. In the end we can account for 74 percent of the decline in entry earnings between the immigrant cohort entering in the 1980-82 period and that entering in 2000-02 with a combination of general new entrant effects (39 percent), shifts in the source country composition (16 percent), and the flattening of the foreign experience profile (24 percent). However, the change in educational composition of new immigrant arrival cohorts actually moved in the opposite direction, indicating that immigrant entry earnings would have fallen even more (-5 percent) in the absence of this compositional shift.

Thus, declines in immigrant earnings over the last two decades point, in part, to more general problems for new entrants to the labour market, whether immigrants or not. They also indicate a need for concern over the ability of immigrants – particularly those from non-European and non-English speaking countries – to transfer to Canada human capital acquired in the source country labour market. This is a concern over and above more standard discussions about transferability of credentials and formal education.

While we focus in this paper almost exclusively on entry earnings, they, of course, only constitute part of the picture of how immigrants adapt to the Canadian economy. The sharply worse entry earnings in the 1990s were accompanied by strong increases in earnings growth after arrival, implying that immigrants might have been able to overcome initial disadvantages. This is in contrast to the 1980s, when successive cohorts of immigrant entrants faced lower entry earnings without offsetting increases in post-arrival growth rates (Baker and Benjamin 1994). We argue that focusing on entry earnings is useful for two reasons. First, politicians and policy-makers may, reasonably, heavily discount later parts of the immigrant earnings profile, worrying more about high levels of hardship just after arrival. Entry earnings are also of interest because to some extent they reflect initial transferability of the human capital an immigrant brings to Canada. This transferability is generally seen as an issue of particular concern in understanding immigrant adaptation (e.g., Reitz 2001).

We begin by describing our data, setting out the main patterns we are seeking to explain and making a case that the data provide results similar to those from more commonly used datasets such as the Census. We then describe our empirical specification, with the results from implementing that specification following. We investigate various potential explanations for the sharp declines in returns to foreign experience, which, as we mentioned earlier, is one of the dominant patterns in the data. The next section contains the results of a decomposition exercise in which we apportion the decline in entry earnings to components related to the general decline in earnings for all new entrants, shifts in the source country composition of the immigrant inflow, and declines in returns to foreign experience. The final section contains conclusions.

Overall Data Patterns

Data Description

We examine earnings patterns using three datasets. For immigrants, we use a special dataset based on immigrant administrative data and tax data called the Immigrant Database (IMDB). For the Canadian born, we use both the Survey of Consumer Finances (SCF) and the Survey of Labour and Income Dynamics (SLID). Both are large, nationally representative household surveys that can be used to generate statistics representative of the Canadian born population. We use all available years for the individual level files from the SCF, 1981, 1982, 1984-1997, and use the SLID for the period 1997 through 2003 (using the overlapping years of 1996 and 1997 to account for possible differences in design across the two Statistics Canada surveys). We also use the IMDB tax year samples for the years 1981, 1982, 1984-2003, dropping the 1983 tax year data to improve comparability with the SCF, for which the 1983 data do not exist.

The IMDB consists of a linkage of the landing records for all the immigrants arriving in Canada after 1980 to their tax records in subsequent years. The landing records consist mainly of the information taken by immigration officials as part of processing the immigrant application. From this we know the individual's source country, gender, and education level and age at time of arrival. Applicants are placed in one of three broad assessment categories, information on which forms part of our data: independents (applicants who are assessed based only on their skills – education, experience, language ability, etc.); family class (applicants who enter based on family relationships to people living in Canada); and refugees. This information from the landing records is linked to the individual tax records for subsequent years. This means, in part, that we do not observe individuals who do not file tax forms, though since we focus on individuals with positive earnings, this is unlikely to cause problems. We also do not know if immigrants obtain extra education or training after arriving in Canada since education is not reported on the tax form, and thus we classify immigrants based on education at time of arrival.

The SCF was conducted annually up to 1997 as an add-on to the Labour Force Survey. From the SCF, we obtain data on annual earnings, age, education, and gender for domestic born Canadians in order to generate a benchmark for the immigrant data. The SLID is a longitudinal survey; however, it is used in this paper to generate cross-sections of data that are representative of the Canadian born population for the relevant survey year. We use it in this way so as to match the cross-sectional information available in the SCF data. Ideally, we would use the SCF over the entire time period of interest; however, the SCF ceased to be collected after the 1997 survey year.

The earnings measure upon which we focus is real annual earnings, deflated using the CPI. We have no way of pro-rating earnings of immigrants according to how long they were in the country in their landing year. In response, we do not use earnings data from the landing year. Thus, our entry earnings measure corresponds to the first full year after landing in Canada. Given that we are using annual earnings, our dependent variable will reflect variation in hours and weeks worked as well as wages, which is worth noting for immigrants, who tend to have high unemployment rates just after arrival (Reitz 2001). For immigrants, earnings patterns for a given education at arrival group may also reflect educational upgrading, which we view as part of immigrant assimilation.

We divide the immigrant sample into cohorts defined by year of landing in Canada. Even though the IMDB is a true panel, in order to match with the SCF we carry out our analysis by forming synthetic cohorts. That is, we treat the data as a series of cross-sections. In each year we identify the individuals who entered Canada in a given period and calculate their average earnings. The set of these averages across years constitutes the annual earnings path for the cohort. As we will see below, an educational breakdown is crucial for understanding movements in overall earnings. Thus, we define cohorts by both landing year of entry and education level. Such a definition is only reasonable if individual values for the education variable do not change over the period the cohort is followed. For immigrants, this condition is met because their education at arrival is linked to their earnings in each year in our data. For the Canadian born, this requirement is more problematic. To ensure that education status is unlikely to change over time for given Canadian born cohorts, we focus our analysis on individuals (either Canadian born or immigrant) whose age is greater than or equal to 25 (which we call the age of entering the mature labour market). Given this, we assume year of landing is the same as the year of labour market entry in our comparisons to Canadian born earnings. We also specify a maximum age of 64 for our samples. In this analysis we focus only on men, addressing the very different patterns for females in another paper.

Immigrants are assigned to a given cohort according to the year of obtaining landed immigrant status in Canada. We define seven cohorts: 1980-82, 1983-86, 1987-89, 1990-92, 1993-96, 1997-99, and 2000-02. These groupings are chosen to reflect a combination of immigration policy regimes and cyclical conditions. Thus, 1980-82 contains the beginning of a recession and a period in which immigration inflows were relatively large. The 1983-86 cohort entered during a period of economic recovery but also a period in which the immigration door was basically shut to independents: applicants could only enter the country through the family or refugee classes or if they had already arranged employment. In 1986, the arranged employment restriction was removed, and the proportion of the inflow accounted for by independents increased again. However, the inflows in the next five to eight years are still dominated by family and refugee class immigrants. Thus, the 1987-89 cohort entered during a period with this type of immigration policy in an economic boom, and 1990-93 is a period with similar policy but a recession. The period 1993-96 exhibits no strong trends in the labour market, and in policy is marked by a move toward giving greater priority to independent class immigrants. The period 1997-99 reflects a period of strong labour market conditions, while 2000-02 represents a period of turbulent macroeconomic conditions. In our interpretations, we do not try to relate our results directly to policy regimes, but we do feel it is useful to organize the cohorts so that they are not a muddle of policies and labour market conditions.[1] We also organize the Canadian born by cohort, in this case defined by their year of labour market entry (i.e., the year in which they turn 25), with cohorts defined using the same year groups as for immigrants.

Due to access restrictions to the confidential IMDB data, we carried out our estimation in two steps. First, we estimated a log earnings model over the individual data of the IMDB that contained provincial dummy variables as well as dummy variables for each year-of-arrival/education/survey year combination.[2] Three separate models were estimated for the three education groups. Next, the synthetic cohort sample was generated by predicting the log earnings for each cell, holding the province of residence effect at the default value (Ontario). Therefore, provincial variation in earnings was removed from the synthetic cohort sample. For immigrants, we carried this exercise out separately for four separate age-at-arrival categories: 25-29, 30-34, 35-39, and 40-44. The end result was an immigrant synthetic cohort sample containing predicted log earnings for approximately 2900 cells (year of arrival/education/survey year/age-at-arrival combinations). It is this sample we use in subsequent estimation. Later in the paper we also make use of data created in the same way but broken down by country of origin. Weighted least squares regression is employed throughout the analysis, with the weights based upon the estimates of the standard errors of the predicted log earnings from the first stage regression analysis.

The Overall Pattern in Male Immigrant Earnings

We begin by using our data to establish the broad patterns in immigrant earnings in the past two decades. Thus, Figure 1 contains separate earnings–Canadian experience profiles for each immigrant cohort with cycle effects removed. The plots correspond to fitted average earnings from a regression of average log earnings on a set of cohort dummy variables, a spline function in years since entering the Canadian labour market (YSE) variable with a linear segment over the range 1 to 9 years and a second linear segment over the range 10 and more years, interactions of the 1 to 9 YSE spline segment and the cohort dummy variables, education dummy variables, and a de-trended unemployment rate variable. We use the acronym YSE rather than the more conventional YSM (for years-since-migration) since we also use an equivalent definition for the Canadian born in which YSE represents years since entering the Canadian labour market for the domestic born. While the spline approach to the specification of YSE effects is unconventional in the immigration literature, we investigated a number of different parameterizations of the YSE profiles and found that this approach appeared to best represent the underlying patterns in the data. The de-trended unemployment rate variable was included in an attempt to strip out cyclical variation and focus on long

FIGURE 1
Predicted Differences in Log Earnings Relative to Entry Earnings of 1980-82 Immigrant Arrival Cohort, Immigrant Men

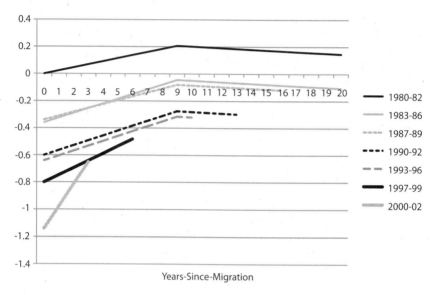

Years-Since-Migration

Source: Authors' estimations based on the IMDB, SFC, and SLID data described in the text.

term patterns. We normalize the plots relative to the entry earnings for the 1980-82 cohort.

The most striking pattern in Figure 1, and the point of emphasis in this paper, is the dramatic fall in real earnings at time of arrival across cohorts. Relative to the 1980-82 entry cohort, earnings at arrival are .6 log points lower for the 1993-96 cohort, and this trend of deteriorating entry earnings accelerates further for the 1997-99 cohort at .8 log points lower and for the 2000-02 cohort at 1.14 log points lower. However, the cohorts with the lowest starting earnings also have the highest earnings growth rates after arrival. The overall pattern can be roughly divided into two periods. In the first, the cohorts entering in the mid- and late 1980s earn approximately .35 log points lower earnings at arrival than the 1980-82 cohort and do not fully catch up to them within the 20 year window. In the second period, the cohorts entering in the 1990s have much lower entry earnings, a pattern that accelerated through the late 1990s, but the cohorts since 1997 have also seen larger post-arrival earnings growth. The fact that the 1980s cohorts fall behind earlier cohorts (and the Canadian born) and do not catch back up has been the source of considerable investigation (e.g., Baker and Benjamin 1994; Bloom, Grenier, and Gunderson 1995; McDonald and Worswick 1998; Grant 1999). The fact that the 1990s entry cohorts have even lower entry earnings is also known (Li 2003; Frenette and Morissette 2003; Aydemir and Skuterud 2005) but has not previously been subjected to an in-depth investigation. The results also match those for the United States, where declines in entry earnings across cohorts have been extensively debated since they were first identified by Borjas (1987).

PATTERNS IN ENTRY EARNINGS BY EDUCATION

Figure 2 presents average entry earnings by cohort and education level. Since our emphasis in the analysis that follows is on entry earnings and is broken down by education, this figure reveals the basic data patterns we are seeking to investigate. The points in these plots are obtained as the coefficients on cohort dummy variables in log earnings regressions (for immigrants only), which include a complete set of cohort dummy variables, the same spline function in YSE as in Figure 1, full interactions of the cohort dummies and the 1 to 9 YSE spline segment, and a de-trended unemployment rate. The regressions were run separately for each education group (high school graduate or lower, post-secondary below a BA, and BA or higher university degree). Thus the plotted points for a given education level correspond to average entry earnings after controlling for cyclical effects.

FIGURE 2
Log Differences in Entry Earnings of Immigrant Arrival Cohorts Relative to 1980-82 Cohorts

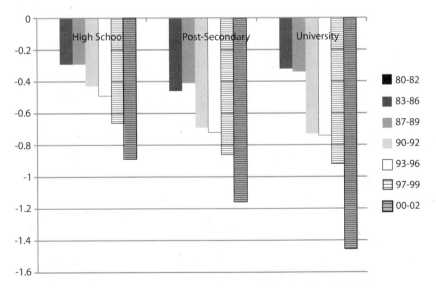

Source: Authors' estimations based on the IMDB, SFC, and SLID data described in the text.

The plots in Figure 2 reveal patterns for each education group that are similar to the intercepts of the profiles for immigrants as a whole in Figure 1. Specifically, they reveal substantial drops in entry earnings in the 1980s, followed by even more dramatic drops in the 1990s and into the early 2000s. As we discuss later, the larger declines in the 1990s are offset by higher post-arrival growth rates for each group. This recovery may to some extent mitigate concerns about the post-1990 immigrants, but if policy-makers are worried about immigrant outcomes just after arrival, then Figure 2 reveals a disturbing pattern. Finally, note that the declines in entry earnings are worse for the post-secondary-below-BA and university educated immigrants than those with high school or less education.

Figure 3 contains the same type of plot as Figure 2 but for Canadian born workers. As we discuss below, we believe that organizing Canadian born workers by cohort, while not standard, is very useful when forming a comparison group for immigrant cohorts. The figure also reveals a decline in entry earnings across Canadian born cohorts.[3]

For the high school educated, the decline across the 1980s is similar in magnitude to that experienced by high school educated immigrants. The declines for more educated Canadian born workers are decidedly less than their immigrant counterparts in both decades. Also, for Canadian born workers, there was a rebound in the 2000 to 2002 cohort. This rebound is especially pronounced for the post-secondary-below-BA group, and the early 1997-99 cohort for this educational grouping also shows a recovery

FIGURE 3
Log Differences in Entry Earnings of Canadian Born Arrival Cohorts Relative to 1980-82 Cohort

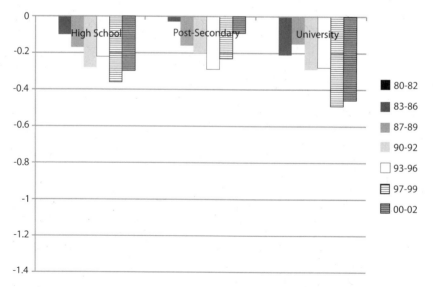

Source: Authors' estimations based on the IMDB, SFC, and SLID data described in the text.

in terms of entry earnings when compared with the 1993-96 cohort. This improvement in the entry earnings for Canadian born near the end of our sample period is not present for immigrants. It is worth emphasizing that the declines across Canadian born cohorts do not look large because we have purposefully plotted them on the same scale as we used for immigrants. However, the Canadian born declines are still substantial: on the order of 20 to 35 percent real declines between the 1980-82 cohort and the 1993-96 cohorts. This fits with the results of Beaudry and Green (2000) and Green and Townsend (forthcoming), who focus specifically on cohort patterns in Canadian earnings.

ESTIMATION APPROACH

General Specification

In classic immigrant earnings decompositions (e.g., Lalonde and Topel 1992), the average earnings in period t for an immigrant in education category s who entered the Canadian labour market in period j is specified as:

$$y^I_{jts} = \mu^I_{js} + a^I_{jts} + b^I_{jts} \qquad (1)$$

where y corresponds to annual earnings and the I superscript refers to immigrants. In this specification, average earnings levels are determined by three processes: μ_{js} (often called cohort effects) represents differences across entry cohorts in their average level of earnings; a_{jts} represents the effects of post-schooling human capital accumulation (the part of earnings generation that is usually captured in a polynomial in years of experience) plus any assimilation of immigrants into the host economy; and b_{jts} represents the impact of macro-economic events on the given cohort. This specification allows for macro events to have different impacts on different vintages of human capital and for the experience profile to vary by cohort. Typically, researchers search for a comparison group, which is used to identify the effects of macro events and the experience profile. The differences between immigrant earnings and those of the comparison group then are interpreted as identifying a combination of the cohort effect (μ_{js}) and the part of the a_{jts} term that corresponds to immigrant assimilation. Perhaps the most common comparison group is Canadian born workers with the same levels of education and total experience as a given immigrant.

While this framework has typically been applied to analyses of immigrant earnings, one could equally well use it in examining Canadian born earnings. Papers by Beaudry and Green (2000) for Canada and MaCurdy and Mroz (1995) for the United States arrange domestic born data by labour market entry cohort. Beaudry and Green (2000) find approximately 20 percent declines in real weekly wages between the 1981 and 1993 cohorts. MaCurdy and Mroz (1995) find similar results using American CPS data. Card and Lemieux (2001) examine skill differentials by cohort for the United States, the United Kingdom, and Canada and argue that the relative size of skill groups within cohorts have impacts on those differentials. Taken together, these papers suggest that earnings outcomes have been quite different across successive generations of new labour market entrants. The implication is that different generations are not perfect substitutes in production and that they experience differently macro events such as technology shocks or the passage of the baby boom through the age structure. This might reasonably be predicted in a simple human capital model where cohorts "lock in" to a specific set of skills (i.e., cease to make further investments) early on in their lives and make investment decisions based on the specific skill price paths they anticipate. In that situation, the most natural comparison group for immigrants is the set of people who are facing the same anticipated paths of prices and the same types of skill investment decisions: other new labour market entrants. We construct a specification based on using Canadian born workers entering the labour market at the same time as a given immigrant cohort as the comparison group intended to capture general macro movements in the economy.[4]

The amount and type of source country human capital an immigrant brings to the host country play a key role in any examination of immigrant human capital investment and earnings after migration. Indeed, work by Friedberg (2000) for Israel indicates that much of the shortfall in earnings for immigrants relative to observationally similar domestic born workers in that country can be accounted for by very low valuation of foreign acquired experience in Israel (see also Schaafsma and Sweetman (2001) for similar results for Canada). For this reason, we use a specification that permits considerable flexibility in the earnings profile based on education and foreign experience. More specifically, we perform all of our estimation separately by education groups, effectively defining cohorts by a combination of year of entry into the labour market (or, more properly, landing year) and education. We also allow immigrants' earnings at arrival and post-arrival earnings growth to vary with years of foreign experience.

Based on this discussion, we adopt a regression specification for the year t log earnings of an individual from cohort, j, and schooling level, s, given by (suppressing the individual specific index for simplicity):

$$y_{jts} = a_{0js}^N + a_{1js}^N YSE09_{jts} + a_{2js}^N YSE10_{jts} + a_{3s}^N UNEMP_t$$
$$+ DIMIG * (\delta_{0js}^I + \delta_{1js}^I YSE09_{jts} + \delta_{2js}^I YSE10_{jts} + \delta_{3s}^I UNEMP_t) \quad (2)$$
$$+ \beta_{1js}^I FEXP_{jts} + \beta_{2js}^I FEXP_{jts}^2 + \gamma_s^I FEXP_{jts} YSE09_{jts}) + u_{jts}$$

where the N superscripts correspond to parameters relevant for Canadian born workers, I superscripts correspond to immigrant parameters, DIMIG is a dummy variable equal to one for immigrants and zero for the Canadian born, UNEMP is a de-trended annual unemployment rate, and FEXP equals years of foreign experience, YSE is the number of years since entry into the Canadian labour market and is calculated as age minus 25 (the age we use as denoting entry into the mature labour market) for the Canadian born and years since landing in Canada for immigrants. The YSE information is included as a spline function with two linear segments over the YSE range of 0 to 9 years (YSE09) and 10 and over years (YSE10). FEXP is calculated as age at arrival minus an assumed school leaving age that differs by level of schooling. We include the UNEMP variable in order to focus attention on long run as opposed to cyclical patterns. Notice that the pattern of subscripts and superscripts implies that each Canadian born cohort (defined both by the year in which workers turned 25 and their schooling) has its own spline function in YSE; each immigrant cohort also has its own spline function in YSE; the intercepts of the immigrant profiles are allowed to vary with years of foreign experience, with this foreign experience profile being allowed to be different for each cohort; and that the slope of the immigrant earnings profile is allowed to vary with FEXP in a way that differs across schooling groups but not by year of arrival. In earlier estimations we allowed the FEXP*YSE09 interaction effect to vary by year of arrival as well as schooling level but found that this made the results harder to interpret, with little pay-off in terms of results. Thus, we adopt the simpler specification here.

In the remainder of the paper, we refer to variation in entry earnings with years of foreign experience as "returns to foreign experience." This phrase should be interpreted cautiously, however. Immigrants who arrive with different numbers of years of foreign experience will face different selection processes, both in terms of the points system and their own motivation. Thus, the derivative of earnings with respect to FEXP might not reflect a simple return on foreign acquired human capital. This should be kept in mind in the discussion that follows.

While the specification given in equation (2) involves the estimation of complete earnings–Canadian experience profiles, we focus our attention on entry earnings patterns as captured in the intercept terms (α_{0js}^N and δ_{0js}^I) and on the FEXP parameters (β_{1js}^I and β_{2js}^I). We do this for two reasons. First, it focuses attention on the period just after arrival when immigrants face considerable adjustment and hardship. Picot and Hou's (2003) work suggests that immigrants are most likely to endure poverty just after arrival. Second, given these early problems, it is probable that politicians and policy-makers will pay particular attention to outcomes for immigrants just after arrival: falling entry earnings are likely to be viewed with concern even if they are ultimately offset by higher post-arrival earnings growth.

ESTIMATION RESULTS

We turn now to our estimates of regression (2). In implementing it, we actually run separate regressions for each of the three education groups.

In each case, the immigrant data is pooled with data from Canadian born workers with the same education level who are in one of the five cohorts defined earlier (i.e., we do not use Canadian born workers who entered the labour market before 1981). We implement a specification with complete flexibility by education group because we believe human capital considerations are likely to play a significant role in understanding changes in entry earnings over time. As we will see, immigrant entry earnings patterns are quite different for the least educated (high school graduate or less) group compared to their counterparts with some post-secondary education.

The Canadian Born

Table 1 contains the estimates of the α_{0js}^N, α_{1js}^N, α_{2js}^N and α_{3s}^N parameters. The first column shows the results for the high school educated. The coefficients denoted as Cohort Dummies correspond to estimates of the intercepts of the cohort profiles (i.e., the entry earnings) measured relative to the intercept of the first (1980-82) entry cohort. With the exception of the last cohort, successive cohorts have declining entry earnings. This is the pattern depicted in Figure 3. The combination of these intercept effects with the cohort-YSE interactions indicate that the 1990s cohorts enter at lower earnings than their 1980s counterparts, but they are at least partially compensated for this by their higher earnings growth rates (although the coefficients on the YSE interaction with the 2000-02 cohort is not statistically significant and of the opposite sign).[5] Thus (again, with the exception of the last cohort) the pattern is similar to that portrayed for immigrants in Figure 1. Finally, the de-trended unemployment rate effect shows that earnings fall in high unemployment periods.

The second column of Table 1 presents results for Canadian born workers with a post-secondary-below-BA education. The patterns are somewhat similar to those for the high school educated, with declining entry earnings through the mid-1990s. However, a small rebound is present for the 1997-99 cohort and in particular for the 2000-02 cohort. The initial earnings for the post-secondary-below-BA educated in the first cohort are similar to those for the high school educated, but the growth rate for the post-secondary-below-BA educated workers is 50 percent higher than for the high school educated. Finally, the results for the university educated in the third column are more like those for the high school educated – with the 1990s cohorts and the early 2000s following a different path from the 1980s cohorts. However, the sizes of the coefficients on the more recent arrival cohorts are larger in absolute value than for the high school group, indicating very large earnings disadvantages at entry. The university educated have much larger lifetime earnings growth rates and, in contrast to both the other groups, appear impervious to cyclical variation.

TABLE 1
Cohort Based Regression Estimates of Average Log Annual Earnings:
Canadian Born Men by Education Group

Variables	High School or Less Educated	Post-Secondary-below-BA Educated	University Educated
Constant	10.15 (.022)*	10.25 (.031)*	10.27 (.048)*
Cohort dummies			
1983-86 cohort	-.10 (.030)*	-.029 (.044)	-.21 (.070)*
1987-89 cohort	-.17 (.031)*	-.16 (.050)*	-.15 (.075)
1990-92 cohort	-.28 (.035)*	-.20 (.038)*	-.29 (.064)*
1993-96 cohort	-.22 (.039)*	-.29 (.055)*	-.28 (.060)*
1997-99 cohort	-.36 (.058)*	-.23 (.071)*	-.49 (.18)*
2000-02 cohort	-.30 (.046)*	-.093 (.080)	-.46 (.13)*
Years since labour market entry (YSE) spline for 0 to 9 years	.022 (.0034)*	.032 (.0043)*	.061 (.007)*
YSE spline for 10 or more years	.0098 (.0028)*	.0067 (.0029)*	.011 (.0043)*
Cohort/ YSE 0-9 spline interactions			
1983-86 cohort	.0050 (.0044)	-.0031 (.0055)	.020 (.0091)*
1987-89 cohort	.011 (.0052)*	.014 (.0071)*	.013 (.011)
1990-92 cohort	.013 (.0065)*	.016 (.0066)	.029 (.010)*
1993-96 cohort	.018 (.0079)*	.034 (.010)*	.034 (.011)*
1997-99 cohort	.021 (.018)	.015 (.019)	.10 (.044)*
2000-02 cohort	-.012 (.026)	-.054 (.045)	.073 (.062)
De-trended unemploy. rate	-.022 (.0039)*	-.021 (.0045)*	-.010 (.0087)
R^2	0.8	0.82	0.85

Note: * (^) significantly different from zero at the 5 (10) percent level of significance.
Source: Authors' estimations based on the IMDB, SCF, and SLID data described in the text.

The patterns for the Canadian born in Table 1 are similar to those generated for males in Beaudry and Green (2000), again using SCF data, in their
discussion of issues of the impact of technological change on the Canadian
labour market. As described earlier, the authors find approximately 20
percent falls in real wages for both the high school and university educated
between the 1981 and 1993 entry cohorts, where cohorts are defined in
a similar way to here.[6] MaCurdy and Mroz (1995), using CPS data from
1976 to 1993, find similar patterns for male US workers. This result points
to the possibility that what we observed for immigrants in Figure 1 is
not just immigrant specific but reflects general declines for new labour
market entrants of all kinds.

HIGH SCHOOL OR LESS EDUCATED IMMIGRANTS

The first column of Table 2 contains the estimates of the δ, β, and γ parameters from specification 2), i.e., the YSE and FEXP related coefficients

TABLE 2
Immigrant Effects Using Foreign Experience Variables

Variables	High School or Less Education	Post-Secondary-below-BA Education	University Education
Immigrant dummy	-.64 (.073)*	-.70 (.064)*	-.39 (.061)*
Cohort dummies			
1983-86 cohort	.019 (.10)	-.18 (.085)*	-.16 (.089)^
1987-89 cohort	-.044 (.10)	.13 (.086)	.044 (.090)
1990-92 cohort	.28 (.12)*	-.12 (.091)	-.16 (.083)*
1993-96 cohort	.26 (.11)*	.0012 (.094)	-.11 (.093)
1997-99 cohort	.35 (.14)*	.045 (.12)	.28 (.20)
2000-02 cohort	.16 (.15)	-.38 (.18)*	-.27 (.24)
Years since labour market entry (YSE) spline for 0 to 9 years	.017 (.0047)*	.017 (.0053)*	.0062 (.0075)
YSE spline for 10 or more years	.0048 (.0040)	.016 (.0040)*	.018 (.0049)*
Cohort-YSE 0 to 9 spline interactions			
1983-86 cohort	.0068 (.0052)	.015 (.0063)*	-.0069 (.010)
1987-89 cohort	-.0054 (.0062)	-.0059 (.0078)	-.0092 (.011)
1990-92 cohort	-.016 (.0076)*	.0035 (.0076)	-.0011 (.011)
1993-96 cohort	-.027 (.0087)*	-.015 (.011)	.0054 (.013)
1997-99 cohort	-.019 (.019)	.019 (.020)	-.036 (.045)
2000-02 cohort	.10 (032)*	.20 (.050)*	.14 (.068)*
Foreign experience (FEXP)	.050 (.0083)*	.088 (.0075)*	.073 (.0058)*
FEXP squared	-.0011 (.00024)*	-.0022 (.00024)*	-.0021 (.00023)*
FEXP-YSE interaction	-.0015 (.00014)*	-.0020 (.00014)*	-.0025 (.00015)*
Cohort-FEXP interactions			
1983-86 cohort	-.024 (.012)*	-.035 (.010)*	.0054 (.0084)
1987-89 cohort	-.0073 (.012)	-.050 (.010)*	-.031 (.0083)*
1990-92 cohort	-.048 (.015)*	-.042 (.012)*	-.034 (.0088)*
1993-96 cohort	-.048 (.014)*	-.041 (.011)*	-.033 (.013)*
1997-99 cohort	-.053 (.016)*	-.067 (.013)*	-.084 (.014)*
2000-02 cohort	-.060 (.019)*	-.069 (.023)*	-.089 (.029)*
Cohort-FEXP squared interactions			
1983-86 cohort	.00061 (.00035)	.0010 (.00034)*	-.00008 (.00032)
1987-89 cohort	.00017 (.00036)	.0014 (.00031)*	.00074 (.00033)*
1990-92 cohort	.0012 (.00043)*	.00095 (.00039)*	.00074 (.00035)*
1993-96 cohort	.00079 (.00040)^	.00056 (.00036)	.00020 (.00049)
1997-99 cohort	.00062 (.00045)	.0011 (.00042)*	.0016 (.00054)*
2000-02 cohort	.00070 (.00054)	.0012 (.00080)	.0020 (.0011)^
De-trended unemployment rate	-.015 (.0045)*	-.014 (.0050)*	-.012 (.0088)
R^2	0.91	0.90	0.94

Notes: * (^) significantly different from zero at the 5 (10) percent level of significance.

The reported coefficients correspond to interactions between the relevant variables and an immigrant dummy variable.

Source: Authors' estimations based on the IMDB, SCF, and SLID data described in the text.

measured relative to the effects for the Canadian born from the same cohort. Thus, the cohort dummy coefficients reported in this table represent movements in entry earnings (for someone with FEXP = 0) across cohorts relative to the movements for the Canadian born seen in Table 1.

Based on Figures 2 and 3, high school immigrant entry earnings fall much more than those for Canadian born new entrants over the period. Immigrant entry earnings fall by .43 log points between the 1980-82 cohort and the 1990-92 cohort and by .89 log points between the first and last cohorts. In contrast, Canadian born entry earnings fall by .28 and .30 log points, respectively, between the same pairs of cohorts. This is strikingly different from what is seen in the cohort dummy coefficients in Table 2. Those coefficients indicate that the 1990-92, 1993-96, and 1997-99 immigrant cohorts have significantly higher earnings than the matching Canadian born cohorts.

The source of the contrast between Tables 1 and 2 and the figures can be found in the inclusion of the FEXP variables in the specification underlying the tables. Indeed, Figure 3 is constructed precisely from the cohort dummy coefficients in Table 1, and the cohort dummy coefficients in Table 2 would show the difference between the immigrant and Canadian born effects presented in Figures 2 and 3 if the FEXP variables were not included.

These FEXP differentials change across cohorts and bear an interesting relationship to returns to Canadian experience obtained by the Canadian born. To make this latter comparison, we need to make an adjustment, since the FEXP and FEXP squared variables are defined relative to school leaving age while YSE and YSE squared variables are defined relative to age 25. Thus, the YSE coefficients in Table 1 (which represent Canadian born returns to experience) refer to a later, flatter part of the experience profile. Comparing the relative values of foreign experience for a high school educated immigrant in the 1980-82 cohort who migrated at age 33 and the Canadian experience of a Canadian born worker of the same age, cohort, and education (i.e., FEXP = 14 in Table 2 and YSE = 8 in Table 1) yields an estimated 1.9 percent increase in earnings for an added year of foreign experience for the immigrant and a 2.2 percent increase for an extra year of experience for the Canadian born worker. Thus, a year of foreign experience is valued at about 87 percent of a year of Canadian experience. However, for the 1993-96 and later cohorts, the returns to experience for the immigrant drop to near zero or negative (-0.6 percent for 1993-96 and -2 percent for 2000-02). To ease interpretation, we use the estimated foreign experience coefficients to plot entry earnings–foreign experience profiles for the first and last cohorts for each education group in Figure 4. An examination of the high school profiles indicates that the fall in returns to foreign experience has very substantial consequences for earnings: because of it, the average entry earnings of an immigrant with 15 years of foreign experience falls by .7 log points between the first and last cohorts.

FIGURE 4
Returns to Foreign Experience at Arrival by Education Group:
1980-82 and 2000-02 Cohorts

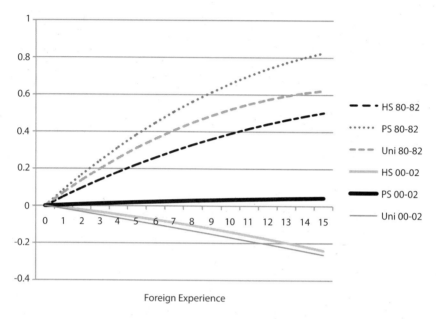

Foreign Experience

Source: Authors' estimations based on the IMDB, SFC, and SLID data described in the text.

Friedberg (2000) finds that returns to foreign experience are near zero for some immigrants to Israel and that this fully explains differences between average immigrant and domestic born earnings (there is no evidence of cohort effects in the Israeli data). Schaafsma and Sweetman (2001) also find that foreign work experience in the host country yields virtually no returns in the Canadian labour market. High school educated immigrants to Canada also face a near zero return to foreign experience, but this is a pattern that has arisen relatively recently. In the case of Canada, the low returns to foreign experience and the fact that this represents a change from earlier cohorts can account for the cross-cohort decline in immigrant earnings relative to those of matched Canadian born cohorts. The difference between the patterns in Figures 2 and 3 and the results in Table 2 arises because the entry earnings results in Figure 2 correspond to immigrants who are age 25 or older at time of arrival in Canada. In the specification in Table 2, in contrast, the coefficients on the cohort dummy variables correspond to earnings just after leaving school (i.e., at FEXP = 0). The declines in entry earnings in Figure 2 then turn out to be accounted for by a combination of declines facing all new entrants to the Canadian labour market (as reflected in Figure 3) and the fact that immigrants in later cohorts receive lower returns for the years of experience they accumulated after leaving school but before migrating to Canada.

The coefficient on the interaction between FEXP and YSE in Table 2 indicates that added years of foreign experience imply a flatter YSE earnings profile. Further, the cohorts with the lowest returns to foreign experience have the highest post-arrival earnings growth rates. Both of these observations fit with the type of human capital investment model discussed in Duleep and Regets (1996) where lower initial earnings for a cohort-FEXP group may reflect both a lower initial transferability of skills and extra time spent investing in order to overcome that problem. More investment just after arrival, in turn, implies a steeper YSE earnings profile because more time is dedicated to earning as the initial investment is reduced and because of returns to that investment.

Finally, the significant negative coefficient on the unemployment rate variable suggests that immigrants are more cyclically sensitive than Canadian born workers who enter the labour market at the same time with the same education.[7] This supports claims that a defining feature of immigrants is their greater variability in reaction to labour market conditions (e.g., Green 1999; McDonald and Worswick 1998).

POST-SECONDARY-BELOW-BA EDUCATED IMMIGRANTS

We present the estimates for post-secondary-below-BA educated immigrants (relative to post-secondary-below-BA educated Canadian born workers) in the second column of Table 2. As with the high school educated, controlling for years of foreign experience with this group reduces the measured decline in earnings across cohorts. However, the pattern of this effect is more complicated than for the high school educated. The fact that the coefficient on the 1987-89 dummy in Table 2 is positive and not statistically significantly different from zero indicates that the combination of general new entrant declines and controlling for foreign experience completely accounts for the 0.41 log point decline between the 1980-82 and 1987-89 cohorts observed in Figure 2. However, these two factors do not fully explain the pattern of immigrant entry earnings in the 1990s. According to Figure 2, the 2000-02 immigrant entry cohort had entry earnings that were almost 1.16 log points below those of the 1980-82 cohort. Canadian born entry earnings fell approximately .09 log points across the same pair of cohorts, implying that the immigrant cross-cohort decline was 1.05 log points greater. The Table 2 coefficients indicate that the 2000-02 immigrant cohort had entry earnings that were .38 log points lower than those of the Canadian born cohort entering the labour market at the same time, once one controls for foreign experience. Thus, .65 log points of the overall 1.16 log point decline is left unexplained by either general new entrant effects or declining returns to foreign experience.

The coefficients related to foreign experience again indicate that returns to foreign experience declined across cohorts. An added year of foreign experience would add 1.9 percent to average annual earnings for an immigrant who is 33 at arrival and in the 1980-82 cohort. This compares to a 2.6 percent effect of an extra year of Canadian experience for a 35 year old Canadian born worker with a post-secondary-below-BA education. By the 1993-96 cohort, the foreign experience differential for that 35 year old entrant had fallen to 0.1 percent and to -0.1 percent for the 2000-02 cohort. Also as with the high school educated, the YSE earnings profile is flatter the more foreign experience an immigrant has, fitting with the simple investment model of immigrant earnings paths.

University Educated Immigrants

The last column in Table 2 contains the results for university educated immigrants. The patterns in this column are most similar to those for the post-secondary-below-BA educated. The changes in average entry earnings for the last cohort relative to the first are similar to those for the post-secondary-below-BA educated for both immigrants and the Canadian born. Thus, as with the post-secondary-below-BA educated, university immigrants experience a cross-cohort decline in entry earnings that is on the order of .5 log points greater than that experienced by the Canadian born. The cohort dummy coefficients in Table 2, however, indicate that immigrant entry earnings decline by .27 log points more than those for the Canadian born once we control for foreign experience. Thus, as with the post-secondary educated immigrants, a combination of general declines for all new entrants and foreign experience effects can account for some of the cross-cohort drop in immigrant entry earnings, but about 18 percent (the 0.27 log point relative decline from the first to the last cohort reported in Table 2 compared to the overall 1.46 log point drop displayed in Figure 2) is still unaccounted for.

Like the other two education groups, the university educated witnessed a sizeable fall in returns to foreign experience across cohorts; however, the returns to foreign experience (relative to the Canadian born) are generally lower for all cohorts. Considering first the 1980-82 cohort, a 35 year old university educated immigrant had a return to a year of foreign work experience that was only 23 percent of the return to a year of work experience for a Canadian born worker of the same age and cohort. However, the estimates from Table 2 indicate that a 35 year old university educated immigrant in the 2000-03 cohort faced a negative return to foreign work experience (-2.16 percent). As with the high school educated, earnings implications of the drop in returns to foreign experience are substantial: an approximately .8 log point drop in average entry earnings for an immigrant with 15 years of foreign experience between the first and last cohorts. This is shown graphically in Figure 4.

Finally, earnings for university educated immigrants are cyclically sensitive. Their overall level of sensitivity is lower than that for less educated immigrants but is significantly higher than that for the university educated Canadian born, whose earnings show no substantial (or statistically significant) relationship to the cycle.

Overall, the results in the first tables and figures indicate that we can account for much if not all of the fall in immigrant entry earnings in both the 1980s and 1990s for the high school educated and in the 1980s for the post-secondary-below-BA educated with a combination of general declines for all new entrants and declining returns to foreign experience. For the post-secondary-below-BA educated in the 1990s and the university educated in both decades, these two factors appear to account for approximately 60 percent of the overall decline. We turn now to investigating potential sources of the decline in returns to foreign experience and of the unexplained portions of the decline for the more educated immigrants and to generating a more formal decomposition of cross-cohort declines in immigrant entry earnings.

THE ROLE OF SHIFTS IN THE COUNTRY OF ORIGIN COMPOSITION

In this section we investigate the role of changes in the source country composition of immigration as a possible explanation for the declining entry earnings across immigrant arrival cohorts. Recall that accompanying the decline in the returns to foreign experience has been a move toward lower initial earnings and higher earnings growth rates among the most recent cohorts. All of this could arise if the composition of immigrant source countries has shifted away from countries from which it is easy to transfer human capital to the Canadian economy (e.g., the United States, United Kingdom, and Europe) and toward countries where the skills acquired in the labour market are either less well matched to the Canadian labour market or come from sources that are not as well known in Canada (perhaps including much of Asia and Africa). Thus, changes in the source country composition are potential candidates for explaining the patterns described earlier.

To investigate this explanation, we re-estimated our main specification separately for three source country groups: the United States, the United Kingdom, Australia, and New Zealand (what we call our English group); France, Germany, Holland, Denmark, Belgium, Switzerland, Sweden, Norway (our northwestern European group); and the rest of the world. In each case we again use Canadian born new entrants as a benchmark. The results of this exercise are presented in Tables 3-5.[8] We do not intend

TABLE 3
Immigrant Effects Using Foreign Experience Variables:
Northwestern European Source Countries

Variables	High School or Less Education	Post-Secondary-below-BA Education	University Education
Immigrant dummy	-1.84 (.19)*	-.35 (.083)*	-.17 (.085)*
Cohort dummies			
1983-86 cohort	.058 (.13)	-.021 (.081)	-.0006 (.010)
1987-89 cohort	.099 (.12)	.21 (.083)*	.22 (.10)*
1990-92 cohort	.55 (.16)*	.11 (.073)	.24 (.11)*
1993-96 cohort	.27 (.14)*	.26 (.083)*	-.16 (.097)
1997-99 cohort	.61 (.16)*	.19 (.10)^	.41 (.20)*
2000-02 cohort	.21 (.28)	-.069 (.14)	.10 (.21)
Years since labour market entry (YSE) spline for 0 to 9 years	.0076 (.013)	.0088 (.0081)	-.0044 (.0097)
YSE spline for 10 or more years	-.011 (.012)	-.0039 (.0083)	.024 (.0095)*
Cohort-YSE 0 to 9 spline interactions			
1983-86 cohort	.0034 (.011)	-.013 (.0090)	-.0099 (.012)
1987-89 cohort	-.0019 (.011)	-.051 (.0095)*	-.0095 (.014)
1990-92 cohort	.0006 (.014)	-.0088 (.0095)	.0044 (.013)
1993-96 cohort	.019 (.014)	-.0019 (.012)	.042 (.015)*
1997-99 cohort	.062 (.024)*	.032 (.024)	-.0087 (.046)
2000-02 cohort	.17 (070)*	.20 (.059)*	.12 (.077)*
Foreign experience (FEXP)	.21 (.019)*	.042 (.0093)*	.052 (.0091)*
FEXP squared	-.0058 (.00052)*	-.00057 (.00028)*	-.00068 (.00031)*
FEXP-YSE interaction	-.00053 (.00052)	-.0025 (.00037)*	-.0027 (.00039)*
Cohort-FEXP interactions			
1983-86 cohort	-.0079 (.0059)	-.012 (.0040)*	-.0014 (.0042)
1987-89 cohort	-.010 (.0058)^	-.015 (.0041)*	-.025 (.0046)*
1990-92 cohort	-.047 (.0072)*	-.030 (.0041)*	-.037 (.0044)*
1993-96 cohort	-.038 (.0065)*	-.044 (.0038)*	-.047 (.0045)*
1997-99 cohort	-.064 (.0084)*	-.042 (.0052)*	-.047 (.0049)*
2000-02 cohort	-.061 (.013)*	-.048 (.0069)*	-.054 (.0080)*
De-trended unemployment rate	-.016 (.0088)^	-.012 (.0067)^	.0031 (.011)
R^2	0.56	0.74	0.72

Notes: * (^) significantly different from zero at the 5 (10) percent level of significance.

The reported coefficients correspond to interactions between the relevant variables and an immigrant dummy variable.

Source: Authors' estimations based on the IMDB, SCF, and SLID data described in the text.

TABLE 4
Immigrant Effects Using Foreign Experience Variables:
English Source Countries

Variables	High School or Less Education	Post-Secondary-below-BA Education	University Education
Immigrant dummy	.47 (.077)*	-.17 (.057)*	-.024 (.059)
Cohort dummies:		.	
1983-86 cohort	-.20 (.059)*	-.20 (.058)*	-.047 (.076)
1987-89 cohort	-.055 (.062)	-.068 (.063)	.034 (.081)
1990-92 cohort	-.045 (.066)	-.13 (.059)*	.075 (.074)
1993-96 cohort	.27 (.090)*	.055 (.073)	.064 (.074)
1997-99 cohort	.17 (.17)	-.23 (.11)*	.35 (.19)^
2000-02 cohort	-.24 (.17)	-.66 (.16)*	-.079 (.17)
Years since labour market entry (YSE) spline for 0 to 9 years	.018 (.0068)*	-.0091 (.0059)	-.0062 (.0077)
YSE spline for 10 or more years	.0027 (.0061)	.0091 (.0051)^	.035 (.0054)*
Cohort-YSE 0 to 9 spline interactions			
1983-86 cohort	.0045 (.0068)	.011 (.0068)^	-.0094 (.0097)
1987-89 cohort	.0034 (.0075)	.00018 (.0079)	-.0014 (.011)
1990-92 cohort	.014 (.0091)	.0111 (.0078)	-.0021 (.011)
1993-96 cohort	-.016 (.012)	-.0074 (.012)	.0044 (.013)
1997-99 cohort	.021 (.031)	.029 (.023)	-.060 (.045)
2000-02 cohort	.15 (057)*	.19 (.058)*	.125 (.071)^
Foreign experience (FEXP)	-.063 (.008)*	.057 (.0048)*	.056 (.0043)*
FEXP squared	.0026 (.00021)*	-.0011 (.00014)*	-.00082 (.00015)*
FEXP-YSE interaction	-.0016 (.00025)*	-.00061 (.00018)*	-.0033 (.00020)*
Cohort-FEXP interactions			
1983-86 cohort	.00015 (.0024)	-.0071 (.0020)*	.0061 (.0020)*
1987-89 cohort	-.0041 (.0024)^	-.0035 (.0018)*	-.0081 (.0022)*
1990-92 cohort	-.0073 (.0028)*	-.0078 (.0020)*	-.011 (.0025)*
1993-96 cohort	-.029 (.0039)*	-.015 (.0024)*	-.021 (.0027)*
1997-99 cohort	-.030 (.0075)*	-.0060 (.0040)	-.032 (.0037)*
2000-02 cohort	-.025 (.0065)*	-.0083 (.0057)	-.026 (.0066)*
De-trended unemployment rate	-.0077 (.0052)	-.0044 (.0052)	.0010 (.0090)
R^2	0.65	0.78	0.80

Notes: * (^) significantly different from zero at the 5 (10) percent level of significance.

The reported coefficients correspond to interactions between the relevant variables and an immigrant dummy variable.

Source: Authors' estimations based on the IMDB, SCF, and SLID data described in the text.

TABLE 5
Immigrant Effects Using Foreign Experience Variables:
Other Source Countries

Variables	High School or Less Education	Post-Secondary-below-BA Education	University Education
Immigrant dummy	-.52 (.053)*	-.71 (.048)*	-.50 (.058)*
Cohort dummies			
1983-86 cohort	-.13 (.048)*	-.25 (.054)*	-.067 (.078)
1987-89 cohort	-.080 (.052)	-.054 (.060)	.074 (.081)
1990-92 cohort	-.0040 (.058)	-.17 (.054)*	-.13 (.073)^
1993-96 cohort	.039 (.053)	-.036 (.063)	-.026 (.072)
1997-99 cohort	.16 (.073)*	-.12 (.081)	.13 (.19)
2000-02 cohort	-.0037 (.064)	-.53 (.11)*	-.46 (.17)*
Years since labour market entry (YSE) spline for 0 to 9 years	.016 (.0050)*	.025 (.0054)*	.018 (.0076)*
YSE spline for 10 or more years	.0042 (.0042)	.014 (.0042)*	.0094 (.0051)^
Cohort-YSE 0 to 9 spline interactions			
1983-86 cohort	.0063 (.0054)	.011 (.0064)^	-.011 (.0097)
1987-89 cohort	-.0076 (.0063)	-.011 (.0078)	-.023 (.011)*
1990-92 cohort	-.018 (.0078)*	-.0063 (.0078)	-.016 (.011)
1993-96 cohort	-.029 (.0088)*	-.024 (.011)*	-.010 (.013)
1997-99 cohort	-.022 (.019)	.016 (.020)	-.047 (.045)
2000-02 cohort	.10 (033)*	.19 (.058)*	.125 (.069)^
Foreign experience (FEXP)	-.030 (.0049)*	.058 (.0039)*	.059 (.0038)*
FEXP squared	-.00067 (.00013)*	-.0014 (.00012)*	-.0018 (.00013)*
FEXP-YSE interaction	-.0014 (.00016)*	-.0019 (.00015)*	-.0020 (.00016)*
Cohort-FEXP interactions			
1983-86 cohort	-.0019 (.0018)	-.0034 (.0016)*	-.00022 (.0018)
1987-89 cohort	.00079 (.0018)	-.0039 (.0015)*	-.0098 (.0015)*
1990-92 cohort	-.0064 (.0021)*	-.0095 (.0018)*	-.013 (.0018)*
1993-96 cohort	-.017 (.0020)*	-.017 (.0017)*	-.023 (.0022)*
1997-99 cohort	-.027 (.0021)*	-.028 (.0021)*	-.035 (.0026)*
2000-02 cohort	-.036 (.0029)*	-.030 (.0040)*	-.031 (.0052)*
De-trended unemployment rate	-.016 (.0046)*	-.019 (.0050)*	-.019 (.0090)*
R^2	0.90	0.94	0.93

Notes: * (^) significantly different from zero at the 5 (10) percent level of significance.

The reported coefficients correspond to interactions between the relevant variables and an immigrant dummy variable.

Source: Authors' estimations based on the IMDB, SCF, and SLID data described in the text.

to discuss these results in detail, but a few summary comments can be made. The cohort and immigrant dummy variable coefficients in the tables indicate that in the first cohort, English country immigrants have superior earnings compared to Canadian born new entrants with the same level of education. This superiority is maintained across cohorts, though it declines to some extent. In contrast, both northwestern European immigrants and those from the rest of the world face substantial earnings deficits relative to the Canadian born in the first cohort, and this deficit either gets worse or improves only slightly across cohorts.

Of greatest interest to us are differences in returns to foreign experience and changes in those returns across cohorts for immigrants from different source countries. To aid in discussion of these patterns, we present fitted earnings-foreign experience profiles (based on Tables 3-5) for the first and last cohorts of university educated immigrants from the three source country groups in Figure 5. Canada experienced a dramatic shift in the source country composition of immigration over our period (Baker and Benjamin 1994). The proportion of high school educated immigrants in the English and northwestern European source country groups fell from .23 and .04, respectively, in the first cohort to .07 and .03 in the last cohort in our data. Based on the estimates in Tables 3-5, such a shift would imply lower average entry earnings and flatter returns to foreign experience for immigrants as a whole. Thus, shifts in the source country composition can

FIGURE 5
Returns to Foreign Experience at Arrival by Source Region:
University Education, 1980-82 and 2000-02 Cohorts

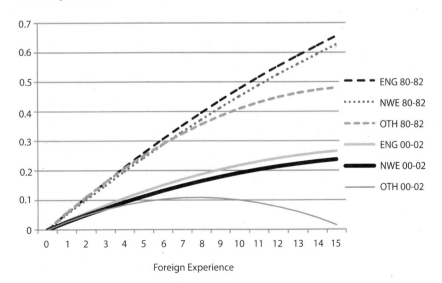

Foreign Experience

Source: Authors' estimations based on the IMDB, SFC, and SLID data described in the text.

account for some of the patterns we observe. However, the fact that the earnings-foreign experience profiles depicted in Figure 5 become flatter over time for all source country groups suggests that changes in the source country composition (at least at the level of aggregation we employ) is not the sole explanation for overall declining returns to foreign experience.

DECOMPOSING THE DECLINE IN ENTRY EARNINGS

To this point we have argued that both general new entrant effects and declines in the return to foreign experience (partly caused by shifts in source country composition) are major causes of the declines in entry earnings witnessed for immigrant cohorts in the 1980s and 1990s. We now turn to using a Oaxaca type decomposition to assess the magnitude of the contribution of each force. In this decomposition exercise, we first use estimates in Table 1 and Tables 3-5 to form fitted entry earnings for a set of cohort×foreign-experience×source-country groups. We do this separately for each education level. We combine these estimated earnings according to the proportion of a given cohort accounted for by a given experience group from a given source country, and then combine the results according to the proportion from each source country group in the given cohort. This creates fitted versions of actual entry earnings for each cohort, which we normalize in order to express the movements relative to the first cohort in our sample. In the first stage of the decomposition, we subtract from each of these relative immigrant cohort entry earnings numbers the decline in entry earnings for the matching Canadian born cohort (again measured relative to the first cohort). The resulting counterfactual series shows the decline in immigrant earnings that would have happened if the general worsening in outcomes for all new labour market entrants had not occurred. In the second stage, we recreate the counterfactual but use only the source country proportions from the first cohort in creating the fitted earnings for all cohorts. Since we again subtract the Canadian born cohort effects, the resulting counterfactual series shows what would have happened to immigrant entry earnings if neither the general decline in new entrant conditions nor the changes in source country composition had occurred. In the third stage, we recreate the fitted earnings for each cohort-experience group but use the returns to foreign experience estimated for the first cohort for all cohorts to effectively eliminate the decline in returns to foreign experience. Because we again eliminate general new entrant effects and hold source country composition constant, a comparison between the counterfactual earnings at this third stage and those created at the second stage shows the impact of declines in returns to foreign experience over and above the declines that are accounted for by changes in the source country composition.

We present the results from the decomposition exercise conducted for each education level separately in Tables 6a-c. The results in Table 6a indicate that general new entrant effects explain roughly half of the declines across the 1980s cohorts (between the 1980-82 and 1987-89 cohorts), which fits with the patterns discussed earlier. The shift in the country composition away from the English and northwestern European countries pushes the results further in the same direction, so that if the new entrant effect had not occurred and the source country composition had not changed, immigrant new entrant earnings would have declined by only 30 percent of the amount of the actual decline over the 1980s. The changes in returns to foreign experience after controlling for source country changes work in the same direction, reinforcing the role of the new entrant effect and the country composition effect. The combined effect of these factors explains 79 percent of the fall in immigrant high school earnings over this decade. Over the 1990s (1987-89 through 1997-99 cohorts), new entrant effects explain 52 percent of the decline; source country composition changes actually move in the wrong direction to explain any of the decline; but the return to foreign experience alone can explain the entire decline. Taking these three factors together, we can in fact over-explain the decline in entry earnings over the decade, indicating that entry earnings of the immigrant arrival cohort (1997-99) would in fact have been higher than that of the 1987-89 cohort in the absence of new labour market entrant effects, changes in the source country composition, and changes in the return to foreign experience. For the whole period (i.e., from the 1980-82 to the 2000-02 cohorts), the three components together account for 90 percent of the decline, with general new entrant effects explaining 33 percent and the decline in the return to foreign experience explaining 55 percent.

For the post-secondary-below-BA educated in Table 6b, we again explain roughly half (59 percent) of the decline in the 1980s through new entrant effects. In the 1990s, the role of the decline in returns to foreign experience once again emerges as the dominant effect, explaining 90 percent of the overall decline in entry earnings of immigrants. As in the high school case, when all three factors are combined, they over-explain the decline in entry earnings for immigrants across the 1990s. Over the entire period, the new entrant effect only explains 10 percent of the decline in immigrant entry earnings, the country composition effect accounts for 14 percent, and the return to foreign experience effect can account for 35 percent.

The university educated results in Table 6c are similar to the results for both the high school educated and the post-secondary-below-BA educated. We can explain over 80 percent of the declines across the whole period with the three effects. General new entrant effects (39 percent) and declines in the returns to foreign experience (27 percent) are particularly important in terms of explaining the overall decline.

TABLE 6A
Counterfactual Results, High School or Less

Component	1980s (1980-82 to 1987-89 Cohort)	1990s (1987-89 to 1997-99 Cohort)	Whole Period (1980-82 to 2000-02 Cohort)
Total	-.34	-.38	-.91
	(1.0)	(1.0)	(1.0)
New entrant effect	-.17	-.19	-.30
	(.49)	(.52)	(.33)
Country composition effect	-.070	.015	-.020
	(.21)	(-.042)	(.022)
Return to foreign experience effect	-.031	-.38	-.50
	(.09)	(1.02)	(.55)
Sum of counterfactual effects	-.27	-.55	-.82
	(.79)	(1.52)	(.90)

Note: Number in parentheses is proportion of the total decline accounted for by the given component.
Source: Authors' estimations based on the IMDB, SCF, and SLID data described in the text.

TABLE 6B
Counterfactual Results, Post-Secondary-below-BA

Component	1980s (1980-82 to 1987-89 Cohorts)	1990s (1987-89 to 1997-99 Cohorts)	Whole Period (1980-82 to 2000-02 Cohorts)
Total	-.27	-.35	-.92
	(1.0)	(1.0)	(1.0)
New entrant effect	-.16	-.07	-.093
	(.59)	(.20)	(.10)
Country composition effect	-.098	-.031	-.13
	(.36)	(.09)	(.14)
Return to foreign experience effect	.021	-.32	-.32
	(-.077)	(.90)	(.35)
Sum of counterfactual effects	-.24	-.42	-.55
	(.87)	(1.19)	(.59)

Note: Number in parentheses is proportion of the total decline accounted for by the given component.
Source: Authors' estimations based on the IMDB, SCF, and SLID data described in the text.

TABLE 6C
Counterfactual Results, University

Component	1980s (1980-82 to 1987-89 Cohorts)	1990s (1987-89 to 1997-99 Cohorts)	Whole Period (1980-82 to 2000-02 Cohorts)
Total	-.15	-.51	-1.17
	(1.0)	(1.0)	(1.0)
New entrant effect	-.15	-.34	-.46
	(1.02)	(.67)	(.39)
Country composition effect	-.061	-.073	-.18
	(.41)	(.14)	(.16)
Return to foreign experience effect	-.007	-.35	-.32
	(.044)	(.68)	(.27)
Sum of counterfactual effects	-.21	-.86	-0.96
	(1.47)	(1.49)	(.82)

Note: Number in parentheses is proportion of the total decline accounted for by the given component.
Source: Authors' estimations based on the IMDB, SCF, and SLID data described in the text.

TABLE 6D
Counterfactual Results, All Education Groups

Component	1980s (1980-82 to 1987-89 Cohorts)	1990s (1987-89 to 1997-99 Cohorts)	Whole Period (1980-82 to 2000-02 Cohorts)
Total	-.28	-.26	-.92
	(1.0)	(1.0)	(1.0)
New entrant effect	-.16	-.24	-.36
	(.56)	(.92)	(.39)
Country composition effect	-.078	-.04	-.15
	(.27)	(.15)	(.16)
Return to foreign experience effect	.075	-.32	-.22
	(-.26)	(1.26)	(.24)
Education composition effect	-.11	.19	.049
	(.37)	(-.73)	(-.05)
Sum of counterfactual effects	-.27	-.41	-.68
	(.93)	(1.61)	(.74)

Note: Number in parentheses is proportion of the total decline accounted for by the given component.
Source: Authors' estimations based on the IMDB, SCF, and SLID data described in the text.

In Table 6d, we create a decomposition for all of the education groups combined. Thus, we combine the results from Tables 6a-c using the proportion of immigrants in each education category in each cohort. We also add a final line to the decomposition showing the effects of holding the education composition constant at the proportions from the first cohort. We can explain 93 percent of the 1980s declines in entry earnings, more than 100 percent of the 1990s declines, and 74 percent of the declines across the whole period. These results are similar to what was found in each of the education-specific decompositions of Tables 6a-c. New entrant (56 percent), country composition (27 percent), and education composition (37 percent) effects are all important factors in terms of explaining the decline in entry earnings of new immigrants in the 1980s. Returns to foreign experience become relatively more important in the 1990s; and over the entire period, general new entrant effects account for 39 percent of the decline, while the changing country composition accounts for 16 percent, and declining returns to foreign experience (after controlling for country composition) accounts for 24 percent.

A striking result is the changing role of educational composition in the 1990s. The sign of this effect switches from being negative in the 1980s to being positive (and large in magnitude at 73 percent) in the 1990s, indicating that the education composition had switched to favouring immigrants who would be expected to have higher entry earnings due to their education. This is consistent with the changes in the immigrant selection system in August 1993, which greatly increased the points allocated for post-secondary education for principal applicants evaluated under the points system (McWhinney 1998).

It is worth noting that in a similar decomposition done without controlling for country composition effects, the returns to foreign experience effects for the whole period for all education groups combined accounted for 34 percent of the decline. Thus, roughly half of the total effect of declining returns to foreign experience arises because of the changes in source country composition within our crude categorization. The portion attributed to declining returns to foreign experience net of country composition shifts is somewhat unsatisfactory, since we do not have a convincing explanation for its source.

CONCLUSIONS

We examine movements in entry earnings across cohorts of Canadian immigrants, trying to understand the sources of those movements. We argue that focusing on entry earnings is of interest if, for example, policy-makers have very high discount rates when it comes to concerns over how immigrants fare in the Canadian economy. We make use of a unique dataset (the IMDB) in which immigrant landing records are linked to subsequent tax records. Comparing that data to survey data for the Canadian born, we find the same general patterns described in other papers (e.g., Li 2003): large declines in entry earnings over the 1980s are followed by even larger declines in the 1990s and early 2000s. Our goal is to try to understand why immigrants since the early 1980s have consistently fared worse in terms of earnings just after arrival.

One possible explanation for the immigrant entry earning pattern is that it is not unique to the immigrant experience. We argue that domestic born workers entering the Canadian labour market at the same time as a given cohort of immigrants provide a good benchmark for capturing the effects of general movements in the economy. Following those workers allows for the possibility that economic events affect young workers differently from those already established in their jobs, partly because, like newly arrived immigrants, those workers are involved in investing in new human capital. As in Beaudry and Green (2000) and Green and Townsend (forthcoming), we find that successive cohorts of Canadian born labour market entrants are also faring worse in terms of their entry earnings, although entry earnings are found to have improved somewhat in the late 1990s and into the early 2000s. Defining earnings movements for these workers as general new entrant effects, we find that such effects account for roughly 40 percent of the total decline in immigrant entry earnings between the early 1980s and the early 2000s. These general new entrant effects explain roughly 50 percent of the declines in entry earnings of immigrants in the 1980s.

The strongest pattern in the decline in immigrant earnings over and above those experienced by other new entrants is the decline in returns to foreign experience. While immigrants obtained returns to foreign experience that were on par with the returns obtained by domestic born workers for their Canadian experience in the early 1980s, by the 1990s immigrants were effectively receiving a zero return on their foreign experience. This decline can account for one-quarter of the overall decline in immigrant entry earnings between the early 1980s and early 2000s. Further investigation of this phenomenon reveals that we can account for about half of it as arising from shifts in the source country composition of immigration toward countries from which one would expect it is harder to transfer human capital to Canada. However, some of the decline in returns to foreign experience still remains after controlling for source country composition changes (enough to account for 24 percent of the overall decline in entry earnings over our period).

We can break the movements in immigrant entry earnings into three periods. In the 1980s, a substantial decline in these earnings was most strongly related to the fact that earnings were declining for all new labour market entrants, immigrants and non-immigrants. Thus, movements in the macro economy affecting all new workers were the dominant force shaping the experience of new immigrants. In the 1990s, these macro effects continued to be important, but the single most important factor in the ongoing decline in immigrant earnings was the virtual eradication of returns to foreign experience. By the mid-1990s, an immigrant just out of school and another immigrant with the same level of schooling but 20 years of experience outside of Canada could expect to have the same average entry earnings in Canada. This occurred at a time when shifts in immigration policy resulted in a strong increase in the average education level of new immigrants. Without these shifts, average entry earnings would have fallen a further 20 percent in the 1990s, according to our calculations. On the other hand, in the early 2000s (the third period) Picot and Hou (2009) argue that highly educated immigrants were particularly negatively affected by the information technology bust. Our results suggest that general macro movements played less of a role in explaining entry earnings movements in this period but that returns to foreign acquired experience continued to be low.

Overall, our results point to two main areas of policy concern. The first is why new labour market entrants in general have been doing so much worse over the past two decades. This is not necessarily an issue that would be directly addressed through immigration policy, but it does have ramifications for how immigrants are faring in the Canadian labour market. The second area of concern is the very low rates of return that immigrants from countries other than the United Kingdom, the United States, and Europe have been receiving for labour market experience acquired before migrating. While more focus has previously been placed on issues relating to recognition of foreign educational credentials,[9] problems related to transferring human capital acquired through experience also appear to be of substantial importance.

Notes

We are grateful to Elizabeth Ruddick and the Strategic Policy, Planning and Research Branch of CIC for their support of this project at its initial stages and for many useful conversations about the data and immigration in general. We also wish to thank Paul Beaudry, Craig Dougherty, Nicole Fortin, Thomas Lemieux, Ted McDonald, and Jeffrey Reitz for helpful comments. All remaining errors and omissions are our own.

1. Antecol, Cobb-Clark, and Trejo (2003) analyze the relationship between differences in immigration policy and differences in immigrant outcomes across countries.
2. The SCF is not perfectly representative, and the survey weights were used in all regressions.
3. Recall that we define time of entry for Canadian born cohorts by the year they turn 25.
4. In a companion piece (Green and Worswick 2004), we provide further discussion of using Canadian born new entrants to control for macro effects. That paper focuses on making comparisons across cohorts in present value terms. The decline in returns to foreign experience, which is the focus of this paper, is evident in some of the results in that paper but was not investigated there.
5. Green and Townsend (forthcoming) provide an extensive investigation of this pattern, arguing that it fits with an implicit contract model.
6. In contrast to the point estimates in Table 1, Beaudry and Green (2000) find that the experience-earnings profiles are parallel across cohorts. This difference arises because that paper uses weekly earnings, while the need to match the IMDB dictates that here we must examine annual earnings.
7. Aydemir (2003) provides a thorough examination of the effect of business cycles on immigrant outcomes.
8. We do not include interactions of the FEXP squared variable and the cohort dummies in this specification because their inclusion made the estimates less stable, probably because of the smaller underlying samples.
9. Ferrer, Green, and Riddell (2006) argue that lower returns to foreign acquired education may actually reflect lower literacy skills in English and French.

References

Antecol, H., D. Cobb-Clark, and S. Trejo. 2003. "Immigration Policy and the Skills of Immigrants to Australia, Canada and the United States." *Journal of Human Resources* 38 (1): 192-218.

Aydemir, A. 2003. "Effects of Business Cycles on the Labour Market Participation Rate and Employment Rate Assimilation of Immigrants." In *Canadian Immigration Policy for the Twenty-First Century,* edited by C. Beach, A. Green, and J. Reitz. McGill-Queen's University Press.

Aydemir, A., and M. Skuterud. 2005. "Explaining the Deteriorating Entry Earnings of Canada's Immigrant Cohorts, 1966-2000." *Canadian Journal of Economics* 38 (2): 641-7.

Baker, M., and D. Benjamin. 1994. "The Performance of Immigrants in the Canadian Labour Market." *Journal of Labor Economics*. 12 (3): 369-405.

Beaudry, P., and D.A. Green. 2000. "Cohort Patterns in Canadian Earnings: Assessing the Role of Skill Premia in Inequality Trends." *Canadian Journal of Economics* 33 (4): 907-36.

Bloom, D.E., G. Grenier, and M. Gunderson. 1995. "The Changing Labour Market Position of Canadian Immigrants." *Canadian Journal of Economics* 28 (4b): 987-1005.

Borjas, G. 1987. "Self-Selection and the Earnings of Immigrants." *American Economic Review* 77 (4): 531-53.

Card, D., and T. Lemieux. 2001. "Can Falling Supply Explain the Rising Return to College for Younger Men? A Cohort Based Analysis." *Quarterly Journal of Economics* 116: 705-46.

Duleep, H.O., and M. Regets. 2002. "The Elusive Concept of Immigrant Quality: Evidence from 1970-1990." IZA Discussion Paper 631.

Ferrer, A., D.A. Green, and W.C. Riddell. 2006. "The Effect of Literacy on Immigrant Earnings." *Journal of Human Resources* (spring): 380-410.

Frenette, M., and R. Morissette. 2003. "Will They Ever Converge? Earnings of Immigrants and Canadian-Born Workers over the Last Two Decades." Statistics Canada, Analytical Studies Branch, Research Paper.

Friedberg, R.M. 2000. "You Can't Take It with You? Immigrant Assimilation and the Portability of Human Capital." *Journal of Labor Economics* 18 (2): 221-51.

Grant, M.L. 1999. "Evidence of New Immigrant Assimilation in Canada." *Canadian Journal of Economics* 32 (4): 930-55.

Green, D.A. 1999. "Immigrant Occupational Attainment: Assimilation and Mobility over Time." *Journal of Labor Economics* 17 (1): 49-79.

Green, D.A., and J. Townsend. Forthcoming. "Understanding the Wage Patterns of Canadian Less-Skilled Workers: The Role of Implicit Contracts." *Canadian Journal of Economics*.

Green, D.A., and C. Worswick. 2004. "Immigrant Earnings Profiles in the Presence of Human Capital Investment: Measuring Cohort And Macro Effects." Institute for Fiscal Studies, IFS Working Paper W04/13.

LaLonde, R.J., and R.H. Topel. 1992. "The Assimilation of Immigrants in the U.S. Labor Market." In *Immigration and the Work Force*, edited by G.J. Borjas and R.B. Freeman. Chicago: University of Chicago Press.

Li, P.S. 2003. "Initial Earnings and Catch-up Capacity of Immigrants." *Canadian Public Policy* 29 (3): 319-37.

MaCurdy, T., and T. Mroz. 1985. "Measuring Macroeconomic Shifts in Wages from Cohort Specifications." Mimeo, Stanford University.

McDonald, J.T., and C. Worswick. 1998. "The Earnings of Immigrant Men in Canada: Job Tenure, Cohort, and Macroeconomic Conditions." *Industrial and Labor Relations Review* 51 (3): 465-82.

McWhinney, M. 1998. "A Selection Criteria Chronology, 1967-1997: Critical Changes in Definitions, the Point System, and Priority Processing." Strategic Research and Review Branch, Citizenship and Immigration Canada (April).

Picot, G., and F. Hou. 2003. "The Rise in Low-Income Rates among Immigrants in Canada." Research Paper, Analytical Studies Branch, Statistics Canada, No. 198.

– 2009. "Immigrant Characteristics, the IT Bust, and Their Effect on Immigrant Earnings." Statistics Canada, Analytical Studies Branch Research Paper No. 315.

Reitz, J.G. 2001. "Immigrant Success in the Knowledge Economy: Institutional Change and the Immigrant Experience in Canada, 1970-1995." *Journal of Social Issues* 57 (3): 579-613.

Schaafsma, J. and A. Sweetman. 2001. "Immigrant Earnings: Age at Immigration Matters." *Canadian Journal of Economics* 34 (4): 1066-99.

Sweetman, A., and C. Warman. 2008. "Integration, Impact, and Responsibility: An Economic Perspective on Canadian Immigration Policy." In *Immigration and Integration in Canada in the Twenty-First Century*, edited by J. Biles, M. Burstein, and J. Frideres, 19-44. Montreal and Kingston: McGill-Queen's University Press.

5

VISIBLE MINORITY STATUS, IMMIGRANT STATUS, GENDER, AND EARNINGS IN CANADA: A COHORT ANALYSIS

TED MCDONALD AND CHRISTOPHER WORSWICK

Dans cet article, nous nous demandons si le fait d'appartenir à certains groupes raciaux influence les revenus des immigrants et ceux des personnes nées au Canada, hommes et femmes. Par une analyse de cohortes, nous comparons les revenus des Blancs et ceux des membres de minorités visibles à différents niveaux d'expérience de travail en permettant aux rendements à l'expérience de varier selon la cohorte d'arrivée pour les immigrants et selon la cohorte d'entrée sur le marché du travail pour les personnes nées au Canada. Nous utilisons les données des fichiers maîtres de quatre recensements canadiens de la période 1991-2006 pour estimer des profils de revenus par genre et par éducation pour chacun des quatre grands groupes raciaux – Blancs, Noirs, personnes d'origine chinoise, personnes d'origine sud-asiatique. Notre analyse montre que l'évolution des différences de revenus parmi les minorités visibles au Canada est fortement influencée par l'âge, le niveau d'éducation, la cohorte et le statut d'immigrant. Chez les personnes nées au Canada, parmi les membres de minorités visibles et entrées récemment sur le marché du travail, ces différences sont faibles; de plus, parmi les personnes nées dans des groupes ethniques historiquement désavantagés (comme les Noirs et les personnes d'origine chinoise et sud-asiatique), on observe des rendements élevés à l'expérience de travail canadienne. Chez les immigrants, on observe, parmi ceux qui sont arrivées plus récemment, une baisse marquée des revenus initiaux dans certains groupes (tout particulièrement ceux de Chine et d'Asie du Sud); toutefois, au sein de toutes les minorités visibles, chez les immigrants arrivés plus récemment, on observe de forts rendements à l'expérience de travail. Cela signale donc que des progrès notables ont été réalisés dans l'intégration des immigrants – et en particulier ceux des minorités visibles – au marché du travail canadien.

Canadian Immigration: Economic Evidence for a Dynamic Policy Environment, ed. T. McDonald, E. Ruddick, A. Sweetman, and C. Worswick. Montreal and Kingston: Queen's Policy Studies Series, McGill-Queen's University Press.

In this chapter, we examine the extent to which race matters to the earnings of Canadian born and immigrant men and women in Canada. We employ a cohort based approach that lets us compare the earnings of white and visible minority groups at different levels of work experience after allowing for the returns to work experience to vary by immigrant arrival cohort for immigrants and by labour market entry cohort for the Canadian born. We use data from the master files of four consecutive Canadian Censuses over the period 1991-2006 and estimate earnings profiles by gender and broad education group separately for each of the four most numerous racial groups in Canada: whites, blacks, Chinese, and South Asians. Our analysis illustrates the importance of age, education, cohort, and immigrant status in terms of understanding the evolution of differences in earnings across visible minority groups in Canada. Our results indicate that differences in earnings across visible minority groups for recent labour market entry cohorts of the Canadian born are small, and there is evidence that recent cohorts of the Canadian born from historically disadvantaged groups such as blacks, Chinese, and South Asians are experiencing strong returns to Canadian work experience. For immigrants, we see pronounced declines in entry earnings for more recent arrivals from certain groups (especially the Chinese and South Asians); however, we also see associated strong returns to work experience for more recent immigrant arrival cohorts in each of the visible minority categories. This is an encouraging sign of significant progress in the integration of immigrants, particularly those from visible minority groups, into the Canadian labour market.

INTRODUCTION

Successful integration of immigrants into the Canadian labour market and the elimination of discrimination along ethnic, racial, and gender lines have been at the forefront of Canadian public policy for many decades. Unlike similar policy challenges in most other countries, the existence of large scale immigration into Canada means that these two policy goals are inherently linked, and a lack of success along one dimension can lead to negative consequences for our success along the other. The elimination of "preferred countries" as part of the Canadian immigration policy changes in 1967 caused a dramatic shift in the shares of immigrant source countries, away from traditional source countries from which came immigrants unlikely to be visible minorities to non-traditional source countries from which came immigrants likely to be visible minorities. This shift has resulted in a sizeable inflow into the Canadian labour market of new workers who are members of visible minority groups, leading to greater potential for the manifestation of discrimination by employers, co-workers, and others. In addition, in terms of degree of support for women's labour market participation, cultural differences across immigrant groups and within the domestic born society have led to differential rates of labour force participation by visible minority groups and resulted in policy challenges in terms of ensuring equality of opportunity for women in Canada. Finally, not just adult immigrants but also the children who arrived with them and their children born in Canada are more likely than ever to be members of visible minority groups and face a similar potential risk of discrimination by employers.

The goal of this paper is to pull together the best available data related to the labour market performance of immigrants and non-immigrants, visible minorities and non-visible minorities, and men and women and to analyze the patterns of earnings differences by immigrant status, visible minority status, and gender. The ultimate goals are to provide useful benchmarks that may enlighten public policy in this area and to provide possible explanations for the underlying patterns in the data. We adopt a cohort approach, defining immigrant cohorts based on the year in which they arrived in Canada and defining Canadian born cohorts based on the year in which they entered the labour market. This enables us to compare the earnings of visible minority groups at different levels of work experience but also to allow for the returns to work experience to vary by immigrant arrival cohort for immigrants and by labour market entry cohort for the Canadian born.

Review of the Literature

In developing our empirical model, we draw from a number of distinct yet related strands of the literature, including racial/ethnic discrimination, immigrant earnings, and labour market cohort differences in earnings. In what follows, we briefly summarize recent research in each area, with emphasis on recent literature for Canada.

Ethnic and Racial Discrimination

In the economics literature, much attention has been devoted to the issue of labour market discrimination.[1] In particular, a large literature exists on racial and ethnic discrimination in the United States,[2] due in large part to the long-standing issue of poor labour market outcomes for African-Americans and the availability of high quality data both from the US Census and US surveys such as the Current Population Survey. Although some important work has been published in the sociology field,[3] labour market discrimination based on race or ethnicity remains an under-researched topic in the economics literature for Canada.[4] Recent work has sought to compare various labour market outcomes for members of different groups based on self-reported ethnicity. For example, Pendakur and Pendakur (1998) use the 1991 Canadian Census and find significant earnings disadvantage between different visible minority groups and the white population in Canada. They (2002) use Canadian Census files from 1971 through 1996 to estimate earnings equations for Canadian born female and male workers and find that earnings differentials between white and visible minority Canadians narrowed through the 1970s, were stable through the 1980s, and expanded between 1991 and 1996.[5] Pendakur and Woodcock (2008) use linked employer-employee data to examine whether immigrant and minority workers' poor access to high-wage jobs is attributable to poor access to jobs in high-wage firms. They find that for some immigrant groups, the sorting of these workers across firm types accounts for as much as half of the economy-wide wage disparity they face.

In contrast, the literature on gender discrimination in Canada is extensive.[6] While our research does not focus specifically on analyzing gender discrimination, we carry out our analysis separately for men and women. This yields estimates of how gender differences in labour market outcomes vary across the different visible minority groups studied.

Labour Market Performance of Immigrants

Since a large number of Canadians who are members of visible minorities are also immigrants, an analysis of the relationship between ethnicity and labour market outcomes must necessarily also consider the relationship between immigrant status and labour market outcomes. The economics literature on the labour market experiences of immigrants in their new countries is extensive, and much of it has focused on the earnings of immigrants relative to comparable domestic born.[7] These studies often estimate human capital earnings equations, typically across pooled sets of cross-sectional survey datasets, and focus on the relationship between an immigrant's year of arrival and years-since-migration, and the immigrant's earnings. Some of these studies find a decline in the success of recent immigrant cohorts in terms of their labour market outcomes for the same number of years of residence in Canada (at least over the early years after migration).[8] Attention has also focused on other direct measures of immigrant labour market adjustment such as unemployment rates (e.g., McDonald and Worswick 1997; Chiswick, Cohen, and Zach 1998) and labour force participation (e.g., Schoeni 1998; Cobb-Clark 2000). Recently, researchers have also focused on differences between immigrants and the Canadian born in other dimensions that are likely to affect the employment and earnings of immigrants and by extension their general labour market success. These include a growing literature on the educational attainment of first and/or second-generation immigrants (e.g., Chiswick and Miller 1994; Gang and Zimmermann 2000), an issue that we take up in this paper.

Labour Market Entry Cohort Effects in Earnings of the Canadian Born

An important related literature has analyzed the earnings of men and women from different birth cohorts to investigate whether more recent labour market entry cohorts have been at a disadvantage in terms of earnings compared with earlier cohorts. Beaudry and Green (1999) use 17 cross-sectional surveys from the SCF data covering the period 1971-93 to track the earnings of different cohorts defined in terms of birth year and level of educational attainment. They find that the age-earnings profiles of Canadian men have been deteriorating for more recent cohorts compared with older cohorts. They also do not find evidence that the returns to experience have been increasing over time, implying a permanent earnings disadvantage for more recent birth cohorts relative to earlier cohorts. A similar pattern was found in the United States by MaCurdy and Mroz (1995).

Immigrant Cohort Differences and Canadian Born Cohort Differences

Green and Worswick (2002) carried out an analysis that benchmarked recent arrival cohorts of immigrants to Canada with recent labour market entry cohorts of the Canadian born. They found that the cross-cohort declines for Canadian born men (found by Beaudry and Green 1999) can explain up to one-third of the decline in immigrant labour market entry cohort earnings over the period 1981-96. The approach involves comparing cohorts of immigrants to Canadian born workers entering the labour market at the same time. The analysis employed a unique dataset that links immigrant landing and tax records (the Longitudinal Immigrant Database, known as the IMDB) to get immigrant data, as well as a series of representative surveys (the Statistics Canada Surveys of Consumer Finances) to get Canadian born data. In both of these studies (Beaudry and Green 1999; Green and Worswick 2002), the data did not contain information on race and ethnicity. Therefore, our research extends this work in an important way, allowing us to explore whether these relationships differ according to race and ethnic background. For example, we can determine whether the declines across labour market entry cohorts of Canadian born workers are larger for persons from visible minority groups.[9]

SPECIFICATION OF THE EARNINGS MODEL

Earnings outcomes are analyzed through the estimation of human capital earnings equations. The following reduced-form model is estimated separately for men and women. In addition, following Beaudry and Green

(1999), the model is estimated separately for three education groupings (high school or less, post-secondary without a university degree, and university degree). This grouping allows for separate labour market entry cohort effects for different types of workers and different returns to years of experience according to these groups:

$$Y_{it} = X_{it}\beta + \beta_1 YSE_{it} + \beta_2 YSE_{it}^2 + \sum_{k=1}^{K-1} coh_k(\alpha_k + \alpha_{k1}YSE_{it} + \alpha_{k2}YSE_{it}^2) + \varepsilon_{it} \qquad (1)$$

where i indexes individuals, and the dependent variable Y_{it} is the natural logarithm of weekly earnings. The vector X_{it} contains the de-trended unemployment rate, fixed effects for province of residence, and other demographic characteristics. The YSE_{it} variable captures the length of time since the person entered the Canadian labour market.[10] It appears in linear and quadratic form and is interacted with dummy variables for a set of K labour market entry cohorts. The analysis is carried out over the pooled sample of all four census years (1991, 1996, 2001, 2006), allowing for the observation of earnings of each labour market entry cohort at up to four time periods. This in turn allows for an analysis of the earnings of the same labour market entry cohort at different numbers of years since entry into the labour market (or potential experience). This model is estimated separately for Canadian born men and women in different visible minority groups (e.g., white, black, Chinese, South Asian). We define these groups based on the self-identification of whether an individual belongs to a visible minority group, and if so, to which group that individual belongs. Although other visible minority groups are identified in the data (e.g., West Asian, Hispanic, Japanese, Korean), we focus on white, black, Chinese, and South Asian, since those are the four largest ethnic groups in Canada, according to the 2006 Census.[11] As well, smaller visible minority groups may not yield sufficient sample sizes to obtain meaningful estimates, particularly given our focus on Canadian born members of particular visible minority groups by education level and gender.

For immigrants, a model similar to equation (1) is employed, which allows for labour market entry cohort effects but also allows for the effects of pre-migration experience, as is done in Green and Worswick (2002):

$$Y_{it} = X_{it}\delta + \delta_{f1}FX_{it} + \delta_{f2}FX_{it}^2 + \delta_1 YSE_{it} + \delta_2 YSE_{it}^2 + \sum_{k=1}^{K-1} coh_k(\gamma_k + \gamma_{k1}YSE_{it} + \gamma_{k2}YSE_{it}^2) + \varepsilon_{it} \quad (2)$$

where FX_{it} is the number of years of foreign work experience of the immigrants. Also, the YSE_{it} variable is equivalent to the common years-since-migration variables in the immigration literature since it measures the number of years-since-entry into the Canadian labour market (or entry into Canada, in this case). Following Green and Worswick (2002), a more flexible specification of the returns to foreign experience allows for differential returns to foreign experience by arrival cohort. However, in order to reduce the amount of notation in the equation, these effects are left out of equation (2).

One important distinction between the approach employed by Green and Worswick (2002, 2010) relative to the current study is that Green and Worswick build in the Canadian born cohort effects into equation (2). Their motivation for this is that these effects are interpreted as general new labour market entrant effects, which are experienced by both the Canadian born and immigrants. In the current study, we allow these new entrant effects to be absorbed into the immigrant cohort differences (which vary with YSE) in equation (2). We take this approach since we are concerned about the possibility of changes in unobservables across labour market entry cohorts within a given visible minority group of Canadian born individuals. Consequently, we do not want to automatically assign these Canadian born cohort effects for the visible minority group as new entrant effects for the immigrants of that visible minority group. However, one can still generate immigrant effects that are comparable with those of Green and Worswick (2002, 2010) by taking the difference of the predicted log earnings for the relevant immigrant cohort using equation (2) and subtracting from that the predicted log earnings from equation (1) for the relative Canadian born cohort.

Equation (2) is estimated separately for men and women and separately by education group. In addition, the model is estimated separately according to the visible minority group of the immigrants. This allows for a differentiation of the effects of visible minority group and immigrant effects such as excess returns to YSE between immigrants and the Canadian born.

Ideally, for a project of this kind, one would use a data source with more annual observations than the Census. Beaudry and Green (1999), for example, use a set of Surveys of Consumer Finances in order to estimate accurately these cohort-specific age-earnings relationships. Unfortunately, the SCF data do not have information on visible minority status and therefore are not suitable for a study of this kind. The Census is carried out less frequently; however, the rich information on visible minority status, coupled with the large sample sizes of each Census year, make Census data the best choice for an analysis of this kind. A second methodological issue relates to changes in the categories for visible minority group available in the Canadian Census files. We take care to reduce the risk of compositional shifts in the different visible minority group categories across Census years.

Data and Sample Selection

Data from the 1991, 1996, 2001, and 2006 master files from the Canadian Census are employed in the analysis. Estimation was carried out at the Research Data Centre at the University of New Brunswick at Fredericton. The sample is restricted to include those individuals age 25 to 64 with positive labour market earnings who have more than half of their annual earnings generated from wages and salaries. Our dependent variable is the average weekly earnings in the reference year. The earnings data are inflated into 2006 Canadian dollars using the CPI index.

As noted above, our two main groups of interest are immigrants who arrived age 25 or older, and the Canadian born. Consequently, we exclude immigrants who were younger than 25 at the time of arrival. This approach to defining the immigrant sample is consistent with that of Green and Worswick (2002, 2010) and makes it likely that the immigrant's education was acquired outside of Canada.

Carrying out a separate analysis of the earnings of aboriginal Canadians, we found lower levels of education and earnings for both aboriginal men and women relative to their counterparts among the remaining Canadian born population. However, since the focus of this study is on the intersection of visible minority status and immigrant status and their relationships with earnings, we do not report estimates for aboriginal Canadians but instead leave these results for analysis in a separate paper.

Given the extremely large sample sizes obtained from combining data from four consecutive 20 percent Census files, we adopted the approach of taking a 10 percent random sample each of white men and white women from each Census file. For visible minority groups, we utilized 100 percent of the observations of blacks, Chinese, and South Asians. After imposing our age restriction and omitting individuals with zero weeks worked during the Census year, we are left with the following sample sizes: for men, 367,667 whites, 63,733 blacks, 100,414 Chinese, and 93,627 South Asians; for women, 323,388 whites, 58,581 blacks, 90,978 Chinese, and 62,269 South Asians.

Table 1 presents the educational distributions for each visible minority group by immigrant status and gender. For Canadian born women, the Chinese and South Asian groups have very high fractions with a university degree at 49.7 and 46.9 percent, respectively. White women and black women both have much lower rates of having a university degree (just over 20 percent) and higher rates of having no more than a high school diploma (roughly 40 percent for each) and post-secondary education but below a university degree (at roughly 40 percent). For the case of immigrant women, the educational distributions are similar across the white, Chinese, and South Asian groups, with approximately 30 percent of women having a university degree. The Chinese and South Asian immigrant women are more likely to have no more than a high school diploma (at over 40 percent) than are the white immigrant women (at 35.5 percent). Black immigrant women are the least likely to have a university degree (12.6 percent).

For Canadian born men, the overall patterns in the educational distributions are similar to those found for Canadian born women. White men have lower rates of having a university degree than do their female

TABLE 1
Educational Distribution by Immigrant Group and Visible Minority Group

	White	Black	Chinese	South Asian
Women				
Canadian born				
HS or less	42.4	36.0	22.5	24.1
PS – no univ. degree	37.3	40.2	27.9	29.0
Univ. degree	20.3	23.8	49.7	46.9
Immigrant				
HS or less	35.5	42.2	44.8	41.5
PS – no univ. degree	34.3	45.2	26.3	24.6
Univ. degree	30.3	12.6	28.9	33.9
Men				
Canadian born				
HS or less	44.6	47.0	25.1	33.9
PS – no univ. degree	37.2	34.9	28.6	26.4
Univ. degree	18.2	18.1	46.4	39.7
Immigrant				
HS or less	30.3	40.2	37.4	33.9
PS – no univ. degree	37.6	37.7	21.0	25.4
Univ. degree	32.2	22.1	41.7	40.7

Source: Authors' compilations based on data from Census of Canada, 1991-2006.

counterparts, while the opposite is true for black Canadian born men. Also, South Asian Canadian born men have lower rates of having a university degree (39.7 percent) than do their female counterparts (46.9 percent). It is important to recall that our samples condition on positive labour market earnings; therefore, the labour market participation selection may mean that differential selection issues between men and women within a visible minority group may affect the sign and magnitude of differences in educational probabilities. For immigrant men, Chinese and South Asian men have the highest rates of having a university degree, at 41.7 and 40.7 percent, respectively. Black immigrant men have the lowest rates of having a university degree (22.1 percent) and the highest rates of having no more than a high school diploma.

The high rates of university education for individuals in the Chinese and South Asian visible minority groups in part reflect the changes in the immigrant selection system over time. After the introduction of the points system in 1967, the steady growth in the share of the immigrant inflow arising from China and South Asia coincided with an increase in the points allocated to education over time, meaning that immigrants from these countries are likely to be both younger on average than immigrants from traditional source countries (who would typically fall into our white group) and more likely to have needed to have a high level of education in order to gain admission under the points system. However, cultural attitudes toward education are likely also important, and the high levels of education for the Canadian born individuals in the Chinese and South Asian groups likely reflect the high level of importance placed on education in their families.

In Table 2, sample means for weekly earnings are presented by immigrant status, visible minority group, gender, and education group. The strong returns to education are apparent, and this is true across all visible minority groups, by immigrant status and for both genders. In the lower panel of the table, the sample means are normalized so as to be a fraction of the equivalent sample means for Canadian born white men with the same level of education. For Canadian born women, the Chinese have 10 percent higher earnings in the high school or less and post-secondary but no degree categories, but 8 percent less earnings than the white Canadian born women do in the university degree category. Black and South Asian Canadian born women have similar earnings to the white women in the high school and post-secondary categories but 15 percent lower earnings in the university category. For immigrant women, the patterns are similar but without the Chinese earnings advantage at the lower two educational levels. Also, South Asian immigrant women with degrees have only 67 percent of the weekly earnings of white Canadian born women with degrees. For men, the Canadian born differences in mean earnings are larger, with black men and South Asian men earning roughly two-thirds to three-quarters of the earnings of white men at the same education level. White immigrant men have earnings comparable to those of white Canadian born men for each education category. However, immigrant men in the other visible minority categories have lower earnings, with the differences for black and South Asian men being similar to those of their counterparts among the Canadian born men. For Chinese immigrant men, the differences relative to the white immigrant men are larger than the Chinese/white differences found for Canadian born men.

These comparisons of mean weekly earnings in part reflect differences across the groups in factors that determine earnings, such as years of work experience. Given that earnings typically rise with the increase in human capital gained from work experience, we would expect older groups in our sample to have higher earnings than younger groups. The substantial changes in source country composition and the growth of visible minority groups across birth cohorts in Canada mean that the white groups are likely to have more years of work experience than the black, Chinese, and South Asian groups, and this difference is likely to be present both for immigrants and for the Canadian born. Sample means for total years of potential work experience (since the age of 25) are presented in Table 3. As expected, the white cell of each row has higher years of work experience than any of the other rows. This is consistent with the idea of a shift away from whites in both the immigrant intake and across successive waves of birth cohorts of the Canadian born in Canada. Given that greater work experience is associated with higher earnings, it is important to control for work experience in our analysis so as to compare different groups

TABLE 2
Weekly Earnings by Immigrant Group and Visible Minority Group

	White	Black	Chinese	South Asian
Women				
Canadian born				
HS or less	441.4	424.2	486.7	434.7
PS – no univ. degree	548.8	507.3	603.4	531.4
Univ. degree	803.3	673.6	741.7	684.5
Immigrant				
HS or less	427.0	418.9	391.9	402.8
PS – no univ. degree	502.9	549.1	511.9	527.4
Univ. Degree	691.9	735.4	624.0	540.3
Men				
Canadian born				
HS or Less	722.55	531.88	569.72	504.54
PS – no univ. degree	842.34	613.14	738.87	612.75
Univ. degree	1109.74	743.73	873.45	755.29
Immigrant				
HS or Less	712.66	536.48	480.29	542.29
PS – no univ. degree	859.98	660.85	645.46	694.86
Univ. degree	1088.78	791.90	781.36	798.90

Earnings as a percent of equivalent earnings for Canadian born whites
with same education level

	White	Black	Chinese	South Asian
Women				
Canadian born				
HS or less	1.00	0.96	1.10	0.98
PS – no univ. degree	1.00	0.92	1.10	0.97
Univ. degree	1.00	0.84	0.92	0.85
Immigrant				
HS or less	0.97	0.95	0.89	0.91
PS – no univ. degree	0.92	1.00	0.93	0.96
Univ. degree	0.86	0.92	0.78	0.67
Men				
Canadian born				
HS or Less	1.00	0.74	0.79	0.70
PS – no univ. degree	1.00	0.73	0.88	0.73
Univ. degree	1.00	0.67	0.79	0.68
Immigrant				
HS or less	0.99	0.74	0.66	0.75
PS – no univ. degree	1.02	0.78	0.77	0.82
Univ. degree	0.98	0.71	0.70	0.72

Source: Authors' compilations based on data from Census of Canada, 1991-2006

of Canadian born and immigrants (by visible minority status) at the same career stage. In addition, given the substantial changes to both the Canadian labour market and Canadian immigration policy over the past 40 years, it is important to allow for these experience effects to vary by both immigrant arrival cohort and (Canadian born) labour market entry cohort. In the next section, we estimate the regression models specified in equations (1) and (2) that allow for this level of flexibility.

TABLE 3
Potential Work Experience by Immigrant Group and Visible Minority Group

	White	Black	Chinese	South Asian
Women				
Canadian born				
HS or less	17.2	12.4	13.0	10.1
PS – no univ. degree	15.2	10.4	10.7	6.5
Univ. degree	13.6	7.7	8.3	5.0
Immigrant				
HS or less	23.8	21.2	20.3	20.4
PS – no univ. degree	21.5	21.0	18.3	20.3
Univ. degree	19.1	19.0	15.5	17.1
Men				
Canadian born				
HS or less	16.3	11.2	11.7	9.3
PS – no univ. degree	15.3	10.4	10.9	7.2
Univ. degree	15.3	9.5	9.2	6.4
Immigrant				
HS or less	24.2	20.1	21.1	19.5
PS – no univ. degree	22.9	20.7	20.5	20.4
Univ. degree	20.7	19.2	17.1	18.6

Source: Authors' compilations based on data from Census of Canada, 1991-2006

REGRESSION RESULTS AND EXPERIENCE/EARNINGS PROFILES

Equations (1) and (2) are estimated separately across the Canadian born and immigrant sub-samples defined by education (high school or less, post-secondary but no degree, and university degree), gender and visible minority group (whites, blacks, Chinese, and South Asians). Given the very large number of regressions as well as coefficient estimates obtained in each regression, we do not present the regression estimates[12] and instead generate and plot the predicted log of weekly earnings by years-since-entry into the Canadian labour market separately for each sub-sample defined by immigrant status, education, race, and gender. In order to reduce the number of figures somewhat, we follow Beaudry and Green (1999) and present experience/earnings[13] profiles for the high school or less group and the university degree group only. Figures 1a to 1h present the cohort-specific experience/earnings profiles for Canadian born men by education level and visible minority status. Each cohort's profile is predicted over the years-since-entry into the Canadian labour market for which the cohort is observed in the survey year range of the data (1991-2006).

In the figures for immigrants, the predicted experience/earnings profiles are generated for the case of immigrants arriving in Canada at age 25. This is the youngest age for which a person in our sample entered Canada.

By choosing the case of adult immigrants entering Canada with relatively little foreign work experience, we are able to focus the comparison on differences between immigrants and the Canadian born that are driven by visible minority status and differences in returns to foreign education, but to limit the role of differential returns to foreign experience by visible minority group and cohort. In a companion paper, we explore the role of age at arrival and return to foreign work experience for immigrants by visible minority status.

In Figure 1a, the experience/earnings profiles by labour market entry cohort are presented for white, Canadian born men with education at the high school diploma level or lower. In general, no clear cohort differences are apparent since the different profiles are very close together. The only exceptions relate to the early cohorts, where there is some evidence of small positive cohort differences in which the more recent entry cohort has higher weekly earnings than the earlier arrival cohort at the same years of experience. This finding is surprising, given that Beaudry and Green (1999) find negative cohort effects in the experience/earnings profiles of Canadian born men in this education group using the SCF data over the period 1971-91. It is possible that for more recent data the evidence of declining cohort effects in the Canadian born earnings is not clear cut. Green and Worswick (2010), using combined SCF and SLID data over the range 1981 through 2003 and using annual earnings as the dependent variable, find evidence of cohort effects for the earlier arrival cohorts, but they also find evidence of an improvement in entry earnings for more recent arrival cohorts. We repeated the estimation used to generate Figure 1a over all racial groups of Canadian born men pooled together and similarly found no clear evidence of cohort effects. Another possibility is that more recent cohorts had lower entry earnings but greater returns to experience. The profiles in Figure 1a for the earlier cohorts are consistent with that hypothesis, since the 1970s cohorts have steeper profiles than the 1950s and 1960s cohorts over the 20 plus range of experience. Unfortunately, we do not observe these cohorts over our sample range at low values of experience, so it is impossible to say whether entry earnings were higher for the 1950s and 1960s cohorts compared with the 1970s and more recent cohorts.

In Figure 1b, the experience/earnings profiles of each labour market entry cohort are presented for black Canadian born men with high school or less education. As was the case in Figure 1a, it is difficult to identify a clear pattern in terms of cohort differences. For the early cohorts, observed near the end of their careers, the experience/earnings profiles are downward sloping and in some cases the different cohort profiles cross. For these earlier cohorts there is some evidence that the entry earnings may have declined in real terms. However, there is also evidence that the profiles are steeper in this case, indicating an initial disadvantage that is overcome with more years in the labour market. It should be stressed that these differences are small, and in general labour market entry cohort differences do not appear to be important for black Canadian born men. However, it is clear that these cohort profiles lie below the equivalent profiles in Figure 1a for white Canadian born men, with the differences approximately in the 10 to 20 percent range. This is consistent with the view that the former group face discrimination in Canada, since holding education fixed at the high school or less level and for the same level of potential experience we see lower weekly earnings for the black Canadian born men than for the white Canadian born men in a given labour market entry cohort.

Next, the experience/earnings profiles for different labour market entry cohorts of Chinese Canadian born men are presented in Figure 1c. The cross-cohort pattern is complicated, with evidence of a decline across cohorts. The most recent cohort (2002-06) had a very low entry earnings level followed by a high return to work experience, so that after only four years in the labour market their earnings were approximately equal to the cohort (1997-2001) that entered just before them. Taken together, the experience/earnings profiles for Chinese Canadian born men are similar to those of black Canadian born men in terms of earnings at experience levels of 10 years and higher. However, entry earnings are lower for the most recent cohorts, indicating that the Chinese group of Canadian born men may face greater difficulty becoming established in the Canadian labour market.

Equivalent experience/earnings profiles are presented in Figure 1d for the case of South Asian Canadian born men with no more than high school education. The cohort pattern is clearer in this case, indicating that over the cohort range of 1977-81 through 1997-2001, the more recent arrival cohorts had higher real weekly earnings than did the earlier arrival cohorts. This pattern is particularly clear over the 1987-91 through 1997-2001 cohort range, where the slopes of each profile are similar. For the most recent arrival cohort, 2002-06, their entry earning are lower than those of the two cohorts that entered the labour market right before them; however, their rate of return to work experience is especially high, so that the initial disadvantage is more than eliminated after four years in the labour market. It is also worth noting that the entry earnings for the more recent arrival cohorts are higher for the South-Asian Canadian born men than for the Chinese Canadian born men. Given the strong positive returns to experience for the recent cohorts of South Asian Canadian born men relative to either the black Canadian born men and the Chinese Canadian born men, the weekly earnings after five years of experience are higher for the South Asian men relative to either the Chinese or the black men and are comparable with those of the white men. Should this rate of growth of weekly earnings continue in future years, this group of South Asian Canadian born men could have by far the highest weekly earnings of any of the visible minority group of men with high school or less education.

Figures 1e through 1h present equivalent experience/earnings profiles by cohort for the four visible minority groups of Canadian born men but for the case of university degree holders. Evidence of positive cohort effects is present in Figure 1e for white Canadian born men. Once again, this is contrary to what one would expect given the findings of negative cohort effects for earlier arrival cohorts by Beaudry and Green (1999). However, the closeness of the profiles of the earlier arrival cohorts to each other and the steepening of the profiles for more recent cohorts may indicate a possible reason for the difference in results. If the sample range were over the 1970s and 1980s (as was the case in Beaudry and Green (1999)), we would not see the most recent arrival cohorts and we would only observe the earlier arrival cohorts for lower values of years of experience. Given the changing slopes across the cohort profiles, it is possible that over this range of experience these earlier arrival cohorts might have somewhat higher real earnings than did the later cohorts. However, given that our sample data range only begins in 1991, we are unable to see this range of experience for these cohorts.[14]

It is interesting to note that the white Canadian born men with degrees have similar entry earnings as the white Canadian born men with high school or less education at least for the more recent entry cohorts. However, the former group have much higher returns to experience than the latter group, such that by 10 years of work experience, log weekly earnings are over 25 percent higher for the university group than for the high school group.

From Figure 1f, we see that black Canadian born men with university degrees have similar entry earnings to white Canadian born men with degrees. However, the returns to experience are generally not as large (although there is some variability in the slopes across the profiles, with many of the cohort profiles crossing). There is some evidence of a steepening of the profiles for the more recent cohorts, indicating an increase in the return to work experience.

In both Figure 1g and 1h, more recent cohorts of Chinese and South Asian Canadian born men with university degrees have higher earnings than did the earlier cohorts of men with the same education and in the same visible minority group. In the Chinese case, the mid-career weekly earnings are higher than those of the equivalent cohorts of both white and black Canadian born men with degrees. For more recent cohorts, entry earnings are also higher for this group relative to those of the recent cohorts of white and black men with degrees. For South Asian men with degrees, their mid-career earnings are among the lowest of the four groups (comparable to those of black men) and are clearly the lowest in terms of late career earnings. However, this group of men also has the strongest positive cohort effects.

FIGURE 1a. White Canadian Born Men, High School or Less

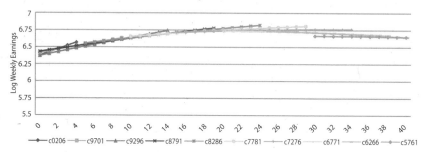

FIGURE 1b. Black Canadian Born Men, High School or Less

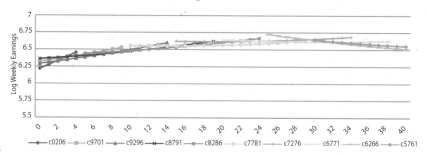

FIGURE 1c. Chinese Canadian Born Men, High School or Less

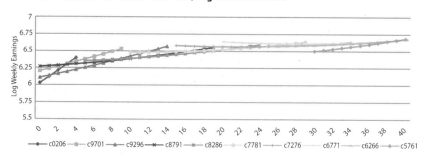

FIGURE 1d. South Asian Canadian Born Men, High School or Less

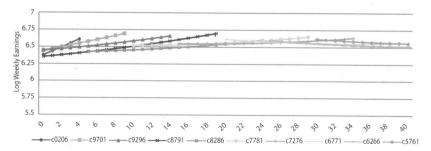

Source: Authors' compilations based on data from Census of Canada, 1991-2006.

FIGURE 1e. White Canadian Born Men, Degree or More

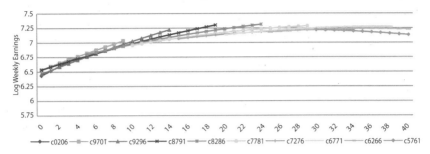

FIGURE 1f. Black Canadian Born Men, Degree or More

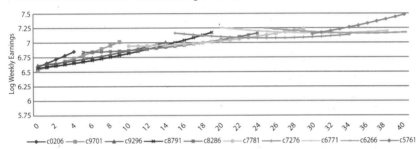

FIGURE 1g. Chinese Canadian Born Men, Degree or More

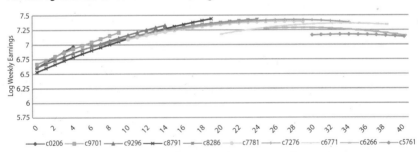

FIGURE 1h. South Asian Canadian Born Men, Degree or More

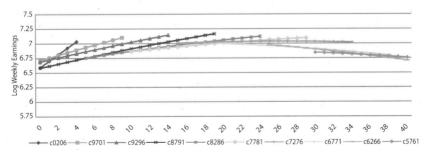

Source: Authors' compilations based on data from Census of Canada, 1991-2006.

In Figures 2a through 2h, equivalent cohort-specific earnings/experience profiles to those in Figures 1a through 1h are plotted by education level and visible minority status but for the case of immigrant men who arrived in Canada at age 25. Green and Worswick (2002, 2010) find that approximately 40 percent of the decline in entry earnings across immigrant arrival cohorts over the 1980s and 1990s can be attributed to the decline in returns to foreign work experience (virtually to zero). Given that the immigrant men considered in these graphs have very little foreign work experience, the decline in returns to that experience is unlikely to have a big impact on their earnings, so whatever entry effects are apparent are not likely due to differences in the return to foreign work experience.

In the first four figures, related to immigrant men with high school education or less, we see very low entry earnings for the more recent cohorts relative to what was the case in Figures 1a through 1d for Canadian born men. Strong negative cohort effects are present in Figure 2a and Figure 2c for white immigrant men and Chinese immigrant men, respectively. For black immigrant men and South Asian immigrant men, the cohort pattern is less clear, with some evidence of negative cohort effects but also strong evidence of a steepening of the experience/earnings profiles, reflecting high rates of return to Canadian work experience. This latter result is true in all four of the high school figures, at least for the case of the most recent immigrant arrival cohort.

In Figures 2e through 2h, similar patterns to those illustrated in Figures 2a-2d are found. For white immigrant men with degrees, there is evidence of negative cohort effects, especially for the more recent arrival cohorts. However, there is also evidence of a steepening of the experience/earnings profile, especially for the 1980s and 1990s cohorts relative to the 1970s and 1960s cohorts. The effect is so pronounced that while these later cohorts arrived at a significant earnings disadvantage, they quickly overcame this disadvantage. The patterns are similar for black immigrant men with degrees (Figure 2f), with even larger returns to Canadian work experience evident for the most recent arrival cohort. There is also evidence that the immigrants who arrived in Canada in the late 1980s and in the early 1990s struggled in the labour market in terms of weekly earnings relative to their counterparts among white immigrant men with degrees. In Figure 2g, a pattern of dramatic declines in entry earnings are present across immigrant arrival cohorts for Chinese immigrant men (with degrees), coupled with an equally impressive increase in the returns to years-since-entry in Canada. The log earnings at entry of the 2002-06 cohort are approximately 5.85 and are by far the lowest entry earnings of any of the immigrant groups of men with university degrees. However, by four years of residence in Canada, this cohort's average weekly earnings are comparable to those of the other recent arrival cohorts. Comparing these experience/earnings profiles to those of South Asian immigrant men with degrees (Figure 2h), we see similarities

FIGURE 2a. White Immigrant Men Arrived Age 25, High School or Less

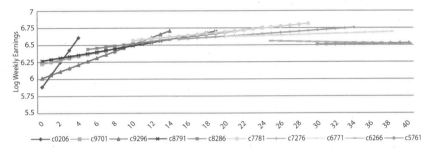

FIGURE 2b. Black Immigrant Men Arrived Age 25, High School or Less

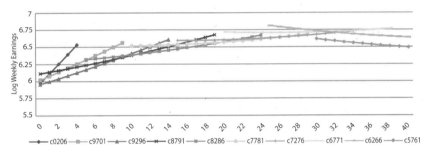

FIGURE 2c. Chinese Immigrant Men Arrived Age 25, High School or Less

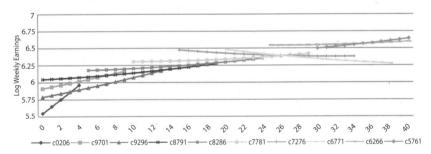

FIGURE 2d. South Asian Immigrant Men Arrived Age 25, High School or Less

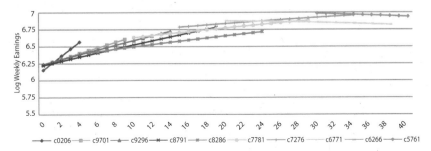

Source: Authors' compilations based on data from Census of Canada, 1991-2006.

FIGURE 2e. White Immigrant Men Arrived Age 25, Degree or More

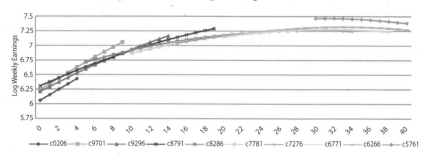

FIGURE 2f. Black Immigrant Men Arrived Age 25, Degree or More

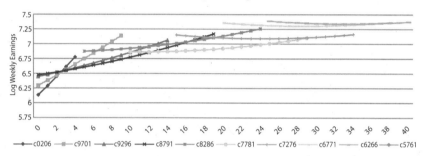

FIGURE 2g. Chinese Immigrant Men Arrived Age 25, Degree or More

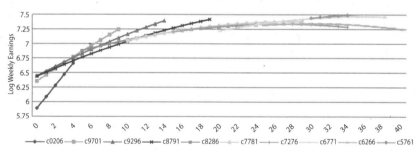

FIGURE 2h. South Asian Immigrant Men Arrived Age 25, Degree or More

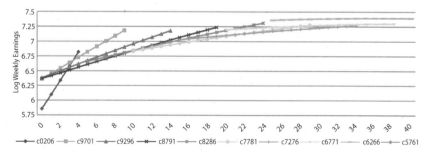

Source: Authors' compilations based on data from Census of Canada, 1991-2006.

in 1) strong negative cohort effects in terms of entry earnings, and 2) large increases in returns to post-migration work experience (or YSE) across immigrant arrival cohorts. In fact, for the South Asian men, the most recent cohort is predicted to have higher log weekly earnings than the other recent arrival cohorts after only four years in Canada.

In Figures 3a through 3d, cohort-specific experience/earnings profiles are presented for the case of Canadian born women with high school education or less by visible minority group. For white women, we see a steepening of the profiles for more recent cohorts, a shifting down of the entry earnings, and a steepening of the earnings profile. By extrapolating the lines out of the sample year range, one can imagine that the entry earnings may have shifted down somewhat for more recent arrival cohorts, but it is not possible to ascertain that this is the case. In Figure 3b for black women and in Figure 3d for South Asian women, the patterns are similar, with a shifting down of entry earnings and a steepening of the profile indicating higher returns to work experience for more recent labour market entry cohorts of Canadian born women. However, for recent cohorts of South Asian women there has actually been a shifting up of the profiles, indicating that these cohorts have had higher earnings than the cohorts that preceded them for the same number of years in the Canadian labour market. For Chinese Canadian born women with high school or less education, the profiles overlap more for the earlier cohorts, and the returns to work experience are modest over the range 10 years and higher. For the most recent cohorts, the entry earnings have shifted down and a steepening of the profile is apparent for the 1997-2001 cohort and the 2002-06 cohort.

Next we consider the experience/earnings profiles of Canadian born women with university degrees by visible minority group. The profiles in Figures 3e through 3h are similar to those found in Figures 3a through 3e, though with a number of important differences. First, entry earnings are much higher for each visible minority group in the case of a university degree compared to a high school diploma. Returns to work experience are greater for black Canadian born women with degrees than for their counterparts with high school or less education. Also, the cohort differences do not seem as large in Figure 3f relative to what is presented in Figure 3b. However, evidence of a steepening of the profile is present in both cases for black Canadian born women. Comparing Figure 3g to Figure 3c, we see that Chinese Canadian born women with degrees have strong positive cohort effects across virtually all of the labour market entry cohorts in contrast to what was found for Chinese Canadian born women with high school or less education. In the former case, we also see strong returns to work experience. The patterns of cross-cohort differences in the profiles are similar in Figure 3h when compared to Figure 3g, indicating that South Asian Canadian born women with degrees also have strong positive cohort effects similar to what is found for Chinese Canadian born women with degrees.

FIGURE 3a. White Canadian Born Women, High School or Less

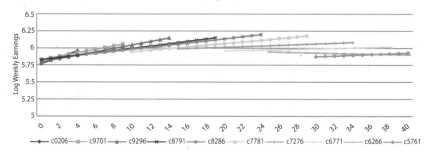

FIGURE 3b. Black Canadian Born Women, High School or Less

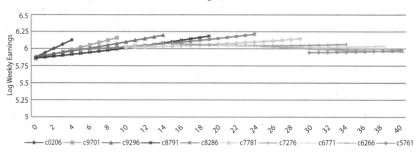

FIGURE 3c. Chinese Canadian Born Women, High School or Less

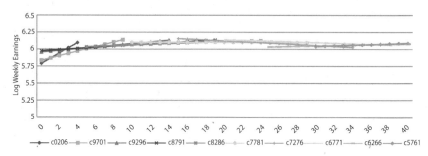

FIGURE 3d. South Asian Canadian Born Women, High School or Less

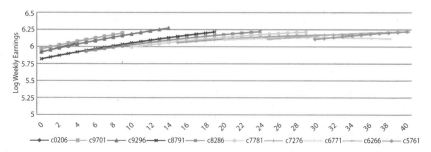

Source: Authors' compilations based on data from Census of Canada, 1991-2006.

FIGURE 3e. White Canadian Born Women, Degree or More

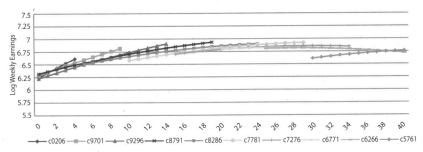

FIGURE 3f. Black Canadian Born Women, Degree or More

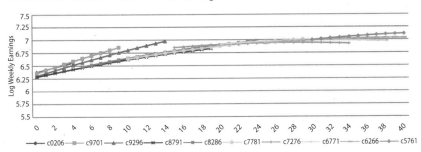

FIGURE 3g. Chinese Canadian Born Women, Degree or More

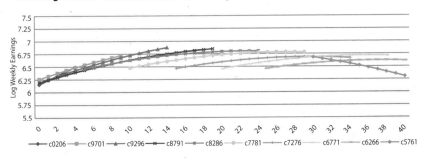

FIGURE 3h. South Asian Canadian Born Women, Degree or More

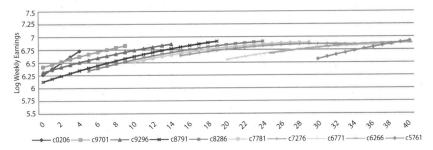

Source: Authors' compilations based on data from Census of Canada, 1991-2006.

In Figures 4a through 4h, equivalent experience/earnings profiles are presented for immigrant women by education category and by visible minority group. Figure 4a presents the experience/earnings profiles for the white immigrant women with high school education or less who arrived in Canada at age 25. Large cohort difference are present that are generally consistent with a shifting down of the entry earnings for more recent cohorts and with a steepening of the profile for these recent cohorts. The main exception is the 2002-06 cohort, which has a large entry earnings effect and a downward sloping profile.[15] This may be due to relatively small sample sizes for this particular cohort. Based on the profiles in Figure 4b, we see that black immigrant women with high school or less education who arrived at age 25 have similar overall profiles to the white immigrant women. The cohort differences for the middle cohorts 1977-81 through 1987-91 are not as pronounced as in the case of Figure 4a; however, evidence of declining entry earnings and increases for more recent cohorts in returns to experience is found. Comparing the two figures, it is hard to see clear evidence that the black immigrant women have lower earnings than the white immigrant women when comparing across equivalent immigrant arrival cohorts (with the exception of the 2002-06 cohort). In both Figure 4c and Figure 4d, there is evidence of decreasing entry earnings for more recent cohorts of Chinese and South Asian immigrant women, coupled with increasing returns to experience for these more recent cohorts. There is some evidence of low earnings for the earliest arrival cohorts in the case of the Chinese immigrant women, which is not present for the South Asian immigrant women; however, in virtually all other respects the figures are very similar.

Figures 4e through 4h present by visible minority group equivalent experience/earnings profiles for immigrant women arriving in Canada at age 25 with a university degree. In all four graphs, there is evidence of large increases in the slopes of the profiles for more recent arrival cohorts relative to the earlier cohorts. These effects are sufficiently large that they clearly overcome the fact that entry earnings have generally shifted down, especially for the Chinese and South Asian women. For the white and black women, there is evidence that the entry earnings may have shifted upwards between the late 1980s and the late 1990s. The trend then reverses again based on the relatively poor performance of the 2002-06 cohort. It is important to note that these entry earnings for the most recent immigrant cohorts are much lower than the entry earnings for the Canadian born women of the same visible minority group and the same labour market entry cohort. The evidence supports the view that white and black immigrant women with university degrees start off in the Canadian labour market at a large wage disadvantage but experience relatively high returns to Canadian work experience so that after 10 years in Canada, their weekly earnings are comparable to those of Canadian born women of the same visible minority group with

FIGURE 4a. White Immigrant Women Arrived Age 25, High School or Less

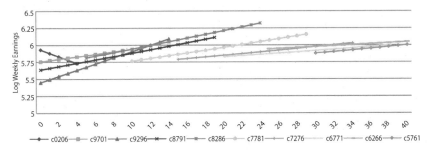

FIGURE 4b. Black Immigrant Women Arrived Age 25, High School or Less

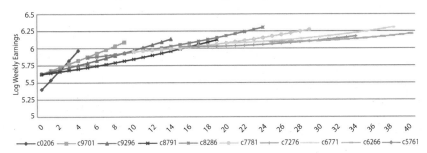

FIGURE 4c. Chinese Immigrant Women Arrived Age 25, High School or Less

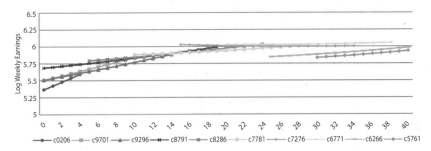

FIGURE 4d. South Asian Immigrant Women Arrived Age 25, High School or Less

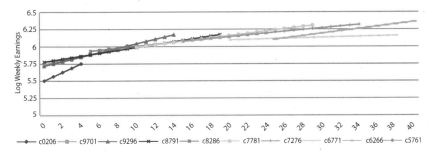

Source: Authors' compilations based on data from Census of Canada, 1991-2006.

FIGURE 4e. White Immigrant Women Arrived Age 25, Degree or More

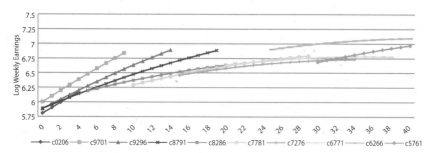

FIGURE 4f. Black Immigrant Women Arrived Age 25, Degree or More

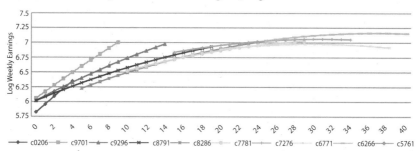

FIGURE 4g. Chinese Immigrant Women Arrived Age 25, Degree or More

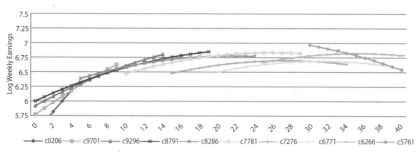

FIGURE 4h. South Asian Immigrant Women Arrived Age 25, Degree or More

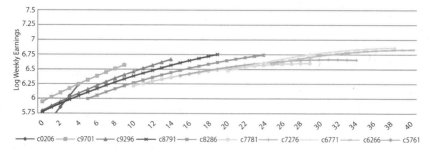

Source: Authors' compilations based on data from Census of Canada, 1991-2006.

the same education. However, this is not the case for Chinese and South Asian immigrant women, who have lower earnings than their Canadian born counterparts over their entire careers.

Given the large number of figures presented above, detailed comparisons of earnings across groups in different figures are difficult in many instances. In order to facilitate such comparisons, we present in Tables 4 and 5 the predicted weekly earnings of 30 year old men and women by immigrant status, visible minority group, and education level for the 1982-86 and 1997-2001 entry cohorts. These numbers are generated from the regression models used to create Figure 1a through Figure 4h. In each case, the log weekly earnings value from the relevant cohort's profile was taken and transformed into level earnings. We focus on age 30, since we see it as an age at which the individuals should be well established in the labour market but which still allows for comparisons for recent labour market entry cohorts for the Canadian born. These two cohorts were selected since we wanted to select a recent cohort (1997-2001) and an earlier one (1982-86) for which members are observed at age 30 in our data. In addition to presenting the predicted weekly earnings for each group, we also present the prediction as a proportion of the prediction for whites of that gender and immigrant status. The goal is to identify those groups with large wage gaps relative to the corresponding group of whites, and to see if there is variation in these differences across the two labour market entry cohorts.

In Table 4, we see that for the case of the 1982-86 cohort, Canadian born men with high school only education in the three visible minority groups earn 81 to 89 percent of the predicted earnings of white Canadian born men with high school education. However, when we consider the 1997-2001 cohort, the proportion is basically unchanged for black men but has risen to 85 percent (from 82 percent) for Chinese men and to 104 percent (from 88 percent) for South Asian men. This indicates that the cross-cohort movement for the Canadian born men in the lowest education category has been toward a reduction in differences across visible minority categories. For university men, the proportions are close to 1 in each case, with Chinese men having a distinct earnings advantage over white men. In general, the situation improves further for the case of the 1997-01 cohort, with the exception of black men who earn 97 percent of the weekly earnings of white men. For immigrant men (in the lower panel of Table 4), a similar overall picture emerges. Chinese men in the high school group are at a distinct disadvantage at 77 percent of white earnings in the 1982-86 cohort and 73 percent of white earnings in the 1997-2001 cohort. However, the remaining results indicate either small earnings disadvantages or advantages relative to white immigrant men. For example, the Chinese university educated men have 17 and 16 percent higher weekly earnings than do white immigrant men with university degrees in the 1982-86 and 1997-2001 cohorts, respectively.

TABLE 4
Predicted Weekly Earnings in Dollars of a Male Aged 30, by Education Level and Period of Entry into the Canadian Labour Market

	High School Only		Degree	
	1982-86	1997-01	1982-86	1997-01
Canadian born				
White	702	691	901	917
Black	627 (.893)	620 (.897)	933 (1.04)	886 (.966)
Chinese	573 (.816)	588 (.851)	1008 (1.12)	1080 (1.18)
South Asian	619 (.882)	719 (1.04)	859 (.953)	1026 (1.12)
Immigrant				
White	626	581	824	825
Black	555 (.887)	552 (.950)	966 (1.17)	852 (1.03)
Chinese	483 (.772)	422 (.726)	971 (1.18)	960 (1.16)
South Asian	607 (.970)	627 (1.08)	780 (.947)	917 (1.11)

Notes: Proportion of predicted weekly earnings for whites presented in parentheses; earnings are in constant 2006 dollars. For Canadian born, period of entry is the period in which the individual turned 25. For immigrants, period of entry is the period in which the immigrant turned 25 and immigrated to Canada.
Source: Authors' compilations.

In Table 5, equivalent sample means are presented for the case of women. For Canadian born women with no more than a high school diploma, the three visible minority groups actually have higher weekly earnings than those of white women in each labour market entry cohort. The same is not true for women with a university degree in the 1982-86 cohort, with South Asian Canadian born women earning only 85 percent of the earnings of white Canadian born women. However, there is evidence of improvement for all three groups by the 1997-2001 cohort, with only the Chinese Canadian born women facing an earnings disadvantage relative to the white Canadian born women. For immigrant women, the patterns in predicted earnings are similar. Women in each visible minority group have earnings that are similar to those of white immigrant women with the exception of Chinese immigrant women in the 1997-2001 cohort. Among degree holders, black women have earnings that are at least as high as white women in each cohort, but Chinese women in the most recent cohort have only 81 percent of the earnings of white women in the same cohort.

The proportions presented in Table 5 can be compared to those in Table 2. The statistics in Table 2 are based on sample means that do not control for average age or average cohort differences across the visible minority groups. As shown in Table 3, the white groups of both men and women have higher years of potential work experience than do any of the visible minority groups, indicating both their having more work experience and being on average from an earlier labour market entry cohort. Once we predict cohort specific weekly earnings for the case of age 30 and particular labour market entry cohorts, we see that the earnings advantage experienced by white men and white women relative to their counterparts in each of the visible minority groups (and immigrant status groups) is greatly diminished and in a number of cases emerges as earnings advantages for certain visible minority groups.

TABLE 5
Predicted Weekly Earnings in Dollars of a Female Aged 30, by Education Level and Period of Entry into the Canadian Labour Market

	High School Only		Degree	
	1982-86	1997-01	1982-86	1997-01
Canadian born				
White	368	386	669	730
Black	398 (1.08)	411 (1.06)	654 (.978)	768 (1.05)
Chinese	419 (1.14)	405 (1.05)	640 (.957)	690 (.945)
South Asian	376 (1.02)	446 (1.16)	569 (.851)	784 (1.07)
Immigrant				
White	335	346	488	652
Black	352 (1.05)	356 (1.03)	506 (1.04)	735 (1.13)
Chinese	328 (.979)	290 (.838)	594 (1.22)	530 (.813)
South Asian	378 (1.13)	360 (1.04)	402 (.824)	553 (.848)

Notes: Proportion of predicted weekly earnings for whites presented in parentheses; earnings are in constant 2006 dollars. For Canadian born, period of entry is the period in which the individual turned 25. For immigrants, period of entry is the period in which the immigrant turned 25 and immigrated to Canada.
Source: Authors' compilations.

CONCLUSIONS

Our analysis has identified a number of key differences in the experience/earnings profiles, in constant 2006 dollars, of labour market entry cohorts by visible minority group. Among Canadian born men, strong similarities are present across different visible minority groups. For white men with no more than a high school level of education, we see relatively small differences across labour market entry cohorts. This is also true for black men, with some evidence of small declines for recent cohorts in entry earnings and also evidence that the returns to work experience may have risen for these recent cohorts. This pattern is much clearer for the case of Chinese and South Asian Canadian born men with high school education. For these latter two groups, declines in entry earnings have occurred across the more recent arrival cohorts, and this pattern has been coupled with a steepening of the experience/earnings profiles, so that the disadvantage experienced at entry does not persist and the earnings of these cohorts converge to those of the earlier cohorts after only five years in the labour market. Among Canadian born men with university degrees, white men have higher earnings than black men and South Asian men but generally have lower earnings than Chinese men. Once again, entry earnings are similar across the four visible minority groups, but returns to experience are especially high for Chinese men. For all four groups, cross labour-market entry cohort differences are captured both in the intercept (lower for more recent cohorts) and in the slope (steeper for more recent cohorts).

For the case of immigrant men, analysis was carried out for men arriving at age 25 in Canada. A general finding across the different education groups and visible minority groups was that entry earnings declined for more recent arrival cohorts, but at the same time the experience/earnings profiles steepened, indicating an increase in returns to post-migration work experience. Among immigrants with only a high school level of education, white men have higher earnings than black men and much higher earnings than Chinese men. However, South Asian immigrant men have the highest earnings, both in terms of entry earnings and at various points on the experience/earnings profile. For immigrant men with university degrees, the cross-cohort patterns in terms of the experience/ earnings profiles are similar to what was found for immigrant men with high school education only. The cross-cohort patterns are consistent with lower entry earnings for recent arrival cohorts and with a steepening of the profiles.

The analysis for women's earnings yields a number of similar relationships to those found for men. In cases where more recent labour market entry cohorts of either immigrants or the Canadian born have particularly low entry earnings, this is often coupled with a steepening of the experience/earnings profile, indicating increased returns to work experience. For Canadian born women, strong similarities are found across the four visible minority groups in terms of the cross-cohort patterns in their experience/earnings profiles. For Chinese and South Asian women with high school only education, strong negative cohort effects at entry are combined with a steepening of the profiles. For the case of the Canadian born women with degrees, we again do not see large differences across the four visible minority groups. In general, the more recent labour market entry cohorts have higher weekly earnings in the middle part of their careers than did the cohorts that preceded them.

For immigrant women, differences across the visible minority groups in terms of their cohort specific experience/earnings profiles are easier to identify. For immigrant women with high school or less education, negative cohort effects are apparent in terms of entry earnings coupled with a steepening of the experience/earnings profiles for these cohorts.

For immigrant women with university degrees, greater differences across visible minority groups are apparent. Chinese women and South Asian women in recent immigrant arrival cohorts have had very low entry earnings in Canada, roughly 20 percent lower than those of white women and black women in the same immigrant arrival cohorts.

To make different comparisons across the various groups easier, predicted weekly earnings were generated for whites and for each visible minority group by gender, education, and immigrant status at the age of 30. The focus was placed on the 1982-86 and 1997-2001 labour market entry cohorts.[16] Wage gaps were found between each visible minority group and their white counterparts in a number of cases and were especially large for high school men. However, in many cases these differences were present for the 1982-86 cohort but greatly diminished or even turned to an advantage by the 1997-2001 cohort. The general pattern is one of an improvement in the relative earnings of each visible minority group relative to comparable whites.

It should be stressed that while our econometric models include immigrants who arrived in Canada between the ages of 25 and 64, much of the discussion in this study has focused on the Canadian born and immigrants who arrived in Canada at age 25. We have not discussed the earnings of older arrivals in any detail, since our goal was to eliminate as much as possible the role of foreign work experience in order to focus on the role of visible minority status in the determination of earnings outcomes of different labour market entry cohorts of men and women. In general, however, we find that, as with earlier literature, the return to foreign experience for immigrants from each ethnic group is low or negligible. In future work, we plan to expand the analysis to consider both immigrants who arrived in Canada at older ages and immigrants who arrived in Canada as children.

Our analysis illustrates the importance of age, education, cohort, and immigrant status in terms of understanding the evolution of differences in earnings across visible minority groups in Canada by gender. While one can easily generate sample means for earnings and make comparisons across different visible minority groups, this ultimately involves comparing different people who are at different stages of their career progression, who may have entered the Canadian labour market in very different economic conditions, and who may face different challenges in terms of having their education recognized by Canadian employers. Our results indicate that differences in earnings across visible minority groups for recent labour market entry cohorts of the Canadian born are small, and there is extensive evidence that recent cohorts of the Canadian born from historically disadvantaged groups such as blacks, Chinese, and South Asians are experiencing strong returns to work experience, indicating that their future earnings are likely to be high. For immigrants, we see strong declines in entry earnings for certain groups (especially the Chinese and South Asians); however, we also see strong returns to foreign work experience often accompanying these declines. Finally, there is evidence that the cross-cohort trend is toward relatively better earnings outcomes for members of visible minority groups in Canada relative to their white counterparts, and this is true within both the Canadian born population and the immigrant population. Clearly, successful integration of recent immigrants into the Canadian labour market remains a key policy challenge. However, the strong returns to work experience of more recent immigrant arrival cohorts in each of the visible minority categories is an encouraging sign that significant progress may be occurring on this policy front.

NOTES

The authors would like to acknowledge helpful comments from an anonymous referee and financial assistance from SSHRC. All empirical analysis of the Census master files was conducted at the UNB Research Data Centre in Fredericton, NB.

1.   Examples of theoretical studies include Becker (1971), Arrow (1973), Bulow and Summers (1986), and Francois (1998).
2.   For recent examples, see Chandra (2000), Borjas (2001), and Antecol and Cobb-Clark (2007, 2009), Antecol (2001).
3.   See, for example, Li (2001) and Reitz (1998).
4.   An important theme in the Canadian literature is on the issue of discrimination against aboriginal people in Canada. See, for example, Kuhn and Sweetman (2002).
5.   See also Antecol (2001), Hum and Simpson (1999), Sweetman and Dicks (1999), and Pendakur and Pendakur (2007).
6.   For examples of recent empirical work on gender discrimination for Canada, see Fortin and Huberman (2002), Baker and Fortin (2001), and Doiron and Riddell (1994).
7.   There is a large body of work on this topic. See for example, Chiswick (1978), Long (1980), Borjas (1985, 1995), and Duleep and Regets (1997) for immigrants to the United States, and Beach and Worswick (1993), Baker and Benjamin (1994), McDonald and Worswick (1998), Grant (1999), Schaafsma and Sweetman (2001), and Aydemir and Skuterud (2008) for immigrants to Canada.
8.   Reitz (2001) uses the 1981, 1986, 1991, and 1996 Census files to explore this relationship.
9.   See also Aydemir and Skuterud (2005) for a related study using Canadian Census data for the period 1981 through 2001.
10. Given that the Census data does not contain years of experience, this will be inferred using the Mincer Identity ($EXP_m \equiv$ Age-Years of Education-5). This approach is problematic for the case of people spending time out of the labour market outside of education. It is more likely to be a problem for women than for men, and should be kept in mind when comparing the estimates of the returns to experience between women and men.

11. We use these categorizations (ethnic labels) in accord with the Census and the previous literature while recognizing that they can be problematic.
12. These are available upon request from the authors.
13. Recall that, for both the Canadian born and the immigrant samples, year of experience are defined as years since the person turned age 25 (or AGE-25). This is consistent with the Beaudry and Green (1999) interpretation of age 25 being the age at which a person enters the mature labour market.
14. In the future, we plan to explore this possibility by accessing the earlier 1981 and 1986 Census master files. However, these files are not yet available through the RDC system.
15. Earnings of the 2002-06 arrival cohort are based only on a single Census file. Thus, it is variation within this cohort that is allowing the return to experience for the cohort to be estimated rather than cross-census variation.
16. Readers should be aware that these cohorts entered the Canadian labour market at different points of the business cycle, and this may have implications for observed differences in earnings. While we control for general economic conditions in all of the regressions through the inclusion of the detrended unemployment rate, there may still be other macroeconomic effects that have different impacts on earnings of different entry cohorts. However, we do not pursue this issue in the analysis.

REFERENCES

Antecol, H. 2001. "Why Is There Interethnic Variation in the Gender Wage Gap? The Role of Cultural Factors." *Journal of Human Resources* 36 (1): 119-43.
Antecol, H., and D.A. Cobb-Clark. 2007. "Identity and Racial Harassment." *Journal of Economic Behaviour and Organization*
– 2009. "Racial Harassment, Job Satisfaction, and Intentions to Remain in the Military." *Journal of Population Economics* 22 (3): 713-38.
Arrow, J.K. 1973. "The Theory of Discrimination." In *Discrimination in Labor Markets*, edited by O. Ashenfelter and A. Rees. Princeton: Princeton University Press.
Aydemir, A., and M. Skuterud. 2005. "Explaining the Deteriorating Entry Earnings of Canada's Immigrant Cohorts, 1966-2000." *Canadian Journal of Economics* 38 (2): 641-7.
– 2008. "The Immigrant Wage Differential within and across Establishments." *Industrial and Labor Relations Review* 61 (3): 334-52.
Baker, M., and D. Benjamin. 1994. "The Performance of Immigrants in the Canadian Labour Market." *Journal of Labor Economics* 12 (3): 369-405.
Baker, M., and N. Fortin. 2001. "Occupational Gender Composition and Wages in Canada, 1987-1988." *Canadian Journal of Economics* 34 (2): 345-76
Beach, C.M., and C. Worswick. 1993. "Is There a Double-Negative Effect on the Earnings of Immigrant Women in Canada?" *Canadian Public Policy* 19 (1): 36-53.
Beaudry, P., and D.A. Green. 1999. "Cohort Patterns in Canadian Earnings: Assessing the Role of Skill Premia in Inequality Trends." *Canadian Journal of Economics* 33 (4): 907-36
Becker, G.S. 1971. *The Economics of Discrimination.* 2nd ed. Chicago: University of Chicago Press.

Borjas, G.J. 1985. "Assimilation, Change in Cohort Quality, and the Earnings of Immigrants." *Journal of Labor Economics* 3: 463-89.

– 1992. "National Origin and the Skills of Immigrants in the Postwar Period." In *Immigration and the Work Force*, edited by G. Borjas and R.B. Freeman, 17-47. Chicago: University of Chicago Press.

– 1995. "Assimilation and Changes in Cohort Quality Revisited: What Happened to Immigrant Earnings in the 1980s?" *Journal of Labor Economics* 13 (2): 201-45.

– 2001. "Long-Run Convergence of Ethnic Skill Differentials, Revisited." *Demography* 38 (3): 357-61.

Bulow, J., and L. Summers (1986). "A Theory of Dual Labor Markets with Application to Industrial Policy, Discrimination, and Keynesian Unemployment." *Journal of Labor Economics* 4 (3): 376-414.

Chandra, A. 2000. "Labor Market Dropouts and the Racial Wage Gap: 1940-1990." *American Economic Review* 90 (2): 333-8.

Chiswick, B.R. 1978. "The Effect of Americanization on the Earnings of Foreign-Born Men." *Journal of Political Economy* 86 (5): 897-921.

Chiswick, B.R., and P.W. Miller. 1994. "Language Choice among Immigrants in a Multi-Lingual Destination." *Journal of Population Economics* 7: 119-31.

Chiswick, B., Y. Cohen, and T. Zach. 1997. "The Labor Market Status of Immigrants: Effects of Unemployment Rate at Arrival and Duration of Residence." *Industrial and Labor Relations Review* 50 (2): 289-303.

Cobb-Clark, D.A. 2000. "Do Selection Criteria Make a Difference? Visa Category and the Labour Market Status of Immigrants to Australia." *Economic Record* 76 (1): 15-31.

Doiron, D., and W.C. Riddell. 1994. "The Impact of Unionization on Male-Female Earnings Differences in Canada." *Journal of Human Resources* 29 (2): 504-34.

Duleep, H.O., and M.C. Regets. 1997. "Measuring Immigrant Wage Growth Using Matched CPS Files." *Demography* 34 (2): 239-49.

Fortin, N., and M. Huberman. 2002. "Occupational Gender Segregation and Women's Wages in Canada: A Historical Perspective." *Canadian Public Policy* 28 (Supplement): 11-39.

Francois, P. 1998. "Gender Discrimination without Gender Difference: Theory and Policy Responses." *Journal of Public Economics* 68 (1): 1-32.

Gang, I.N., and K.F. Zimmermann. 2000. "Is Child Like Parent? Education Attainment and Ethnic Origin." *Journal of Human Resources* 35 (3): 550-69.

Grant, M.L. 1999. "Evidence of New Immigrant Assimilation in Canada." *Canadian Journal of Economics* 32 (4): 930-55.

Green, D.A., and C. Worswick. 2002. "Earnings of Immigrant Men in Canada: The Roles of Labour Market Entry Effects and Returns to Foreign Experience." Paper presented at 2002 Cerf Conference on Immigration, Calgary.

– 2010. "Entry Earnings of Immigrant Men in Canada: The Roles of Labour Market Entry Effects and Returns to Foreign Experience." In *Canadian Immigration: Economic Evidence for a Dynamic Policy Environment*, edited by T. McDonald, E. Ruddick, A. Sweetman, and C. Worswick. Montreal and Kingston: Queen's Policy Studies Series, McGill-Queen's University Press.

Hum, D., and W. Simpson. 1999. "Wage Opportunities for Visible Minorities in Canada." *Canadian Public Policy* 25 (3): 379-94.

Kuhn, P., and A. Sweetman. 2002. " Aboriginals as Unwilling Immigrants: Contact, Assimilation and Labour Market Outcomes." *Journal of Population Economics* 15 (2): 331-55.

Li, P.S. 2001. "The Market Worth of Immigrants' Education Credentials." *Canadian Public Policy* 27 (1): 23-38.

Long, J.E. 1980. "The Effect of Americanization on Earnings: Some Evidence for Women." *Journal of Political Economy* 88 (3): 620-9.

MaCurdy, T., and T. Mroz. 1995. "Measuring Macroeconomic Shifts in Wages from Cohort Specifications." Working paper, Department of Economics, Stanford University.

McDonald, J.T., and C. Worswick. 1997. "Unemployment Incidence of Immigrant Men in Canada." *Canadian Public Policy* 23 (4): 353-73.

– 1998. "The Earnings of Immigrant Men in Canada: Job Tenure, Cohort and Macroeconomic Conditions." *Industrial and Labor Relations Review* 51 (3): 465-82.

Pendakur, K., and R. Pendakur. 1998. "The Colour of Money: Earnings Differentials among Ethnic Groups in Canada." *Canadian Journal of Economics* 31 (3): 518-48.

– 2002. "Colour My World: Have Earnings Gaps for Canadian Born Ethnic Minorities Changed over Time?" *Canadian Public Policy* 28 (4): 489-512.

– 2007. "Minority Earnings Disparity across the Distribution." *Canadian Public Policy* 33 (1): 41-61.

Pendakur, K., and S. Woodcock. 2008. "Glass Ceilings or Glass Doors? Wage Disparity within and between Firms." Discussion Paper, Department of Economics, Simon Fraser University.

Reitz, J.G. 1998. *Warmth of the Welcome: The Social Causes of Economic Success for Immigrants in Different Nations and Cities.* Boulder, CO: Westview Press.

– 2001. "Immigrant Success in the Knowledge Economy: Institutional Change and the Immigrant Experience in Canada, 1970-1995." *Journal of Social Issues* 57 (3): 579-613.

Schaafsma, J., and A. Sweetman. 2001. "Immigrant Earnings: Age at Immigration Matters." *Canadian Journal of Economics* 34 (4): 1066-99.

Schoeni, R. 1998. "Labor Market Assimilation of Immigrant Women." *Industrial and Labor Relations Review* 51(3): 483-504.

Sweetman, A., and G. Dicks. 1999. "Education and Ethnicity in Canada: An Intergenerational Perspective." *Journal of Human Resources* 34 (4): 668-96.

6

IMMIGRATION POLICY AND THE SELF-EMPLOYMENT EXPERIENCE OF IMMIGRANTS TO CANADA

HERBERT J. SCHUETZE

Dans cette étude, une approche empirique est utilisée – comme c'est le cas de très nombreuses recherches sur les revenus des immigrants salariés – pour analyser la tendance à devenir travailleurs indépendants que l'on observe chez les immigrants qui s'installent au Canada. L'impact des politiques d'immigration sur les résultats du travail indépendant y est évalué, d'une part en se basant sur les moments où ont eu lieu des changements dans la politique canadienne d'immigration, et d'autre part en utilisant des comparaisons avec les États-Unis au cours des mêmes périodes. Dans les deux pays, j'observe ainsi, dans le processus d'assimilation chez les immigrants, une transition entre le travail salarié et le travail indépendant; mais, au Canada, contrairement à ce que l'on observe aux États-Unis, ce processus d'assimilation n'est pas stable au cours de la période étudiée, c'est-à-dire de 1971 à 2002. Un changement dans le profil d'assimilation se produit en particulier au cours de la période qui correspond en gros au moment où la politique canadienne d'immigration a subi des transformations majeures – dont la mise en place du système de points –, à la fin des années 1960. Par contre, rien n'indique dans les données canadiennes qu'il y ait eu un changement dans le profil d'assimilation au moment de la création de la catégorie « gens d'affaires » parmi les travailleurs qualifiés. Toutefois, une comparaison avec les résultats de l'immigration aux États-Unis suggère que la politique d'immigration canadienne peut avoir jouer un rôle plus important qu'il n'y paraît quand on ne considère que les résultats au Canada.

This study utilizes an empirical approach, similar to the large number of studies examining immigrant earnings in the wage sector, to study the self-employment propensities of immigrants arriving in Canada. In addition, the impact of immigration policy mechanisms on self-employment outcomes are identified using the timing of changes in Canadian immigration policy and comparisons to immigrant outcomes over the same period in the

Canadian Immigration: Economic Evidence for a Dynamic Policy Environment, ed. T. McDonald, E. Ruddick, A. Sweetman, and C. Worswick. Montreal and Kingston: Queen's Policy Studies Series, McGill-Queen's University Press.

United States. I find that the assimilation process among immigrants to both countries involves a transition from wage employment to self-employment. In Canada, unlike the United States, this assimilation process is not stable across the years examined, 1971 to 2001. In particular, a shift in the assimilation profile occurred that roughly coincides with major changes implemented in the late 1960s in Canadian immigration policy, including the introduction of the points system. There is little evidence of a shift in the assimilation profile around the time of the introduction of the "business" class of skilled workers in the Canadian data. However, comparison to immigrant outcomes in the United States suggests that Canadian immigration policy, particularly the introduction of the business class of skilled immigrants, may have played a bigger role than suggested by the results for Canada alone.

INTRODUCTION

Self-employment represents a considerable fraction of the labour market activity of Canadian immigrants. Census data show that in 1995 over 15 percent of prime-aged Canadian immigrant workers were self-employed. The importance of immigrants as a source of entrepreneurial capital has not gone unnoticed by policy-makers. In 1978 in Canada, a second group of immigrant workers was added to the "skilled worker" entry category with the creation of the "business" class entry program. The stated goal of this program was to spark economic activity in Canada by attracting entrepreneurial talent and/or investor funds. Indeed, Canada is not alone in attempting to attract entrepreneurs; immigration policies in Australia and Germany, as examples, include special visas and entry requirements that facilitate immigration by would-be entrepreneurs.

Perhaps because of the importance of self-employment among immigrants, a number of research studies have attempted to identify the reasons for the high incidence of this labour market activity among immigrants as compared to the domestic born. Some researchers have suggested that cultural factors related to country of origin may provide an advantage to immigrants in self-employment and help to explain their higher propensities toward self-employment. Diversity in traditions of commerce (Light 1984), in the ability to supply ethnic goods and services (Light and Rosenstein 1995), and attitudes toward entrepreneurship that are related to one's religion (Carroll and Mosakowski 1987; Clark and Drinkwater 2000; Rafiq 1992) have all been suggested as possible cultural advantages in self-employment. However, empirical support for the hypothesis that self-employment rates among immigrant groups are correlated with home country self-employment rates has been mixed. While Yeungert (1995) found that immigrants from countries with high self-employment rates are more likely to become self-employed in the United States, Fairlie and Meyer (1996) found no correlation.

Another hypothesis related to ethnic advantage suggests that the presence of ethnic concentrations or "enclaves" in the host country creates opportunities for potential immigrant entrepreneurs. It is argued that ethnic enclaves provide their members with greater access to capital through the pooling of investment resources (Light 1972), a supply of local labour (Light and Bonacich 1988), and consumers with tastes for goods that ethnic entrepreneurs are better positioned to provide (Aldrich et al. 1985). Ethnic enclaves may also influence the decision to become self-employed through social network effects if the choice of employment sector is influenced by network members. However, evidence for such an enclave effect has also been mixed. As Parker (2004, 121-2) points out, while some studies find that the presence and size of ethnic enclaves positively impact the probability of self-employment among members (Flota and Mora 2001; Le 2000; Lofstrom 2002), many do not (Borjas and Bronars 1989; Clark and Drinkwater 1998, 2000, and 2002; Razin and Langlois 1996; Yuengert 1995). Even within studies there is no consensus. For example, Borjas (1986) and Boyd (1990) find support for an enclave effect among some ethnic groups but not among others.

In contrast to the above hypotheses, a number of researchers argue that the high rates of immigrant self-employment result not because of an endowed advantage in self-employment but because immigrants are disadvantaged in the wage employment sector. These researchers contend that ethnic minorities faced with discrimination from employers in the wage and salary sector turn to self-employment as a way to advance in such segmented labour markets (Li 1998; Light 1972; Mata and Pendakur 1998; Metcalf, Modood, and Virdee 1996; Min 1984; Moore 1983; Phizacklea 1988; Sowell 1981; Wong and Ng 2002).

Despite the rather large literature explaining differences in the *levels* of self-employment, however, relatively few studies have examined the *process of entry* into self-employment by immigrants or the factors that influence this process. Studies that do examine the transition into self-employment by immigrants include Li (2001a, 2001b) and Frenette (2002), using Canadian data, and Borjas (1986) and Lofstrom (2002), using US data. However, because these studies are limited to a single country over a short period of time, they do not provide much insight into the role of immigration policy in the process of becoming self-employed[1] – a topic of focus in this paper. A recent paper by Antecol and Schuetze (2005), which most closely resembles the present study, focuses on self-employment outcomes of immigrants across Australia, Canada, and the United States. However, unlike the focus of Antecol and Schuetze (2005) that of the present study is on the effects of changes in immigration policy over time within Canada, using outcomes in the United States as a comparator.

More specifically, the goals of this paper are twofold. The first is to establish the key features of the self-employment experiences of immigrants to Canada. In particular, Canadian Census data is used to examine the self-employment outcomes of immigrants in the context of an empirical approach similar to the relatively large number of studies examining immigrant outcomes in the wage sector (e.g., Baker and Benjamin (1994) and Bloom, Grenier, and Gunderson (1995) on Canada, and Borjas (1995) and Funkhouser and Trejo (1998) on the United States). Given the stated goal of the immigrant business program to attract entrepreneurial immigrants to Canada, the focus here, unlike in wage sector studies that concentrate on earnings outcomes, is on the path into self-employment among immigrants. Therefore, the primary outcome of interest is whether or not immigrants choose self-employment (i.e., the propensity toward self-employment). Because cross-section studies on immigrant outcomes confound secular changes in cohort outcomes with the within-cohort business start-up process (see, for example, Borjas (1985) or LaLonde and Topel (1992), pairs of data files are used to perform an empirical decomposition that allows identification of "assimilation" patterns (changes in self-employment incidence within an arrival cohort) for comparison across immigrant cohorts of different vintages. In addition, changes in self-employment propensities across cohorts with the same number of years in Canada are identified to determine the effects of the recent declines in immigrant cohort outcomes in the wage sector. The method used allows for identification of the performance of self-employed immigrants relative to some base group (primarily the self-employed Canadian born). However, it has been shown that the results of similar analyses in the wage sector are sensitive to the choice of base group (Baker and Benjamin 1994; Lalonde and Topel 1992). Therefore, a number of different base groups, including earlier arrival cohorts, are used for comparison.

The second goal is to shed light on the impacts of available immigration policy mechanisms on self-employment outcomes among immigrants to Canada. To achieve this, the timing of changes in Canadian immigration policy, such as the introduction of the Canadian points system and the acceptance of business class immigrants, is compared to changes in immigrant self-employment outcomes. This comparison is made possible by examining immigrant self-employment outcomes across a number of years of Canadian Census data from 1971 to 2001. In addition to examining changes in policy within Canada, I repeat the analysis using Census data from the United States between 1970 and 2000. Comparison over the same time period of immigrant self-employment outcomes in Canada to those in the United States, whose immigration policies and experiences differ significantly from Canada's, provides a difference in differences setting. This approach allows insights into the effectiveness of immigration policy on self-employment outcomes.

The remainder of the paper is organized as follows. The next section outlines the relevant policy developments in Canada over the period examined and highlights important differences between Canadian and US policies relevant to immigrant self-employment outcomes. The third and fourth sections depict the empirical strategy used to identify the key elements of immigrants' self-employment experience and describe the data and estimation results. The final section concludes the paper.

POLICY BACKGROUND

This section provides a brief overview of some of the more salient developments in Canada's immigration policy and compares Canadian immigration policy to that of the United States. Particular attention is given to those policy changes/differences that are likely relevant to self-employment outcomes among immigrants and to the period in which cohort assimilation profiles can be determined from the available data (roughly 1956 to 2001). For a more exhaustive history of Canada's immigration policy, see, for example, Green and Green (1992), and for a comparison between Canadian and US policy, see Borjas (1993).

Within Canada over the relevant time frame, one can identify two points at which there were significant policy developments that directly or indirectly may have affected self-employment outcomes among immigrants. The first well-known major change in Canadian policy occurred in the 1960s. Over this period the right to sponsor family members for immigration to Canada was extended to immigrants from non-traditional source countries, and in 1967 a points system was introduced. This system introduced a new class of non-sponsored immigrants to Canada (skilled workers) that was somewhat objectively evaluated on the basis of skills. This newly developed class of independent immigrants, along with the sponsorship of immigrant family members from non-traditional source countries, led to a significant change in the composition of immigrant cohorts arriving in Canada. Green (1995) shows that a shift in source regions occurred subsequent to these changes and suggests that the impacts of these policies were most evident among cohorts arriving after 1970. In particular, he finds that after 1970 the composition of immigrants to Canada was increasingly made up of immigrants from Asia rather than from the more traditional regions of Western Europe, the United Kingdom, and the United States. Not surprisingly, it has also been shown that the composition in terms of labour market characteristics changed over this period; most notably, the skill level of immigrants arriving after 1970 increased relative to prior cohorts (Borjas 1993; Antecol, Cobb-Clark, and Trejo 2003).

While it appears that these shifts in composition likely had impacts on the self-employment outcomes of immigrants, the precise nature of the impacts is unclear. Given that immigrant cohorts were increasingly comprised of visible minorities, one might expect that self-employment propensities among post-1970 cohorts would have increased. In addition, given that previous research shows that education or skill level is positively correlated with the probability of self-employment in the overall population, increases in skill level among immigrants arriving after 1970 may have also led to increases in self-employment. However, the probability of self-employment may also be affected by the level of self-employment in the source country and the presence of ethnic enclaves in the receiving country. Thus, it is unclear in which direction these changes likely shifted immigrant self-employment rates.

A second relevant change in immigration policy occurred in 1978, when a further category of "skilled workers" was added with the creation of the "business" class of immigrants. The stated goal of the new legislation was to spark economic activity in Canada by attracting entrepreneurial talent and/or investor funds. To this end, three sub-categories of business class immigrants were eventually developed. Initially, these included the entrepreneur and self-employment streams. In 1986 the third, the investor stream, was added. While these programs have undergone a good deal of fine-tuning since their inception, the primary difference between immigrants applying under the business class and other skilled workers is the criteria used to assess their skills and the threshold required to be granted entry. Increased weight is placed on prior experience (business experience) for all business class immigrants and on the availability of investment funds for those entering under the investor and entrepreneur categories. The minimum points required for immigrants entering under the business class are also significantly lower than those required for entry under the other skilled worker category (in 2003, only 35 points out of a possible 100 were required of business class immigrants compared to 75 points among other skilled workers).

A list of some of the program requirements as of 2003 helps to illustrate the differences between the three streams in the business class. Immigrants entering under the investor stream "must make a C$400,000 investment that is used by the provinces for economic development and job creation."[2] There is no requirement for investors to run a business. However, immigrants entering under the entrepreneur and self-employment streams must own and manage a business in Canada. What primarily distinguishes these two streams is the fact that those entering under the entrepreneur program must "create at least one full-time job equivalent for Canadian citizens or permanent residents for a period of at least one year within three years of arrival in Canada." The self-employed need only provide work for themselves.

Figure 1 illustrates the percent of total immigration comprised of business immigration in Canada as well as the percent attributable to the two streams requiring ownership of a business (self-employed plus

FIGURE 1
Business Immigration to Canada, 1980-2001
Percent of Total Immigration

Source: Author's compilation.

entrepreneur) for the period 1980 to 2001.[3] While immigrants were slow to respond to this policy change, by the late 1980s a significant number of immigrants were entering Canada annually under the business class program. Between 1980 and 1986 Canada received an annual inflow of nearly 6,000 business class immigrants, accounting for an average of 6 percent of overall immigration. By the late 1980s and early 1990s the number of business class immigrants had increased to over 15,000 annually, increasing their proportion of overall immigration flow to 9 percent. The number had doubled by 1993 to more than 30,000 immigrants and accounted for 13 percent of immigration flow. All of the increase in the early to mid-1990s is attributable to an increase in the number of immigrants entering under the investment stream, which does not require immigrants to run a business. Increases among the other two streams were confined to the period including the early 1980s up until the late 1990s, after which there was a slight decline. Overall, there was substantial growth in the representation of business immigrants over the period examined. Given that the intent of this program is to attract immigrants with high entrepreneurial spirit and that many of the immigrants entering under this program were required to maintain a business of some form upon entry to Canada, one would expect that this policy led to increases in self-employment propensities among immigrants, particularly in the first few years after migration.

Finally, as noted above, the analysis that follows exploits important differences between Canadian and US immigration policies to help identify the role of such policy in immigrant self-employment outcomes. In contrast to the Canadian points system's focus on the skills of potential immigrants, US immigration policy in recent decades has placed greater emphasis on family reunification. As a result, the composition of US immigrants differs substantially from that of Canadian immigrants over the period examined. Of significance is the relative differential in skill level (measured by years of education) between immigrants and the domestic born across the two countries. Borjas (1993) and Antecol, Cobb-Clark, and Trejo (2003) provide evidence that immigrants to the United States have lower observable skill levels than domestic born workers, whereas immigrants to Canada are (on average) more highly skilled than the Canadian born. While there is debate about the role of the points system in these outcomes, the differences in skill outcomes highlight the benefits of comparing the immigrant self-employment experiences across the two countries.

EMPIRICAL FRAMEWORK

Adopting the framework developed by Borjas (1986), the following cross-sectional self-employment probability equation can be estimated by probit for the group of employed immigrants:

$$P_t = \Phi(X_t'\beta_t + \sum_k^K \delta_{kt}) \tag{1}$$

where P_t is the probability of self-employment in year t, X_t is a vector of observable characteristics related to the self-employment decision, Φ is the normal cumulative distribution function, k indexes a series of five-year arrival cohorts identified by the earliest year of arrival among those in the cohort, and the $\delta_{k,t}$ are cohort-year specific intercepts.

Estimation of the assimilation process in terms of business start-up using the coefficient estimates of the $\delta_{k,t}$ from equation (1) are unreliable if there exist time-varying, cohort-specific fixed effects that impact the probability of self-employment. Baker and Benjamin (1994) find that more recent cohorts of immigrants to Canada have poorer earnings outcomes in the wage sector than earlier cohorts. If these changes in immigrant "quality" affect self-employment earnings differently, the use of single cross-section will not be appropriate. Instead, estimates of "assimilation" that are free of this potential fixed effect bias and identification of the effects of changes in cohort quality on the self-employment decision can be obtained using quasi-panel methods. Thus, equation (1) is estimated at two points in time (year t and t+10). While the Canadian Census is conducted in five year intervals, the decision was made to examine 10 year intervals. This was done to be consistent with the comparative analysis carried out using data from the US Census, which is conducted only every 10 years.

The decomposition of the cross-section change in the probability of self-employment can be stated as follows. Consider the predicted probability of self-employment for a cohort group k in year t+10 evaluated at the average values of immigrant characteristics in that year ($\overline{X}$). This probability is given by:

$$\hat{P}_{k,t+10} = \Phi(\overline{X}\hat{\beta}_{t+10} + \hat{\delta}_{k,t+10})\qquad(2)$$

For this same cohort, the predicted probability of self-employment in year t evaluated at $\overline{X}$ (i.e., at the average characteristics of immigrants in year t+10) is:

$$\hat{P}_{k,t} = \Phi(\overline{X}\hat{\beta}_{t} + \hat{\delta}_{k,t})\qquad(3)$$

The predicted probability of the cohort in year t+10 that has the same number of years since migration as cohort k in year t, evaluated at $\overline{X}$ is

$$\hat{P}_{k+10,t+10} = \Phi(\overline{X}\hat{\beta}_{t+10} + \hat{\delta}_{k+10,t+10})\qquad(4)$$

Given the definitions in equations (2) and (4), the cross-section change in the self-employment propensity over 10 years from census year t+10 is equal to $\hat{P}_{k,t+10} - \hat{P}_{k+10,t+10}$. Following Borjas (1985) this change can be decomposed into two components as follows:

$$\hat{P}_{k,t+10} - \hat{P}_{k+10,t+10} = (\hat{P}_{k,t+10} - \hat{P}_{k,t}) + (\hat{P}_{k,t} - \hat{P}_{k+10,t+10})\qquad(5)$$

The first term on the right-hand side of equation (5) gives the change in the probability of self-employment experienced by cohort k over the 10 year period. In other words, it gives the quasi-panel estimate of "assimilation."[4] The second term gives the difference in the probability of self-employment between two cohorts with the same number of years since migration. This difference provides an estimate of the impact of changes in cohort "quality" on the propensity to choose self-employment. It will be negative if more recent cohorts are more likely to choose self-employment (for example, if wage employment outcomes for more recent cohorts are worse relative to self-employment).

These estimates will be biased if there are unobserved time effects (other than assimilation) that change over the 10 year period. This is likely the case given the recent trends in self-employment in Canada. A common solution in the literature is to normalize the changes in immigrant outcomes to some base group (n). Borjas (1986) normalizes changes in the self-employment propensities among immigrants utilizing Canadian born workers as a base group. However, Baker and Benjamin (1994) examine immigrant earnings assimilation in the wage and salary sector for Canada and show that the results are sensitive to the choice of base group. Thus, I experiment with a number of different base groups, including Canadian born workers and previous cohorts of immigrants.

Suppose that for base group n, in year t, the following probit equation determines the probability of self-employment.

$$P_{n,t} = \Phi(X_t'\theta_t) \qquad (6)$$

Thus, the predicted probability of self-employment for a member of the base group with similar characteristics as the average immigrant (at t+10) is given by:

$$\hat{P}_{n,t} = \Phi(\overline{X}\theta_t) \qquad (7)$$

The quasi-panel decomposition can be normalized as follows:

$$\hat{P}_{k,t+10} - \hat{P}_{k+10,t+10} = [(\hat{P}_{k,t+10} - \hat{P}_{k,t}) - (\hat{P}_{n,t+10} - \hat{P}_{n,t})] + [(\hat{P}_{k,t} - \hat{P}_{k+10,t+10}) - (\hat{P}_{n,t} - \hat{P}_{n,t+10})] \quad (8)$$

Here, the first term on the right-hand side of equation (8) gives the estimate of within-cohort self-employment growth for a representative immigrant net of changes in the probability of self-employment for a representative individual with similar characteristics from the base group over the 10 year period. Similarly, the second term provides an estimate of the difference in the probability of self-employment between two cohorts with the same number of years since migration net of changes in this probability for a similar individual from the base group.

ESTIMATION AND RESULTS

The primary data used in the analysis are drawn from the Canadian Census Public Use Microdata Files conducted in 1971, 1981, 1991, and 2001. These data were chosen in order to coincide as much as possible with the data available for the United States.[5] The data files are pooled across pairs of census files conducted across 10 year intervals (1971-81, 1981-91, and 1991-2001). For comparison, the analysis is repeated using data drawn from the US Census 1970 1/100, 5 percent SMSA and County Group file, and the 1980, 1990, and 2000 Public Use A samples, which contain 5 percent random[6] samples of the population. The pooled years for the United States are 1970-80, 1980-90, and 1990-2000. While not ideal, the use of census data in this context is the best possible approach. Currently available panel data on Canadian immigrants, while useful in a number of settings, do not include information on Canadian born outcomes.

In all cases the samples are restricted to males who are employed in the survey week (the week prior to the survey), who are not in the armed forces, and who are not in school in the survey week. Because of the prevalence of self-employment in the agricultural sector among non-immigrants and the recent decline of that sector in North America, the samples are further restricted to individuals employed in non-agricultural industries.[7] To control for aging within cohorts across each of the 10 year time frames, the samples are restricted to individuals aged 18 to 54 in year t and to those aged 28 to 64 in year t+10. Because detailed information on year of arrival for immigrants in the eastern provinces and the Northern Territories is not made available publicly (there are too few observations to protect confidentiality), data drawn from the Canadian Census files are restricted to Quebec, Ontario, and the western provinces. Due to the large sample sizes of the US Census data, 40 percent random samples of non-immigrants were taken. Weights were applied throughout the calculations to the US samples to account for the unbalanced samples taken and the fact that the 1990 US Census was a non-random sample of the population.[8]

In order to derive the decompositions suggested by equations (5) and (8), it is necessary to estimate the probit models of the probability of self-employment for immigrants and the base group as indicated in equations (1) and (6) for the years t and t+10. The self-employment indicator used in these probit equations is based on the class of worker variables in the various census files.[9] The definition of self-employed includes individuals who indicate that they work for themselves in incorporated or unincorporated businesses and individuals in professional practices. The self-employed definition excludes unpaid family workers. Year of arrival cohort indicators are generated for five-year groupings of immigrants as outlined in Appendix Table A1. Throughout the paper I will refer to cohorts based on the two digit descriptor of the first year of the five year grouping (for example, the 1971-75 arrival cohort will be referred to as the "71" cohort). In identifying demographic and economic variables that influence the relative returns in the two sectors to include in the analysis, I am guided by previous research (e.g., Fairlie and Meyer (1998); Schuetze (2000); Kuhn and Schuetze (2001)) using Canadian and US data on the determinants of self-employment. I include age as a quadratic, indicator variables for the level of education achieved, indicator variables for marital status, and controls for source country of immigrants.[10]

Age has been found to have a positive effect on the probability of self-employment. This relationship might be explained by the fact that older workers are more likely to have accumulated entrepreneurial abilities, business links, and savings or capital necessary for self-employment. An increase in educational attainment is also often found to be positively associated with self-employment, perhaps because of the skills necessary to succeed. Previous research indicates that married men are more likely to be self-employed than those in other marital status categories. This is likely because married men are more likely to be in a family with a second income and fringe benefits that extend coverage to the entire family. Finally, given the substantial changes in the composition of immigrants to Canada over the period examined (documented in Baker and Benjamin 1994), it is important to control for place of birth.[11]

To make the decomposition more tractable, I place some constraints on the coefficients. In particular, I restrict the coefficients on the demographic and economic variables to be the same across years for immigrants and the Canadian born such that $\beta_t=\beta_{t+10}=\beta$ and $\theta_t=\theta_{t+10}=\theta$. In other words, I allow the impacts of these variables to differ across immigrants and the Canadian born but restrict them to be the same within these groups across the 10 year period examined. With these assumptions the various decompositions, each with a different base group, can be derived using the pooled data files from the estimation of a single equation by interacting the coefficients with indicator variables for survey year and immigration status. This derivation is possible because the base groups used in the analysis are comprised of either Canadian born workers or cohorts of earlier immigrants. To overcome the classic problem of distinguishing between cohort, age, and period effects, I impose the identifying restriction (common to the literature) that the period effect is the same for immigrants and the base group. In essence, the period effect is estimated from the Canadian born, and this information is used to identify cohort and assimilation effects for immigrants. The regression results for the various pairs of data are presented in Appendix Table A1. Because the coefficient estimates are similar to those found in previous studies, I will not elaborate on these here.

As a first step of an empirical progression toward identifying the process of assimilation into self-employment, I generate estimates of assimilation constructed using cross-sectional information from a single year of data (year t+10) for each of the samples. In particular, equation (1)[12] is estimated for each of the end year (t+10) samples of immigrants, and the year of arrival cohort indicators coefficients are utilized to generate estimates of changes in self-employment rates with time in Canada. These results are presented in Table 1[13] and provide these rate changes over several overlapping 10 year periods since migration. For example, using only the 1981 cross-section, it is estimated that the probability of self-employment in the first 10 years in Canada increases by 3.2 percentage points. This estimate is derived as the difference between the predicted probabilities of self-employment between an immigrant in the 1966-1970 ("66") cohort and a similar immigrant in the 1976-80 ("76") cohort. While this approach is somewhat naïve, it is presented here to motivate the decomposition analysis that follows.

Ignoring potential cohort-specific differences among immigrants for the moment, the results in Table 1 suggest that the assimilation process is quite unstable across years. In particular, there appears to be a substantial difference in the business start-up process derived from the 1981

TABLE 1
Predicted Cross-Section Results: Canada

	Census Years		
Cohort	1981	1991	2001
56-66	0.045		
	(0.009)		
61-71	0.022	0.020	0.003
	(0.010)	(0.010)	(0.011)
66-76	0.032	-0.003	0.007
	(0.010)	(0.009)	(0.009)
71-81		0.012	0.012
		(0.009)	(0.010)
76-86		0.057	0.008
		(0.008)	(0.009)
81-91			-0.005
			(0.009)
86-96			0.042
			(0.008)

Note: Values in parentheses are standard errors derived from bootstrapping.
Source: Author's compilation.

cross-section and those derived from the 1991 and 2001 cross-sections. There is a significant increase in the self-employment propensities in the first and subsequent 10 year periods in the 1981 census, while only the first 10 year periods in the 1991 and 2001 censuses show significant growth. The instability of these cross-section results is, as I will show, indicative of substantial changes in cohort specific self-employment outcomes.

As a second step toward identifying the process of assimilation into self-employment, the self-employment assimilation profiles of immigrants net of year-of-arrival cohort effects are derived using the decomposition given by equation (5) and the three pairs of data files. Before we examine the results of these decompositions, Table 2 highlights some of the trends in predicted outcomes derived from the coefficient estimates. In particular, each pair of columns represents a synthetic cohort over a 10 year period, such that reading across the paired columns gives an indication of changes in the self-employment propensity over the 10 year period. In all cases the predicted self-employment propensities are derived holding constant individual characteristics (the Xs) at the average of immigrants in year t+10 from each of the census pairs. Reading across the sets of

TABLE 2
Summary of Selected Trends in Predicted Values: Canada

Table Entry	Census Years					
	1971-81		1981-91		1991-2001	
	1971	*1981*	*1981*	*1991*	*1991*	*2001*
Predicted probability Cdn born controlling for characteristics*	0.110 (0.002)	0.131 (0.002)	0.136 (0.002)	0.148 (0.001)	0.149 (0.001)	0.164 (0.001)
Predicted probability average immigrant**	0.106 (0.004)	0.145 (0.003)	0.154 (0.003)	0.169 (0.002)	0.173 (0.002)	0.179 (0.002)
Gap*** Most recent arrival and similar Cdn born	-0.066 (0.005)	-0.032 (0.008)	-0.022 (0.009)	-0.028 (0.006)	-0.022 (0.006)	-0.029 (0.006)

Notes: Values in parentheses are standard errors derived from bootstrapping.
* The predicted probability of self-employment for a Canadian born with the characteristics of the average immigrant in year t+10; t is the start year of the period t+10 the end year.
** The predicted probability of self-employment for an immigrant with the characteristics of the average immigrant in year t+10.
*** The predicted probability "gap" in the self-employment rates between the most recent arrival cohort and a similar Canadian born.
Source: Author's compilation.

paired columns gives changes in self-employment propensities, holding individual characteristics constant, for later cohorts across a later time period. Reading down allows for a comparison between immigrants and their Canadian born counterparts. A direct comparison is provided for each data pair and across time in row 3, which gives the predicted self-employment rate gap between a representative immigrant from the most recent arrival cohorts in each year and a similar Canadian born cohort.

Consistent with overall trends in self-employment in Canada, these results show secular growth in self-employment among these representative Canadian born individuals and immigrants. Across the 1971-81 and 1981-91 censuses, the self-employment rate grew at a faster rate than among similar Canadian borns. This trend reverses across the 1991-2001 censuses. In almost all years the predicted probability of self-employment for the representative immigrant is greater than that for a similar Canadian born. The one exception is 1970, where the predicted self-employment rates are about equal. While overall predicted rates of self-employment are generally higher among immigrants than among the Canadian born, this is not true for immigrants upon first arrival. The entry gap is negative and statistically significant in all years. In fact, this gap narrows over the period examined, with significant tightening over the 1971-81 period.[14]

Taken together, these findings suggest that immigrants' self-employment propensities increase with years in Canada and/or that previous cohorts of immigrants had higher rates of self-employment.

To sort between these two explanations, Table 3 presents decompositions of the 1981, 1991, and 2001 cross-section assimilation profiles from Table 1 into estimates of assimilation net of cohort effects and "within" cohort effects, and estimates of the effects of changes in cohort quality, "across" cohort effects. The results suggest that secular changes in the composition of immigrant cohorts, which have led to increases in self-employment propensities among immigrants with similar years in Canada in a number of cases, bias the cross-section assimilation growth estimates downward. Except for the 1991-2001 period, estimates of the changes in self-employment propensities with years in Canada increase once cohort fixed effects are taken into account.

TABLE 3
Decomposition of Changes in the Probability of Self-Employment:
Canada (Unadjusted)

| | Census Years | | | | | |
| | 1971-81 | | 1981-91 | | 1991-2001 | |
Cohort(s*)	Within	Across	Within	Across	Within	Across
56 *(66)*	0.063 (0.011)	-0.018 (0.010)				
61 *(71)*	0.059 (0.012)	-0.037 (0.011)	0.034 (0.011)	-0.014 (0.010)		
66 *(76)*	0.087 (0.008)	-0.054 (0.009)	0.023 (0.009)	-0.026 (0.010)	0.013 (0.009)	-0.006 (0.009)
71 *(81)*			0.039 (0.009)	-0.026 (0.010)	0.007 (0.009)	0.004 (0.010)
76 *(86)*			0.061 (0.011)	-0.004 (0.010)	-0.003 (0.011)	0.011 (0.009)
81 *(91)*					-0.002 (0.011)	-0.003 (0.010)
86 *(96)*					0.049 (0.008)	-0.007 (0.008)

Notes: Values in parentheses are standard errors derived from bootstrapping.
* In the columns labelled "Across," the across-cohort outcomes controlling for time in Canada require observations of a second cohort with the same years in Canada (in year t+10) as the primary cohort of observation in year t. These second cohorts are listed in brackets in the first column.
Source: Author's compilation.

To help illustrate this point, consider the cohort of immigrants that arrived between 1971 and 1975 (the "71" cohort group) observed in the 1981 Census, 12 ½ years after arrival (on average), and 10 years later in 1991. As is indicated by the entry in the second column and fourth row of Table 1, this cohort experienced no statistically significant change in self-employment propensity over the first 10 years in Canada using the cross-section estimate of assimilation. However, the decomposition given in the third and fourth columns and fourth row of Table 3 shows that between 1981 and 1991 the probability of self-employment increased by almost 4 percentage points within this cohort. Compared to the "81" cohort 12 ½ years after arrival in the 1991 census, the self-employment propensity of the "71" cohort 12 ½ years after arrival in the 1981 census is 2.6 percentage points lower. Thus, the across-cohort change wipes out most of the within-cohort change in the cross-section estimate.

Looking across the pairs of census years, we find an interesting pattern of assimilation. In all years, the within-cohort increases in self-employment propensities are higher among the most recent arrival cohorts than among cohorts with more potential Canadian labour market experience. Indeed, across the 1991-2001 censuses, the only cohort to experience a statistically significant increase in self-employment was the most recent arrival cohort from the 1991 Census (the "86" cohort). Thus, if it is the case that immigrants "assimilate" into self-employment, it appears that this process is accelerated in the first 10 to 15 years after arrival. Before deriving any conclusions, however, the analysis must control for general trends in self-employment outcomes. The changes observed in Table 3 may simply reflect overall trends in employment compensation that make self-employment more or less attractive.

The results of the final step toward identifying the process of assimilation into self-employment are presented in Table 4. This table provides estimates of the decomposition given by equation (8), which controls for secular trends in self-employment propensities among a comparison group. Following previous research examining the wage sector,[15] three base groups are used in separate decompositions. The first comparison group is that of Canadian born and implies the typical definition of assimilation (growth in excess of the Canadian born population). The second base group is a fixed cohort of prior immigrant arrivals (those prior to 1956 in the 1971-81 analysis, prior to 1961 in the 1981-91 analysis, and prior to 1966 in the 1991-2001 analysis). Here, assimilation of immigrants is defined relative to a particular group of previous immigrants. The final comparison group is a group of prior arrivals with a fixed number of years in Canada. In all years the comparison group is comprised of immigrants with more than 20 years in Canada. This approach has the advantage of holding the point on the assimilation profile among immigrants in the base group fixed. The results in Table 4 are presented for each of the base groups in separate panels.

TABLE 4
Decomposition of Changes in the Probability of Self-Employment: Canada (Adjusted)

Base Group Cohort(s*)	Census 1971–81						Census 1981–91						Census 1991–2001					
	Cdn Borns		Prior to 1956		>20 Years		Cdn Borns		Prior to 1961		>20 Years		Cdn Borns		Prior to 1966		>20 Years	
	Within	Across	Within	Across	Within	Across	Within	Across	Within	Across	Within	Across	Within	Across	Within	Across	Within	Across
56 (66)	0.042 (0.011)	0.002 (0.010)	0.032 (0.013)	0.012 (0.013)														
61 (71)	0.038 (0.012)	-0.016 (0.011)	0.028 (0.014)	-0.007 (0.013)	-0.004 (0.016)	0.026 (0.015)	0.022 (0.012)	-0.002 (0.011)	0.025 (0.013)	-0.005 (0.012)								
66 (76)	0.066 (0.008)	-0.033 (0.010)	0.056 (0.011)	-0.024 (0.012)	0.024 (0.013)	0.008 (0.014)	0.011 (0.008)	-0.014 (0.010)	0.014 (0.011)	-0.016 (0.012)	0.018 (0.008)	-0.021 (0.012)	-0.001 (0.009)	0.008 (0.009)	-0.019 (0.012)	0.026 (0.013)		
71 (81)							0.027 (0.009)	-0.015 (0.010)	0.029 (0.011)	-0.017 (0.012)	0.034 (0.011)	-0.022 (0.012)	-0.007 (0.009)	0.019 (0.010)	-0.025 (0.012)	0.037 (0.013)	0.001 (0.012)	0.010 (0.013)
76 (86)							0.049 (0.011)	0.008 (0.010)	0.052 (0.012)	0.005 (0.012)	0.056 (0.013)	0.001 (0.012)	-0.017 (0.011)	0.025 (0.010)	-0.036 (0.014)	0.043 (0.013)	-0.009 (0.009)	0.017 (0.013)
81 (91)													-0.016 (0.011)	0.011 (0.010)	-0.034 (0.014)	0.029 (0.013)	-0.008 (0.014)	0.003 (0.013)
86 (96)													0.035 (0.008)	0.007 (0.008)	0.017 (0.012)	0.026 (0.012)	0.043 (0.012)	-0.001 (0.012)

Notes: Values in parentheses are standard errors derived from bootstrapping.

* In the columns labelled "Across," the across-cohort outcomes controlling for time in Canada require observations of a second cohort with the same years in Canada (in year t+10) as the primary cohort of observation in year t. These second cohorts are listed in brackets in the first column.

Source: Author's compilation.

It appears that, unlike previous studies on wage outcomes, the choice of base group has little impact on the results here examining choice of labour market sector. Despite small differences in the magnitudes, the general patterns of assimilation and across-cohort changes in self-employment are very similar regardless of base group chosen. The one exception occurs when the fixed cohort of immigrants arriving prior to 1966 is utilized as the base group looking across the 1991-2001 censuses.[16] The overall effect of normalizing the results is to dampen both the within- and across-cohort effects. In fact, a number of the entries in Table 4 are small in magnitude and statistically insignificant. This suggests that much of the growth in self-employment within cohorts and across cohorts with similar years since migration, which was identified in Table 3, is explained by a secular rise in the probability of self-employment. There are, however, some interesting exceptions to this general finding.

First, there is evidence of a significant increase in the propensity toward self-employment net of secular trends across cohorts at the time of entry into Canada between 1971 and 1981. This across-cohort increase of approximately 3 percentage points accounts fully for the decrease in the entry gap found in Table 2 over this period. No similar increases are found across immigrants entering between the other two periods.

Second, it appears that as immigrants integrate into the Canadian labour market, an increasing number choose to become self-employed, leaving open the possibility that the relative returns to self-employment increase.[17] Much of this assimilation, particularly since the 1980s, appears to occur in the first 10 to 15 years after arrival. The estimated rates of assimilation, net of economy-wide secular changes, among the most recent arrivals in each of the three periods are larger in magnitude and more likely to be statistically significant than earlier arrival cohorts. In addition, the magnitudes of the increases in self-employment propensities experienced among immigrant cohorts in their first 10 to 15 years in Canada are substantial. For example, focusing on the first columns of each panel (outcomes relative to those among the Canadian born), the results show that immigrant self-employment rates caught up to or overtook those of similar Canadian borns in the first 10 to 15 years after arrival. For example, the "76" immigrant cohort, which was the most recent arrival cohort in 1981, experienced an estimated increase in the self-employment rate net of secular increases in this same rate among the Canadian born of 5 percentage points between 1981 and 1991. This compares to a negative gap between this cohort and the Canadian born in 1981 of just over 2 percentage points and implies that by 1991 the rate of self-employment for this cohort was nearly 3 percentage points higher than for similar Canadian born individuals.

Third, there appears to be a significant change in the assimilation process as observed across the 1971-81 censuses compared to that observed in the post-1981 periods examined. In particular, the results looking across

1971-81 suggest that, unlike more recent cohorts, immigrant cohorts that arrived prior to 1966 experienced significant increases in self-employment net of secular trends well beyond their first 10 to 15 years in Canada. For instance, the "61" cohort, which would have experienced their second decade in Canada between 1971 and 1981, saw a net increase in self-employment of 4 percentage points. A similar increase occurred over this period among those in the "56" cohort who, therefore, continued to assimilate up until 25 years after arrival. This compares to a process in which assimilation is observed primarily in the first 10 to 15 years after arrival in the 1981-91 period. There is evidence that the propensity toward self-employment net of secular increases among the "71" cohort continued to rise up until 20 years after arrival over the 1981-91 period. However, the rate of growth among these immigrants is generally much lower. Another change in the assimilation process between the 1981-91 and 1991-2001 periods led to a pattern in which assimilation occurred only in the first 10 to 15 years after arrival between 1991 and 2001.

To demonstrate these changes, Figures 2A through 2C illustrate the predicted assimilation profiles of immigrants, through a piece-wise linear splicing of the within-cohort changes net of changes among similarly skilled Canadian borns, for each of the pairs of census data. Looking across these figures the changes in the profiles are easily identifiable; the assimilation profile becomes less linear and more concave over time.[18] It is also clear from the diagrams that the period of time in Canada over which statistically significant assimilation occurs (the solid lines) has decreased in more recent years. These changes in the assimilation pattern coincide with shifts in the probability of self-employment of immigrant cohorts upon entry to Canada. As noted above, the gap between self-employment rates of immigrant cohorts upon entry compared to that of similar Canadian borns fell substantially in the 1971-81 period. Thus, it appears that more recent immigrant cohorts enter Canada with rates of self-employment closer to those of similar Canadian borns and assimilate rapidly into self-employment, while previous cohorts entered Canada with rates of self-employment significantly lower than the Canadian born and assimilated more slowly. Despite these adjustments in path, however, it appears from the diagrams that the longer run self-employment differential between immigrants and the Canadian born did not change. In all cases the longer run differential is somewhere between 3 and 4 percentage points.

The most notable adjustment to the self-employment assimilation pattern of immigrants coincides with the significant policy developments that were implemented in the late 1960s through the introduction of the points system. A significant change in the assimilation pattern occurred within the 1971-81 period. Over this period there was an across-cohort shift in the propensity toward self-employment accompanied by a change in the assimilation profile, which can be observed looking across the 1981

166   *Herbert J. Schuetze*

FIGURE 2.A. Predicted Assimilation Profiles: 1971-81 Census (Canada)

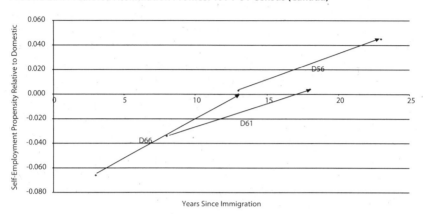

FIGURE 2.B. Predicted Assimilation Profiles: 1981-91 Census (Canada)

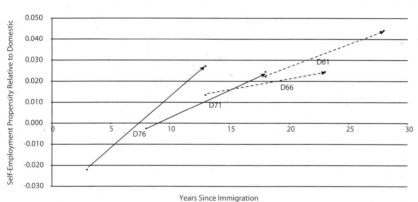

FIGURE 2.C. Predicted Assimilation Profiles: 1991-2001 Census (Canada)

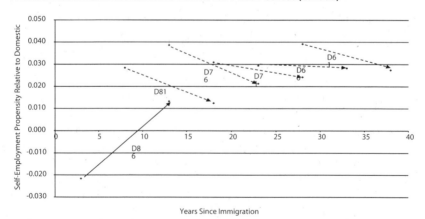

Note: Solid lines indicate statistically significant increases at the 5 percent level of significance.

Source: Author's compilation.

to 1991 censuses. As discussed above, the implementation of the rights to family reunification and the introduction of the points system in 1967 led to substantial changes in the composition of immigrants to Canada. Consistent with the timing of the changes in self-employment outcomes found here, the impacts of these policies in terms of the composition of immigrants were most evident among cohorts arriving after 1970. This leaves open the possibility that the shift in policy in the 1960s and the introduction of the points system are responsible for the changes in self-employment outcomes observed among immigrants to Canada over this period. The unchanging pattern of assimilation of immigrants since the early 1980s suggests that the introduction of the business class had no appreciable effect on the average immigrant's self-employment experience in Canada.

One potential problem with these conclusions is that they do not account for self-employment outcomes in the absence of the policy changes. (In the analysis we don't observe the self-employment outcomes that would have resulted if a points system or the business class immigrant program had not been introduced.) I attempt to account for this in the next section using an informal difference in differences approach.

CANADA-US COMPARISON

In an attempt to separate out the effects of changes in Canadian-specific immigration policy on self-employment outcomes from the effects of broader changes in the composition of immigrants related to the general selection mechanism among potential international migrants, the analysis is carried out using three pairs of census data files from the United States and is then compared to the results for Canada. Changes in immigration policy and the labour market performance of immigrants to Canada and the United States, while differing in important ways, are similar in many respects. Both countries established universal admissions policies in the mid- to late 1960s, resulting in substantial changes in the source country composition of immigrants. Further, wage sector outcomes of immigrants to the two countries are similar in many respects. Over roughly the 30 year period since the early 1970s, immigrant wage employment outcomes of successive cohorts have declined for new arrivals to both countries relative to earlier cohorts.[19] On the other hand, the introduction of a skilled class of immigrants in Canada and not the United States has resulted in a higher fraction of immigrants selected based on skills arriving in Canada compared to the United States.[20] Within the class of skilled workers, Canada also introduced selection based on entrepreneurial or self-employment skills in the 1980s.

All of this suggests that the self-employment experience of immigrants to the United States may provide a reasonable proxy for the likely self-employment outcomes of immigrants to Canada in the absence of selection based on general and entrepreneurial skills. Thus, differences across the two countries can be attributed to the Canadian selection based policies. Conditions unique to the United States make this approach far from ideal. For example, income variance (the return to skill) is higher in the United States, and a much larger number of illegal immigrants enter the United States each year because of its proximity to Mexico. However, the similarities between the two countries' geographic location and social / economic institutions get one as close to ideal as can be achieved.

Table 5 presents a summary of selected trends in predicted values from the analysis of US data. Comparable to the layout of Table 2 for Canada, the first two rows of Table 5 provide the predicted probability of self-employment for each year for an American born worker and a similar immigrant, respectively, while row 3 gives the self-employment rate gap for each year. Consistent with previous studies examining self-employment outcomes among US men (see, for example, Schuetze 2000), the results show little secular change in self-employment rates beyond 1980. Unlike the results for Canada, which showed significant growth in predicted self-employment rates among domestic born workers, the predicted self-employment rates remained stable in the United States

TABLE 5
Summary of Selected Trends in Predicted Values: United States

| | Census Years | | | | | |
| | 1970-80 | | 1980-90 | | 1990-00 | |
Table Entry	1970	1980	1980	1990	1990	2000
Predicted probability domestic born controlling for characteristics*	0.079 (0.002)	0.098 (0.001)	0.122 (0.001)	0.127 (0.001)	0.130 (0.000)	0.129 (0.000)
Predicted probability average immigrant**	0.093 (0.005)	0.125 (0.001)	0.119 (0.001)	0.132 (0.001)	0.132 (0.001)	0.122 (0.001)
Gap*** Most recent arrival and similar domestic born	-0.035 (0.006)	-0.018 (0.003)	-0.038 (0.002)	-0.045 (0.002)	-0.049 (0.002)	-0.059 (0.001)

Notes: Values in parentheses are standard errors derived from bootstrapping.
* The predicted probability of self-employment for a domestic born with the characteristics of the average immigrant in year t+10; t is the start year of the period t+10 the end year.
** The predicted probability of self-employment for an immigrant with the characteristics of the average immigrant in year t+10.
*** The predicted probability "gap" in the self-employment rates between the most recent arrival cohort and a similar domestic born.
Source: Author's compilation.

following the 1970-80 period. Also unlike the results for Canada, Table 5 suggests that the self-employment rate gap between new arrivals and the domestic born widened somewhat over the period examined in the United States. This gap, while predicted to have fallen over the 1970-80 period in Table 5, is predicted to have grown over the 1980-90 and 1990-2000 time periods in the United States. The fact that this gap was stable over the 1980s and 1990s in Canada leaves open the possibility that Canadian immigration policy toward self-employment, which requires business class immigrants to maintain a business in the first few years after arrival, has resulted in higher rates of self-employment among Canadian immigrants upon arrival.

Table 6 provides the results of the full decompositions of the changes in self-employment propensities for the United States. The first column in each of the panels gives the cross-section assimilation pattern constructed from the year-of-arrival cohort indicators for year t+10, while the next two columns decompose these into within- and across-cohort differences without adjusting for secular trends. Because the results were not sensitive to the base group used,[21] only the "adjusted" results using the American born as the base group are presented for the United States. These results are presented in the last two columns of each of the panels. As for Canada, the results of the decomposition show that the cross-section estimates conceal important aspects of the assimilation process. Also similar to a certain extent to the results for Canada is the pattern of assimilation. The results in Table 6 suggest that the probability of self-employment among immigrants to the United States does not increase monotonically with the number of years since migration. Most of the assimilation occurs in the first 10 to 20 years in the United States, with the highest rates in the first 10 to 15 years. In addition, similar to outcomes among Canadian immigrants, rates of self-employment among immigrants to the United States quickly overtake those of similarly skilled America borns. Comparing the relevant gap in each period (year t from each panel of Table 5) to the rate of growth net of secular trends among the most recent arrivals from Table 6 suggests that immigrant self-employment rates exceed those of similar American borns after 10 to 15 years in the 1970-80 and 1980-90 censuses and after 15 to 20 years in the 1990-2000 analysis. Interestingly, this overtaking occurs in both countries and across all periods, despite differences in the size of the entry gaps. The fact that immigrant self-employment rates overtake those of the domestic born despite differences in the general level of self-employment suggests that, regardless of differences in the institutional specific or country specific factors that influence local rates of self-employment, immigrants adapt to local labour market conditions (relatively rapidly, according to the estimates). This result casts doubt on explanations of the higher rates of self-employment that suggest that fixed characteristics such as home country propensities toward self-employment are responsible.

TABLE 6
Decomposition of Changes in the Probability of Self-Employment: United States

Cohort(s*)	Census 1970-80					Census 1980-90					Census 90-2000				
		Unadjusted		Adjusted (Domestic Born)			Unadjusted		Adjusted (Domestic Born)			Unadjusted		Adjusted (Domestic Born)	
	Cross-Section	Within	Across	Within	Across	Cross-Section	Within	Across	Within	Across	Cross-Section	Within	Across	Within	Across
55 (65)	0.011 (0.005)	0.020 (0.011)	-0.009 (0.011)	0.000 (0.011)	0.011 (0.011)	-0.010 (0.003)	0.001 (0.003)	-0.011 (0.004)	-0.005 (0.003)	-0.006 (0.003)					
60 (70)	0.022 (0.005)	0.045 (0.010)	-0.024 (0.010)	0.026 (0.011)	-0.004 (0.010)	-0.015 (0.003)	0.003 (0.004)	-0.018 (0.004)	-0.003 (0.004)	-0.013 (0.003)	-0.004 (0.003)	-0.005 (0.004)	0.001 (0.003)	-0.004 (0.004)	-0.000 (0.003)
65 (75)	0.049 (0.004)	0.086 (0.007)	-0.036 (0.007)	0.066 (0.007)	-0.017 (0.007)	-0.007 (0.003)	0.018 (0.003)	-0.026 (0.003)	0.013 (0.003)	-0.021 (0.003)	-0.014 (0.003)	-0.011 (0.003)	-0.003 (0.003)	-0.010 (0.003)	-0.005 (0.003)
70 (80)						0.024 (0.002)	0.036 (0.003)	-0.011 (0.002)	0.031 (0.003)	-0.006 (0.002)	-0.007 (0.003)	-0.017 (0.002)	0.011 (0.003)	-0.016 (0.002)	0.009 (0.002)
75 (85)						0.069 (0.003)	0.067 (0.002)	0.002 (0.002)	0.062 (0.002)	0.007 (0.002)	0.013 (0.002)	-0.004 (0.003)	0.017 (0.003)	-0.003 (0.002)	0.016 (0.002)
80 (90)											0.036 (0.002)	0.012 (0.002)	0.024 (0.002)	0.013 (0.002)	0.023 (0.002)
85 (95)											0.062 (0.002)	0.051 (0.002)	0.011 (0.002)	0.052 (0.002)	0.010 (0.002)

Notes: Values in parentheses are standard errors derived from bootstrapping.

* In the columns labelled "Across," the across-cohort outcomes controlling for time in the US require observations of a second cohort with the same years in the US (in year $t+10$) as the primary cohort of observation in year t. These second cohorts are listed in brackets in the first column.

Source: Author's compilation.

Finally, despite changes in the entry gap, the pattern of assimilation appears to be much more stable in the United States than in Canada across the various periods examined. For example, in the United States, the period of assimilation is about the same across the time periods. Immigrants entered the country with rates of self-employment that were below those of similar American borns, but these rates rose relative to the American born for approximately 10 to 15 years after arrival (up to 20 years after arrival in the 1980-90 panel). The similarity in the pattern of assimilation across the time periods is illustrated in Figures 3A through 3C, which plot out the predicted self-employment rates of immigrants relative to similar American borns through time in the United States for each of the time periods, separately. With a couple of exceptions, these profiles appear to be alike. First, over the 1990-2000 period there is evidence of a decline in the propensity toward self-employment among earlier arrival cohorts of immigrants relative to the American born. Second, looking across the assimilation profiles, it appears that the predicted longer run self-employment rate differential between immigrants and the American born has declined in more recent years. For example, in the 1970-80 analysis, the longer run predicted immigrant male self-employment rate differential approaches 4 percentage points. In the more recent profiles, while it is difficult to make out the longer run trend, it is clear that the self-employment rate differentials are lower.[22]

Treating the results for the United States as the counterfactual outcome for Canada in the absence of selection based on general and entrepreneurial skills suggests that Canadian immigration policy, particularly the introduction of the business class of skilled immigrants, may have played a bigger role than suggested by the results for Canada alone. The entry gap increased in the United States after 1980 but remained stable in Canada over the same time period. In addition, the longer run (through years since migration) relative self-employment rate of immigrants to the United States declined beyond the 1980s, while this rate remained stable in Canada. The main differences in policy between the two countries over this period were the introduction in Canada of the skilled class of workers in the late 1960s and the business class of skilled workers in the 1980s. The results suggest that these policies may have helped to avoid the declines in self-employment rates along the assimilation path that were observed in the United States. Given the caveats listed above, however, this interpretation is open to debate.

CONCLUSIONS

A number of interesting conclusions can be drawn from the observed self-employment patterns among male immigrants. The results for both Canada and the United States suggest that the assimilation process

FIGURE 3.A. Predicted Assimilation Profiles: 1970-80 Census (United States)

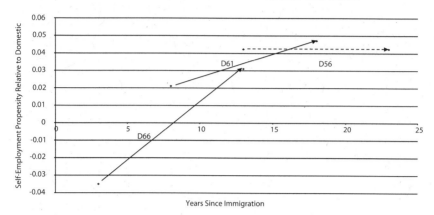

Years Since Immigration

FIGURE 3.B. Predicted Assimilation Profiles: 1980-90 Census (United States)

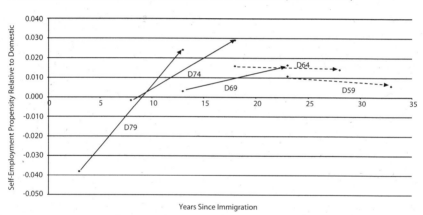

Years Since Immigration

FIGURE 3.C. Predicted Assimilation Profiles: 1990-2000 Census (United States)

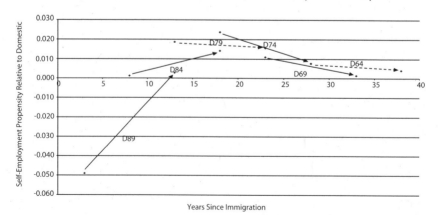

Years Since Immigration

Note: Solid lines indicate statistically significant increases at the 5 percent level of significance.
Source: Author's compilation.

likely involves a transition from wage employment to self-employment for many immigrants. In all years and in both countries, I find positive and statistically significant growth in the self-employment propensities of newly arriving immigrants, over and above that of similar domestic borns and previous cohorts of immigrants. This may be because, relative to wage employment, self-employment typically requires greater financial investment, the development of contacts, and greater country-specific knowledge. Given that all of these typically take time to acquire, it is perhaps unsurprising that a period of integration is required. In addition, the growth pattern in the probability of self-employment is not monotonic across years since migration. In Canada and the United States, most of the relative growth in self-employment tends to occur in the first 10 to 15 years after migration.

However, in Canada, unlike in the United States, this assimilation process is not stable across the years examined. In particular, a shift occurred in the assimilation profile which roughly coincides with major changes to Canadian immigration policy implemented in the late 1960s, including the introduction of the points system. Unlike immigrant cohorts that arrived after 1970, cohorts that arrived prior to 1966 experienced increases in self-employment, net of secular trends, well beyond their first 10 to 15 years in Canada. At the same time, a comparison of more recent immigrant cohorts to earlier cohorts at the point of entry to Canada suggests that more recent cohorts at this stage in the assimilation process chose self-employment. This shift in the self-employment propensity led to a decline in the gap between the predicted self-employment rate of a representative immigrant upon entry and that of a similar Canadian born. Interestingly, this shift in the gap occurred following the major policy developments in the late 1960s in Canada.

Despite the changes in the assimilation profiles of Canadian self-employed immigrant males, there is little difference in the self-employment probabilities of immigrant male cohorts with similar years since migration that have been in Canada for more than 10 to 15 years. Taken together, the results looking at Canada alone are consistent with the notion that Canadian policy developments over this period have led to higher self-employment propensities upon entry, while at the same time leading to a reduction in the amount of assimilation and the time frame over which assimilation occurred. However, over the long run (measured in years since migration) it appears that there was no appreciable effect of these policies. In other words, it is as if there is some "natural rate" of self-employment among immigrants that is higher than that of the Canadian born, and the changes in policy adjusted the *path to* the natural rate but not the *level of* self-employment.

One potential problem with the conclusions drawn is that they do not account for immigrant self-employment outcomes in the absence of the policy changes. Using immigrant self-employment outcomes in the

United States over the same time period to generate a counterfactual outcome suggests that Canadian immigration policy, particularly the introduction of the business class of skilled immigrants, may have played a bigger role than suggested by the results for Canada alone. In the United States the entry gap increased after 1980, and the longer run relative self-employment rate fell, while in Canada these differential rates remained stable over the same period. In addition, the longer run (through time in the country) self-employment rate of immigrants to the United States declined beyond the 1980s, while this rate remained stable in Canada. The results suggest that the introduction of the skilled class of workers and the business class of skilled workers in Canada may have helped to avoid the declines in self-employment rates along the assimilation path that were observed in the United States.

While previous researchers have attempted to explain differences in the level of self-employment between immigrants and the domestic born, this is one of the first papers in the literature to exam the dynamic process that results in the propensity of self-employment among immigrants overtaking that of similar Canadian born individuals. The fact that policy appears to affect immigrants differently at different times in their assimilation process suggests that examinations of the overall relative level of self-employment among immigrants may be misleading. Overall changes in the relative level of self-employment are confounded by potentially important changes across the time path into self-employment among immigrants. Much more work is needed to understand why so many immigrants opt for self-employment. Future research should build on the findings here and examine how factors influence immigrant self-employment outcomes along the various segments of the time path into self-employment. This study suggests that immigration policy plays a role. However, because identification of the link between policy and self-employment outcomes through time is achieved using the timing of policy, future research that is able to examine a more direct link is also warranted.

NOTES

Funding for this research was provided by SSHRC (Grant # 410-2003-1823) and a research grant from Metropolis RIIM. I am grateful to Janice Chow and Hui Feng for competent research assistance. I am solely responsible for any omissions or errors.

1. One further concern with Li (2001a and 2001b) is that the nature of the data used does not allow him to control for secular changes in self-employment, which may confound the underlying transition rates.
2. Program requirements can be found on the CIC web page: http://www.cic.gc.ca/english/irpa/fs-business.html.

3. These figures are derived from published numbers in Employment and Immigration Canada, "Immigration Statistics" Cat. No. mp 22-1, various years.

4. For this estimate of assimilation to be unbiased, it must be assumed that cohort specific fixed effects are equal across time. This may not be true in this setting if, for example, the composition of the cohort changes through the re-migration of immigrants based on skills.

5. The full analysis was also conducted using 1986-96 Canadian Census files. These results, which are similar in many respects to those utilizing the 1991-2001 files, are available from the author upon request. The analysis was not carried out for the 1976-86 period because information on the year of immigration was not collected in the 1976 Census. The 2006 Census was not utilized because it falls outside of the time frame available for the United States.

6. The one exception is the 1990A sample. See the discussion below.

7. Agricultural industries include agricultural production and services, forestry, fishing, hunting, and trapping.

8. All results in the tables are generated from the output of probit analysis. All regressions utilize the sample weights provided in the censuses (choosing the weight option in Stata).

9. These variables are the same across years within census files and are very similar across the Canadian and US censuses.

10. I experimented with a number of different specifications, including some with additional variables (such as a proxy for experience age-total years of schooling) to those used in the final analysis. The results were not sensitive to the specification choice.

11. It should also be noted that, following several studies from the immigration literature on wage earnings outcomes that find age at immigration to be an important determinant (see, for example, Schaafsma and Sweetman (2001)), the analysis was redone including age at arrival. These results (available from the author) do not differ substantially from those below.

12. These estimates are derived from the coefficient estimates presented in Appendix Table A2 and therefore differ slightly from those that would be derived from a simple cross-sectional regression estimated using only the t+10 data. This is because of the restrictions placed on the coefficients that are noted above.

13. Standard errors for the assimilation estimates in this and the remaining tables are derived through the method of bootstrapping. This method was chosen over the use of the "Delta" method for ease of calculation and because the bootstrap method provides more reliable estimates in this setting. The bootstrap estimates were generated specifying the number of replications to be 1000 and drawing bootstrap samples equal in size to those of the original sample.

14. In results not presented here, I find that the decline in the entry gap is greater when no controls for place of birth are included. This suggests that changes in the source country composition of immigrants have resulted in higher rates of self-employment among more recent cohorts of immigrants.

15. The base groups are chosen based on the approaches taken in Borjas (1985) and LaLonde and Topel (1992) and subsequently taken in Baker and Benjamin (1994).

16. It appears that changes in the labour market led to larger increases in self-employment rates among this older fixed cohort of immigrants than for similar Canadian borns. This occurred despite relatively small increases in self-employment among immigrants as a whole. This suggests that, in the improving labour market between 1991 and 2001, this older immigrant cohort adapted much more like the Canadian born than younger immigrants. To test for sensitivity to the somewhat arbitrary choice of cut-off year, a number of different older fixed cohorts were used with no change in results.

17. It was pointed out that the "within" increases in self-employment may be explained by a transition from unemployment directly into self-employment. To examine this possibility, I redid the analysis, restricting attention to those who were not employed or self-employed. The results do not support this hypothesis.

18. Some caution should be taken in interpreting these profiles. Treating them as predictions of the pattern of assimilation that a recent cohort will follow may be misleading because the profiles use outcomes of earlier cohorts to predict the pattern of assimilation for a newly arriving immigrant.

19. There is some evidence, however, that immigrants to the United States fare better over time than those to Canada. See Parent and Worswick (2004), for a nice discussion.

20. See Antecol, Cobb-Clark, and Trejo (2003).

21. The one exception pertains to the 1990-2000 period. This outcome is discussed below.

22. One caveat with this interpretation is that these differences may result from the fact that the predicted profiles in each of the time periods are evaluated at different values of the characteristics.

REFERENCES

Aldrich, H., J. Cater, T. Jones, D. McEvoy, and P. Velleman. 1985. "Ethnic Residential Concentration and the Protected Market Hypothesis." *Social Forces* 63: 996-1009.

Antecol, H., D. Cobb-Clark, and S. Trejo. 2003, "Immigration Policy and the Skills of Immigrants to Australia, Canada, and the United States." *Journal of Human Resources* 38 (1): 192-218.

Antecol, H., and H.J. Schuetze. 2005. "Immigration, Entrepreneurship and the Venture Start-Up Process." In *International Handbook Series on Entrepreneurship*, vol. 2, edited by S.C. Parker, Z.J. Acs, and D.R. Audretsch. Kluwer Academic Publishers.

Baker, M., and D. Benjamin. 1994. "The Performance of Immigrants in the Canadian Labor Market." *Journal of Labor Economics* 12 (3): 369-405.

Beach, C.M., and C. Worswick. 1993. "Is There a Double-Negative Effect on the Earnings of Immigrant Women?" *Canadian Public Policy* 19 (1): 36-53.

Bloom, D, G. Grenier, and M. Gunderson. 1995. "The Changing Labour Market Position of Canadian Immigrants." *Canadian Journal of Economics* 28: 987-1005.

Borjas, G. 1985. "Assimilation, Changes in Cohort Quality and the Earnings of Immigrants." *Journal of Labour Economics* 3: 463-89.

– 1986. "The Self-Employment Experience of Immigrants." *Journal of Human Resources* 21 (4): 485-506.

– 1993. "Immigration Policy, National Origin and Immigrant Skills: A Comparison of Canada and the United States." In *Small Differences That Matter: Labor Markets and Income Maintenance in Canada and the United States,* edited by D. Card and R. Freeman, 21-44. Chicago: University of Chicago Press.

– 1995. "Assimilation and Changes in Cohort Quality Revisited: What Happened to Immigrant Earnings in the 1980s?" *Journal of Labor Economics* 13 (2): 201-45.

Borjas, G., and S. Bronars. 1989. "Consumer Discrimination and Self-Employment." *Journal of Political Economy* 97: 581-605.

Boyd, R.L. 1990. "Black and Asian Self-Employment in Large Metropolitan Areas: A Comparative Analysis." *Social Problems* 37: 258-69.

Carroll, G.R., and E. Mosakowski. 1987. "The Career Dynamics of Self-Employment." *Administrative Sciences Quarterly* 32: 570-89.

Clark, K., and S. Drinkwater. 1998. "Ethnicity and Self-Employment in Britain." *Oxford Bulletin of Economics and Statistics* 60: 383-407.

– 2000. "Pushed Out or Pulled In? Self-Employment among Ethnic Minorities in England and Wales." *Labour Economics* 7: 603-28.

– 2002. "Enclaves, Neighbourhood Effects and Employment Outcomes: Ethnic Minorities in England and Wales." *Journal of Population Economics* 15: 5-29.

Fairlie, R., and B. Meyer. 1996. "Ethnic and Racial Self-Employment Differences and Possible Explanations." *Journal of Human Resources* 31 (4): 757-93.

Flota, C., and M.T. Mora. 2001. "The Earnings of Self-Employed Mexican-Americans along the US-Mexico Border." *Annals of Regional Science* 35: 483-99.

Frenette, M. 2002. "Do the Falling Earnings of Immigrants Apply to Self-Employed Immigrants?" Business and Labour Market Analysis, Statistics Canada Cat. No. 11F0019MIE – No. 195.

Funkhouser, E., and S. Trejo. 1998. "Labor Market Outcomes of Female Immigrants in the United States." In *The Immigration Debate: Studies on the Economic, Demographic, and Fiscal Effects of Immigration,* edited by J.P. Smith and B. Edmonston, 239-288. Washington, DC: National Academy Press.

Green, A.G. 1995. "A Comparison of Canadian and U.S. Immigration Policy in the Twentieth Century." In *Diminishing Returns,* edited by D. DeVoretz. Toronto: CD Howe Institute and Laurier Institution

Green, A.G., and D.A. Green. 1995. "Canadian Immigration Policy: The Effectiveness of the Point System and Other Instruments." *Canadian Journal of Economics* 28: 1006-41.

Hiebert, D. 2002. "The Spatial Limits to Entrepreneurship: Immigrant Entrepreneurs in Canada." *Tijdschrift voor economische en sociale geografie* 93 (2): 173-190.

Kuhn, P.J., and H.J. Schuetze. 2001. "Self-Employment Dynamics and Self-Employment Trends: A Study of Canadian Men and Women, 1982-1995." *Canadian Journal of Economics* 34 (3): 760-84.

Lalonde, R.J., and R. Topel. 1992. "The Assimilation of Immigrants in the US Labor Market." In *Immigration and the Workforce,* edited by G.J. Borjas and R. Freeman, 67-92. Chicago: University of Chicago Press.

Le, A.T. 2000. "The Determinants of Immigrant Self-Employment in Australia." *International Migration Review* 13: 183-214.

Li, P. 1998. *The Chinese in Canada.* 2nd ed. Toronto: Oxford University Press.

– 2001a. "Immigrants' Propensity to Self-Employment." IMDB Research Paper Series, Citizenship and Immigration Canada: Strategic Policy, Planning and Research.

– 2001b. "Economic Returns of Immigrants' Self-Employment." IMDB Research Paper Series, Citizenship and Immigration Canada: Strategic Policy, Planning and Research.

Light, I. 1972. *Ethnic Entrepreneurs in America*. Berkeley: University of California Press.

– 1984. "Immigrant and Ethnic Enterprise in North America." *Ethnic and Racial Studies* 7: 195-216.

Light, I., and E. Bonacich. 1988. *Immigrant Entrepreneurs: Koreans in Los Angeles, 1965-1982*. Berkeley: University of California Press.

Light, I., and C. Rosenstein. 1995. *Race, Ethnicity and Entrepreneurship in Urban America*. New York: Aldine de Gruyter.

Lofstrom, M. 2002. "Labor Market Assimilation and the Self-Employment Decision of Immigrant Entrepreneurs." *Journal of Population Economics* 15: 83-114.

Mata, F., and R. Pendakur. 1998. "Immigration, Labour Force Integration and the Pursuit of Self-Employment." RIIM Working Paper No. 98-05.

Metcalf, H., T. Modood, and S. Virdee. 1996. *Asian Self-Employment: The Interaction of Culture and Economics*. London: Policy Studies Institute.

Min, P.G. 1984, "From White Collar Occupations to Small Business: Korean Immigrants' Occupational Adjustment." *Sociological Quarterly* 25: 333-52.

– 1988. *Ethnic Business Enterprise: Korean Small Business in Atlanta*. New York: Center for Migration Studies.

Moore, R.L. 1983. "Employer Discrimination: Evidence from Self-Employed Workers." *Review of Economics and Statistics* 655: 496-501.

Parent, D., and C. Worswick. 2004. "Immigrant Labour Market Performance and Skilled Immigrant Selection: The International Experience." CIRANO Working Paper 2004RP-07.

Parker, S.C. 2004. *The Economics of Self-Employment and Entrepreneurship*. Cambridge: Cambridge University Press.

Phizacklea, A. 1988. "Entrepreneurship, Ethnicity and Gender." In *Enterprising Women*, edited by S. Westwood and P. Bhachu. London: Routledge.

Rafiq, M. 1992. "Ethnicity and Enterprise: A Comparison of Muslim and Non-Muslim Owned Asian Businesses in Britain." *New Community* 19: 43-60.

Razin, E., and A. Longlois. 1996. "Metropolitan Characteristics and Entrepreneurship among Immigrants and Ethnic Groups in Canada." *International Migration Review* 30: 703-27.

Schaafsma, J., and A. Sweetman. 2001. "Immigrant Earnings: Age at Immigration Matters." *Canadian Journal of Economics* 34 (4): 1066-99.

Schuetze, H.J. 2000. "Taxes, Economic Conditions and Recent Trends in Male Self-Employment: A Canada-U.S. Comparison." *Labour Economics* 7: 507-44.

Sowell, T. 1981. *Markets and Minorities*. New York: Basic Books.

Wong, L., and M. Ng. 2002. "The Emergence of Small Transnational Enterprise in Vancouver: The Case of Chinese Immigrant Entrepreneurs." *International Journal of Urban and Regional Research* 26 (3): 508-30.

Yuengert, A.M. 1995. "Testing Hypothesis of Immigrant Self-Employment." *Journal of Human Resources* 30 (1): 194-204.

APPENDIX

A1. Variable Definitions: Immigrant Arrival Cohorts

Cohort Name	Definition
Canada	
46	In Census 71-81 analysis, these are immigrants who arrived prior 1946
51	Immigrants who arrived between 1951 and 1955
56	Immigrants who arrived between 1956 and 1960
	In Census 81-91 analysis, these are immigrants who arrived prior to 1956
61	Immigrants who arrived between 1961 and 1965
66	Immigrants who arrived between 1966 and 1970
71	Immigrants who arrived between 1971 and 1975
76	Immigrants who arrived between 1976 and 1980
81	Immigrants who arrived between 1981 and 1985
86	Immigrants who arrived between 1986 and 1990
91	Immigrants who arrived between 1991 and 1995
96	Immigrants who arrived between 1996 and 2000
United States	
D50	Immigrants who arrived prior to 1950
D55	Immigrants who arrived between 1950-1959*
D60	Immigrants who arrived between 1960-1964
D65	Immigrants who arrived between 1965-1969 (1965-1970 in the 1970 Census)
D70	Immigrants who arrived between 1970-1974
D75	Immigrants who arrived between 1975-1979 (1975-1980 in the 1980 Census)
D80	Immigrants who arrived between 1980-1984
D85	Immigrants who arrived between 1985-1989 (1985-1990 in the 1990 Census)
D90	Immigrants who arrived between 1990-1994
D95	Immigrants who arrived between 1995-1999 (1995-2000 in the 2000 Census)

Source: Author's compilation.

A2. Probit Model Estimation Results for Canada

Coef.\Year	1971-81		1981-91		1986-96	
	Coef.	Std	Coef.	Std	Coef.	Std
Age	0.099	0.005	0.068	0.003	0.114	0.004
agel	-0.005	0.010	0.010	0.007	-0.041	0.008
agesq	-0.001	0.000	-0.001	0.000	-0.001	0.000
agesql	0.000	0.000	0.000	0.000	0.001	0.000
ed2	0.085	0.045	0.033	0.047	0.037	0.056
ed3	0.065	0.045	0.039	0.046	0.027	0.054
ed4	0.073	0.047	0.014	0.046	-0.013	0.054
ed5	0.059	0.046	0.079	0.048	0.016	0.055
ed6	0.112	0.051	0.051	0.048	0.033	0.055
ed7	0.117	0.050	0.180	0.047	0.103	0.054
ed8	0.126	0.050	0.040	0.047	-0.028	0.054
ed9	0.198	0.061	0.193	0.050	0.163	0.056
ed10	0.441	0.048	0.144	0.049	0.095	0.055
ed11			0.292	0.046	0.242	0.054
ed12					0.182	0.059
ed13					-0.002	0.057
ed14					-0.091	0.073
edl2	0.054	0.069	0.190	0.067	0.301	0.082
edl3	0.121	0.070	0.220	0.065	0.255	0.077
edl4	0.118	0.076	0.246	0.067	0.337	0.077
edl5	0.065	0.070	0.285	0.069	0.431	0.081
edl6	-0.044	0.077	0.260	0.072	0.318	0.081
edl7	0.097	0.079	0.133	0.066	0.309	0.078
edl8	0.018	0.080	0.171	0.068	0.332	0.078
edl9	-0.072	0.105	0.207	0.074	0.333	0.082
edl10	-0.163	0.074	0.145	0.070	0.200	0.080
edl11			0.088	0.064	0.251	0.077
edl12					0.253	0.088
edl13					0.331	0.082
edl14					0.165	0.103
mstat2	0.264	0.022	0.197	0.016	0.059	0.017
mstat3	0.048	0.075	0.109	0.035	0.023	0.028
mstat4	0.205	0.043	0.043	0.022	-0.082	0.020
mstat5	0.168	0.042	0.097	0.039	-0.100	0.072
mstatl2	-0.032	0.046	-0.047	0.036	0.003	0.039
mstatl3	0.057	0.152	0.042	0.072	-0.030	0.061
mstatl4	-0.073	0.089	-0.064	0.049	-0.026	0.045
mstatl5	-0.103	0.087	-0.121	0.082	-0.023	0.148
Y81/Y91/Y01	0.105	0.014	0.052	0.009	0.029	0.007
immig	0.465	0.222	-0.066	0.164	0.583	0.188
immgy81/91/96			-0.014	0.028	0.004	0.041

A2. Probit Model Estimation Results for Canada (continued)

Coef.\Year	1971-81		1981-91		1986-96	
	Coef.	Std	Coef.	Std	Coef.	Std
D56	-0.087	0.049				
D61	-0.296	0.066	-0.061	0.040	0.067	0.038
D66	-0.579	0.062	-0.107	0.032	0.006	0.031
D71	-0.233	0.040	-0.185	0.036	-0.023	0.031
D76	-0.325	0.052	-0.268	0.047	0.016	0.034
D81			-0.078	0.036	0.009	0.038
D86			-0.250	0.035	-0.167	0.036
D91					-0.001	0.041
D96					-0.153	0.043
D56Y	0.133	0.059				
D61Y	0.185	0.078	0.089	0.051	-0.067	0.068
D66Y	0.435	0.070	0.043	0.042	-0.014	0.054
D71Y			0.112	0.045	0.031	0.052
D76Y			0.234	0.056	-0.063	0.055
D81Y					-0.084	0.058
D86Y					0.147	0.054
constant	-3.780	0.105	-3.056	0.078	-3.718	0.089
Pseudo R-Square	0.0318		0.0274		0.0346	
Obs.	104246		203908		266093	

Source: Author's compilation.

7

HOW FAR DOES THE POINTS SYSTEM STRETCH? THE SPOUSES OF SKILLED WORKER PRINCIPAL APPLICANTS

ARTHUR SWEETMAN AND CASEY WARMAN

Le système de points de la politique canadienne d'immigration – mis en place pour sélectionner les demandeurs principaux dans la catégorie «travailleurs qualifiés et professionnels» (DP-TQ) ayant des résultats supérieurs sur le marché du travail – peut-il prédire efficacement les résultats des conjoints ou conjointes de ces demandeurs sur le marché du travail? Et quelle est la situation de ces demandeurs et de leur conjoint ou conjointe sur le marché du travail? Nos résultats montrent que le système de points permet de bien sélectionner les DP-TQ ayant de meilleurs résultats sur le marché du travail, en comparaison avec les immigrants des autres catégories étudiées. De plus, il n'y a aucune différence statistique, en matière de résultats sur le marché du travail, entre les hommes et les femmes qui font une demande en tant que DP-TQ. Le nombre de points accordés aux conjoints des DP-TQ est, en moyenne, seulement légèrement inférieur à celui de leur partenaire. Par contre, les résultats des conjoints ne semblent pas aussi bons que leurs caractéristiques mesurées par le système de points permettraient de prédire. Cet écart ne semble pas provenir de différences entre les taux de rendement économique associés aux points, c'est-à-dire la pente de la courbe entre les revenus et le nombre de points. Toutefois, l'ordonnée à l'origine de cette courbe est très élevée et négative pour les conjoints, ce qui suggère que les conjoints, et en particulier les conjointes, ont des revenus de départ plus bas et ce pour des raisons qui ne sont pas reliées au nombre de points. Dans la catégorie «famille», les immigrants qui font une demande en tant que couple reçoivent beaucoup moins de points, et ont de plus faibles résultats sur le marché du travail, que les conjoints ou conjointes de DP-TQ.

How well does the Canadian immigration points system, which is intended to select skilled worker principal applicants (SWPAs) with superior labour market outcomes, predict the labour market outcomes of their spouses? And, how well do SWPAs and their spouses do

Canadian Immigration: Economic Evidence for a Dynamic Policy Environment, ed. T. McDonald, E. Ruddick, A. Sweetman, and C. Worswick. Montreal and Kingston: Queen's Policy Studies Series, McGill-Queen's University Press.

in the labour market? The points system successfully selects SWPAs with better labour market outcomes than the other immigrant groups studied. Also, there is no statistically distinguishable difference in labour market outcomes between male and female SWPAs. Spouses of SWPAs have imputed points that are on average lower than those of their partners, but not dramatically lower. However, the outcomes of spouses do not appear to be quite as good as might be expected based on their characteristics as measured by the points system. This gap does not appear to derive from differences in the economic rate of return to immigration points, that is, the slope of the relationship between earnings and points. Rather, the intercept term of the relationship is very large and negative for spouses, suggesting that spouses, and especially female spouses, start from a low base level of earnings for reasons unrelated to immigration points. Family class immigrants who immigrate as couples have much lower imputed points, and lower labour market outcomes, than SWPA spouses.

Introduction

Of the 247,243 individuals who immigrated and became permanent residents of Canada in 2008, 43,360 or 17.5 percent were assessed under the points system; that is, they were skilled worker principal applicants (SWPAs). From a slightly different point of view, the assessed group represented 29.1 percent of the 149,072 economic class immigrants. However, an additional 40.5 percent of the economic class, or 24.4 percent of the total permanent resident flow, comprised the spouses and dependants of these SWPAs.[1] It is unclear what portion of the 60,376 people in the skilled worker spouses and dependents sub-category were spouses since statistics are reported for the grouping as a whole, but 50,875 were over age 15. Clearly, the direct effect of the points system on immigrant labour market outcomes is limited by the scale of the relevant immigration stream. However, points may also have an indirect effect if the spouse's characteristics are correlated with those of the SWPA.

In this paper we focus on a narrow set of related questions. Primarily, how well does the Canadian immigration points system, which is intended to select principal applicants with superior labour market outcomes, predict the labour market outcomes of their spouses? And, how well do the spouses of SWPAs do in the labour market? Tangentially, since we employ a subset of the family class as a comparison group, we also explore limited aspects of family class immigration. Perhaps most interestingly, we ask counterfactual questions about the points each subgroup would have had, and compare the economic rate of return on those points across subgroups.

Currently, if the SWPA has a spouse, the points system acknowledges the "jointness" of the immigration process by attributing some points to the principal applicant based on the characteristics of his/her spouse, with an emphasis on the spouse's education. In fact, having a spouse can make meeting the minimum number of points required for entry somewhat easier for the principal applicant since these spousal points increase the score but the pass mark is not affected. (Therefore, the effective minimum for a principal applicant without a spouse is higher than that for one with a spouse who has any characteristics for which points may be assigned.) Of course, families select for themselves who will serve as the principal applicant and who will be defined as the spouse for immigration purposes. In contrast to the current selection system's approach, previous versions have focused exclusively on the principal applicant. From time to time there are calls for changes to the way families are assessed, but very little is known about the functioning of the current points system with respect to them.

LITERATURE REVIEW

Given the dearth of data directly linking labour market outcomes to the Canadian points system, most work on labour market outcomes has used the Census or other general purpose datasets to look at immigrant labour market outcomes. These studies find a general deterioration in labour market outcomes from the 1970s through to the first decade of 2000, perhaps with modest business cycle upturns in the late 1980s and 1990s (e.g., Baker and Benjamin 1994; Bloom, Grenier, and Gunderson 1995; Grant 1999; Warman and Worswick 2004; Frenette and Morissette 2005; Aydemir and Skuterud 2005; and Green and Worswick 2010).

A small number of researchers have had access to administrative data with information about the immigration system. Picot, Hou, and Coulombe (2007) explore immigrant entry class. Focusing on low income, they find continued declines in labour market outcomes, especially among economic class immigrants, beyond 2000. De Silva (1997) looks at males who arrived in the early 1980s and finds a convergence with time-since-migration in outcomes by economic class. Sweetman and Warman (2009) provide a broad overview of labour market outcomes by immigrant class using the same data as this paper, but their focus is on predicting outcomes for the new "Canada experience class."

Aydemir (forthcoming) uses the first two years of the Longitudinal Survey of Immigrants to Canada (LSIC) – the first two waves of the data used in this paper – but we have access to all three waves over four years. His research is the most closely related to that here, and he finds that while those selected by the points system (principal applicants and others jointly) have higher measured skills than the family class, two years after landing their skills have limited power in predicting labour market success. His is also the only other paper of which we are aware that looks, albeit briefly and only in the short term, at spousal outcomes.

He finds evidence of positive assortative matching, implying that the higher skills of the principal applicant imply higher skills for the spouse as well, but those skills do not translate into appreciably better outcomes than those of individuals in other visa categories.

In considering Aydemir's results, two issues arise that are particularly relevant. First, there is the well known difficulty that, starting in the 1980s or earlier, immigrants have had in transferring foreign human capital to the Canadian labour market and in developing Canada-relevant human capital. For example, Schaafsma and Sweetman (2001), Aydemir and Skuterud (2005), Picot and Sweetman 2005, Ferrer and Riddell (2008), and Green and Worswick (2010) all find almost no return to foreign work experience for recent cohorts of immigrants. Language and characteristics associated with changing source countries are also important correlates of the decline. The return to education is lower for immigrants than for the Canadian born, but this does not appear to have changed much in recent decades. Perhaps immigration points do not matter as much as when the system was initially conceptualized. Second, there are issues about timing and immigration class. It is possible that the start-up of economic class immigrants is slower because they have fewer local contacts (information) and/or institutional support than do family class immigrants and refugees. Hence, by the third wave, after four years in Canada, the SWPAs may have relatively better labour market outcomes and the system's points become better predictors.

HYPOTHESES REGARDING SPOUSAL/GENDERED GAPS IN OUTCOMES

Given that we are addressing how the operation of the selection system interacts with spousal pairs, gender and family issues may play an important role. Three classes of hypotheses are therefore worth mentioning since they may assist in interpreting our findings.

The family investment hypothesis: The basic idea of the family investment hypothesis is that immigrants' decisions about labour market integration strategies and investments in Canada-specific human capital are made in the context of families, with particular individuals taking different roles. Gendered implications arise when women immediately after landing take on jobs that have relatively little growth potential but provide for the family in the short run and subsidize men's investment in human capital, which is expected to have longer-term payoffs. Baker and Benjamin (1997) find evidence consistent with this hypothesis for Canada. Subsequently Dowhan and Duleep (2002), looking primarily at US results but also addressing the Canadian literature (especially Worswick 1996, 1999), suggest that more recent cohorts of immigrant women may have modified their labour market activities so that their pattern of activities is more similar to that of men.

Tied mobility: When families relocate for economic reasons, it is common that the move is instigated by one member finding or anticipating a good job match. The other members are "tied" to this primary mover, and the quality of any job-worker match for them in the new region is not, on average, likely to be as good as that for the primary mover. Overall, the family may benefit from the move, but, any after-the-fact observation of labour market outcomes will show a gap between the principal and "tied" movers. Loprest (1992) discusses, very generally, how differences in job mobility between men and women can have detrimental effects on wage growth for women, producing wage gaps. A gender aspect to this may exist if female partners are more likely to be the "tied" movers. Of course, expected labour market outcomes are conditional on individual characteristics, and therefore it is plausible that any potential gap should be measured conditional on observed labour market relevant characteristics. If immigrant women also have characteristics that are less valuable in the labour market, then the spousal gaps may be particularly large since the gaps measured without conditioning on characteristics will have (at least) two sources.

Social or cultural influences and discrimination: It is entirely possible that any observed differences between SWPAs and their spouses may follow from Canadian and/or immigrant source country "cultural norms"/ discrimination regarding men's and women's roles. A large literature looks at differences in male-female labour market outcomes. Antecol (2000, 2003) provides particularly relevant analyses of immigrant and ethnic differences in these gendered gaps in labour market outcomes within the immigration context. It appears plausible that source country gender norms are, at least in the short run, to some degree observed in the receiving country's labour market.

DATA DESCRIPTION AND EMPIRICAL STRATEGY

The Longitudinal Survey of Immigrants to Canada

The data used in the estimation come from the Longitudinal Survey of Immigrants to Canada (LSIC). It contains a sample of new immigrants who applied through a Canadian mission abroad, were age 15 or older at the time of landing, and immigrated between 1 October 2000 and 30 September 2001. They are then interviewed in three waves: at six months, two years, and four years after landing. The response rate at the first interview was just over 60 percent, and of those who responded at the first interview, about 65 percent continued through to the third wave.

   In addition to the usual reasons for non-response, both return and/or onward migration are issues for the sample in question since the survey is restricted to those residing in Canada; Aydemir and Robinson (2008) suggest that almost 25 percent of all new immigrants leave the country within five years, with over 80 percent of those departing doing so in the first year after landing. Moreover, given that all respondents in the LSIC landed from abroad (as opposed to landing from within Canada), the national return and onward migration rate is likely to underestimate departures in the survey's sample since economic class immigrants had to apply through a mission abroad at the time of the survey and are also more likely to depart, whereas refugee claimants may land from within the country and are more likely to stay. Aydemir and Robinson find that around 25 percent of immigrants who arrived under the skilled worker class left within the first year after arrival, and that four years after landing (which would correspond to wave 3 in our data) around 33 percent had left. We employ the weights provided by Statistics Canada throughout the analysis to make the sample representative.

We restrict our sample to those who were between the ages of 19 and 62 at the time of the first interview (around six months after landing). We check the sensitivity of the results to this sampling by re-estimating for a few different age groupings, and we do not find important differences.

The primary goal of our paper is to study immigrant selection. We are not interested in immigrants' earnings conditional on having a job; rather, we are interested in earnings (or being employed/unemployed) conditional upon entering Canada in a particular immigrant class or subclass, or having been assigned a particular number of immigration points. Our empirical strategy matches our substantive questions. For the earning regressions we therefore present the results for weekly earnings from the main job and assign respondents $1 in earnings if they did not have paid employment.[2] We include those respondents with zero earnings in the analysis since we think that this best reflects the policy question we are posing, which concerns the entire flow of immigrants and not exclusively those who gain employment.[3] Another option would be to look at hourly earnings. The key systematic difference between weekly and hourly measures is that gaps tend to be larger for weekly earnings since hourly wages and weekly hours are positively correlated. We think that weekly earnings better reflect the overall economic outcomes in which we are interested given that this measure combines both the rate of pay and the intensity. Earnings are converted into real terms by using the Consumer Price Index. Since there is a 12 month gap between the landing of the first and last immigrants, we use a moving average of the monthly CPI over the reference period for each immigrant to better control for differences in the price level.[4]

Although our focus is on spousal pairs, the survey is a random sample of individual new immigrants, not families. There are no spousal pairs in the data; although there are both SWPAs and spouses of SWPAs who are respondents, they are not related. However, each SWPA respondent is asked a limited set of questions about his/her spouse, and we are able to use this information to construct a category for the spouses of the SWPAs in the data.[5] Therefore, given the available data, and the substantive issues being pursued, we identify four subgroups for comparison:

- respondents of the LSIC who are SWPAs;
- spouses of the SWPAs who are respondents of the LSIC – spouses of the first group (these spouses are not respondents of the survey, but the SWPAs are asked questions that allow us to determine their spouses' labour market outcomes and, therefore, include their spouses as a group for analysis – we refer to this group as "Spouses");
- respondents of the LSIC who are spouses of SWPAs not in the survey (we refer to this group as "Other Spouses" since they are spouses of SWPAs *other* than those in the survey); and
- respondents of the LSIC who are members of the family class who immigrate as a spousal couple (we refer to this group as the "Family Class").[6]

We do not have sufficient information to estimate the Spouses' points; rather, we assign each the points of his/her SWPA partner. This assigning of points is, of course, the central motivation for the paper. We want to see if the points of the SWPA are predictive of the spouse's labour market outcomes. Further, to form a comparison group, and to answer other related questions, we calculate (counterfactual) individual points for Other Spouses based on their own characteristics, even though in practice they are not assigned points by the immigration system. We can, therefore, compare and contrast these two sets of SWPA spouses. Given the sampling scheme, these two groups of spouses should have, within sampling error, the same distribution of characteristics since (after the weights are applied) they are independent random draws from the same population. For both spousal categories we employ the labour market outcome of the spouse himself or herself, but the immigration points assigned are the principal applicant's points for Spouses in accordance with the motivation for the paper.

Restricting the Family Class to those who immigrate as a couple serves to make it, in one sense, more similar to the skilled worker category, but on other dimensions it makes it less similar since the members of the family class who immigrate as a couple are parents and grandparents of their sponsors. However, it is not similarity that is of primary importance for this comparison group. Rather, it is the group among the family class that can be most easily adjusted in terms of immigration levels. The other adult family class subcategory is "spouses and partners." This subclass is already given substantial processing priority and is not obviously subject to government policy with respect to the size of the flow. (The government cannot mandate sponsors to find new spouses to sponsor, but there is a queue of individuals interested in sponsoring parents and grandparents.)

Therefore, this subgroup of the family class is the most appropriate for the policy counterfactual we wish to pursue since, were there a policy change, it would be this subgroup that would expand.

Given that we are interested in the before-the-fact ability of the points system to predict, at the time of selection, subsequent labour market outcomes for both SWPAs and their spouses, we restrict the sample for the economic and family class to spousal couples who immigrated together. We also remove respondents who had a new spouse after landing or who were divorced or separated during the sample period. Finally, we further restrict the sample in terms of age so that *both* the respondent and her / his spouse are between the ages of 19 and 62 at the time of the first cycle.

The actual points assigned to each SWPA in the immigration process are not available in the survey data. However, an estimate of the immigration points can be constructed from the survey responses. Although it may be interesting to estimate points for each individual under the points systems in place at the time of immigration, and / or the time of application to immigrate, as well at the current one, it is not possible to accurately construct the system that was previously in place using the information provided in the LSIC. Most immigrants would likely have been assessed under the points system in place between 1997 and 2002. However, we are unable to determine more than half of the possible points that may have been awarded under that regime since we lack information regarding such criteria as demographic factors and personal suitability, as well as the occupational factors related to the designated occupations list, which in turn prevents us from determining points for other factors (the education and training factor, and the experience factor). We therefore only estimate points for the current system.

For the current points system, we are able to construct most factors using the survey responses in the LSIC. However, there are some items where we cannot perfectly assign points given some limitations in the data. For the arranged employment factor, we are able to determine if the respondents had arranged employment, but we are unable to determine if they were on a work visa or had a Human Resources and Skills Development Canada (HRSDC) approved job when they were applying to immigrate. We can determine most of the points for the education factor, but lack certain information, such as the duration of the respondents' degrees or diplomas. To determine the points attained from language, we use the categorical self-assessed language ability of the respondent. For the age selection factor, we can measure the points accurately. For the work experience selection factor, since we do not know the exact work history of the respondent, we use information derived from potential experience. We lack some information to create the adaptability factor, particularly with respect to information on the spouses; the LSIC lacks information on whether the spouse had been in Canada on a work visa prior to immigration.[7] Although we do not know if each individual had been in Canada on a student visa, we use information on whether the highest degree was received in Canada. As will be seen, the imputed points are sometimes less than the current 67 cut-off, and this is in most cases because the above-mentioned omissions cause our index to be biased down relative to the actual points. We are, however, able to esti-mate the bulk of the points reasonably well, and our index is consistent across groups, providing comparability. It can be thought of as a proxy for the major items in the current points system. In the regressions that follow, we rescale the points variable in order to rescale the coefficient; we divide the points variable by 10 so the coefficient is 10 times larger than it would otherwise be.

Model Specification

The analysis initially focuses on a baseline understanding of the gaps in outcomes between the four groups (classes) defined above and estimates a model of the form:

$$Y_i = \beta_0 + \beta_1 msm_i + \beta_2 Class_i + \left[\beta_3 Female_i + \beta_4 Female_i * Class_i \right] + \varepsilon_i \quad (1)$$

where i indexes individuals, Y is (the natural logarithm of) weekly earn-ings or the dichotomous variable employment, msm is months-since-migration, $Class$ is a vector of indicators for immigration class (Spouse, Other Spouse, and Family Class), and $Female$ is an indicator for the gender of the individual. The portion in brackets is estimated in some specifica-tions but not others. When the dependent variable is earnings, ordinary least squares regression is employed. Probit regression is used when the dependent variable is the dichotomous employment variable. We estimate equation (1) separately for each wave of the data since we want to see the evolution of the gaps in earnings over time. Months-since-migration is the only control variable in the regression since it provides improved com-parability across individuals. It is modelled linearly in all cases in order to employ a common specification, although for the wave 1 regression a quadratic term is statistically significant. Restricting the specification to be linear for all three waves does not alter the substantive interpretation. Subsequently the model is expanded to include the points and the inter-actions of points with the variables in the regression (1):

$$Y_i = \beta_0 + \beta_1 msm_i + \beta_2 Class_i + \beta_3 Points_i + \beta_4 Points_i * Class_i +$$
$$\left[\beta_5 Female_i + \beta_6 Female_i * Class_i + \beta_7 Points_i * Female_i + \beta_8 Points_i * Female_i * Class_i \right] \quad (2)$$
$$+ \varepsilon_i$$

where the other elements of equation (2) are defined as (1). This allows us to look at how controlling for points, the index of each skilled worker principal applicant's human capital employed by the immigration system changes the average earnings of each immigration class relative to the earlier regressions. The models also contrast the rate of return to points for each immigration class.

EMPIRICAL RESULTS

Descriptive Statistics

Table 1 presents descriptive statistics for the four groups examined in this study. Looking across the table, it is clear that the SWPAs have the highest point average, followed fairly closely by Other Spouses. Family Class points are substantially lower. For each of these three groups, where we can calculate points, the full distribution is seen in Figure 1. Clearly, the shapes of the three distributions are quite dissimilar. Family Class has a profile that is skewed to the left with a lower mode, and SWPAs have a very tight distribution that is mostly above the 67 point threshold and is skewed to the right. Other Spouses have a distribution that is intermediate between the two, but more similar to the SWPAs. Recall that for all groups the points are an underestimate since some factors are missing.

The fraction of each group with a university degree, in Table 1, mirrors the imputed points in that almost 90 percent of SWPAs have a university degree, as do just under 70 percent of spouses in both categories, but only 12 percent of the Family Class have one. It is reassuring that the two groups of spouses have, within sampling error, the same average age, percent female, and percentage of people with a university degree, since they should be independent random draws from the same population with the same distribution of characteristics. Note that both spousal groups are slightly younger than the SWPAs, but the Family Class is almost two decades older, consistent with the idea that they are parents and grandparents of their sponsors.

It is worth comparing the educational outcomes of these new immigrants to those of the existing Canadian population (including the Canadian born and earlier immigrants). To do this, we employ the 2000 Labour Force Survey public use file and calculate mean levels of education for different age groups by gender. For those between 27 and 39 years of age, 21.6 percent of men and 23.8 percent of women report having a university degree. Clearly, both the SWPAs and their spouses have average levels of education dramatically in excess of that for the existing Canadian population. However, there is sometimes concern about the comparability of international definitions of community college and university. We therefore estimate the percentage of the Canadian born with any type of post-secondary certificate, diploma, or degree and find that 56.7 percent of men and 59.4 percent of women have some type of post-secondary certification. This is clearly too broad a category, but even

TABLE 1. Means by Immigrant Class

	Skilled Worker Principal Applicants (SWPAs)		Spouses (of SWPAs in the survey)		Other Spouses (of SWPAs not in the survey)		Family Class (parents and grandparents)	
	Means	s.e.	Means	s.e.	Means	s.e.	Means	s.e.
Points	70.77	0.31	70.77	0.31	60.05	0.47	28.35	1.11
Percent ≥ 67 points	0.75	0.01	0.75	0.01	0.40	0.01	0.04	0.01
Age at wave 1	36.57	0.17	34.89	0.18	34.92	0.19	53.87	0.29
University degree[a]	0.89	0.01	0.69	0.01	0.67	0.01	0.12	0.02
% Female	0.18	0.01	0.82	0.01	0.83	0.01	0.51	0.03
Wave 1								
Weekly earnings[b]	425.65	16.28	156.58	7.63	177.81	7.76	155.83	11.96
Positive weekly earnings	640.81	20.47	389.45	12.91	394.00	11.21	365.83	10.79
ln(earnings)[b]	4.13	0.09	2.32	0.08	2.62	0.09	2.49	0.18
ln(positive earnings)	6.21	0.03	5.77	0.03	5.81	0.03	5.84	0.03
Hours worked[c]	27.33	0.57	14.63	0.54	16.54	0.57	18.74	1.37
Positive hours[d]	38.77	0.35	34.61	0.50	34.68	0.49	43.42	0.92
Employed[e]	0.70	0.01	0.42	0.01	0.48	0.01	0.43	0.03
Months since migration	6.66	0.03	6.66	0.03	6.62	0.03	6.68	0.06
Wave 2								
Weekly earnings[b]	609.34	16.85	289.70	9.68	308.46	12.18	233.35	12.67
Positive weekly earnings	761.19	17.87	461.49	11.34	471.15	15.47	378.79	9.46
ln(earnings)[b]	5.16	0.08	3.73	0.09	3.90	0.09	3.62	0.17
ln(positive earnings)	6.44	0.02	5.94	0.02	5.96	0.02	5.87	0.03
Hours worked[c]	37.64	0.47	24.12	0.55	26.69	0.57	27.12	1.36
Positive hours[d]	41.34	0.34	35.51	0.39	36.38	0.41	42.74	0.84
Employed[e]	0.91	0.01	0.68	0.01	0.73	0.01	0.63	0.03
Months since migration	26.43	0.02	26.43	0.02	26.51	0.03	26.53	0.05
Wave 3								
Weekly earnings[b]	699.57	16.61	341.96	10.23	374.95	10.96	232.05	15.26
Positive weekly earnings	863.51	16.43	527.46	10.94	544.83	11.52	405.24	15.74
ln(earnings)[b]	5.35	0.08	3.96	0.09	4.21	0.09	3.37	0.18
ln(positive earnings)	6.62	0.02	6.10	0.02	6.11	0.02	5.88	0.04
Hours worked[c]	38.88	0.40	25.45	0.55	27.97	0.53	25.09	1.37
Positive hours[d]	41.26	0.30	36.19	0.37	35.25	0.40	41.37	1.00
Employed[e]	0.94	0.01	0.70	0.01	0.79	0.01	0.61	0.03
Months since migration	49.38	0.02	49.38	0.02	49.30	0.02	49.41	0.04

Notes: Sample age 19 to 62 at the time of the first wave. The notation ln( ) implies natural logarithm. Standard error (s.e.) in the column to the right of the mean. [a] At time of landing; [b] weekly earnings include people with zero earnings; people with zero earnings are given $1 prior to taking the natural logarithm; [c] includes people with zero hours; [d] includes only workers with positive hours worked; [e] defined as working positive hours.
Source: Authors' calculations.

FIGURE 1
Kernel Density Estimates of Imputed Points

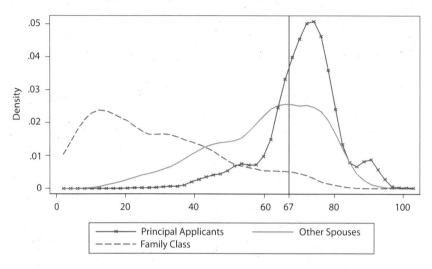

Source: Authors' compilation.

it is well below that for new immigrants both in the SWPA category and
for their spouses. In contrast, the percentage of Family Class immigrants
with a university degree is substantially lower than any of the numbers
for the Canadian population. As this group is also older, we generated
comparable numbers for the Canadian population aged 45 to 59. We find
that 21.4 percent of the men and 16.8 percent of the women hold university
certificates, and 52.2 percent of the men and 45.9 percent of the women
hold some type of post-secondary certification. Thus even when Family
Class is compared to the older age group, this set of new immigrants is
seen to have a low average level of education.[8]

Table 1 also shows various labour market outcomes at waves 1, 2, and
3. Given that our substantive policy question involves selection, the focus
is on the weekly earnings of all immigrants, including those with zero
earnings and hours of work, although we also show the average earnings
and hours of those with strictly positive employment income. For all four
groups there is a clear improvement in labour market outcomes as time
in Canada increases. Without adjusting for characteristics (which would
make the gaps appear smaller), SWPAs consistently have higher earnings,
hours, and employment rates than the other three groups. Compared to
Spouses and Other Spouses, the Family Class appears to have a similar
start in finding employment despite their much lower level of education
and lower points. This is consistent with the idea that they receive assistance and benefit from the local knowledge of their family members/
sponsors. However, by the second wave two years after landing, and

more so in the third wave four years after landing, this subgroup of the Family Class has fallen behind the spouses in terms of employment rates and earnings.

Regressions Addressing Only Immigration Category

The first three columns of Table 2, in accord with the functioning of the immigration system, do not distinguish the gender of the immigrant and, in fact, do not control for any respondent characteristics. The variable months-since-migration, which is not shown, is included purely as a control. We believe that the first three regressions in these, and subsequent, tables are the most important for selection policy, at least in the short run. Compared to the SWPAs, which is the omitted category, Spouses earn approximately 85 percent less [$(e^{-1.808}-1)*100\% = -83.6\%$] in wave 1.[9] The gap is similar, although the point estimates are not quite as large, for the other two groups. Though enormous, and controlling for months since migration does increase the gaps' sizes somewhat, these gaps are consistent with the differences in earnings displayed in Table 1.

TABLE 2
OLS (ln) Weekly Earnings Regressions

	Wave 1	Wave 2	Wave 3	Wave 1	Wave 2	Wave 3
Spouses	-1.808***	-1.425***	-1.397***	-0.510**	-0.051	-0.474**
	[0.125]	[0.119]	[0.120]	[0.236]	[0.204]	[0.224]
Other spouses	-1.502***	-1.240***	-1.152***	-0.345	-0.377*	-0.486**
	[0.128]	[0.120]	[0.120]	[0.244]	[0.225]	[0.236]
Family class	-1.642***	-1.520***	-1.982***	-0.916***	-0.283	-0.916***
	[0.206]	[0.205]	[0.210]	[0.297]	[0.237]	[0.273]
Female				-0.769***	-0.217	-0.076
				[0.238]	[0.203]	[0.203]
Female x spouse				-0.991***	-1.513***	-1.071***
				[0.333]	[0.291]	[0.305]
Female x oth sp				-0.803**	-0.877***	-0.748**
				[0.341]	[0.306]	[0.314]
Female x family				-0.919**	-2.274***	-2.030***
				[0.429]	[0.388]	[0.409]
Observations	3,742	3,742	3,742	3,742	3,742	3,742
R-squared	0.07	0.05	0.05	0.10	0.09	0.07

Notes: Sample restricted to households for which both spouse and respondent were age 19 to 62 at the time of the first wave. Sample includes zero $ earners, with zero set to $1 prior to taking ln. Robust standard errors in brackets.
* significant at 10 percent; ** significant at 5 percent; *** significant at 1 percent. All regressions include controls for months since migration.
Source: Authors' calculations.

The earnings gaps reduce slightly for both categories of spouses in waves 2 and 3 with the smallest being about 68 percent [$(e^{-1.152}-1)*100\%=$ -68.4%]. However, the gap increases by wave 3 for the Family Class. Of course, as seen in Table 1, earnings are going up for all four groups. Overall, SWPAs and Family Class appear to have early success relative to the two spousal groups. Spouses in both categories subsequently have gaps that remain quite large but become slightly smaller compared to the SWPAs. In contrast, the Family Class's labour market outcomes decline relative to the SWPA's as time in Canada increases. Note that the R^2s for these regressions containing only the immigration classes as regressors are about 0.05. This can be compared with "common" earnings regressions where the sample comprises only those with positive earnings and the specification includes regressors such as age (or experience), education, geographic residence indicators, and others, which typically have R^2s of roughly 0.30.

A gendered analysis is undertaken in columns 3, 4, and 5. In these regressions the omitted (comparison) group is *male* SWPAs. The uppermost three coefficients in each regression reflect the earnings gap between them and males who are members of the respective groups. The Female coefficient measures the gap between male and female SWPAs, and finally, the interactions with the female indicator estimate the gap between males and females in each of the other three immigration categories. Introducing the interactions reduces the magnitude of the first three coefficients compared to the regressions in the first set of columns, indicating that the gap between males across the classes is smaller than that when the sexes are combined. Of course, SWPAs are disproportionately male and Spouses disproportionately female, so the number of male spouses is small. Family Class males are also seen to have appreciably lower earnings than both Spouses and Other Spouses who are male.

In wave 1 the Female coefficient, measuring the gender gap among SWPAs, is appreciable, but the gap is eliminated by wave 3. It is plausible that female SWPAs are slower in obtaining employment initially, but there is no appreciable gender difference in earnings beyond the first wave. Of course, the selection process by which families choose the woman rather than the man to be the principal applicant plays a role since, as seen in Table 1, 82 percent of families choose the man. Male-female gaps for the other three groups are seen in the final three regression coefficients. For the Spouse*Female and Other Spouse*Female coefficients, the gap is appreciable and is roughly constant across the three waves of the survey, but the interaction coefficient for the Family Class increases after the first wave and becomes even larger as, apparently, the men in that class preferentially find employment.

Table 3 has exactly the same structure as Table 2 but looks at the marginal effects (evaluated at the mean values of the variables) of being employed, using probit regressions. The pattern in the first three columns is quite similar to that for earnings. For example, six months after landing, in wave 1, the Spouses have 28.5 percent lower probability of being employed than the SWPAs, but that probability remains approximately constant across time.

TABLE 3
Marginal Effects from Probit Estimates on Employment

	Wave 1	Wave 2	Wave 3	Wave 1	Wave 2	Wave 3
Spouses	-0.286***	-0.281***	-0.305***	-0.059	-0.079*	-0.144***
	[0.021]	[0.022]	[0.022]	[0.042]	[0.041]	[0.040]
Other spouses	-0.234***	-0.229***	-0.218***	-0.008	-0.051	-0.06
	[0.021]	[0.023]	[0.023]	[0.044]	[0.043]	[0.043]
Family class	-0.272***	-0.360***	-0.460***	-0.158***	-0.134**	-0.258***
	[0.031]	[0.039]	[0.038]	[0.050]	[0.057]	[0.058]
Female				-0.103**	-0.061*	-0.056
				[0.041]	[0.037]	[0.036]
Female x spouse				-0.205***	-0.175***	-0.120**
				[0.056]	[0.062]	[0.058]
Female x oth sp				-0.194***	-0.146**	-0.121*
				[0.058]	[0.064]	[0.064]
Female x family				-0.185**	-0.320***	-0.263***
				[0.073]	[0.089]	[0.090]
Observations	3,742	3,742	3,742	3,742	3,742	3,742

Notes: Sample restricted to households for which both spouse and respondent were age 19 to 62 at the time of the first wave. Robust standard errors in brackets.
* significant at 10 percent; ** significant at 5 percent; *** significant at 1 percent. All regressions include controls for months since migration.
Source: Authors' calculations.

Overall, for the SWPAs, gender is not predictive of labour market outcomes, but it is predictive for the other three groups, with women in the Family Class having the lowest outcomes (largest gaps) relative to the other groups. Also, though not proving either, these results are consistent with both the family investment hypothesis and the idea of tied mobility.

Regressions Addressing Immigration Category and Points

Extensions of Tables 2 and 3 are presented in Tables 4 and 5, where results from estimating equation (2) are presented for earnings and employment, respectively. These models introduce points, and points interacted with immigration class and gender, as regressors. Total immigration points is the summary measure of individual characteristics employed by the immigration system, and understanding that measure's relationship to outcomes is therefore valuable.

TABLE 4
OLS (ln) Weekly Earnings Regressions

	Wave 1	Wave 2	Wave 3	Wave 1	Wave 2	Wave 3
Spouses	2.834***	0.943	1.072	4.588***	1.451	2.049
	[0.847]	[0.802]	[0.822]	[1.456]	[1.261]	[1.373]
Other spouses	1.050	-0.551	-1.650**	4.213***	3.828***	2.189*
	[0.679]	[0.634]	[0.649]	[1.363]	[1.100]	[1.323]
Family class	3.073***	0.857	-0.178	4.676***	3.004***	1.446*
	[0.687]	[0.638]	[0.653]	[0.888]	[0.753]	[0.823]
Points/10	0.667***	0.396***	0.287***	0.734***	0.435***	0.307***
	[0.083]	[0.073]	[0.076]	[0.092]	[0.084]	[0.086]
Points/10 * spouse	-0.656***	-0.335***	-0.349***	-0.717***	-0.205	-0.356*
	[0.118]	[0.111]	[0.115]	[0.206]	[0.175]	[0.195]
Points/10 * oth sp	-0.306***	-0.044	0.134	-0.633***	-0.606***	-0.383*
	[0.098]	[0.091]	[0.094]	[0.200]	[0.168]	[0.198]
Points/10 * family	-0.665***	-0.246*	-0.206	-0.843***	-0.492***	-0.359**
	[0.132]	[0.132]	[0.134]	[0.177]	[0.141]	[0.165]
Female				1.808	1.082	0.570
				[1.438]	[1.245]	[1.349]
Female * spouses				-3.907*	-1.691	-1.850
				[2.037]	[1.799]	[1.951]
Female * oth sp				-4.690**	-5.501***	-4.567**
				[1.891]	[1.584]	[1.819]
Female * family				-3.412**	-3.605***	-2.499*
				[1.593]	[1.380]	[1.504]
Points/10 * female				-0.353*	-0.176	-0.085
				[0.203]	[0.174]	[0.189]
Points/10 * f * sp				0.400	0.013	0.105
				[0.289]	[0.251]	[0.276]
Points/10 *f*oth sp				0.586**	0.722***	0.615**
				[0.275]	[0.234]	[0.267]
Points/10 * f * fam				0.262	0.16	-0.019
				[0.281]	[0.257]	[0.269]
Observations	3,742	3,742	3,742	3,742	3,742	3,742
R-squared	0.10	0.07	0.07	0.13	0.11	0.09

Notes: Sample restricted to households for which both spouse and respondent were age 19 to 62 at the time of the first wave. Sample includes zero $ earners, with zero set to $1 prior to taking ln. Robust standard errors in brackets.
* significant at 10 percent; ** significant at 5 percent; *** significant at 1 percent. All regressions include controls for months since migration.
Source: Authors' calculations.

TABLE 5
Marginal Effects from Probit Estimates on Employment

	Wave 1	Wave 2	Wave 3	Wave 1	Wave 2	Wave 3
Spouses	0.341***	0.074	0.097	0.641***	0.119	0.261*
	[0.125]	[0.111]	[0.106]	[0.131]	[0.161]	[0.140]
Other spouses	-0.003	-0.169	-0.280*	0.514***	0.331***	0.218
	[0.124]	[0.120]	[0.144]	[0.152]	[0.108]	[0.148]
Family class	0.295***	-0.041	-0.119	0.443***	0.165***	0.071
	[0.085]	[0.114]	[0.145]	[0.054]	[0.057]	[0.096]
Points/10	0.088***	0.045***	0.037**	0.103***	0.050***	0.039**
	[0.015]	[0.013]	[0.015]	[0.017]	[0.015]	[0.016]
Points/10 * spouse	-0.093***	-0.048***	-0.052***	-0.122***	-0.029	-0.065**
	[0.021]	[0.017]	[0.017]	[0.036]	[0.027]	[0.031]
Points/10 * oth sp	-0.024	0.000	0.016	-0.085**	-0.072**	-0.048
	[0.018]	[0.015]	[0.016]	[0.035]	[0.030]	[0.035]
Points/10 * family	-0.088***	-0.022	-0.026	-0.120***	-0.052**	-0.041*
	[0.023]	[0.020]	[0.019]	[0.031]	[0.025]	[0.024]
Female				0.330	0.094	0.030
				[0.227]	[0.224]	[0.242]
Female * spouses				-0.677***	-0.179	-0.382
				[0.162]	[0.328]	[0.422]
Female * oth sp				-0.678***	-0.763***	-0.697**
				[0.135]	[0.214]	[0.343]
Female * family				-0.468***	-0.524*	-0.336
				[0.114]	[0.279]	[0.400]
Points/10 * female				-0.062*	-0.022	-0.012
				[0.035]	[0.031]	[0.034]
Points/10 * f * sp				0.091*	0.000	0.028
				[0.050]	[0.040]	[0.045]
Points/10 *f*oth sp				0.105**	0.087**	0.073
				[0.048]	[0.041]	[0.047]
Points/10 * f * fam				0.038	0.021	-0.006
				[0.053]	[0.042]	[0.042]
Observations	3,742	3,742	3,742	3,742	3,742	3,742

Notes: Sample restricted to households for which both spouse and respondent were age 19 to 62 at the time of the first wave. Robust standard errors in brackets.
* significant at 10 percent; ** significant at 5 percent; *** significant at 1 percent. All regressions include controls for months since migration.
Source: Authors' calculations.

In wave 1 of the first set of columns in Table 4, the coefficient on points, which is the rate of return in terms of earnings for SWPAs, is 6.7 percent (each additional point increases earnings by 6.7 percent). This implies that a shift from 20 points to 80 points (a quite large, but not unrealistic, increment as seen in Figure 1) would imply an approximately 400 percent increase in earnings. Given that the mean SWPA earnings seen in Table 1 are about 270 percent of the mean earnings for the Family Class, this ratio seems reasonable.

Spouses, who are assigned their partner's points, have an intercept term at wave 1 that is positive and statistically significant, but the coefficient on the interaction between points and Spouse is negative and roughly comparable to that for their partners. Since those groups with interaction terms have a total return to points that is the sum of the points coefficient and the coefficient representing the gap, this implies that Spouses have earnings that are completely unrelated to their SWPA partner's immigration points. However, their intercept is higher than that for the SWPAs. In contrast, for Other Spouses, where the points are their own, the intercept term is not statistically significant, and the rate of return to points is roughly half of that for SWPAs. For Family Class the rate of return on points is negative and almost exactly equal in magnitude to that of the SWPAs, suggesting that the net effect of points for the Family Class is zero, but the class has a positive and statistically significant intercept.

In subsequent waves, as time in Canada increases, the situation changes dramatically. First, the rate of return to points decreases by just under two-thirds, suggesting that some of the value of points lies in finding a (good) job quickly. Second, the intercept terms for Spouses, Other Spouses, and the Family Class all decrease in value. For the Spouses, and for the Family Class, they become statistically insignificantly different from zero, and for the Other Spouses the coefficient becomes negative and statistically significant. Moreover, the rate of return on points for the Other Spouses and the Family Class groups, where we can measure individual points, is not statistically different from that for the SWPAs. For the Spouses, to whom we assigned their partner's points, the rate of return on those points is negative, and the coefficient's point estimate is slightly larger than that for their partner, suggesting approximately zero relationship between their partner's points and their earnings, or that having a higher earning SWPA decreases the Spouses' earnings slightly.

The first three columns of Table 5, looking at employment, tell a similar story but one that is perhaps even stronger (more precise), since some of the statistically insignificant point estimates that were estimated imprecisely in the earnings regressions are both close to zero and have relatively small standard errors in this case, giving us confidence that the coefficients are actually close to zero rather than just being poorly estimated.

What does this all mean? It suggests that, where we can measure the points for the individual, the rate of return to characteristics is similar regardless of immigrant class. (The one caveat with this conclusion is, as mentioned, that some of the point estimates for the coefficients on the interaction terms for points in the earnings regressions are large and have large standard errors; thus it could be that more precise estimates from a larger sample would tell a slightly different story.) However, the intercepts for the Other Spouses in Tables 3 and 5 suggest less labour market activity than the SWPAs, which is consistent with the evidence in Table 1. Overall, the results also suggest that, at the level of the individual, a partner's points are not good predictors of spousal labour market outcomes. Of course, while the rates of return to points for individuals do not appear to differ across classes, the average level of points does. Further, in general, the magnitude of most of the coefficients diminishes appreciably across the waves as workers integrate in the economy.

Turning next to the fourth, fifth, and sixth columns of Table 4, where a gendered analysis is undertaken, we focus on the final column based on the data in wave 3 after four years in Canada. First, it is worth noting that for SWPAs the rate of return to points is not statistically significantly different by gender. Second, unlike SWPAs, it appears that male Spouses and Other Spouses and Family Class members have intercept terms indicating higher earnings than their female partners. Third, in terms of points, male members of the Family Class and spouses in both categories have a rate of return to points that is effectively zero. Female Other Spouses have a large and statistically significant return to points in excess of that for male SWPAs. The other two coefficients on points interactions are not statistically different from zero, indicating no difference from the males in those groups, which is to say approximately zero return to immigration points.

As was the case with the analysis that did not distinguish between genders in the first three columns of Tables 4 and 5, the employment regressions in the last three columns of Table 5 have a pattern that is mostly similar to that for earnings in Table 4. However, in terms of employment the Other Spouses do not appear to receive a benefit to their points above and beyond that for males, and their intercept term is not statistically different from zero.

CONCLUSION

Understanding the labour market implications of employing an immigration selection mechanism that, for families, chooses entire nuclear families by (almost exclusively) evaluating the characteristics of one family-selected member is the goal of this paper. In exploring this issue we compare labour market outcomes for four distinct groups: (1) skilled worker principal applicants (SWPAs), (2) their spouses (Spouses), (3) the spouses of other SWPAs not surveyed (Other Spouses), and (4) Family Class immigrants. In all cases we restrict the sample to individuals who enter as couples; for the Family Class this implies that the sample is composed of parents and grandparents of sponsors. For the first, third, and fourth groups we use each individual's own characteristics to impute immigration points, but for the second group, Spouses, we assign them those of their SWPA. Assigning points to Spouses accords with the central motivation of the paper: to explore the relationship between the SWPA's points and her/his spouse's outcomes. The Other Spouses and Family Class serve as comparison groups and allow us to examine the relationship between outcomes and each individual's own characteristics. In all cases the individual's own labour market outcomes are the focus of the analysis, and we analyze, first, weekly earnings, including in the sample respondents with no earnings, and, second, employment. If a policy decision were made to alter the relative magnitudes of the flow of Economic and Family Class immigrants to Canada, the trade-off would likely be between these (sub)groups since the other adult immigrants in Family Class are spouses and partners of sponsors, which is a group where the size of the flow is not particularly amenable to public policy.

What do we observe? First, as expected, there is clearly an integration process for all four groups, with both wages and employment rates generally increasing across the survey waves. However, the Family Class appears to plateau earlier than the others – at wave 2 after two years in Canada. Also, the Family Class appears to obtain, relative to their characteristics, labour market success slightly earlier than both groups of spouses.

Second, controlling for neither gender nor points (that is, looking at the gross outcomes of the system, which is arguably what we care about as the outcome of selection policy), SWPAs have much higher earnings than the spouses of that category – about 70 percent higher when the gap is at its smallest after four years, and the gap for the Family Class is even larger. Gaps in employment are comparably large. These results indicate that the immigration system is able to select SWPAs with much stronger labour market outcomes than these other groups. This is at odds with some interpretations of earlier evidence discussed in the literature review, which suggest that immigration categories are not associated with appreciable longer-term differences in labour market outcomes.

Third, when gender is taken into account, but with no controls for characteristics, no gender gap is observed among the SWPA group. Large gender gaps are, however, observed within both sets of spouses and the Family Class. Of course, only about 18 percent of SWPAs are women, and conversely a small fraction of spouses are men – the composition of these groups is far from random. Care is, therefore, needed in interpreting these findings since a disproportionate number of women with the highest earnings potential are in the SWPA category instead of the spousal one. It is difficult to distinguish between the family investment and tied mover hypotheses in the data, which have elements that are consistent with either or both. Perhaps most interesting is that the SWPAs find jobs more quickly than their spouses, and many have (as buried in the points system) pre-arranged employment, which does not "prove" the understudied tied mover hypothesis but is consistent with it. Members of the Family Class also find employment quite quickly, relatively speaking, presumably by using their sponsors' local knowledge.

Fourth, looking at gender once we control for characteristics as measured by points, we find that among principal applicants there is, as with the third point, still no male-female earnings or employment gaps by the third wave, although there is a gap at six months after landing.

Fifth, although the spouses of SWPAs are not assessed under the points system, their distribution of characteristics, as measured by the points index and as observed in the Other Spouses group, is associated with immigration points that look more like those of SWPAs than the subgroup of the Family Class studied here. This is clearly consistent with a role for positive assortative mating. The SWPAs and both sets of spouses have education levels that are dramatically above those for the existing Canadian population, and Canada is one of the most highly educated countries in the world. Those who enter in the skilled worker category, both principal applicants and spouses, have remarkably high levels of education. In this sense, the points system has both direct and indirect effects.

Sixth, for Spouses, the points of their SWPA partner have very little if any predictive power for their labour market outcomes (the slope coefficient on "points" is statistically indistinguishable from zero). The correlation between Spouses' labour market activities and their SWPA partners' points is, surprisingly, not very high. However, this suggests that, while at the level of the population there is a correlation between both the points and education of SWPAs and their spouses, it is not strong enough – or other phenomena are also at play – to influence the Spouse's individual labour market outcomes appreciably. We (and readers) can only speculate on the reasons for this observation, which hopefully will be the subject of future research. The finding, however, implies that Spouses do not do as well in the labour market as might be expected based on the simple correlation between their points and those of the SWPAs.

Seventh, in contrast to point 6, the data for the Other Spouses show that points derived from their own characteristics have substantial predictive power for labour market outcomes. Again, there is some evidence that Other Spouses do not do as well as might be expected given the points they are observed to have. This is consistent with the evidence obtained by Aydemir (forthcoming). However, while initially the spouses of SWPAs appear to have a lower rate of return on points than do the SWPAs, by the third wave there is no statistically significant difference.[10] Ignoring gender, the gap in total earnings between SWPAs and Other Spouses appears to result both from an intercept shift and a lower distribution of points for the latter, and not the rate of return to those points (value of each point). However, once gender is factored in, the situation is seen to be more complex. Male spouses have a zero (or negative) return to their characteristics as measured by points, but females have quite a high return. Consistent with the above-mentioned analysis ignoring points, Other Spouses have a large negative intercept term. In general, when spousal points can be observed for women, the pattern is that low-skilled women have very low earnings/employment compared to men, but their outcomes improve more quickly with increasing points as the gap diminishes with increasing skills (as measured by immigration points). In short, points matter more to women than to men, but women seem to start from a base position of lower labour market outcomes. It is not clear that we can distinguish between the various sources of gendered labour market outcome gaps discussed in the section on hypotheses regarding spousal/gendered gaps, and it is likely that more than one source is operating. However, we clearly need to distinguish between the rate of return to points (the slope) and the base from which women start (the intercept). It is the intercept that needs to be the focus of future research.

Eighth, as with the Other Spouses, we find evidence of a very substantial negative intercept shift for females in the Family Class group. For reasons unrelated to characteristics as captured in the immigration points, women appear to have lower earnings. However, in this case, unlike that for Other Spouses, there is no benefit to increasing points for women (or men) in the Family Class. Of course, very few in this category (male or female) have an appreciable number of points, and the average age in this group is much older than that for spouses. It is possible that at low levels of skills the rate of return is low because of the operation of minimum wage legislation and the like.

In sum, the points system does identify SWPAs with superior labour market outcomes among the groups studied. There is no statistically distinguishable difference in labour market outcomes between male and female SWPAs. Their spouses have points that are somewhat, but not dramatically, lower, and both SWPAs and their spouses have education levels that are remarkably high compared to the Canadian population. However, the outcomes of spouses do not appear to be quite as good as might be expected based on their characteristics as measured by the points system. This gap does not appear to derive from the economic rate of return to immigration points (the slope coefficient). Rather, the intercept is very large and negative, suggesting that spouses, and especially female spouses, start from a very low earnings and employment base.

Notes

We thank the Canadian Labour Market and Skills Researcher Network for funding aspects of this research under contract to Human Resources and Skills Development Canada (HRSDC). We would like to thank the following for helpful comments on this program of research: David Gray, Jennifer Hunt, Michael McCormick, Patrizio Piraino, one anonymous referee from the CLSRN, participants at the CLSRN 2007 Workshop on Immigration in Canada, the Metropolis Policy-Research Seminar on Temporary Migration at the University of Ottawa, and the 2008 Canadian Economic Association Meetings. While the research and analysis are based on data from Statistics Canada, the opinions expressed do not represent the views of Statistics Canada, and all errors are the authors' responsibility.

1. The remainder of the economic class comprised principal applicants, spouses, and dependants who were sub-categorized as either entrepreneurs, self-employed, investors, provincial/territorial nominees, or live-in caregivers. There are three major immigration classes – economic, family, and refugees – each of which has subclasses as well as a small "other" category. See CIC (2009) for further information; all statistics regarding the 2008 immigrant flows are from this source.

2. Note that we assign $1 only to allow the natural logarithm transformation to be applied as required for the regressions. This is a normalizing transformation to improve the regression's statistical properties, and it requires strictly positive inputs. Assigning individuals $1 is roughly equivalent to recognizing that they have zero earnings.

3. There is appreciable diversity in selecting the sample for analysis with respect to earnings. In stark contrast to our approach, Baker and Benjamin (1994) include only those who worked 40 or more weeks in the year, thereby focusing on those with substantial labour market success, which accords with their policy question, but this would be inappropriate for our approach.

4. For example, for an immigrant interviewed at cycle 1, we take an average of the CPI over his/her six month reference period.

5. While there is sufficient information for us to include the spouses of the SWPAs as observations in our analysis, the reverse is not possible, and the un-surveyed SWPAs associated with the SWPA spouses in the sample cannot be included in the analysis.

6. We exclude same-sex couples from this part of the analysis since there are too few observations to do separate analysis, and gays and lesbians are found to have very different labour market outcomes compared to heterosexuals in Canada (see Carpenter 2008, and LaFrance, Warman, and Woolley 2009). Also, although some questions about spouses are posed to survey respondents other than SWPAs, we do not include these other spousal groups since they are not relevant to our substantive question and/or insufficient information is collected to be useful.

7. We also re-estimate the results excluding the points that come from the spouse's adaptability, and given that only a small percent of the points come from the spouse, we find very similar results (for example, we excluded the points received for the spouse's Canadian education).

8.   We do not provide standard errors on these estimates from the Labour Force Survey; however, the sample size for the annual file is sufficiently large that the standard errors are extremely small.
9.   This formula is used since the coefficient is for an indicator (dummy) variable in a regression where the dependent variable is transformed using the natural logarithm.
10. Recall that the rate of return is, for earnings, the value of each additional point (percent increase in earnings for each additional point) and not the aggregate value of the total points of an individual. It is the slope of the relationship between earnings and points.

REFERENCES

Antecol, H. 2000. "An Examination of Cross-Country Differences in the Gender Gap in Labour Force Participation Rates." *Labour Economics* 7 (4): 409-26.
– 2003. "New Evidence on Culture and the Gender Wage Gap: A Comparison across Ethnic Origin Groups." *Research in Labour Economics* 22: 451-68.
Aydemir, A. Forthcoming. "Immigrant Selection and Short-Term Labour Market Outcomes by Visa Category." *Journal of Population Economics*.
Aydemir, A., and M. Skuterud. 2005. "Explaining the Deteriorating Entry Earnings of Canada's Immigrant Cohorts: 1966-2000." *Canadian Journal of Economics* 38 (2): 641-71.
Aydemir, A., and C. Robinson. 2008. "Global Labour Markets, Return and Onward Migration." *Canadian Journal of Economics* 41 (4): 1285-1311.
Baker, M., and D. Benjamin. 1994. "The Performance of Immigrants in the Canadian Labour Market." *Journal of Labour Economics* 12: 369-405.
– 1997. "The Role of the Family in Immigrants' Labour Market Activity: An Evaluation of Alternative Explanations." *American Economic Review* 87: 705-27.
Bloom, D.E., G. Grenier, and M. Gunderson. 1995. "The Changing Labour Market Position of Canadian Immigrants." *Canadian Journal of Economics* 28 (4b): 987-1005.
Carpenter, C. 2008. "Sexual Orientation, Work, and Income in Canada." *Canadian Journal of Economics* 41 (4): 1239-61.
Citizenship and Immigration Canada (CIC). 2009. *Facts and Figures 2008: Immigration Overview*. Minister of Public Works and Government Services Canada, No. Ci1-8/2008E-PDF.
De Silva, A. 1997. "Earnings of Immigrant Classes in the Early 1980s in Canada: A Reexamination." *Canadian Public Policy* 23: 179-99.
Dowhan, D.J., and H.O. Duleep. 2002. "Revisiting the Family Investment Model with Longitudinal Data: The Earnings Growth of Immigrant and U.S.-Born Women." IZA Working Paper No. 568.
Ferrer, A., and W.C. Riddell. 2008. "Education, Credentials and Immigrant Earnings." *Canadian Journal of Economics* 41 (1): 186-216.
Frenette, M., and R. Morissette. 2005. "Will They Ever Converge? Earnings of Immigrant and Canadian-Born Workers over the Last Two Decades." *International Migration Review* 39 (1): 228-57.
Grant, M.L. 1999. "Evidence of New Immigrant Assimilation in Canada." *Canadian Journal of Economics* 32 (4): 930-55.

Green, D.A., and C. Worswick. 2010. "Entry Earnings of Immigrant Men in Canada: The Roles of Labour Market Entry Effects and Returns to Foreign Experience." In *Canadian Immigration: Economic Evidence for a Dynamic Policy Environment*, edited by T. McDonald, E. Ruddick, A. Sweetman, and C.Worswick. Montreal and Kingston: Queen's Policy Studies Series, McGill-Queen's University Press.

Lafrance, A., C. Warman, and F. Woolley. 2009. "Sexual Identity and the Marriage Premium." Working Paper 1219, Department of Economics, Queen's University.

Loprest, P.J. 1992. "Gender Differences in Wage Growth and Job Mobility." *American Economic Review* 82 (2): 526-32.

Picot, G., and A. Sweetman. 2005. "The Deteriorating Economic Welfare of Immigrants and Possible Causes." Statistics Canada, Analytical Studies Research Paper No 262.

Picot, G., F. Hou, and S. Coulombe. 2007. "Chronic Low Income and Low-Income Dynamics among Recent Immigrants." Statistics Canada, Analytical Studies Research Paper No. 294.

Schaafsma, J., and A. Sweetman. 2001. "Immigrant Earnings: Age at Immigration Matters." *Canadian Journal of Economics* 34 (4): 1066-99.

Sweetman, A., and C. Warman. 2009. "Temporary Foreign Workers and Former International Students as a Source of Permanent Immigration." CLSRN Working Paper no. 25. At http://www.econ.ubc.ca/clsrn//workingpapers.php.

Warman, C.R. and C. Worswick. 2004. "Immigrant Earnings Performance in Canadian Cities: 1981 through 2001." *Canadian Journal of Urban Research* 13 (1): 62-84.

Worswick, C. 1996. "Immigrant Families in the Canadian Labour Market." *Canadian Public Policy* 22 (4): 378-96.

– 1999."Credit Constraints and the Labour Supply of Immigrant Families in Canada." *Canadian Journal of Economics* 32 (1): 152-70.

APPENDIX 1
IMPUTING POINTS

TABLE A1
Points Categories

Category	Maximum Points
Education	25
Language ability	24
Work experience	21
Age	10
Arranged employment	10
Adaptability	10
Total available points	100
Required for pass	67

Source: www.cic.gc.ca

Education: 6 categories for education (25, 22, 20, 15, 12, and 5 points with 0 points as the default).

Language ability: 24 categories for each of the possible points from language ability (ranging from 1 to 24 points with 0 points as the default).

Work experience: 4 categories for work experience (21, 19, 17 and 15 points with 0 points as the default).

Age: 5 categories for age (10, 8, 6, 4, and 2 points with 0 points as the default).

Arranged employment: 1 category for prearranged employment (10 points with 0 points as the default).

Adaptability: 6 categories for adaptability (10, 9, 8, 5, 4, and 3 points with 0 points as the default).

8

THE PORTABILITY OF HUMAN CAPITAL OF MALE TEMPORARY FOREIGN WORKERS: YOU CAN BRING IT WITH YOU

CASEY WARMAN

De nombreuses recherches ont montré que les revenus des immigrants récents dans plusieurs pays occidentaux se sont détériorés. L'une des principales causes de ce phénomène est la faible transférabilité du capital humain étranger; un autre facteur en jeu – tout particulièrement important au Canada – est la baisse du rendement à l'expérience étrangère. A partir de données provenant des Recensements du Canada, cette étude montre que, contrairement aux immigrants reçus, les travailleurs temporaires étrangers – y compris ceux qui viennent de pays d'origine non traditionnels (c'est-à-dire d'ailleurs que des États-Unis et d'Europe) – n'ont aucune difficulté à transférer leur capital humain étranger, et que le rendement à l'expérience de travail étrangère est très élevé. Ces résultats montrent qu'il est donc possible que le capital humain que des travailleurs étrangers ont acquis dans leur pays d'origine soit reconnu sur le marché du travail canadien.

A large body of research has found that the earning outcomes of recent immigrants have worsened in many western countries. The lack of portability of foreign human capital has been shown to be one of the main causes, with the fall in the returns to foreign work experience being particularly important in Canada. Using Canadian Census data, this study finds that, unlike recently landed immigrants, temporary foreign workers face no difficulty transferring their foreign human capital and, in particular, obtain very high returns to their foreign work experience. This is also true for temporary foreign born workers from non-traditional countries of origin. This demonstrates that it is possible for foreign born workers to obtain recognition for their foreign acquired human capital in the Canadian labour market.

Canadian Immigration: Economic Evidence for a Dynamic Policy Environment, ed. T. McDonald, E. Ruddick, A. Sweetman, and C. Worswick. Montreal and Kingston: Queen's Policy Studies Series, McGill-Queen's University Press.

INTRODUCTION

Many developed countries are becoming more reliant on immigrants to meet labour shortages due mainly to an aging workforce. However, despite this apparent demand, most research has found deteriorating labour market outcomes for immigrants over the past several decades. One of the difficulties recent immigrant cohorts have encountered is the lack of portability of the human capital they acquired prior to immigrating. For example, Friedberg (2000) finds that the earnings disadvantage encountered by immigrants relative to the domestic born in Israel can be fully explained by the low returns to foreign education and foreign work experience.

In Canada, while returns to foreign acquired education are often found to be lower than for Canadian acquired education, these returns have been relatively steady over the period in which immigrant outcomes have been declining.[1] Instead, one of the main causes of the deterioration in labour market outcomes of recent immigrant cohorts has been the fall in returns to their foreign work experience. Aydemir and Skuterud (2005) find that in Canada, between one-quarter to one-half of the fall in entry earnings is due to the decline in the returns to foreign work experience. While there has been extensive research into immigrant outcomes, little is known about another group of foreign born workers in Canada, namely, temporary foreign workers (TFWs).

This study compares the returns to foreign human capital of male recently landed immigrants and male temporary foreign workers.[2] Starting in 1991, the Canadian Census began to include information allowing for the identification of temporary residents, thus making this analysis possible. One might expect TFWs not to encounter the same difficulties in receiving returns to their foreign human capital; while immigrants are selected by the government through broad policies designed to target both economic and social goals, the TFW program is driven by employers, who are likely better able to assess the transferability of the worker's skills to the Canadian labour market. Although the immigration and temporary foreign worker systems addressed in this study are particular to Canada, the comparison of immigrants with TFWs provides an unmatched opportunity to obtain further understanding of the portability of immigrants' foreign human capital. As well, given the recent introduction of the Canadian Experience Class, under which some former TFWs and former international students who meet certain criteria are able to immigrate to Canada, understanding the economic outcomes of TFWs is even more important.

Results from this paper show, similar to previous research, that recently landed immigrants receive no returns to their foreign work experience; conversely, TFWs appear to receive a large positive return. In addition, while immigrants do receive positive returns to years of foreign schooling, TFWs receive higher returns. More importantly, TFWs from non-traditional countries of origin receive high returns to both their foreign experience and foreign education. This demonstrates that it is possible for foreign born workers to obtain recognition for their foreign acquired human capital in the Canadian labour market, even if they come from non-traditional backgrounds.

RETURNS TO FOREIGN WORK EXPERIENCE AND FOREIGN
EDUCATION LITERATURE

As with research in the United States (Borjas 1985, 1995; Lubotsky 2007) where declining labour market outcomes of immigrant cohorts are found, research in Canada overwhelmingly indicates that entry earnings of successive cohorts have fallen over the past several decades. Immigrant entry earnings fell during the 1980s (Baker and Benjamin 1994; Bloom, Grenier, and Gunderson 1995) and continued to fall during the 1990s (Warman and Worswick 2004; Frenette and Morissette 2005; Aydemir and Skuterud 2005) and in the first half of the 2000s (Picot, Hou, and Coulombe 2008). One of the main causes for this decline has been the difficulty immigrants in Canada have encountered in receiving returns to their foreign work experience.

Evidence suggests that foreign work experience is heavily discounted for immigrants in this country. Schaafsma and Sweetman (2001) find that foreign work experience renders virtually no returns in Canada. Further, using the 1981 through 2001 Canadian Census data, Aydemir and Skuterud (2005) find that there has been a large decline in the returns to foreign work experience. Green and Worswick (2004) similarly find that the returns to foreign experience fell for immigrants entering during the 1990s relative to the 1980s cohorts.

While immigrants and the Canadian born receive very similar returns to education obtained in Canada, immigrants receive a lower return to years of foreign education (Schaafsma and Sweetman 2001). The results found by Ferrer, Green, and Riddell (2006) reveal that foreign universities generate less usable literacy skills, and this can help explain the lower returns to foreign education. Sweetman (2004) also finds that lower school quality of the sending country (based on test scores from international literacy and numeracy surveys) is associated with the lower returns. However, there does not appear to be any fall in these returns over the period in which immigrant entry earnings have fallen (Aydemir and Skuterud 2005).

Despite some evidence that the lower returns to foreign *education* can be attributed to quality differences between Canada and the source country, it would appear more difficult to pin down the reasons for the lower returns to foreign work *experience*. For example, while differences in usable language ability can account for much of the lower returns to foreign acquired university education relative to that acquired in Canada, Ferrer, Green, and Riddell (2006) do not find any relationship between language ability and the low returns to foreign work experience. Goldmann, Sweetman, and Warman (2009) take another approach, examining the role that matching between source country and Canadian occupation plays in the economic outcomes of immigrants in the first four years after landing. Potentially, the lower returns to foreign experience could be attributable to a mismatch between the work experience in the source country and the job performed in Canada. Although Goldmann, Sweetman, and Warman (2009) find that immigrants who obtain a successful match achieve much higher earnings than do immigrants who fail to match, they find that, regardless, immigrants receive no returns to their years of potential foreign work experience. This is surprising, since it would be expected that immigrants who obtain a successful match would possess higher quality foreign work experience and therefore would experience some benefit to additional years of work experience, especially relative to immigrants not working in the same type of occupation as the last job they performed prior to immigrating.

In addition to the recent large change in source regions and the resulting poorer language ability, and the worsening conditions experienced by all new entrants in Canada, the selection process of economic immigrants has seen changes over the period in which overall immigrants' entry outcomes have deteriorated. Beach, Green, and Worswick (2006) note "a major change in the point system ... away from specific occupational preferences and towards broader emphasis on educational credentials, language facility and young families, again with an eye to human capital and skills development of the host country." One potential consequence of moving toward a system that does not put much emphasis on the demand for specific skills in the labour market is that even if immigrants enter Canada with a high level of human capital in terms of education and work experience, there is no guarantee that their skills will be useful or in demand in the Canadian labour market.

TFWs should not experience the same difficulty in receiving returns to their foreign human capital that has been experienced by immigrants. TFWs are chosen by employers, leading to a two-way selection process in which, in addition to the employer choosing the TFW, the TFW must decide to come to Canada to work in the occupation. Despite the long history of the TFW program in Canada, there is very little empirical evidence on the economic outcomes of TFWs in Canada.[3] Sweetman and Warman (2009) examine the entry outcomes of immigrants who had been in Canada on either a work or student permit prior to immigration relative to immigrants without any pre-immigration Canadian human capital. They find that TFWs who immigrated to Canada had superior outcomes in terms of both earnings and employment.

BRIEF DESCRIPTION OF IMMIGRANT AND TFW PROGRAMS IN CANADA

In Canada, immigrants enter under three main classes: humanitarian, family, and economic. Only immigrants entering under the economic class are evaluated based on their labour market skills under the points system.[4] Starting in the mid-1990s, the proportion of immigrants who entered under the economic class increased, and a large emphasis was placed on education. Yet these changes did little to reverse the poor entry outcomes of immigrants. Immigrants entering through the points system receive points for their education, work experience, and other skills that should help them integrate into the Canadian economy. Currently, immigrants can receive a maximum of 25 points for education and 21 points for work experience out of a required 67 points for a pass. However, insufficient consideration is given to how these skills will be valued by employers in the Canadian labour market. As well, immigrants in the other two main classes, family and humanitarian, are not evaluated based on skills. They are admitted to Canada not under economic considerations but according to social objectives, even though most of these immigrants will enter the labour market.

TFWs are usually brought in for economic reasons to fill short-term labour shortages and make the economy work more efficiently. The TFW program is actually a group of programs, although under each program the TFWs are selected by employers. The main group of TFWs are high-skilled workers who are brought in to fill gaps where the Canadian labour force temporarily lacks necessary skills.[5] To enter under the high-skilled TFW program, a worker normally must have a job offer. The employer has to prove to Human Resources and Skills Development Canada (HRSDC) that there is a labour market shortage for the job that they are bringing in the TFW to fill, or that bringing in the worker will provide a positive benefit to Canada. If HRSDC gives a positive labour market opinion (LMO), the employer is allowed to hire the worker, and then the worker normally must apply to Citizenship and Immigration Canada (CIC) for a work permit.[6]

High-skilled workers can also enter under trade agreements such as the North American Free Trade Agreement and the General Agreement on Tariffs and Trades. However, these workers are unlikely to show up in the Canadian Census population since they are often considered to be visitors.[7] There are also programs to bring in less-skilled workers to perform jobs that Canadians will not do, at least not at the going wage;[8] these include the Live-in-Care-Givers program and the Seasonal Agricultural Workers Program (SAWP).[9] Under SAWP, which began in 1966, employers could annually bring in agricultural workers. In 1981, then called the Foreign Domestic Workers Program, the Live-in-Care-Givers program (as of 1992) formalized the TFW process for domestic workers.[10]

Starting in September 2008, a new class was introduced that created a bridge between the TFW program and the immigration program. With the introduction of the Canadian Experience Class, high-skilled TFWs can now gain permanent resident status relatively quickly, and within Canada.[11] Under this program, TFWs require at least 24 months of work experience in Canada over a 36 month period just prior to making the application, and the work experience needs to be in a managerial or professional occupation (National Occupational Classification O or A) or in technical occupations and skilled trades (NOC B). As well, they need a minimum level of language ability that depends on the occupation in which the work experience was acquired.[12]

DATA AND METHODOLOGY

The 1991, 1996, and 2001 Canadian Census Master Microdata Files are used.[13] The Census gives a sample of the May stock of TFWs who were in Canada for at least a portion of the previous year. Log weekly earnings from wages and salaries are used as the dependent variable and are converted into real terms using the Canadian Consumer Price Index, with 2000 as the base year. Weekly earnings are calculated by dividing total wages and salaries earned in the reference year by the number of weeks worked. Only male respondents aged 30-64 who are not in school full time and who have positive earnings from wages and salaries are used. The lower part of the age restriction is used to ensure that the education obtained is from the sending country. The sample is examined for people with at most 30 years of schooling and at most 45 years of potential experience, since there are few individuals above these thresholds.

In the Census, TFWs are part of the non-permanent resident population, which also includes students and refugee claimants.[14] The non-permanent resident category does not differentiate as to the type of non-permanent resident to which the respondent belongs. While students are removed, the sample still contains refugee claimants.[15] However, Schellenberg (2001) finds that 60 to 70 percent of inland determination refugee claimants who were authorized to work did not receive a wage or salary. As previously discussed, temporary residents can work under a wide range of possible programs as a TFW in Canada, and the type of program that the TFW entered under is not identified in the Census data.

The analysis is restricted to foreign born workers who are either TFWs or recently landed immigrants. Only recently landed immigrants will have encountered the same entry conditions and will have been in Canada a similar length of time as the TFWs. The immigrant cohorts analyzed are the 1986-90 cohort for the 1991 Census, the 1991-95 cohort for the 1996 Census, and the 1996-2000 cohort for the 2001 Census. The choice of immigrant cohorts minimizes any difference in the time in Canada for the immigrants and TFWs. Given that the two variables of interest are returns to foreign work experience and returns to foreign schooling, the Canadian born are not examined in this study.

While restricting the sample to recently landed immigrants helps to reduce differences in the duration in Canada, it does not fully control for possible differences among these two groups or allow one to fully differentiate between domestic and foreign work experience. The master files give the precise year of immigration, and many studies have used year of immigration to try to differentiate between domestic and foreign work experience and schooling. However, since it is possible for immigrants to live in Canada prior to obtaining immigration status, an error in estimating variables based on year of immigration to Canada still exists. While information on year of entry into Canada is not available, the Census has information on the place of residence five years prior to the Census date.[16] Table 1 displays this information for immigrants and TFWs. Many of the immigrants lived in Canada five years prior to the Census date. For example, 20 percent of the 1995 immigrant cohort and almost half of the 1992 immigrant cohort were present in Canada in May 1991. Given that the year of entry into Canada may be inaccurately measured, it becomes difficult to fully differentiate between Canadian and foreign experience and schooling. Therefore, studies using age at immigration to differentiate between Canadian and foreign experience and education may be incorrectly attributing as foreign human capital that was actually obtained in Canada.

It is equally or maybe even more difficult to determine when TFWs entered the country. While it is possible to get a sense of how long immigrants have been in Canada based on the year of immigration, the same information does not exist for TFWs. Table 1 indicates that between 31 and 39 percent of male TFWs were present in Canada five years prior to the Census. Therefore, to equalize years in Canada, all workers who were

TABLE 1
Proportion Living in Canada Five Years Prior to the Census Survey Date

	1991	*1996*	*2001*
Temporary foreign workers	31.26	39.25	35.62
Immigrants who immigrated between four years and one year prior	18.19	32.04	20.22
Immigrated four years prior	33.57	48.47	28.97
Immigrated three years prior	14.21	29.42	20.91
Immigrated two years prior	13.01	20.42	15.40
Immigrated one year prior	12.26	20.83	12.74

Note: Samples are restricted to foreign born males aged 30 to 64 who are not in school full time and have positive earnings from wage and salaries.

Source: Author's compilation from the 1991, 1996, and 2001 Canadian Census Master Microdata Files.

in Canada five years prior to the Census enumeration are removed. This will also likely further remove any refugees from the non-permanent resident population.

The actual measure of labour market experience is not given in the Census. Instead, potential experience is measured by age minus total years of school minus six. While the estimate of experience is likely measured with error, Drolet (2002), using the Canadian Survey of Labour and Income Dynamics (SLID), finds that the amount of labour market experience for females is particularly overstated by proxy measures of experience. Hum and Simpson (2004), also using the SLID, find that the simple correlation between actual and potential experience is 49.7 percent for female immigrants and 82.2 percent for male immigrants. Due to the large measurement error that has been found using potential experience for females, the sample is restricted to males.

To differentiate between domestic and foreign years of work experience, it is typical to subtract years in the host country from total years of experience to obtain an estimate of host country experience. As just discussed, it is possible for the immigrant to be in the country prior to the date of immigration, and the date of entry is not given for the TFW. Therefore, it is not possible to determine how much of a worker's experience is foreign and how much is domestic. However, given that the sample is restricted to foreign born workers who were not in the country four years prior to the reference year, the amount of Canadian experience is minimal, with the maximum years of Canadian work experience being four (or more precisely three years and seven and half months).[17] Therefore, given the negligible number of possible years of Canadian work experience, *total experience* and *foreign experience* are used interchangeably.

The returns to schooling and experience are examined using the following equation:

$$\ln W_i = \beta X_i + \delta_1 S_i + \delta_2 EXP_i + \delta_3 EXP_i^2 + u_i \tag{1}$$

where S_i represents years of foreign schooling and EXP_i represents years of potential work experience. The matrix X includes a visible minority dummy, seven region of origin categories (United States (omitted category), Central/South America or Caribbean, West/South/North Europe, East Europe, Africa, or Middle East, Asia, and Oceania or other), three mother tongue categories (English (omitted category), French, and other language), eight region of residence categories (Atlantic provinces, Montreal, the rest of Quebec, Toronto (omitted category), the rest of Ontario, the Prairies, Vancouver, the rest of British Columbia), three categories controlling for the size of the population of the place residence (100,000 + (omitted category), 10,000 to 100,000, and less than 10,000) and a married dummy. The sample means are presented in Table 2.

TABLE 2
Sample Means

	Recently Landed Immigrants	Temporary Foreign Workers
Age	39.194	38.843***
Years of schooling	15.045	15.428***
% 12 years or less	0.246	0.232**
% 18 years or greater	0.244	0.301***
Years of experience	18.149	17.415***
Married	0.852	0.779***
Visible minority	0.680	0.547***
United States	0.021	0.159***
Central/South America	0.084	0.126***
West/South/North Europe	0.151	0.205***
Eastern Europe	0.121	0.054***
Africa/Middle East	0.121	0.141***
Asia	0.498	0.310***
Other	0.004	0.005
Atlantic	0.010	0.024***
Quebec (excluding Montreal)	0.011	0.019***
Montreal	0.097	0.164***
Ontario (excluding Toronto)	0.127	0.145***
Toronto	0.459	0.409***
Prairies	0.108	0.104
British Columbia (excluding Van.)	0.022	0.023
Vancouver	0.166	0.113***

Notes: Samples are restricted to male foreign born workers aged 30 to 64 who have been living in Canada less than four years who are not in school full time and who have positive earnings from wage and salaries.
Statistical difference between means: * significant at 10 percent; ** significant at 5 percent; *** significant at 1 percent.
Source: Author's compilation from the 1991, 1996, and 2001 Canadian Census Master Microdata Files.

While the polynomial expression is included in equation (1) to capture the possible non-linearity of labour market experience, it has been found that the quadratic model may not give representative estimates of the returns to experience (Murphy and Welch 1990; Horowitz 2000). Although most of the literature only uses a quadratic model to capture the non-linearity in the experience-earnings profile, a cubic estimator is also used to see if this higher order polynomial is able to capture some of the non-linearity that the quadratic model may not uncover. As well, the returns to experience are also estimated nonparametrically using a partial linear regression model to avoid any potential specification error. Partial linear models estimate part of the model nonparametrically, while the rest of the variables in the model are estimated parametrically:

$$\ln W_i = \beta X_i + \delta_1 S_i + f(EXP_i) + u_i \tag{2}$$

The method suggested by Robinson (1988) is used to estimate equation (2). The first step involves removing the effect of EXP_i by running non-parametric regressions on $\ln W_i$ and each of the independent variables separately. Then a regression is run to obtain the parametric estimates using the residual from these nonparametric regressions, and is estimated by:

$$\ln W_i - E(\ln W_i \mid EXP_i) = (X_i - E(X_i \mid EXP_i))\beta + (S_i - E(S_i \mid EXP_i))\delta_1 + v_i \tag{3}$$

where $E(\ln W_i \mid EXP_i)$, $E(X_i \mid EXP_i)$ and $E(S_i \mid EXP_i)$ are estimated by non-parametric regressions. A nonparametric regression is then estimated on $\ln W_i$ after the parametric effects have been removed. This method proposed by Robinson is referred to as the *double-residual* estimator in the remainder of the paper.

It is likely that the returns to work experience will vary with years of schooling, and therefore the relationship between experience and years of schooling is also investigated. Equation (4) allows for both years of experience and years of schooling to enter nonparametrically:

$$\ln W_i = \beta X_i + f(EXP_i, S_i) + u_i \tag{4}$$

The double-residual technique is again used to calculate equation (4), where the procedure is similar to that outlined when only one variable enters nonparametrically. The nonparametric effects of experience and years of schooling are jointly removed from the dependent variable and each of the independent variables using nonparametric regressions.[18] Then the parametric regression is estimated on the residual from the nonparametric regressions. Finally, a nonparametric regression is estimated using the residual of the parametric regression.

Empirical Results

Sample Characteristics

Before comparing the returns to foreign schooling and experience between TFWs and recently landed immigrants, it is important to get a sense of how similar these two groups are, at least in terms of observable characteristics. Sample means are presented in Table 2. While the differences in age, years of schooling, and years of potential work experience are all statistically significant, the magnitudes of these differences are not large. The average age is very similar for both groups (around 39 years), although immigrants have around half of a year more potential labour market experience and have slightly less schooling. However, the distributions of schooling are different. While immigrants and TFWs have a similar proportion with 12 years or less of schooling, 30 percent of TFWs have 18 years of schooling or more compared to 24 percent of immigrants.

There are large differences in the proportion that are married, with TFWs being much less likely to be married. Immigrants are also more likely than TFWs to be a visible minority (the difference is around 13 percentage points). TFWs are much more likely to be born in the United States or come from Western, Southern, or Northern Europe. Looking at the workers from the non-traditional sending regions, TFWs are more likely than recently landed immigrants to come from Central and South America or Africa and the Middle East but are much less likely to come from Asia. There is a fairly even breakdown in the residential settling patterns between the two groups. The only notable differences are that TFWs are around 5 percentage points less likely than recently landed immigrants to live in Toronto, but are more likely to live in Montreal.

Returns to Experience and Schooling with Experience Entering Nonlinearly

The results for total years of schooling for equations (1) and (3) are displayed in section 1 of Table 3. Both TFWs and immigrants receive positive returns to schooling, with an extra year of school increasing weekly earnings 6 and 4 percent, respectively.[19] It is worth noting that the double-residual and quadratic models yield very similar estimates of the parametric returns to foreign schooling. As well, the estimates of the other parameters were also very similar between the two models.[20]

The experience-earnings profiles are plotted in the upper portion of Figure 1. The corresponding returns for each additional year of experience ($d(E(lnW_i \mid EXP_i))/dEXP_i$) are displayed in the lower portion of Figure 1. It is clear that the recently landed immigrants receive no returns for their labour market experience when first entering Canada. Conversely, the TFWs receive a very high premium for their potential labour market experience. Looking at the upper left-hand graph of Figure 1, the experience-earnings profile is decreasing over the majority of the experience profile for the immigrant sample. This is related to the finding by Schaafsma and Sweetman (2001) that immigrants who arrive at an older age have worse earnings outcomes. The bottom left-hand graph of Figure 1 shows that the returns for an additional year of experience are slightly negative throughout the majority of the distribution.

We might expect foreign born workers who are more similar to the host country population in terms of language and culture to encounter less difficulty transferring their foreign acquired human capital. Aydemir and Skuterud (2005) find that while male immigrant cohorts from western countries endured a modest fall in the returns to foreign work experience between the late 1960s and 1990s, recent cohorts still obtained positive

TABLE 3
Returns to Foreign Experience and Foreign Schooling

	Recently Landed Immigrants		Temporary Foreign Workers	
	Quadratic	Double Residual	Quadratic	Double Residual
1: Full sample				
Experience	-0.004*		0.058***	
	[0.002]		[0.006]	
Experience squared/100	-0.004		-0.104***	
	[0.005]		[0.014]	
Years of schooling	0.038***	0.038***	0.058***	0.060***
	[0.002]	[0.002]	[0.004]	[0.004]
Observations	41,710	41,710	8,396	8,396
R-squared	0.09	0.07	0.23	0.23
2: Non-traditional immigrants[a]				
Experience	-0.012***		0.030***	
	[0.003]		[0.011]	
Experience squared/100	0.011*		-0.044*	
	[0.006]		[0.024]	
Years of schooling	0.033***	0.033***	0.063***	0.063***
	[0.002]	[0.002]	[0.008]	[0.008]
Observations	24,800	24,800	3,633	3,633
R-squared	0.07	0.05	0.10	0.10
3: Traditional-immigrants[b]				
Experience	0.043***		0.073***	
	[0.008]		[0.011]	
Experience squared/100	-0.091***		-0.129***	
	[0.021]		[0.027]	
Years of schooling	0.078***	0.080***	0.028***	0.028***
	[0.005]	[0.005]	[0.008]	[0.008]
Observations	3,829	3,829	2,181	2,181
R-squared	0.14	0.14	0.16	0.11

Notes: [a] Visible minorities with neither English/French as mother tongue from non-western countries; [b] Non-visible minorities with either English/French as their mother tongue from western countries.

See Figure 1 for corresponding plots of returns to experience for section 1 of this table. See Figure 2 for corresponding plots of returns to experience for section 2. See Figure 3 for corresponding plots of returns to experience for section 3. Samples are restricted to foreign born males aged 30 to 64 who have been living in Canada less than four years, are not in school full time, and have positive earnings from wage and salaries. Regressions also control for year, population size of place of residence, region of residence, region of origin, marital status, and language. Robust standard errors are in brackets.

* significant at 10 percent; ** significant at 5 percent; *** significant at 1 percent.

Source: Author's compilation from the 1991, 1996, and 2001 Canadian Census Master Microdata Files.

FIGURE 1
Full Sample

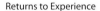

Returns to Experience

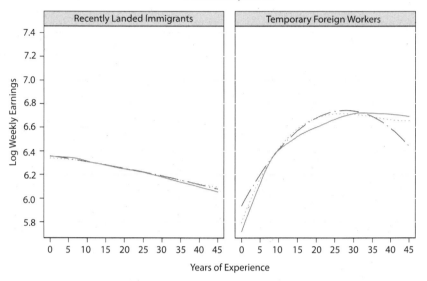

Returns to an Additional Year of Experience

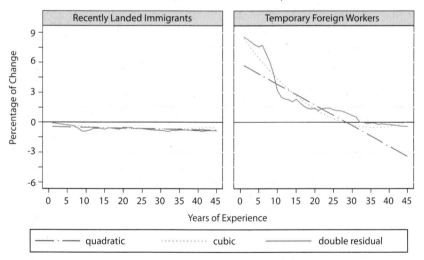

Notes: Samples are restricted to foreign born males aged 30 to 64 who have been living in Canada less than four years, are not in school full time, and have positive earnings from wages and salaries. Model also includes controls for years of schooling, region of birth, region of residence, population size of place of residence, marital status, mother tongue, and visible minority status.

Source: Author's compilation from the 1991, 1996, and 2001 Canadian Census Master Microdata Files.

returns. Conversely, immigrant cohorts from non-western countries saw a larger fall in the returns to foreign work experience, and the 1990s cohorts received no returns to their foreign work experience.

With this in mind, the results in section 1 of Table 3 are re-estimated looking at both foreign born workers who are similar to the host country population and those who are dissimilar. The similar group is defined as workers who speak either English or French, come from a western country (Western Europe, United States, Australia, and New Zealand), and are not a visible minority. The non-similar immigrant group is defined as workers who do not speak English or French, come from a non-western country (Eastern Europe, Asia, Middle East, Africa, South America, or Central America), and are a visible minority. This estimation also allows us to explore if the better outcomes in returns to work experience for TFWs over immigrants are simply due to the TFW program selecting a higher proportion of workers from backgrounds more similar to the host country, or if the higher returns exist within groups.

The results for the sample that is dissimilar to the Canadian population are shown in section 2 of Table 3 and in Figure 2. The returns to schooling are higher for TFWs than immigrants, with the return for an extra year of schooling around 3 percentage points higher for TFWs (see right-hand side of section 2 of Table 3). For recently landed immigrants, the experience-earnings profile has a linear form and trends downward (see upper left graph of Figure 2), and each additional year of experience decreases weekly earnings slightly (see lower left graph of Figure 2). For TFWs, the experience-earnings profile is very steep until around 10 years of experience, and then it flattens out but remains upward sloping throughout the range. In the lower right graph in Figure 2, the double-residual estimate shows that TFWs receive around a 4 percent increase for an additional year of experience for each of the first several years of experience, but a decline with higher levels of experience.

Surprisingly, for the sample that is similar to the Canadian population, TFWs receive lower returns to schooling than do immigrants, with returns to a year of schooling of 3 and 8 percent, respectively (see section 2 of Table 3). This is probably because, unlike what was found for the full sample in Table 2, there are not many TFWs from this group with few years of school, so if the returns to schooling are non-linear, the school-earnings profile is being estimated largely over the part where it flattens out.[21] Restricting the sample to workers with 20 years of schooling or less, the returns to schooling are much closer, with returns of 6.6 percent for TFWs and 8.3 percent for immigrants. The possible non-linearity of schooling is investigated in the next section, where both schooling and experience are estimated nonparametrically. The experience-earnings profiles are very similar for immigrants and TFWs (Figure 3). Both experience-earnings profiles resemble quadratic returns to experience. However, the profile for the immigrants does hit a maximum several years earlier than that for the TFWs, at around 22 years and 30 years respectively.

FIGURE 2
Visible Minorities with Neither English/French as Mother Tongue from Non-Western Countries

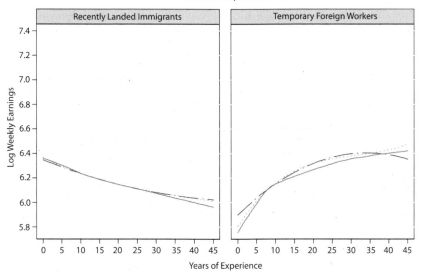

Returns to Experience

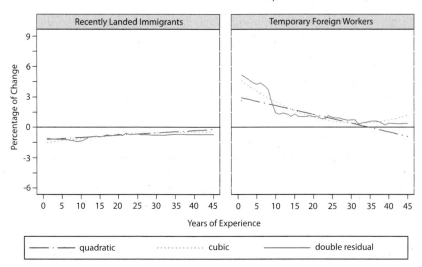

Returns to an Additional Year of Experience

Notes: Samples are restricted to foreign born males aged 30 to 64 who have been living in Canada less than four years, are not in school full time, and have positive earnings from wages and salaries. Model also includes controls for years of schooling, region of birth, region of residence, population size of place of residence, and marital status.

Source: Author's compilation from the 1991, 1996, and 2001 Canadian Census Master Microdata Files.

FIGURE 3
Non-Visible Minorities with Either English/French as Their Mother Tongue from Western Countries

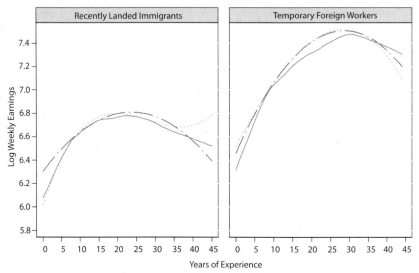

Returns to Experience

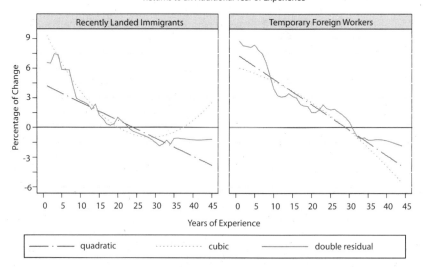

Returns to an Additional Year of Experience

Notes: Samples are restricted to foreign born males aged 30 to 64 who have been living in Canada less than four years, are not in school full time, and have positive earnings from wages and salaries. Model also includes controls for years of schooling, region of birth, region of residence, population size of place of residence, and marital status.

Source: Author's compilation from the 1991, 1996, and 2001 Canadian Census Master Microdata Files.

Experience and Years of Schooling Both Entering Nonparametrically

The nonparametric estimates of the returns to experience and schooling for the full sample are presented in Figure 4. Allowing schooling to enter nonparametrically allows for the possibility that the returns to schooling are non-linear. As well, allowing experience and schooling to enter multiplicatively allows us to explore how the returns to work experience vary for different levels of schooling. For recently landed immigrants, there is a positive return to schooling for workers in the low and mid years of the experience profile, but little return to schooling in the upper years of experience. Further, there are no returns to experience, with earnings actually falling with years of experience. This result is consistent across the different levels of schooling. For TFWs, additional schooling causes a large increase in log weekly earnings throughout the experience profile, especially for the middle years of schooling (10 ≤ years of schooling ≤ 20). There are little returns to experience for TFWs with few years of schooling, with the returns actually being negative in the upper years of the experience profile. However, there are positive returns for the first 20 years of experience for those in upper range of years of schooling.

The results for the visible minority immigrants with neither English nor French as their mother tongue from non-western countries (see Figure 5) are similar to the overall results for immigrants.[22] While the recently landed immigrants enjoy positive returns to schooling, they encounter no returns to experience at low levels of schooling and negative returns at mid and high levels of schooling. TFWs do not encounter the same fall in earnings as experience increases. Further, they encounter very high returns to schooling throughout the experience profile.

Figure 6 displays the results for non-visible minority foreign born workers with either English or French as their mother tongue from a western country. For the TFWs, there are large returns to experience in the mid portion of the schooling profile. For those with a low level of schooling, there is less of a return to experience. However, little emphasis should be placed on the results for less than 10 years of schooling for this group, since there are few TFWs from this subset in this range. There are also high returns to extra schooling from around 10 years to 20 years of schooling throughout most of the experience profile, after which there are actually negative returns. For the recently landed immigrants (lower graph of Figure 6), there are large returns to experience in the mid and upper portion of the schooling profile. As was seen in Figure 3, the experience-earnings profile flattens earlier for the immigrants than for the TFWs, although the opposite is true for years of schooling.

FIGURE 4
Returns to Foreign Experience and Foreign Schooling, Full Sample

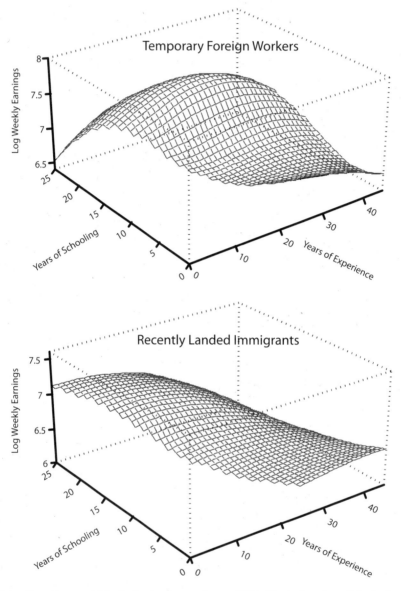

Notes: Samples are restricted to foreign born males aged 30 to 64 who have been living in Canada less than four years, are not in school full time, and have positive earnings from wages and salaries. Model also includes controls for region of birth, region of residence, population size of place of residence, marital status, mother tongue, and visible minority status.

Source: Author's compilation from the 1991, 1996, and 2001 Canadian Census Master Microdata Files.

FIGURE 5
Returns to Foreign Experience and Foreign Schooling, Visible Minorities with Neither English/French as Mother Tongue from Non-Western Countries

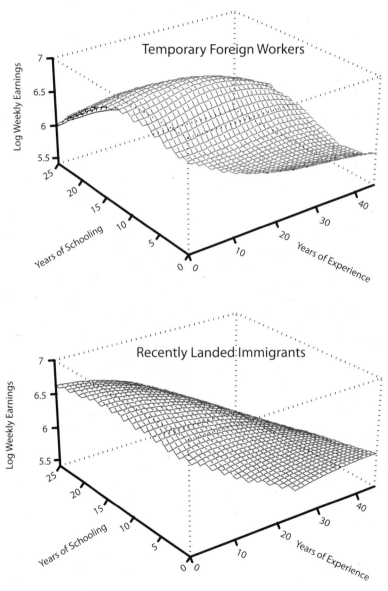

Notes: Samples are restricted to foreign born males aged 30 to 64 who have been living in Canada less than four years, are not in school full time, and have positive earnings from wages and salaries. Model also includes controls for region of birth, region of residence, population size of place of residence, and marital status.

Source: Author's compilation from the 1991, 1996, and 2001 Canadian Census Master Micro-data Files.

FIGURE 6
Returns to Foreign Experience and Foreign Schooling, Non-Visible Minorities with Either English/French as Their Mother Tongue from Western Countries

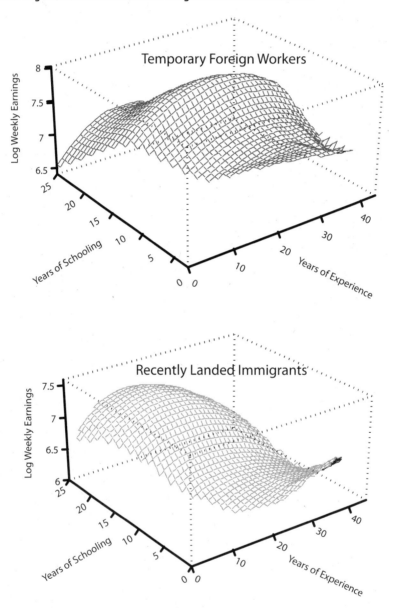

Notes: Samples are restricted to foreign born males aged 30 to 64 who have been living in Canada less than four years, are not in school full time, and have positive earnings from wages and salaries. Model also includes controls for region of birth, region of residence, population size of place of residence, and marital status.

Source: Author's compilation from the 1991, 1996, and 2001 Canadian Census Master Microdata Files.

CONCLUSION

This paper compares the returns to foreign work experience and education of recently landed immigrants and TFWs in Canada using both parametric and semi-parametric techniques. Poor returns to foreign human capital – or more specifically, a fall in the returns to foreign labour market experience – has been found to be one of the major reasons for the decline in the earning outcomes of immigrants in Canada, particularly for immigrants from non-traditional backgrounds.

Another group of foreign born workers who have entered over the same time period but under different policies are TFWs. This study found that, in comparison to recently landed immigrants, male TFWs receive higher returns to their foreign schooling and much higher returns to their labour market experience. Further, when the sample is restricted to visible minorities with neither English nor French as their mother tongue from non-western countries (the group with the greatest difficulty receiving returns to their foreign human capital for recent immigrants cohorts), again we find that TFWs experience positive returns to their work experience while immigrants receive no returns. Furthermore, these TFWs receive higher returns to their foreign schooling.

It is likely that the better outcomes are partially due to differences in ability between immigrants and TFWs that cannot be controlled for in the Census data. Part of the success of male TFWs in receiving higher returns to both their foreign schooling and labour market experience is also likely due to the selection policy under which they enter. Entering under the TFW program, the worker is selected by employers, which minimizes any potential problem receiving recognition for human capital obtained prior to entering Canada. As well, given that the employer must normally demonstrate a labour shortage for the job, the worker will be employed in an area of high demand. Immigrants are chosen by the government. Economic immigrants receive points for their human capital, but without much consideration for how the foreign human capital will be recognized by employers.[23] The other two main immigrant classes, the humanitarian class and the family class, enter the country based on social goals, without consideration for how these immigrants will integrate economically.

The findings in this paper are particularly important given the recent introduction of the Canadian Experience Class, under which some TFWs will become future immigrants. By taking into consideration the needs of employers and the areas of skill shortages in the Canadian labour market, it is possible to bring in immigrants with skills that are in high demand, and consequently the immigrants' foreign schooling and work experience will be better rewarded. However, given that the needs of the economy are always changing, skills that are in high demand in one period may not be in high demand in another, and any advantage may be temporary. Further, many of the TFWs may not desire to become permanent residents.

Nonetheless, the most significant finding is that it is possible for foreign born workers to obtain returns to their foreign acquired human capital and, in particular, positive returns to their foreign work experience, something that has eluded recent immigrants to Canada.

NOTES

This project was originally part of the research program of the Family and Labour Studies Division, Statistics Canada. I would like to thank Charles Beach, Miles Corak, Ross Finnie, David Gray, Gilles Grenier, Stanley Kustec, Yuri Ostrovsky, Elizabeth Ruddick, Saul Schwartz, Arthur Sweetman, Frances Woolley, and Christopher Worswick, and seminar participants at Carleton University and the Canadian Economics Association meetings for their comments. While the research and analysis are based on data from Statistics Canada, the opinions expressed do not represent the views of Statistics Canada.

1. Alboim, Finnie, and Meng (2005) find that in Canada a year of foreign schooling is worth only around 70 percent a year of Canadian school, while a year of foreign work experience is worth around a third of a year of Canadian work experience.
2. It should be noted that in this paper the term "temporary foreign worker" refers to all non-permanent residents working in Canada at the time of the Census and not uniquely to the "temporary foreign worker" program managed by CIC and HRSDC. This distinction is discussed in the section describing Immigrant and TFW Programs in Canada below.
3. Looking at college graduates in the United States, Hunt (2009) finds that immigrants who first entered on a temporary work visa do very well in terms of wages and other measures of productivity relative to other immigrants and the domestic born.
4. Only the primary applicant entering under the economic class is assessed under the points system. The dependants entering under the economic class with the primary applicant are not assessed. However, the primary applicant can receive a maximum of 5 points for the education level of the spouse/ common law partner. See Sweetman and Warman (2009) for an examination of the outcomes of the spouses and role of the points of the principal applicant in predicting their economic outcomes.
5. The share of male TFWs in the weighted sample who are considered high skilled based on the classification of their employment in Canada has risen over the period covered by the data, starting at around 60 percent in 1991 and increasing to over 73 percent in 1996 and 2001.
6. The worker applies to Ministère des Relations avec les Citoyens et de l'Immigration (MRCI) if applying to work in Quebec.
7. Foreign workers who arrive under NAFTA and GATS are exempt from an LMO but still require a work permit.
8. In 2002, the Low-Skilled Worker Pilot Program allowed employers to bring in workers for some jobs that would not qualify under the normal TFW program.

9. TFWs working under the Live-in-Caregiver program are able to apply for permanent resident status after working for 24 months over a three-year period. Conversely, workers under the SAWP are not able to apply for permanent resident status in Canada.
10. It is possible for some temporary residents who do not enter under these programs to work. For example, spouses of foreign students and spouses of some high skilled TFWs are able to work in Canada.
11. It is also possible to apply outside of Canada, as long as it is within one year after last working in the job in Canada being considered.
12. Former international students with at least a two year degree and one year of work experience after the completion of the education can also apply under the Canadian Experience Class if they meet certain criteria.
13. The 2006 Census is not used, since information on years of schooling is not asked; therefore it is difficult to measure the already likely noisy potential work experience.
14. A small number of Minister's permit holders will also be in the sample. Minister's permits give special admission to come to Canada for a short period of time to some people who would not have qualified under the TFW program. The Census excludes non-permanent residents and their family members who are government representatives of a diplomatic body of another country, members of the Armed Forces of another country, or those visiting Canada temporarily.
15. The inclusion of the refugee claimants is likely to bias downward the returns to foreign work experience and foreign education of the TFWs.
16. For example, the 2001 Census would provide information of where the respondent lived in May 1996.
17. It is also possible that people could have been out of the country five years prior to the reference year but in Canada prior to that.
18. See Horowitz and Lee (2001), Yatchew (2003), and Li and Racine (2007) for an explanation of partial linear models and nonparametric functions with multiple variables.
19. The equations were re-estimated separately for each of the three years, which revealed little difference in returns to foreign schooling. An earlier version of the paper also controlled for 14 occupational dummies and hours worked dummies. The results were qualitatively and quantitatively similar. However, given that occupation and hours worked are likely endogenous, the results presented do not include these controls.
20. The estimates of the other variables are not presented here due to space considerations but are available upon request.
21. For English/French speaking non-visible minorities from western countries, only 6 percent of TFWs have 12 years of schooling or less compared to 15 percent of immigrants.
22. However, given that immigrants from "non-traditional" countries of origin have relatively poorer economic outcomes than immigrants from "traditional" countries of origin, increasing their weight with respect to immigrants who enter Canada would reduce the overall economic outcomes of the immigrant population.
23. Currently, economic immigrants can receive a maximum of 10 points if they have arranged HRSDC employment in an area of skill shortage or had previous employment that was arranged or exempt.

REFERENCES

Alboim, N., R. Finnie, and R. Meng. 2005. "The Discounting of Immigrants' Skills in Canada." *Immigration and Refugee Policy* 11 (2), ISSN 0711-0677.

Aydemir, A., and M. Skuterud. 2005. "Explaining the Deteriorating Entry Earnings of Canada's Immigrant Cohorts: 1966-2000." *Canadian Journal of Economics* 38 (2): 641-71.

Baker, M., and D. Benjamin. 1994. "The Performance of Immigrants in the Canadian Labor Market." *Journal of Labor Economics* 12 (3): 369-405.

Beach, C., A.G. Green, and C. Worswick. 2006. "Impacts of the Point System and Immigration Policy Levers on Skill Characteristics of Canadian Immigrants." Queen's Economics Department Working Paper No. 1115.

Bloom, D.E., G. Grenier, and M. Gunderson. 1995. "The Changing Labor Market Position of Canadian Immigrants." *Canadian Journal of Economics* 28 (4b): 987-1005.

Borjas, G.J. 1985. "Assimilation, Change in Cohort Quality, and the Earnings of Immigrants." *Journal of Labor Economics* 3 (4): 463-89.

– 1995. "Assimilation and Changes in Cohort Quality Revisited: What Happened to Immigrant Earnings in the 1980s?" *Journal of Labor Economics* 13 (2): 201-41.

Drolet, M. 2002. "Differentials: Does Measurement Matter?" Canadian Public Policy 28 (1): 1-16.

Ferrer, A., D.A. Green, and W.C. Riddell. 2006. "The Effect of Literacy on Immigrant Earnings." *Journal of Human Resources* 41 (2): 380-410.

Frenette, M., and R. Morissette (2005) "Will They Ever Converge? Earnings of Immigrant and Canadian-Born Workers over the Last Two Decades." *International Migration Review* 39 (1): 228-57.

Friedberg, R.M. 2000. "You Can't Take It with You? Immigrant Assimilation and the Portability of Human Capital." *Journal of Labor Economics* 18 (2): 221-51.

Goldmann, G., A. Sweetman, and C. Warman. 2009. "The Economic Return on New Immigrants Human Capital: The Impact of Occupational Matching." CLSRN Working Paper 30, UBC Department of Economics.

Green, D.A., and C. Worswick. 2004. "Immigrant Earnings Profiles in the Presence of Human Capital Investment: Measuring Cohort and Macro Effects." Mimeo.

Horowitz, J.L. 2000. "Semiparametric Models." Unpublished manuscript. Prepared for the *International Encyclopedia of Social and Behavioral Sciences*.

Horowitz, J.L., and S. Lee. 2001. "Semiparametric Methods in Applied Econometrics: Do the Models Fit the Data?" *Statistical Modelling* 2 (1): 1-20.

Hum, D., and W. Simpson. 2004. "Reinterpreting the Performance of Immigrant Wages from Panel Data." *Empirical Economics* 29 (9): 129-47.

Hunt, J. 2009. "Which Immigrants Are Most Innovative and Entrepreneurial? Distinctions by Entry Visa." NBER Working Paper 14920.

Li, Q., and J.S. Racine. 2007. *Nonparametric Econometrics: Theory and Practice.* Princeton University Press.

Lubotsky, D. 2007. "Chutes or Ladders? A Longitudinal Analysis of Immigrant Earnings." *Journal of Political Economy* 115 (5): 820-67.

Murphy, K.M., and F. Welch. 1990. "Empirical Age-Earnings Profiles." *Journal of Labor Economics* 8 (2): 202-29.

Picot, G., F. Hou, and S. Coulombe. 2008. "Poverty Dynamics among Recent Immigrants to Canada." *International Migration Review* 42 (2): 393-424.

Robinson, P.M. 1988. "Root-N-Consistent Semiparametric Regression." *Econometrica* 56 (4): 931-54.

Schaafsma, J., and A. Sweetman. 2001. "Immigrant Earnings: Age at Immigration Matters." *Canadian Journal of Economics* 34 (4): 1066-99.

Schellenberg, G. 2001. "Inland Determination Refugees before and after Landing." IMDB Research Paper Series, CIC.

Sweetman, A. 2004. "Immigrant Source Country Educational Quality and Canadian Labour Market Outcomes." Analytical Studies Research Paper Series, no 234. Statistics Canada, Ottawa.

Sweetman, A., and C. Warman. 2009. "Temporary Foreign Workers and Former International Students as a Source of Permanent Emmigration." CLSRN Working Papers 34, Department of Economics, UBC.

Warman, C., and C. Worswick. 2004. "Immigrant Earnings Performance in Canadian Cities: 1981 through 2001." *Canadian Journal of Urban Research* 13 (1): 62-84

Yatchew, A. 2003. *Semiparametric Regression for the Applied Econometrician*. Cambridge University Press.

9

ASSIMILATION OR STRATIFICATION? THE SOURCES OF EARLY DIFFERENTIATION OF IMMIGRANT ETHNO-RACIAL GROUPS IN THE CANADIAN HOUSING MARKET

MICHAEL HAAN

Dans cet article, je compare la capacité de deux théories – la théorie de l'assimilation et la théorie de la stratification sociale – à expliquer les écarts, sur le plan de l'accession à la propriété, que l'on observe chez les immigrants faisant partie de sept groupes différents de minorités visibles au Canada. Grâce à l'analyse de la chronologie des évènements, à l'échantillonnage bootstrap et aux données des trois vagues de l'Enquête longitudinale auprès des immigrants du Canada (ELIC), j'analyse le phénomène d'accession à la propriété chez les immigrants arrivés entre octobre 2000 et septembre 2001, et ce, pendant les quatre années suivant leur immigration. La richesse des données de l'ELIC me permet ainsi de déterminer si les différences que l'on observe entre les différents groupes sont dues à des contraintes de crédit ou au manque d'argent des immigrants au moment de l'immigration. Or, je conclus que ces deux facteurs ont, de façon surprenante, peu d'effets sur l'accès à la propriété des immigrants arabes, noirs, philippins, latino-américains, sud-asiatiques et blancs. Je discute ensuite des implications de ces résultats au Canada et dans d'autres pays.

In this paper I compare the ability of assimilation and stratification theories of immigrant integration to explain differences in the home ownership levels of seven recently arrived immigrant visible minority groups in Canada. I use event history analysis, bootstrap sampling, and three waves of the Longitudinal Survey of Immigrants to Canada (LSIC) to model the home ownership status of the October 2000-September 2001 arrival cohort in their first four years after arrival. Given the richness of LSIC data, it is possible to determine if differentiation between groups occurs because of either credit constraints or entry wealth. I find these factors to have surprisingly little effect on the home ownership

Canadian Immigration: Economic Evidence for a Dynamic Policy Environment, ed. T. McDonald, E. Ruddick, A. Sweetman, and C. Worswick. Montreal and Kingston: Queen's Policy Studies Series, McGill-Queen's University Press.

propensities of Arab, black, Filipino, Latin American, South Asian, and white immigrants. I discuss the implications of these results for Canada and other countries.

Introduction

Researchers interested in home ownership in both Canada (Edmonston 2004; Haan 2005a; Mendez, Hiebert, and Wyly 2006; Skaburskis 1996) and the United States (Borjas 2002; Freeman and Hamilton 2004; McConnell and Redstone Akresh 2008; Megbolugbe and Cho 1996; Painter, Yang, and Yu 2003a) have shown that although access to home ownership is declining among immigrants on average, there are sizeable and often unexplained differences between ethno-racial groups. Notably, some groups, such as the Chinese, are likely to buy homes soon after arrival in their host country (Painter, Yang, and Yu 2003b), whereas others, such as blacks, are not (Balakrishnan and Wu 1992; Skaburskis 1996). In the United States, the gap between the group with the highest and lowest tenure rates is about 27 percentage points (Callis and Cavanaugh 2005). In Canada, the difference is about the same (Haan 2007a).

Given that housing tenure is tied so closely to neighbourhood quality, residential stability, public safety, and numerous other positive outcomes (Flippen 2001b; Green and White 1997; Krivo and Kaufman 2004; Massey and Denton 1993; Myers, Megbolugbe, and Lee 1998; Oliver and Shapiro 1995), early differences between groups shape well-being and access to opportunity far into the future (Di 2007; Orfield and McArdle 2006). Consequently, understanding which factors shape housing careers – and differences in housing careers – is of vital importance, particularly during the early years, when, as I show below, the seeds of longer-term differentiation are sown.

Since most immigrant housing research relies on either assimilation or stratification theory for guidance, in this paper I compare the abilities of these two theories to explain the differences in access to owner-occupied housing across ethno-racial groups. I use event history analysis, bootstrap sampling, and three waves of the Longitudinal Survey of Immigrants to Canada (LSIC) to model the home ownership status of the October 2000-September 2001 arrival cohort in their first four years. Given the richness of LSIC data, I take a first look at how credit constraints and entry wealth affect the home ownership propensities of Arab, black, Chinese, Filipino, Hispanic, South Asian, and white immigrants. Although I find that these factors (as well as standard household demographic and socio-economic characteristics) are important for all groups, Arab, black, and Chinese immigrants remain statistically distinguishable from the white reference group.[1]

In the sections below, I first review assimilation and stratification theories, followed by a discussion of recent trends in the Canadian housing market. Then, I describe the novel explanatory factors in LSIC, followed by a description of the study methodology and presentation and discussion of results.

IDENTIFYING ASSIMILATION AND STRATIFICATION

As mentioned above, a good deal of research on immigrant home ownership (and other immigrant socio-economic characteristics) looks to either assimilation or stratification for theoretical guidance. Although there are variants of both theories here, I use Alba and Nee's definition of assimilation as "minority participation in mainstream socio-economic institutions (e.g., the labour market) on the basis of parity with ethnic-majority individuals of similar socio-economic origins" (Alba and Nee 1997). Unexplained, and often large, initial gaps between immigrant groups and the domestic born dissipate over time, as language skills improve and knowledge of the host society increases. Consequently, duration of residency in the new country and language fluency often take centre stage with assimilation, because they capture a newcomer's growing ability to participate in mainstream institutions (Alba and Logan 1992; McConnell and Redstone Akresh 2008), such as labour and housing markets. Relating assimilation to housing tenure, differences in home ownership levels may exist between groups, but they should disappear after adjusting for duration, fluency, and the many other standard factors known to matter for housing status, such as life course, demographic, and socio-economic factors.

Some researchers feel that current immigrant inflows, although useful as a theoretical starting point, complicate the application of assimilation. Foremost among these complications is the increased recruitment of non-European immigrants, resulting in a growing proportion of non-white arrivals (Hou 2004; Picot and Sweetman 2005) and, consequently, the presence of longer-term cultural and physical differences. As a result, groups face differences in their context of reception (Boyd 2003; Portes and Zhou 1993), affecting access to resources such as owner-occupied housing (Rosenbaum and Friedman 2007) and creating a "rank order" of ethno-racial groups over time (Marger 2008).

The mechanisms that potentially create the rank order are numerous but could include redlining, residential steering, and mortgage discrimination by banks (Elmelech 2004; Flippen 2001b; Yinger 1998). Although these barriers are often unobserved (and therefore difficult to measure), they emerge after immigrant group members have arrived in the host country, suggesting that differentiation under stratification largely occurs post-arrival, because it is within the host society that individual groups encounter differential treatment.

As this differential treatment pertains to housing, given that the primary factors (language fluency and duration) used to capture assimilation are measured in most datasets (including the LSIC used here), and that the factors behind stratification are not, distinguishing between assimilation and stratification often translates into interpreting the differences between groups (immigrants and the Canadian born, whites and non-whites, etc.) that diminish after controls as proof of assimilation, with the remaining gaps pointing to stratification.

Given that this is the convention, research that includes new information has the potential to advance immigrant incorporation debates considerably. With this in mind, my contribution here is to longitudinally model the effect of credit constraints and entry wealth, two fairly critical omissions in the area of housing research, alongside more commonly included factors.

Before moving on to look at whether these variables might impact access to home ownership, however, below I first provide some background information on the Canadian housing market. I outline the broad contours of home ownership trends in Canada, then show how immigrant ethno-racial groups have diverged in recent years, using the Canadian born as a benchmark. This provides a platform for the multivariate analysis that appears later in the paper.

Background: The Decline of the Canadian Immigrant Home Ownership Advantage

Two noteworthy trends have characterized the Canadian housing market in recent history. First, home ownership levels among the Canadian born have risen since 1981, moving from roughly 70 percent to 73 percent in 2001. Second, immigrant levels of ownership have declined alongside these gains (Table 1).

TABLE 1
Percentage of Immigrants and the Canadian Born Who Are Home Owners in 1981 and 2001

	1981	2001
Immigrant	72.7%	68.8%
Canadian born	70.3%	73.1%

Note: Contains all persons aged 25-55

Source: 1981 and 2001 Censuses of Canada.

In 1981, when immigrants held a sizeable advantage over their Canadian born counterparts, nearly 73 percent of all dwellings with foreign born owners were owner-occupied.[2] By 2001, however, this advantage had disappeared, due to an immigrant decline in ownership alongside rising Canadian born levels. Collectively, this produced a 7 percentage point relative drop in the home ownership levels of Canadian immigrants.[3] Although not shown here, these declines are evident in Montreal, Toronto, and Vancouver as well as (though to a lesser extent) in Canada's smaller cities, suggesting that the decline has been a national phenomenon. Further, the shift in immigration settlement patterns over time (largely the declining popularity of Montreal in favour of places with high home ownership) has shielded an even greater decline (Haan 2005b).

To explain this decline, it is useful to see if subgroups share the main trend. It is possible to group immigrants in any number of ways, but a common and often informative division to make, particularly when comparing assimilation and stratification theory, is by ethno-racial category. Further support for this division can also be drawn from the long heritage of (often American) research that finds wide, and largely unexplained, differences in home ownership propensities across groups (Alba and Logan 1992; Balakrishnan and Wu 1992; Bianchi, Farley, and Spain 1982; Flippen 2001a; Jackman and Jackman 1980; King and Mieszkowski 1973; Krivo and Kaufman 2004; McConnell and Redstone Akresh 2008).

Consistent with previous research, Table 2 shows that the 1981-2001 immigrant home ownership decline does indeed differ by group. As only one example of this, consider that alongside a 1 percentage point drop for whites over the 20 year period is a 32 point decline for Arabs. What is perhaps most interesting, however, is that aside from whites and Arabs, all other groups actually *increased* their access to home ownership

TABLE 2
Percentage of Immigrants Who Are Home Owners in 1981 and 2001
by Race/Ethnicity in Canada

	1981			2001		
	% Owner	*Rank*	*% of All Imms.*	*% Owner*	*Rank*	*% of All Imms.*
Arab	72.1	3	7.1	40.2	8	17.2
Black	40.6	7	5.2	42.4	6	14.3
Chinese	74.8	1	6.6	78.3	1	8.0
Filipino	56.4	5	2.1	59.4	5	5.3
Latin Am.	33.3	8	1.5	40.7	7	3.3
South Asian	62.3	4	0.2	64.3	3	4.6
White	73.9	2	73.0	72.8	2	40.0
Other immigrants	45.9	6	4.3	60.9	4	7.4

Note: Contains all foreign born persons aged 25-55.

Source: 1981 and 2001 Censuses of Canada.

in this period. For most, this is a good-news story; the gap between non-white immigrants and both white immigrants and the Canadian born has narrowed.

At the same time, most ethno-racial immigrant groups continue to lag well behind both white immigrants and the Canadian born, two commonly used reference groups. Only the Chinese eclipsed whites in access to home ownership between 1981 and 2001, with a fairly consistent pattern among all other groups except Arabs. Furthermore, it is the shrinking numbers of immigrants from high home ownership groups (like whites and the Chinese) that is behind the aggregate decline, suggesting that researchers interested in reversing the declining immigrant access to home ownership should focus on identifying the reasons behind differences between groups. With that in mind, the question for the remainder of this paper is whether these differences more accurately reflect assimilation or stratification.

DISSECTING THE DECLINE IN IMMIGRANT HOME OWNERSHIP

Part of explaining differences across ethno-racial groups (and of assessing the relative utility of assimilation versus stratification in doing so) requires an identification of when disparities emerge. Most housing research (Borjas 2002; Krivo and Kaufman 2004; Kurz and Blossfeld 2004) focuses on a single point in time, but as Dowell Myers and his colleagues have shown (Myers 1999; Myers and Lee 1998; Myers, Megbolugbe, and Lee 1998), these results mislead when they do not look at timing (see Borjas 1985) for an earlier discussion related to immigrant earnings). Cross-sectional disparities between groups can stem from either differences in attainment rates or from immediate differences at time of entry being carried forward.[4] The difference is analogous to comparing y-intercept values (differences at time 0) to slope coefficients (different rates of attainment over time) in a standard regression. In terms of weighing the explanatory utility of assimilation versus stratification, it is critical to know if groups differ due to processes extant in the new country or from processes that existed at time of entry.

In Canada, early differentiation appears to be most relevant for explaining home ownership gaps (Table 3). Although significant differences between groups (recent and more established) existed in both 1981 and 2001, home ownership levels fell for nearly all recent (<5 years) arrivals between the time points, but increased for all of the more established groups but Arabs. For some groups, like Latin Americans and South Asians, the increase was quite substantial, at 12 percent and 7.7 percent, respectively, whereas all recent arrivals but Latin Americans experienced losses between 1981 and 2001. This is true even for Chinese and whites, Canada's housing "high achievers" (Haan 2007b).

TABLE 3
Home Ownership Levels of 1977-1981 and 1997-2001 Immigrant Arrivals to Canada by Ethno-Racial Group

	1981		2001		1981-2001 Decline	
	Non-Recent (%)	Recent (%)	Non-Recent (%)	Recent (%)	Non-Recent (%)	Recent (%)
Arab	72.1	72.2	48.3	18.6	-49.5	-288.0
Blacks	43.0	24.2	45.5	17.7	5.4	-36.8
Chinese	82.4	50.6	86.4	46.0	4.6	-10.0
Filipino	61.6	42.3	63.8	36.8	3.4	-14.9
Latin Am.	38.0	18.8	43.2	25.5	12.0	26.2
South Asian	66.3	44.3	71.8	35.1	7.7	-26.1
White	75.4	45.3	76.7	30.8	1.8	-47.2
Other immigrants	55.4	20.7	64.8	36.2	14.5	42.7

Note: Contains all persons aged 25-65.
The last two columns are not percentages like the first four, but instead represent a proportional change in the percent of home owners in each group.
Source: 1981 and 2001 Censuses of Canada.

Consequently, three things are evident from Tables 1-3. First, a good deal of the home ownership immigrant decline is due to "shift share," or the growing numbers of low home ownership groups immigrating to Canada. Second, differentiation across immigrant ethno-racial groups seems to occur in the years immediately after arrival. Finally, there is "path dependency" in terms of access, suggesting that the early years are critical for understanding both why groups face different levels of access to home ownership and why aggregate immigrant home ownership levels are falling.

But, to return to our main question, are these early differences better explained by assimilation or stratification theory? That is to say, will the differences disappear when adjustments for standard characteristics, particularly duration and fluency, are introduced? What impact will credit constraints and entry wealth have? How much of the difference between groups will remain after adjusting for these factors?

Analytically, demonstrating the importance of the early years of residence in Canada is important, because it directs researchers to unique data sources. Most housing research relies on the Census, which, despite its strengths (comparability over a long term, large sample size, etc.), is rather limited in the information it contains. Focusing on the early years, however, allows for an exploration of some new data sources, such as the LSIC used in the remainder of this paper.[5] These surveys contain information not available elsewhere, thereby holding considerable promise for furthering our understanding of immigrant home ownership attainment and the assimilation-stratification debate. In the section below, I describe credit history and entry wealth data, two unique pieces of information in the LSIC.

ENTRY WEALTH AND THE LACK OF CREDIT HISTORY

As mentioned earlier, a good deal of housing research on immigrant home ownership tends to cite differences between immigrant ethno-racial groups that persist after adjustments as evidence of stratification. As a result, debates about the explanatory power of the two theories advance when the effect of new characteristics is observed. One such characteristic in the LSIC is the lack of credit history. Since a high percentage of Canada's immigrants now hail from developing nations (Badets and Chui 1994; Picot and Sweetman 2005), group differences may increasingly stem from difficulties garnering the necessary resources to buy a home. Often, lesser developed parts of the world do not have well developed credit industries, so newcomers from these regions may lack the requisite credit history to obtain a mortgage. Therefore, the differences in attainment profiles among recent arrivals could stem from the inability of certain groups to obtain the necessary funds for a home purchase, explaining a portion of the between-group disparities. Credit history differences are likely to vary, at least in part, by country of origin, and might therefore also differ by ethno-racial group. Consequently, what might be seen as evidence for stratification in studies without this information could actually be a function of credit history.[6]

One of the ways to avoid domestic requirements for prior credit history is to bring wealth into Canada from a previous country of residence. If these savings are large enough, credit agencies and mortgage lenders, and therefore the risk of mortgage discrimination, can be avoided altogether; even if they cannot, an applicant with a sizeable down payment will still be more attractive to a mortgage lender, regardless of preconceived notions about that person, thereby boosting the probability of ownership. In either regard, access to owner-occupied housing, and the differences between groups, could depend in part on entry wealth.

Both the lack of credit history and entry wealth are measured in the LSIC. The expectation is that lower levels of entry wealth will negatively affect the probability of ownership, and that a lack of prior credit history will do the same. Descriptive statistics for these variables appear in Table 4 below.

Looking first at credit constraints, 95 per cent of Chinese arrivals brought at least some savings to Canada with them, with a median amount of around $20,000.[7] This appears to have provided them with an edge over other groups; about half of blacks, for example, brought savings, with a median amount of $10,000. At the same time, compared to the 9.3 percent of blacks who were home owners after six months, 12.5 percent of Chinese owned their dwellings.[8]

TABLE 4
Self-Reported Credit Problems and Wealth Characteristics by Ethno-Racial Group, 2000-01 Immigrants to Canada

	Arab	Black	Chinese	Filipino
% that brought savings	70.6%	51.1%	95.4%	82.2%
Median savings at entry	$8,000	$10,000	$20,000	$12,000
% that report credit constraints are a problem for getting a mortgage	20.1%	14.1%	9.4%	14.5%
Percent home owner at six months	6.0%	9.3%	12.5%	17.4%

	Latin Am.	S. Asian	White	Other
% that brought savings	72.9%	75.2%	82.7%	88.4%
Median savings at entry	$14,000	$14,000	$14,000	$50,000
% that report credit constraints are a problem for getting a mortgage	27.6%	15.2%	16.4%	19.2%
Percent home owner at six months	11.9%	14.8%	18.1%	18.2%

Note: Median savings at entry and income are only reported for those with positive values.
Source: Longitudinal Survey of Immigrants to Canada, wave 1.

Differences in entry wealth and credit history, two factors that relate to assimilation and stratification, are both characteristics that immigrant households take with them from a previous country. These characteristics are therefore fixed, and lend more support for assimilation theory's explanatory power. That is not to say that differences in these two characteristics will not impede access to opportunity, but that the differences between groups do not stem from physical characteristics – a white immigrant without entry wealth or a credit history is as unlikely to receive the support to buy a home as is someone who is Filipino. Furthermore, there would be clear policy interventions (discussed more fully later in the paper) that can be made from finding that entry wealth and credit history matter to home ownership. Given this, I will interpret differences that diminish after controlling for credit constraints as support for assimilation theory.

METHODOLOGY

Sample

The study sample is drawn from the LSIC, a three-wave study of about 20,000 people aged 15 and over (at wave 1) who were randomly selected from the approximately 165,000 immigrants who settled in Canada between October 2000 and September 2001. To be part of the LSIC sample, respondents needed to have applied for admission to Canada through a mission abroad (Statistics Canada 2003). Respondents were interviewed at six months, two-years, and four years after arrival. This study reduces the full sample to contain only people aged 25-65 (at time 1), not living with their parents and residing in one of Canada's 27 Census Metropolitan Areas. The latter restrictions had very little impact on overall sample size.

Dependent Variable

A key feature of the LSIC is that it gathers information in event history format,[9] so that the timing of key events is recorded for each individual. Given this feature, person-month observations can be calculated by determining the amount of time in months before an individual purchased a home. The dependent variable is therefore a binary indicator signalling that a longitudinal respondent has purchased a home. Those who immediately bought their dwelling were given a value of 1 at time point 1, and immediately exit the sample after contributing one person-month record. Those who never buy a home have values of 0 for all time points, and contribute between 48 and 52 person-month observations (depending on the date of their final interview). Differential contributions per respondent are typical of event history data and can be modelled without bias (Allison 1995).

Independent Variables

Another key feature of event history data is the possibility of allowing characteristics to vary over time. If individuals experience a life change (their marital status changes, they get a raise, they move to another city, etc.), it is possible to model the effect of this change. Consequently, event-history analysis conceptualizes people as having characteristics that can change over time. That said, not all characteristics are dynamic (entry wealth, skin colour, etc.), so event history formatted data contains both fixed and time-varying information.

The regressions include a number of demographic and household level control factors (age, marital status, and household structure), as well as labour market (employment status, number of jobs, logged income) and human capital characteristics such as education. One other noteworthy addition is the inclusion of monthly mortgage interest rates, obtained from the Bank of Canada and appended to every record in the file. Since each respondent arrived at the same time, however, mortgage interest rates, rather than differences between groups, are expected to affect overall access levels. Additional coding information (including whether a variable is fixed or time varying) is provided in Table 5 below.

In addition to these more widely used measures, entry wealth and the presence of previous credit history will also be modelled. Central to the analysis that follows is how these two factors affect the statistical significance of the vector of ethno-racial indicators, which capture the differences in home ownership propensities not explained by other variables in the model. These coefficients are expected to diminish in terms of strength and significance with the introduction of controls in increasingly complex models.

TABLE 5
Variable Coding Information

Time	Coding Details		Focal Explanatory Clusters	Coding Details	
Time (in logged months)	C	TV	**Class of entry**		
Socio-demographic characteristics			Economic class	RC	F
Age	C	TV	Family class	D	F
Married	D	TV	Skilled worker	D	F
# of children	C	TV	Refugee	D	F
Multiple family	D	TV	**CMA indicators**		
Human capital characteristics			Toronto	D	TV
Less than high school	RC	TV	Montreal	D	TV
High school	D	TV	Vancouver	D	TV
Post-secondary	D	TV	Lives elsewhere in Canada	RC	TV
University	D	TV	**Credit constraints**		
Labour market characteristics			No credit	D	TV
# of jobs	C	TV	Interest rate	C	TV
Work: FT or PT	D	TV	Bring savings	D	F
Employed	D	TV	Entry wealth (logged)	C	F
Income (logged)	C	TV			
Can speak English	D	TV			
Can speak French	D	TV			
Doesn't speak English or French	RC	TV			
Race/ethnicity indicators					
Arab	D	F			
Black	D	F			
Chinese	D	F			
Filipino	D	F			
Latin Am.	D	F			
South Asian	D	F			
White	RC	F			
Other immigrants	D	F			

Note: C denotes a continuous variables, whereas D = dichotomous, RC = reference category, TV=time-varying, and F=fixed.

Source: Author's compilation.

Analytical Technique

As mentioned above, event history analysis estimates the probability of an event occurrence, with the ability to use both fixed and time-varying factors as predictors. To do this, it is necessary to recast individual observations as person-month data points, which can be estimated in a standard probit regression framework. To compare fit across models, I use the Bayesian Information Criterion (BIC), where lower values of BIC are preferred (Raftery 1995).

Statistics Canada requires users to estimate standard errors with bootstrap sampling techniques, using provided bootstrap weights. Bootstrapping entails a re-estimation of regressions using a matrix of weight variables and sub-sample of observations, with the main results being the average of these models. The result is a vector of standard errors adjusted for the complex survey design of the LSIC. For this study, I use 750 bootstrap weights.

In preliminary analysis (not shown), access to credit, entry wealth, and Census Metropolitan Area of residence were modelled as endogenous variables, but given the similarities between the results from those models and the exogenous only models, I opt to present the simpler models below.

Multivariate Results

Table 6 shows three probit regression models. Model 1 captures ethno-racial group differences, adjusted for time only, whereas model 2 includes standard demographic and labour market characteristics. Model 3 considers the impact of credit constraints and entry wealth.

Looking first at the time coefficient in model 1, the negative value supports the assertion that housing purchases tend to occur immediately, and that the propensities wane over time.[10] Model 1 also reveals statistically significant differences among all groups but Latin Americans. Model 2 attempts to explain these disparities by adding a series of commonly used socio-economic and demographic characteristics. Most of the socio-economic variables are statistically significant and denote patterns commonly found in other studies. Older married couples with children are more likely to own, as are multiple family dwelling households. Also consistent with other studies is that the relationship between home ownership and education appears to be quite weak in both models. For the most part, the trends for the labour market variables are in the expected direction, with full-time employed workers with higher incomes more likely to be home owners. One unexpected result is that the ability to speak English has no effect on home ownership in the early years, and the French coefficient is actually slightly negative and significant.

TABLE 6
Probit Coefficients of the Correlates of Home Ownership among a Cohort of Immigrants to Canada

	Model 1		Model 2		Model 3	
	Coefficient	SE	Coefficient	SE	Coefficient	SE
Time (logged)	-0.165***	0.009	-0.310***	0.018	-0.319***	0.018
Arab	-0.333***	0.033	-0.255***	0.038	-0.218***	0.039
Black	-0.210***	0.042	-0.193***	0.046	-0.147**	0.047
Chinese	-0.113***	0.025	-0.088***	0.027	-0.155***	0.028
Filipino	0.087***	0.033	-0.055	0.036	0.013	0.036
Latin American	-0.037*	0.048	-0.009	0.050	0.014	0.047
South Asian	0.045*	0.024	-0.034	0.025	-0.004	0.026
Other	0.100***	0.036	0.078	0.039	-0.010	0.043
Age			0.008***	0.001	0.001***	0.002
Married			0.285***	0.034	0.268***	0.036
# of children			0.040***	0.009	0.025**	0.010
Multiple family			0.295***	0.028	0.316***	0.029
High school			0.018	0.044	-0.011	0.045
Post-secondary			0.093*	0.040	0.029	0.041
University			0.023	0.039	-0.043	0.041
# of jobs			-0.032*	0.013	-0.024	0.013
Work -FT or PT			0.105***	0.024	0.102***	0.024
Employed			0.888***	0.027	0.080**	0.028
Income (logged)			0.055***	0.009	0.059***	0.008
Speaks English			-0.034	0.019	-0.060**	0.019
Speaks French			-0.114***	0.037	-0.075	0.039
Toronto			-0.156***	0.020	-0.170***	0.021
Montreal			-0.413***	0.035	-0.376***	0.036
Vancouver			-0.130***	0.029	-0.158***	0.030
Interest rate			-0.231***	0.026	-0.237***	0.026
No credit					-0.439***	0.057
Bring savings					-1.201***	0.116
Entry wealth (logged)					0.135***	0.011
Constant	-1.682***	0.028	-0.954***	0.230	-0.303	0.230
BIC	-2124766		-2125569		-2125885	

Notes: $p<0.05$:*; $p<0.01$:**; $p<0.001$:***
Source: Longitudinal Survey of Immigrants to Canada.

The large reductions in BIC between models 1 and 2 point to substantial improvements in model fit, showing that, not surprisingly, standard demographic and socio-economic characteristics do indeed matter for housing tenure status. Although this improvement denotes an important improvement in explanatory power, these factors have been deemed extraneous in this study due to their extensive attention elsewhere. It is worth noting, however, that three of seven groups remain statistically distinguishable from the white reference group.[11]

At this point the evidence supporting assimilation theory is mixed. Filipinos, South Asians, and Other Immigrants are no longer statistically distinguishable from whites, but Arabs, blacks, and Chinese are. The main contribution of this paper is to identify whether credit constraints and entry wealth provide additional support for standard assimilation theory versus stratification. I discuss this prospect below.

The Effect of Access to Credit

I argued earlier that ethno-racial groups might have different access to the necessary resources to purchase a home, resulting in access gaps across groups. These differences could stem from either differences in entry wealth or from credit constraints.

Each of the variables designed to measure this information (no credit, bring savings, and logged entry wealth) are statistically significant predictors of home ownership in Table 6. Credit constraints greatly reduce the probability of home ownership, as does a lack of entry wealth (remember that all coefficients, including time in Canada in months, should be interpreted as the value when all other values in the model are set to zero). Increasing entry wealth increases home ownership propensities, and an additional $10,000 in logged savings brought from the previous country results in a probit coefficient value of 0.135. Both models show that entry wealth and access to credit matter for immigrant access to home ownership.

Turning now to the vector of ethno-racial coefficients in model 3, credit constraints and entry wealth reduce the unexplained differences between groups only slightly. There are reductions in magnitudes of difference for Arabs and blacks compared to model 2, suggesting that entry-level economic resources explain some of the difference. At the same time, however, all of the significant differences in model 2 remain, and the gap actually grows for the Chinese, suggesting that entry level economic resources, at least as measured here, are not a major explanatory factor behind Canada's home ownership "rank order."

CONCLUSION: CANADA'S HOME OWNERSHIP HIERARCHY

In the past 40 years the source of immigrants to Canada and other traditional immigrant recipient countries has shifted radically, to the point where a debate has emerged about whether or not traditional notions of immigrant assimilation bear any relevance today. Traditionally, it was thought that immigrants would converge over time with the Canadian born on a host of outcomes, one of them being home ownership. Home ownership propensities would therefore be rather low at time of entry but would more or less increase monotonically for all groups until little, if any, difference with the Canadian born existed. Researchers since at least Warner and Srole (1945) have realized that this notion is somewhat simplified, because individuals (and groups of individuals) enter their host societies with different levels of resources. As a result, groups would not reach socio-economic parity with the Canadian born at the same time, but with the inclusion of relevant controls, they would more or less progress equally.

Given the growth in immigrant diversity, however, even these basic tenets are being questioned and are in some instances being replaced by another scenario predicated on the assumption of longer-term differentiation and stratification, based on physical or external characteristics. That is, groups that look like the Canadian born should get access to resources enjoyed by the Canadian born; those that don't, wont.

In my attempt to determine which of these two theoretical scenarios better explains home ownership in Canada, I make two contributions in this paper. The first is to estimate the effect of entry wealth and credit constraints, two plausible characteristics for explaining home ownership disparities across groups. As the results show, these factors are both strong and significant predictors of home ownership, and future studies would do well to include them whenever possible. Second, I show that these factors explain very little of the differences between groups. Although the unexplained gap in home ownership levels shrinks slightly for Arabs and blacks, it grows for the Chinese, and all three groups remain statistically distinguishable from whites. This finding is quite provocative and likely extends well beyond the Canadian context, since members of these groups are also heading to other traditional immigrant receiving countries, especially Australia, New Zealand, and the United States.

It is also interesting to note that home ownership levels for the 2000-01 cohort of Chinese immigrants are not as high as they were for earlier same-group members. This suggests that the Chinese are not necessarily a de facto high home ownership group. Since a large share of more recent arrivals hail from mainland China, they are likely to be quite different from their predecessors, many of whom came from Hong Kong and Taiwan. Although there are likely to be wealth differences between cohorts, attitudes about the importance of buying a house versus investing in other goods (like education for children) may also differ. Each visible minority category is itself internally heterogeneous, and the drop in home ownership for the Chinese may be reflecting that heterogeneity.

Turning now to the central question of this paper: which of the two theories better explains the differences between groups? Is the Canadian housing market more accurately characterized by assimilation or stratification theory? Clearly, the answer is mixed. On the one hand, the differences between some groups dissolve with controls, as we would expect under assimilation. On the other hand, three groups remain significantly different from each other, lending support to the claim that the Canadian housing market is stratified along ethno-racial lines (Henry 1989; Hulchanski 1993, 1994; Murdie 1994).

One possible way to explain these findings is to not hold assimilation and stratification in opposition to one another. Social relations and solidarity develop in space (Lindstrom 1997), suggesting that, as shown with the descriptive results, home ownership is path dependent and that early differentiation extends well into the future. It may be the case that immigrants who predominantly enter Canada as renters for whatever reason are much more likely to develop relationships with other renters (Skaburskis 1996), same group or otherwise, thereby discouraging them from leaving their neighbourhoods and statuses, and creating a "culture of tenancy."

At the same time, if we agree with Oliver and Shapiro (1995) that wealth is "used to create opportunities, secure a desired stature, and standard of living, or pass class status along to one's children," then it is critical to look more closely at why several groups continue to have reduced access to home ownership. Why do some groups immediately rent, when housing represents a form of forced savings that will change the resources available in the future? All of this is to say that the primary barrier to understanding Canada's home ownership hierarchy is a significant knowledge gap. We know surprisingly little about recent trends in home ownership among ethno-racial groups in Canada.

In some ways, we also know very little about the markets that ethno-racial group members enter. Although it is true that there is a Canadian housing market, for understanding residential patterns (immigrant or otherwise), it is often more useful to think of metropolitan markets. At the time of writing this paper (July 2009), the Canadian Real Estate Association reports that the average price of an owner-occupied dwelling in Vancouver is $575,949, whereas in Halifax, it is less than half that price at $240,093. Aside from some interesting work being done in Vancouver by Hiebert and colleagues, and in Winnipeg by Tom Carter, we know little about metropolitan housing markets and how ethno-racial groups interact within them.

It is hard to imagine that earnings in the two CMAs of Vancouver and Halifax will level the disparity in the housing market, suggesting that part of rectifying housing tenure differences could involve understanding why people choose to live where they do in Canada. Aside from some work at Statistics Canada with the LSIC (Statistics Canada 2003), little is known about the factors behind a household's choice of location in Canada. To the extent that local markets probably determine accessibility, this is an important part of the puzzle.

Furthermore, there are significant gaps in what is known about housing markets *within* CMAs. Looking at a metropolitan housing market as unified rather than heavily channelled and fractured restricts certain fields of inquiry that might yield explanatory dividends. Many of the ethnic enclaves of Canada's cosmopolitan cities are highly desirable places for co-ethnics to live, and it is possible that same-group households seeking a place to live will choose to rent in an enclave instead of buying outside of their enclave.

Once the reasons for remaining differences between groups are uncovered, there will be significant room for policy intervention. What these policies might look like is uncertain, but practices in other countries may be instructive. In Australia, designated underwriting by the federal government is one practice, and another is "shared ownership," in which the federal government is essentially a co-owner and pays a portion of a household's mortgage. The owner may then buy out the government's share when this option becomes affordable. In New Zealand, public housing units are built, and after some time, sold to inhabitants. This has the benefit of preserving community, enabling a purchase decision, and allowing the government to constantly renew and replenish its public housing stock. Even the United States, one of the more private (at least until recently) housing markets, has policies to enable immigrant home ownership.

In Canada, however, no such federal plan exists, and in 2007 a special UN envoy strongly urged Canada to begin thinking about a national housing strategy to address issues like the ones outlined above (as well as others such as homelessness and the lack of public housing). Altering any of these policies (or designing an overall strategy) for the Canadian context would no doubt pose problems, but a necessary first step is illustrating the need for such interventions. This study begins to illustrate such a need; whether seen through the lens of assimilation or stratification, nearly half of Canada's immigrant groups experience unexplained gaps in their access to home ownership. What is more troubling is how resilient these gaps are over time (Haan 2007b).

At first blush, targeted policies may seem discriminatory, in that they provide advantages for immigrants in the housing market relative to the Canadian born. It could, however, be argued with equal force that the few housing policies that do exist in Canada already differentiate between groups. A good example of this is the so-called universal benefit known as the Home Buyers Plan, which allows first-time home buyers in Canada to withdraw up to $25,000 of their RRSP contributions without penalty. However, it is difficult for recent immigrants to immediately benefit from the plan since the RRSP is a Canadian program. Policies could and should exist to make housing as accessible for immigrants as for those who were either born in Canada or have been here for a long time.

Given that the majority of future housing demand is likely to come from immigrants, policy interventions will affect not only immigrant well-being but also that of the nearly five million Canadians on the verge of retirement, many of whom expect their dwelling to be a cornerstone of their retirement portfolios. Whether explained by assimilation or stratification, the declines in immigrant home ownership levels are a cause for concern for the future and warrant further research. We do not know, for example, how beliefs about paying interest on borrowed money impact access for some groups; another question to be explored might be whether newcomers are delaying buying homes until after they are able to gain access to their ethnic enclave.

Answering such questions will of course only raise others. For example, in this paper I assume that time, credit history, and assets operate equally on each group. Each of these assumptions is questionable, and each could easily be the topic of a separate paper.[12]

NOTES

I would like to thank the Social Sciences and Humanities Research Council of Canada for providing financial support for this project. Additionally, I thank Barry Edmonston, Ted McDonald, John Myles, and an anonymous reviewer for reading over early drafts of this paper. All errors and omissions are solely my fault and responsibility.

1. Attempting to explain differences across groups is not meant to imply within-group homogeneity. Some groups are more alike than others – for example, although most people who identified as Filipino were born in the Philippines, those who identified as black could have come from one of 50 different countries the world over. Consequently, it should be noted that the ethno-racial categories used in this paper are intended primarily to capture differences in reception based on ascribed group characteristics and tendencies rather than actually existing biological or social difference. For consistency, I use the term "ethno-racial" throughout the paper.
2. Only one respondent (the highest earner) per dwelling is chosen, and this person is between the ages of 25 and 65.
3. These figures refer only to Canada's seven largest census metropolitan areas, where over 85 percent of all immigrants live.
4. Or a combination of these two components.
5. Or the Longitudinal Survey of Immigrants to Australia, the New Zealand Longitudinal Immigrant Survey, and the US New Immigrant Survey for other countries
6. Naturally, credit constraints are not solely the result of region of origin. Even within source regions, there is likely to be considerable variation in access to credit, credit history, attitudes toward building credit, etc., that stems from individual characteristics (presence of a co-signer, propensity to take risks, etc.). Since these factors are often unobserved, however, they may be endogenously determined. I discuss this prospect more fully in the methodology section.
7. Only those who reported bringing some savings to Canada (about 74 percent of the sample) are included in these calculations. For the multivariate models presented later, savings amounts were modelled with a dummy variable to denote whether or not persons brought some wealth with them. For those

who did, I entered the amount in logged dollars (giving a value of zero on this variable to those who brought no savings).

8. Some early readers of this paper have expressed concern about the relatively low entry ownership rates of Chinese, stating that typically this group has higher rates than most other groups. Although this does appear anomalous, others (Wang and Lo, 2005) have noted similar declines in the labour market for recent Chinese arrivals.

9. Several terms are used synonymously with event history analysis in the literature, including survival analysis and failure-time analysis, but for consistency I use "event history analysis" throughout the paper.

10. This is in part a function of the length of observation. The full attainment profile more closely resembles a j-shaped curve.

11. The large negative coefficients for the Chinese may be surprising to some, since Chinese are typically conceived as high home ownership groups, but the coefficients reflect the fact that this cohort largely hails from mainland China and is not as well-heeled as its predecessors.

12. Thanks to Ted McDonald for pointing out these assumptions after reading my chapter.

REFERENCES

Alba, R.D., and J. Logan. 1992. "Assimilation and Stratification in the Homeownership Patterns of Racial and Ethnic-Groups." *International Migration Review* 26 (4): 1314-41.

Alba, R., and V. Nee. 1997. "Rethinking Assimilation Theory for a New Era of Immigration." *International Migration Review* 31 (4): 826-74.

Allison, P.D. 1995. *Survival Analysis Using the SAS System : A Practical Guide*. Cary, NC: SAS Institute.

Badets, J., and T. Chui. 1994. *Canada's Changing Immigrant Population*. Toronto: Prentice Hall Canada.

Balakrishnan, T.R., and Z. Wu. 1992. "Home Ownership Patterns and Ethnicity in Selected Canadian Cities." *Canadian Journal of Sociology/Cahiers canadiens de sociologie* 17: 389-403.

Bianchi, S., R. Farley, and D. Spain. 1982. "Racial Inequalities in Housing: An Examination of Recent Trends." *Demography* 19 (1): 37-51.

Borjas, G.J. 1985. "Assimilation, Changes in Cohort Quality, and the Earnings of Immigrants." *Journal of Labor Economics* 3 (4): 463-89.

– 2002. "Homeownership in the Immigrant Population." *Journal of Urban Economics* 52 (3): 448-76.

Boyd, M. 2003. "Educational Attainments of Immigrant Offspring: Success or Segmented Assimilation?" In *Host Societies and the Reception of Immigrants*, edited by J. Reitz, 91-117. La Jolla, CA: Center for Comparative Immigration Studies.

Callis, R.R., and L.B. Cavanaugh. 2005. "Census Bureau Reports on Residential Vacancies and Homeownership." Washington, DC: United States Department of Commerce.

Di, Z.X. 2007. "Do Homeowners Have Higher Future Household Income?" *Housing Studies* 22: 459-72.

Edmonston, B. 2004. "Who Owns? Homeownership Trends for Immigrants in Canada." Winnipeg, MB: Canadian Population Society.

Elmelech, Y. 2004. "Housing Inequality in New York City: Racial and Ethnic Disparities in Homeownership and Shelter-Cost Burden." *Housing, Theory, and Society* 21: 163-75.

Flippen, C.A. 2001a. "Racial and Ethnic Inequality in Homeownership and Housing Equity." *Sociological Quarterly* 42: 121-49.

– 2001b. "Residential Segregation and Minority Home Ownership." *Social Science Research* 30: 337-62.

Freeman, L., and D. Hamilton. 2004. "The Changing Determinants of Inter-Racial Homeownership Disparities: New York City in the 1990's." *Housing Studies* 19: 301-23.

Green, R.K., and M.J. White. 1997. "Measuring the Benefits of Homeowning: Effects on Children." *Journal of Urban Economics* 41: 441- 61.

Haan, M. 2005a. "The Decline of the Immigrant Homeownership Advantage: Life-Cycle, Declining Fortunes and Changing Housing Careers in Montreal, Toronto and Vancouver, 1981-2001." *Urban Studies* 42: 1-22.

– 2005b. "The Decline of the Immigrant Homeownership Advantage: Life-Cycle, Declining Fortunes and Changing Housing Careers in Montreal, Toronto and Vancouver, 1981-2001." Ottawa: Statistics Canada.

– 2007a. "Do I Buy with a Little Help from My Friends? Homeownership-Relevant Group Characteristics and Homeownership Disparities among Canadian Immigrant Groups, 1971-2001." *Housing Studies* 22: 921-44.

– 2007b. "The Homeownership Hierarchies of Canada and the United States: The Housing Patterns of White and Nonwhite Immigrants of the Past 30 Years." *International Migration Review* 33: 433-65.

Henry, F. 1989. *Housing and Racial Discrimination in Canada*. Toronto: Policy and Research, Multiculturalism and Citizenship.

Hou, F. 2004. "Recent Immigration and the Formation of Visible Minority Neighbourhoods in Canada's Large Cities." Ottawa: Statistics Canada.

Hulchanski, D. 1993. "Barriers to Equal Access in the Housing Market: The Role of Discrimination on the Basis of Race and Gender." Toronto: Centre for Urban and Community Studies, University of Toronto.

– 1994. *Discrimination in Ontario's Rental Housing Market: The Role of Minimum Income Criteria*. Toronto: Ontario Human Rights Commission.

Jackman, M., and R. Jackman. 1980. "Racial Inequalities in Homeownership." *Social Forces* 58: 1221-34.

King, T.A., and P. Mieszkowski. 1973. "Racial Discrimination, Segregation and the Price of Housing." *Journal of Political Economy* 81: 590-606.

Krivo, L.J., and R.L. Kaufman. 2004. "Housing and Wealth Inequality: Racial-Ethnic Differences in Home Equity in the United States." *Demography* 41: 585-605.

Kurz, K., and H.-P. Blossfeld. 2004. *Home Ownership and Social Inequality in Comparative Perspective*. Stanford, CA: Stanford University Press.

Lindstrom, B. 1997. "A Sense of Place: Housing Selection on Chicago's North Shore." *Sociological Quarterly* 38: 19-39.

Marger, M.N. 2008. *Race and Ethnic Relations: American and Global Perspectives*. Belmont, CA: Wadsworth/Thomson Learning.

Massey, D.S., and N.A. Denton. 1993. *American Apartheid: Segregation and the Making of the Underclass*. Cambridge, MA: Harvard University Press.

McConnell, E.D., and I.Redstone Akresh. 2008. "Through the Front Door: The Housing Outcomes of New Lawful Immigrants." *International Migration Review* 42: 134–62.

Megbolugbe, I.F., and M. Cho. 1996. "Racial and Ethnic Differences in Housing Demand: An Econometric Investigation." *Journal of Real Estate Finance and Economics* 12: 295-318.

Mendez, P., D. Hiebert, and E. Wyly. 2006. "Landing at Home: Insights on Immigration and Metropolitan Housing Markets from the Longitudinal Survey of Immigrants to Canada." *Canadian Journal of Urban Research* 15: 82-104.

Murdie, R. 1994. "'Blacks in Near-Ghettos?' Black Visible Minority Population in Metropolitan Toronto Housing Authority Public Housing Units." *Housing Studies* 9: 435-57.

Myers, D. 1999. "Cohort Longitudinal Estimation of Housing Careers." *Housing Studies* 14: 473-90.

Myers, D., and S.W. Lee. 1998. "Immigrant Trajectories into Homeownership: A Temporal Analysis of Residential Assimilation." *International Migration Review* 32: 593-625.

Myers, D., I. Megbolugbe, and S.W. Lee. 1998. "Cohort Estimation of Homeownership Attainment among Native-Born and Immigrant Populations." *Journal of Housing Research* 9: 237-69.

Oliver, M.L.. and T.M. Shapiro. 1995. *Black Wealth/ White Wealth.* New York: Routledge.

Orfield, G., and N. McArdle. 2006. "The Vicious Cycle: Segregated Housing, Schools and Intergenerational Inequality." Cambridge, MA: Joint Center for Housing Studies, Harvard University.

Painter, G., L. Yang, and Z. Yu. 2003a. "Heterogeneity in Asian American Home-Ownership: The Impact of Household Endowments and Immigrant Status." *Urban Studies* 40: 505-30.

– 2003b. "Why Are Chinese Homeownership Rates So High?" Los Angeles: Lusk Center for Real Estate, University of Southern California.

Picot, G., and A. Sweetman. 2005. "The Deteriorating Economic Welfare of Immigrants and Possible Causes: Update 2005." Ottawa: Statistics Canada.

Portes, A., and M. Zhou. 1993. "The New Second Generation: Segmented Assimilation and Its Variants." *Annals of the American Academy of Political and Social Science* 530:74-96.

Raftery, A. 1995. "Bayesian Model Selection in Social Research." In *Sociological Methodology*, edited by P.V. Marsden, 111-95. Cambridge, MA: Blackwell.

Rosenbaum, E., and S. Friedman. 2007. *The Housing Divide: How Generations of Immigrants Fare in New York City's Housing Market.* New York: New York University Press.

Skaburskis, A. 1996. "Race and Tenure in Toronto." *Urban Studies* 33 (2): 223-52.

Statistics Canada. 2003. "Longitudinal Survey of Immigrants to Canada: Process, Progress and Prospects." Ottawa: Statistics Canada.

Wang, S., and L. Lo. 2005. "Chinese Immigrants in Canada: Their Changing Composition and Economic Performance." *International Migration* 43 (3): 35-71.

Warner, W.L., and L. Srole. 1945. *The Social Systems of American Ethnic Groups.* New Haven, CT: Yale University Press.

Yinger, J. 1986. "Measuring Racial Discrimination with Fair Housing Audits: Caught in the Act." *American Economic Review* 76 (5): 881-93.

– 1998. "Housing Discrimination Is Still Worth Worrying About." *Housing Policy Debate* 9: 893-927.

10

IMMIGRANT CHILDREN IN ELEMENTARY SCHOOL: AN INTERNATIONAL PERSPECTIVE

ARTHUR SWEETMAN

Cet article analyse, à l'aide des données de la Troisième enquête internationale sur la mathé-matique et les sciences (TEIMS), les résultats obtenus par les enfants immigrants âgés de 9 à 13 ans scolarisés en Australie, au Canada et aux États-Unis. Les résultats des enfants immigrants – particulièrement en sciences – comparés à ceux des enfants nés au pays, sont en moyenne inférieurs dans le cas du Canada et des États-Unis, mais sensiblement les mêmes dans le cas de l'Australie. Toutefois, en Amérique du Nord, à l'âge de 13 ans, les enfants immigrants et les enfants nés au pays obtiennent des résultats beaucoup plus proches qu'à l'âge de 9 ans, ce qui suggère que l'âge joue un rôle dans le rattrapage du retard chez les immigrants. Par ailleurs, après la première année passée au pays, le nombre d'années depuis l'immigration ne semble avoir aucun effet sur les résultats – et ce, dans les trois pays. Il existe cependant une corrélation entre les résultats et les caractéristiques propres à l'école fréquentée par les enfants. Les aptitudes langagières individuelles (selon les déclarations du répondant sur la langue parlée à la maison) et les aptitudes langagières moyennes à l'école que fréquente l'enfant sont, de façon indépendante, fortement reliées aux résultats. Enfin, quand on tient compte de l'effet de ces caractéristiques et d'autres variables, les résultats des immigrants se rapprochent de ceux des enfants nés au pays – et l'écart observé disparait dans le cas de l'Amérique du nord.

Test scores from the Third International Math and Science Survey (TIMSS) are used to compare immigrant children's outcomes in the school systems of Australia, Canada, and the United States in the grades containing children aged 9 to 13. Immigrants' scores, especially in science, are on average usually below those of the domestic born in Canada and the United States, but immigrants in Australia usually have scores comparable to those of the domestic born. In North America, immigrant outcomes are much closer to those of domestic born children at age 13 than at age 9, suggesting that catching up may

---

Canadian Immigration: Economic Evidence for a Dynamic Policy Environment, ed. T. McDonald, E. Ruddick, A. Sweetman, and C. Worswick. Montreal and Kingston: Queen's Policy Studies Series, McGill-Queen's University Press.

be associated with an age effect. In all three countries, years in the host country have almost no impact on test scores beyond the first year after arrival. School level character- istics are found to be correlated with student test score outcomes. Individual language skill (self-reported language use at home) and the average language skill in the student's school have large and independent associations with the test score outcomes. Once these and other characteristics are controlled for, the test scores of immigrants improve relative to those of the domestic born, and in North America the observed gaps are eliminated.

The vast majority of the economics literature on immigration focuses on prime-age males, while a smaller body of work looks at females, and some recent work looks at husband-wife pairs.[1] However, a substantial frac- tion of immigrants arrive in host countries as children, and little research has explored their integration into their new country's educational and social institutions. Since educational quality can have impacts on lifetime outcomes, this appears to be an issue worth understanding.

Several aspects of the integration of immigrant children into the host country's school system are explored here using data from the Third Inter- national Math and Science Survey (TIMSS). The analysis evaluates and compares immigrant and domestic born children's educational outcomes in math and science in three developed, immigrant-receiving English speaking countries: Australia, Canada, and the United States. The survey was structured so that, in addition to background questionnaires given to students and school representatives, students were given the same standardized test in each country with a variety of multiple choice and short answer questions. While test scores have been used as an outcome measure in numerous studies of children's education, their importance for long-term labour market outcomes has been underscored in work using British data by Gregg and Machin (2000) and Currie and Thomas (2001). Both studies demonstrate that scores from standardized tests taken in elementary school are correlated with educational and labour market outcomes at ages 23 and 33. Currie (2009) provides an interesting overview of childhood influences on outcomes in later life.

As far as I am aware, Worswick (2004) is the only other author who explores issues regarding child immigrants' integration into the host country education system as measured by test score outcomes.[2] He uses the first three waves of Statistics Canada's National Longitudinal Survey of Children and Youth (NLSCY) and therefore cannot compare across countries; he also does not look at the cohort, or school-level, correla- tions that will be explored here. In addition to outcomes in math that are addressed in both his and the current study, he looks at reading scores, which are not addressed here; however, his data, unlike the TIMSS, does not have science scores. Overall, he finds that parental language is a key correlate of student outcomes, and that as immigrant children age, their test scores improve relative to those of the Canadian born. The TIMSS data show similar patterns on many dimensions, which is notable since the nature of the TIMSS and NLSCY tests are quite different, with the TIMSS being curriculum based whereas the NLSCY is more attuned to skills for daily living.

A related interesting international literature looks at childhood age at immigration in relation to educational attainment by adulthood and labour market outcomes (Böhlmark 2008; Chiswick and DebBurman 2004; Gonzalez 2003; Schaafsma and Sweetman 2001; Van Ours and Veenman 2006). The consistent finding is that immigrants who arrive in the host country during their pre-teen years have remarkably good outcomes – better than those who arrive as teenagers, and usually at least as good, or better, than the domestic born. One plausible hypothesis that is consistent with this literature and this research is that immigrant children catch up as they age and gain English (or sometimes French in Canada) language skills, and they do well in terms of educational attainment as seen in data that look at ages older than those in the TIMSS.

Immigrants can be identified in the TIMSS data since students were asked if they were born in the country in which they were being educated, and if not, how old they were on arrival. (Unfortunately no questions were asked about their country of origin.) In addition to geographic identifiers, TIMSS data provide information deriving from questions about language use at home and, for the older age group only, about their parents' education. Further, given the clustered nature of the sample (students are sampled within schools), estimates of the fraction of students in each school with given characteristics can be easily calculated; these group-level characteristics can be used to look for linguistic and socio-economic neighbourhood, or cohort, (conditional) correlations.

One of the main messages of the current study is that there is important trans-national heterogeneity in the educational outcomes of immigrant children, as well as some common patterns. For example, immigrants are found to do less well than domestic born children in Canada and the United States, but not in Australia. Rapid integration is observed in all countries, and most importantly, language skills matter everywhere for math, and especially science, achievement. Although immigrant children at younger ages have lower test scores, the gap decreases in Canada and the United States as they age, and the gap is entirely explained by observable characteristics, especially language spoken at home.

Data Description and Methodology

Surveying and testing for the TIMSS were conducted in 42 countries in 1995 (or 1994 for some countries in the southern hemisphere). Immigrant children who had recently arrived in a host country and were not proficient in the language of instruction were not tested, and so the findings observed here are not driven by this type of outlier. More information regarding the TIMSS, the design of the tests, and the education systems in the countries involved can be found in Gonzalez and Smith (1997) and Robitaille (1997).

Two populations of students are studied here. Population 1 includes those in the adjacent grades with the highest number of children aged 9 (grades 3, 4, and 5 in Australia and grades 3 and 4 in Canada and the United States); population 2 contains the grades of those aged 13 (grades 7, 8, and 9 in Australia and grades 7 and 8 in Canada and the United States). The sample sizes across countries are quite different, with Canada having very large datasets.[3]

While two populations are studied here, the TIMSS database includes a third that is not used: those in their last year of secondary school. Sample selection problems arising from differential school dropout rates across countries, and within countries between immigrant and domestic born children, are quite difficult to deal with convincingly. Further, differences in the definition of the last year of secondary school across countries (and within some countries) also render comparisons difficult. While none of these studies explores dropout rates by immigrant status, they show substantial variability across racial and ethnic groups, suggesting that immigrants may have quite different senior high school enrolment rates than the domestic born. An enumeration of enrolment rates in the TIMSS countries by grade is available in Robitaille (1997), but the definitions are not standardized across countries, making comparisons difficult; further, rates are not available for different demographic groups. In contrast, in the two populations under study here, enrolment is extremely high, providing comparability.

Care must be taken in analyzing the TIMSS dataset since it is a stratified and clustered sample. Within each strata (either a country or a region within a country), schools were selected, and within each school, multiple classrooms were tested; therefore there are two levels of clustering. Further, the selection process was not entirely random, so sampling weights are provided. However, in all cases the TIMSS sample encompasses both private and public schools. For more detail on the survey design, see Gonzalez and Smith (1997). The econometric approach adopted here is to view both the sample means and the regression model coefficients as fixed finite-population parameters, and to estimate them and their standard errors, taking the nature of the data into account.

Descriptive Statistics

To facilitate comparisons and provide an intuitive metric for dealing with the test scores, each of the math and science results for each population (male and female combined) is converted to z-scores, and these are used throughout the paper.[4] Thus a score of 0.5 (-0.5) implies being one-half a standard deviation above (below) the three country average for the relevant grade. Table 1, in z-score format, presents the mean math and science scores by sex and immigrant status for each population. Looking at population 1 (approximately age 9) in the upper half of Table 1, it is clear that there are substantial differences across countries.

In both math and science, all of the Australian means, with the exception of the science scores of immigrant females, are above the three country mean, with many of the differences being statistically significant at the 5 percent level. Of course some of the Australian students are also one grade ahead. Notably, immigrant averages are mostly similar to, or above, those of the domestic born. In stark contrast, the results for Canada show substantial differences across the immigrant and domestic born groups, with immigrants having substantially (and statistically significantly) lower outcomes. In Canada only domestic born males, for both math and science, have a mean above the overall mean for population 1 in the three countries. Further, some of the gaps between immigrants and the Canadian born are quite sizeable. In Canada, the differences between immigrants and the domestic born are such that immigrants have apparently lower outcomes in both tests for both genders. The United States has the largest gaps between immigrants and the American born, not because the immigrants do worse there than in Canada, but rather the similarly

TABLE 1
Standardized Test Scores by Country and Immigrant Status

	Australia		Canada		United States	
	Immigrant	*Domestic*	*Immigrant*	*Domestic*	*Immigrant*	*Domestic*
Population 1						
Male						
Math	0.276	0.190	-0.358	0.096	-0.395	0.190
Science	0.221	0.196	-0.439	0.090	-0.420	0.298
Female						
Math	0.108	0.118	-0.468	0.013	-0.523	0.206
Science	-0.010	0.108	-0.505	-0.007	-0.557	0.215
Population 2						
Male						
Math	0.158	0.097	-0.072	0.110	-0.333	-0.071
Science	0.009	0.109	-0.183	0.096	-0.204	0.171
Female						
Math	0.034	0.112	-0.136	0.109	-0.092	-0.136
Science	-0.138	0.018	-0.390	-0.028	-0.169	0.062

Note: The test scores for each population and subject are presented as z-statistics. They, therefore, represent standard deviations from the three country mean; see the text for a discussion.

Source: Author's compilation.

poor immigrant outcomes are combined with higher averages for the domestic born students. Looking at the differences between males and females, within the immigrant and domestic born groups, the males' test scores are at least as high as the females' in every case except one, but the differences are frequently small.

Results for population 2 (approximately age 13), in the lower panel of Table 1, show in many cases a much less pronounced gap between domestic born and immigrants than was observed for population 1. Australia continues to have test results above the three nation average, but most of the differences are no longer statistically significant; immigrants, however, continue to do well there and are not distinguishable from the domestic born in these scores. In Canada (and largely for the United States) the gap between immigrants and the domestic born continues, although it is smaller than that for the younger students, and the gap for sciences tends to be larger than that for math. The domestic born American children in population 2 do not have the above-average scores observed in population 1, and for the most part immigrants do not have scores that are as far below the three country average. Overall, there appears to be a diminution of the gaps between the domestic born and immigrants for the older population for each of the three countries. It is possible that there is an aging effect, whereby outcomes improve and the gap between immigrants and the domestic born is reduced. This is explored in more detail below.

Looking at Table 2, which shows descriptive statistics for population 2, it is clear that immigrant and domestic born children have quite different demographics in all the countries. (Descriptive statistics are not presented for population 1, since they are quite similar to those for population 2, but they are discussed where relevant.) Geographic location categorized as urban, suburban, rural, and isolated (not applicable in some samples) is listed first in each table.[5] As is well known, and demonstrated here in both populations, immigrants are more, or much more, likely to reside in an urban environment, and less likely to live in a rural and isolated one. Immigrants are also less likely in Canada and the United States to live in the suburbs, but the reverse is true in Australia. Inasmuch as school quality varies across these types of geographic regions (and it may do so differently across countries), immigrants will differ from the domestic born. In many of the countries being studied, "urban" includes inner-city schools.

Immigrants are also dramatically more likely not to speak the language of instruction at home, or to speak it only sometimes. Table 2 shows that as many as 30-40 percent more children in immigrant households speak the language of instruction at home only sometimes compared to households where the children were born in the country. For Canada and the United States, the gap is even larger for population 1, in which just over 45 percent of the immigrant children do not speak the language of instruction at home (the sum of those who speak it sometimes and never). The United States, however, has a higher fraction who never speak the

TABLE 2
Sample Means of Selected Demographic Variables for Population 2

	Australia		Canada		United States	
	Immigrant	*Domestic*	*Immigrant*	*Domestic*	*Immigrant*	*Domestic*
Males						
Location						
Urban	0.298	0.311	0.770	0.549	0.579	0.434
Suburban	0.648	0.519	0.172	0.254	0.260	0.308
Rural	0.054	0.171	0.053	0.178	0.128	0.225
Isolated	-	-	0.005	0.018	0.032	0.034
Speaks instruct. lang. at home						
Sometimes	0.326	0.049	0.417	0.048	0.359	0.056
Never	0.035	0.010	0.053	0.010	0.088	0.006
Mother's education						
Some high school	0.186	0.301	0.074	0.110	0.085	0.078
High school	0.191	0.224	0.110	0.194	0.145	0.250
University	0.212	0.166	0.332	0.252	0.316	0.244
Father's education						
Some high school	0.156	0.250	0.050	0.119	0.072	0.084
High school	0.109	0.143	0.103	0.146	0.152	0.223
University	0.290	0.204	0.310	0.264	0.297	0.263
Percentage in the school						
Immigrants	0.210	0.109	0.246	0.077	0.137	0.060
Not language at home	0.184	0.087	0.197	0.082	0.155	0.080
Father has university degree	0.228	0.205	0.342	0.262	0.251	0.255
N	441	3892	448	5912	336	3815
% Immigrants	10.2		7.0		8.1	
Females						
Location						
Urban	0.336	0.368	0.757	0.552	0.609	0.433
Suburban	0.625	0.450	0.757	0.255	0.293	0.330
Rural	0.039	0.182	0.757	0.174	0.067	0.205
Isolated	-	-	0.757	0.019	0.031	0.033
Speaks instruct. lang. at home						
Sometimes	0.249	0.044	0.467	0.044	0.356	0.061
Never	0.035	0.003	0.020	0.006	0.039	0.002
Mother's education						
Some high school	0.206	0.334	0.064	0.131	0.082	0.094
High school	0.154	0.151	0.124	0.184	0.206	0.236
University	0.233	0.171	0.243	0.266	0.221	0.233
Father's education						
Some high school	0.151	0.258	0.042	0.129	0.076	0.098
High school	0.130	0.117	0.117	0.148	0.148	0.203
University	0.298	0.197	0.310	0.264	0.249	0.258
Percentage in the school						
Immigrants	0.177	0.096	0.264	0.077	0.161	0.062
Not language at home	0.139	0.073	0.221	0.079	0.193	0.081
Father has university degree	0.214	0.204	0.308	0.267	0.269	0.259
N	4551	4324	418	5908	277	4013
% Immigrants	9.5		6.6		6.5	

Note: Mother and father's education display only selected values. The full set is elementary or less, some high school, completed high school, completed vocational training, some university, completed university, and unknown. Equivalents are accepted in each case.

Source: Author's compilation.

language of instruction at home in both populations. In contrast to language use at home in Canada and the United States, in Australia there is a substantial drop from population 1 to population 2 in the fraction not regularly speaking the language of instruction at home, from about 50 percent to 25-35 percent. Language ability is clearly crucial to educational attainment, and this variable will be seen to play an important role in the analysis that follows. Given the cross-sectional nature of the data, it is of course not possible to ascertain whether the change in Australia is the result of a different mix of immigrant source countries across the two populations or some type of social "acculturation" process that is quite rapid in Australia.

For population 2 only, the survey includes a question about the highest level of completed education of each parent. This information is provided by the student, and is not asked of the younger population who are not believed to be able to answer about their parents' education with sufficient accuracy.[6] While there is a large "unknown" category that is excluded from this table but included as a separate group in the regression analysis that follows, this variable provides a useful indicator of family background. The categories captured in the survey for each parent are: grade school only, some high school, high school graduate, vocational certificate, some university, completed university, and unknown. In all three countries, immigrant children are seen to almost always have more highly educated parents than the domestic born. The effect is particularly strong in Australia and Canada, which have points systems that screen immigrants on entry, with education being one of the screens. The survey also includes information about the student's age and grade in school, which is coded as "lower grade" or "upper grade" relative to the grade with the highest fraction of students aged 9 (population 1) or 13 (population 2).

Three "school average" variables are employed in the analysis. These variables are the same for each person in a given school and represent the average of the relevant characteristic for that school. Each is a fraction or proportion and therefore is bounded between zero and one. The first is the fraction of students in the school who were not born in the host country – the fraction immigrant. The second is the fraction who never, or only sometimes, speak the language of instruction at home.[7] The third, which is only available for population 2 since this question was not posed to the younger population, is the fraction of parents in the school with a university degree. These three variables are meant to capture neighbourhood, or cohort, effects, and Table 2 illustrates that they differ substantially between foreign and domestic born children. The school-level measures are, by construction, the same for each child – immigrant and Canadian born – in a particular school. Foreign born children, on average, attend schools with two to three times more foreign born children than domestic born children. In all three countries there are clearly "immigrant schools." This effect is particularly strong in both Canada and population 1 in

Australia, where for domestic born children, on average, only 6-8 percent of their classmates are immigrants; for foreign born children, 18-21 percent of their classmates are also foreign born. Clearly immigrants are highly geographically concentrated.

Highly correlated with the fraction immigrant, the fraction of a student's classmates that do not speak the language of instruction at home is much higher if the child is an immigrant rather than domestic born, but, perhaps surprisingly, its effect is not quite as strong. In all three jurisdictions, an immigrant child has roughly twice as many classmates who do not speak the language of instruction at home. The level is, however, quite different across countries; it is between 15-28 percent for immigrant children across the three countries, with the United States and Australia having somewhat lower averages than Canada. Although the changes across populations are not shown in the table, it is interesting to consider them. The reduction in the fraction not speaking the language of instruction is larger in the United States and Australia than in Canada. It is possible that this difference may indicate a slower rate of linguistic integration in Canada; however, we only have one cross-section and there may be differences in composition across age groups

The fraction of children in each school with a father having a university degree is the third neighbourhood variable and is only available for population 2.[8] While the previous two neighbourhood variables are highly correlated with each other, this one is less highly correlated with either. Interestingly, there is no substantial difference in this variable for Australia or the United States, but in Canada immigrant children attend schools where a (statistically significantly) higher fraction of parents have university degrees: 26-27 percent for the Canadian born compared to 31-34 percent for the immigrant born. This accords with previous results from studies employing Canadian data (e.g., Finnie and Mueller 2010; Schaafsma and Sweetman 2001), which show adult immigrants to be more highly educated than the Canadian born, and to attend post-secondary at higher rates.

Regression Results

Ordinary least squares regression results are presented in Tables 3 through 8 (3-5 for population 1, and 6-8 for population 2), with each having the same format. Each table presents results for one country; columns 1 to 4 contain regression results for females, and columns 5 through 8 for males. For each sex, math results are presented first and science results next. Further, two regressions are run for each dependent variable: the first attempts to identify how immigrants do on each test relative to the domestic born without controlling for any variables that might be thought to be associated with immigrant status, and the next controls for a large list of explanatory variables in an effort to identify the influence of other characteristics on the immigrant coefficient.

The measures of school characteristics – the fraction of students who are immigrants, who do not speak the language of instruction at home regularly, and, for population 2 only, who have parents with a university degree – are highly correlated (especially the first two). Therefore, Table 9 presents coefficients for the school average variables from regressions that are otherwise similar to the larger ones in Tables 3 through 8, but each regression includes only a single school average regressor.

TABLE 3
Australia – Population 1: Male and Female Math and Science Regressions

	Females				Males			
	Math		Science		Math		Science	
Immigrant	0.025	0.096	-0.093	0.100	0.134	0.236*	0.062	0.234*
	(0.114)	(0.098)	(0.072)	(0.067)	(0.084)	(0.069)	(0.067)	(0.064)
YSM1	-0.652*	-0.634*	-0.488+	-0.425+	-0.501~	-0.457+	-0.343+	-0.297+
	(0.234)	(0.241)	(0.197)	(0.193)	(0.259)	(0.220)	(0.170)	(0.137)
Lower grade	-0.651*	-0.640*	-0.390*	-0.372*	-0.461*	-0.466*	-0.383*	-0.377*
	(0.079)	(0.079)	(0.084)	(0.080)	(0.082)	(0.081)	(0.102)	(0.096)
Upper grade	0.541*	0.506*	0.350*	0.291*	0.498*	0.461*	0.433*	0.363*
	(0.087)	(0.087)	(0.065)	(0.064)	(0.080)	(0.075)	(0.066)	(0.062)
Speaks instructional language at home								
Never		-0.829*		-0.939*		-0.742*		-0.937*
		(0.222)		(0.209)		(0.169)		(0.123)
Some		-0.176+		-0.366*		-0.166+		-0.365*
		(0.072)		(0.073)		(0.073)		(0.070)
Location								
Urban		-0.042		0.034		-0.172+		-0.008
		(0.128)		(0.094)		(0.087)		(0.10)
Rural		-0.10		0.021		-0.044		0.173
		(0.117)		(0.093)		(0.093)		(0.111)
Proportion in the school								
Immigrant		0.761		0.983+		0.697		1.712+
		(0.517)		(0.425)		(0.680)		(0.766)
Not home language		-0.611		-1.005*		-0.853		-1.307*
		(0.521)		(0.388)		(0.531)		(0.473)
R^2	0.185	0.200	0.111	0.151	0.138	0.157	0.104	0.150

Notes: Standard errors in parentheses: $p<0.10=$~, $p<.05=+$, $p<0.01=*$. N(females)= 4384; N(males)= 4325; N(Schools)= 154; N(Regions)= 8. Also included in the regression are seven regional dummy indicators, four dummy variables indicating age 8, 10, 11, and 12, and an intercept. The indicator variable YSM1 is set to one if years since migration is less than or equal to one.
Source: Author's compilation.

TABLE 4
Canada – Population 1: Male and Female Math and Science Regressions

	Females				Males			
	Math		Science		Math		Science	
Immigrant	-0.275*	-0.136+	-0.420*	-0.172*	-0.326*	-0.196+	-0.484*	-0.259*
	(0.076)	(0.059)	(0.072)	(0.062)	(0.087)	(0.081)	(0.073)	(0.065)
YSM1	-0.316+	-0.367*	-0.211	-0.321	-0.188	-0.228~	-0.049	-0.060
	(0.124)	(0.116)	(0.154)	(0.199)	(0.148)	(0.119)	(0.216)	(0.141)
Lower grade	-0.716*	-0.744*	-0.528*	-0.555*	-0.614*	-0.679*	-0.528*	-0.598*
	(0.048)	(0.042)	(0.055)	(0.051)	(0.072)	(0.065)	(0.057)	(0.049)
English	-0.542*	-0.807*	0.078	-0.135	-0.480*	-0.753*	0.024	-0.140
	(0.068)	(0.143)	(0.053)	(0.091)	(0.062)	(0.166)	(0.060)	(0.113)
Speaks instructional language at home								
Never		-0.397*		-0.427*		-0.295*		-0.396*
		(0.095)		(0.121)		(0.099)		(0.133)
Some		-0.179*		-0.276*		-0.166*		-0.308*
		(0.040)		(0.046)		(0.063)		(0.058)
Location								
Urban		-0.164+		-0.142*		-0.211*		-0.132+
		(0.078)		(0.054)		(0.060)		(0.063)
Rural		-0.225*		-0.174*		-0.201*		-0.160+
		(0.070)		(0.059)		(0.063)		(0.072)
Isolated		0.061		-0.004		-0.181		-0.122
		(0.241)		(0.154)		(0.116)		(0.140)
Proportion in the school								
Immigrant		1.356+		0.490		1.717*		1.058+
		(0.642)		(0.489)		(0.416)		(0.415)
Not home language		-1.459*		-1.217*		-1.596*		-1.598*
		(0.380)		(0.296)		(0.260)		(0.298)
R^2	0.239	0.310	0.138	0.215	0.187	0.263	0.125	0.212

Notes: Standard errors in parentheses: $p<0.10$=~, $p<.05$=+, $p<0.01$=*. N(females)= 6277; N(males)= 6303; N(Schools)= 360; N(Regions)= 7. Also included in the regression are six regional dummy indicators, four dummy variables indicating age 8, 10, 11, and 12, and an intercept. Indicator variables: YSM1, one if years since migration less than or equal to one; English, one if that language, as opposed to French, is the language of instruction.
Source: Author's compilation.

A preliminary exploration of the data (not shown) indicates that, unlike the labour market literature, there is no measurable "assimilation" or integration profile in test scores, except in some cases for the very first year after the immigrant has arrived.[9] Therefore, only a single "year since migration" (YSM1) indicator variable (sometimes called a dummy variable) is included to allow for this effect. Each regression also contains regressors to control for the student's age and grade (either above or below that of the majority of the target age). Children much older than those normally in the grade being surveyed tended to perform quite poorly (though the age coefficients are suppressed). The coefficients of the upper and/or lower variables provide an interesting measure of the value of a year's education and can be used as a benchmark against which the magnitudes of the other coefficients can be measured. For example, in column 5 of Table 4, the immigrant coefficient for Canadian males in math is -0.326, while the lower grade's coefficient is -0.614, suggesting that immigrants, on average, have test scores that are about half a grade behind those of the domestic born.

TABLE 5
United States – Population 1: Male and Female Math and Science Regressions

	Females				Males			
	Math		Science		Math		Science	
Immigrant	-0.626*	-0.292*	-0.702*	-0.316*	-0.453*	-0.207*	-0.607*	-0.307*
	(0.077)	(0.065)	(0.071)	(0.066)	(0.058)	(0.059)	(0.066)	(0.069)
YSM1	0.271	0.359~	0.145	0.250	0.551*	0.583*	0.553+	0.569*
	(0.251)	(0.198)	(0.307)	(0.248)	(0.169)	(0.142)	(0.215)	(0.175)
Lower grade	0.723*	0.717*	0.541*	0.531*	0.755*	0.748*	0.576*	0.569*
	(0.071)	(0.065)	(0.054)	(0.050)	(0.060)	(0.056)	(0.058)	(0.054)
Speaks instructional language at home								
Never		-0.577*		-0.700*		-0.555*		-0.586*
		(0.090)		(0.120)		(0.119)		(0.115)
Some		-0.214*		-0.184*		-0.197*		-0.266*
		(0.056)		(0.052)		(0.060)		(0.066)
Location								
Urban		-0.183+		-0.105		-0.224*		-0.174+
		(0.076)		(0.072)		(0.076)		(0.075)
Rural		-0.249*		-0.192*		-0.274*		-0.194+
		(0.081)		(0.073)		(0.073)		(0.077)
Isolated		-0.380*		0.167+		-0.364*		-0.143~
		(0.091)		(0.080)		(0.074)		(0.080)
Proportion in the school								
Immigrant		-1.721*		-1.742*		-1.466+		-1.361+
		(0.615)		(0.547)		(0.632)		(0.663)
Not home language		-0.574~		-0.948*		-0.750+		-1.003*
		(0.310)		(0.313)		(0.312)		(0.344)
R^2	0.176	0.253	0.118	0.221	0.161	0.246	0.118	0.217

Notes: Standard errors in parentheses: $p<0.10$=~, $p<.05$=+, $p<0.01$=*. N(females)= 4134; N(males)= 4018; N(Schools)= 155; N(Regions)= 4. Also included in the regression are three regional dummy indicators, four dummy variables indicating age 8, 10, 11, and 12, and an intercept. The indicator variable YSM1 is set to one if years since migration is less than or equal to one.
Source: Author's compilation.

TABLE 6
Australia – Population 2: Male and Female Math and Science Regressions

	Females				Males			
	Math		Science		Math		Science	
Immigrant	-0.061	-0.040	-0.146+	-0.107~	0.012	0.038	-0.111	-0.021
	(0.057)	(0.056)	(0.061)	(0.062)	(0.074)	(0.064)	(0.080)	(0.061)
YSM1	-0.565	-0.335	-0.472	-0.276	0.404	0.245	-0.250	-0.292~
	(0.402)	(0.309)	(0.424)	(0.334)	(0.257)	(0.226)	(0.212)	(0.161)
Lower grade	-0.415*	-0.411*	-0.360*	-0.343*	-0.312*	-0.357*	-0.303*	-0.372*
	(0.085)	(0.070)	(0.084)	(0.073)	(0.10)	(0.099)	(0.085)	(0.092)
Upper grade	0.460*	0.522*	0.458*	0.498*	0.527*	0.538*	0.510*	0.561*
	(0.092)	(0.057)	(0.079)	(0.055)	(0.110)	(0.087)	(0.094)	(0.076)
Location								
Urban		-0.027		-0.016		0.060		0.011
		(0.061)		(0.055)		(0.080)		(0.081)
Rural		0.026		-0.004		-0.024		-0.006
		(0.102)		(0.071)		(0.117)		(0.103)
Speaks instructional language at home								
Never		-0.233		-0.175		-0.264		-0.251
		(0.193)		(0.125)		(0.173)		(0.212)
Some		-0.270*		-0.249*		-0.172+		-0.290*
		(0.075)		(0.073)		(0.075)		(0.065)
Mother's education								
<=elem		-0.080		-0.186		-0.138		-0.180
		(0.136)		(0.122)		(0.185)		(0.158)
Some HS		-0.096~		-0.118+		-0.025		-0.040
		(0.052)		(0.051)		(0.071)		(0.067)
HS		-0.162*		-0.153+		-0.039		0.002
		(0.052)		(0.061)		(0.070)		(0.079)
Vocational training		0.036		-0.014		0.100		0.035
		(0.059)		(0.065)		(0.093)		(0.089)
Some university		0.013		0.032		0.182~		0.036
		(0.069)		(0.070)		(0.107)		(0.100)
Unknown		-0.275*		-0.226*		-0.068		-0.143~
		(0.061)		(0.064)		(0.068)		(0.076)
Father's education								
<=elem		-0.342*		-0.385*		-0.367+		-0.530*
		(0.124)		(0.122)		(0.167)		(0.142)
Some HS		-0.104~		-0.150*		-0.105		-0.174*
		(0.057)		(0.052)		(0.074)		(0.059)
HS		-0.058		-0.124+		-0.195*		-0.197*
		(0.060)		(0.063)		(0.071)		(0.067)
Vocational training		0.058		0.063		0.021		0.015
		(0.057)		(0.048)		(0.075)		(0.062)
Some university		0.077		-0.054		-0.026		-0.059
		(0.068)		(0.065)		(0.095)		(0.098)

... continued

TABLE 6
(Continued)

	Females		Males	
	Math	Science	Math	Science
Unknown	-0.014	-0.144*	-0.165+	-0.175+
	(0.053)	(0.049)	(0.077)	(0.070)
Proportion in the school				
Immigrant	-0.192	0.067	-0.145	-0.380
	(0.470)	(0.444)	(0.654)	(0.601)
Not home language	0.118	-0.567~	-0.177	-0.209
	(0.366)	(0.326)	(0.477)	(0.385)
Father has univ. degree	2.167*	1.589*	2.120*	1.658*
	(0.218)	(0.225)	(0.266)	(0.239)
R²	0.074 0.243	0.084 0.223	0.068 0.225	0.078 0.196

Notes: Standard errors in parentheses: p<0.10=~, p<.05=+, p<0.01=*. N(females)= 5021; N(males)= 4551; N(Schools)= 137; N(Regions)= 8. Also included in the regression are seven regional dummy indicators, four dummy variables indicating age 8, 10, 11, and 12, and an intercept. The indicator variable YSM1 is set to one if years since migration is less than or equal to one.
Source: Author's compilation.

Population 1

For population 1 in each country except Australia, the immigrant indicator variable is negative, large, and statistically significant for both males and females in math and science in the smaller regressions (odd-numbered column models with fewer regressors). To facilitate comparisons across countries, the immigrant coefficients from the larger regressions are plotted in Figure 1. In the Australian sample, the coefficient is never statistically different from zero. In all three countries, when the background and school characteristic variables are included in the regressions, the immigrant coefficient becomes more positive. In most cases it remains significant and negative but much smaller in magnitude. In Canada and the United States it becomes insignificant, and in some of the Australian regressions, significantly positive. Almost universally the coefficients on the language spoken at home and "never" indicator variables, which measure how frequently the language of instruction is spoken at home, are negative, large, and statistically significant. Language ability, proxied by the variables available in this dataset, is clearly an important determinant of these children's outcomes. Further, except in Australia, immigrant children are less likely to reside in suburban areas, where test scores are, for the most part, highest. Finally, in almost every regression there is a strong neighbourhood, or cohort, relationship. Children in schools with a higher fraction of immigrants, and a higher fraction of those who do not

TABLE 7
Canada – Population 2: Male and Female Math and Science Regressions

	Females				Males			
	Math		Science		Math		Science	
Immigrant	-0.107	0.000	-0.346*	-0.089	-0.085	-0.051	-0.298*	-0.092
	(0.075)	(0.076)	(0.063)	(0.056)	(0.077)	(0.069)	(0.105)	(0.096)
YSM1	0.032	0.008	-0.438~	-0.345~	0.321	0.210	-0.072	-0.059
	(0.201)	(0.174)	(0.239)	(0.201)	(0.233)	(0.199)	(0.239)	(0.217)
English	-0.688*	-0.764*	0.021	0.070	-0.483*	00.724*	0.115	0.145
	(0.077)	(0.088)	(0.071)	(0.087)	(0.080)	(0.119)	(0.078)	(0.105)
Lower grade	-0.550*	-0.520*	-0.368*	-0.363*	-0.540*	-0.513*	-0.420*	-0.405*
	(0.060)	(0.054)	(0.052)	(0.047)	(0.048)	(0.045)	(0.050)	(0.051)
Location								
Urban		-0.045		0.007		-0.034		-0.070
		(0.053)		(0.041)		(0.062)		(0.052)
Rural		0.109		-0.002		-0.019		0.002
		(0.078)		(0.052)		(0.074)		(0.063)
Isolated		-0.107		-0.188+		-0.189+		-0.250~
		(0.082)		(0.078)		(0.096)		(0.132)
Speaks instructional language at home								
Never		-0.317+		-0.268+		-0.104		-0.331~
		(0.147)		(0.105)		(0.112)		(0.200)
Some		-0.106~		-0.204*		-0.041		-0.210*
		(0.061)		(0.059)		(0.061)		(0.060)
Mother's education								
<=elem		-0.212*		-0.303*		-0.103		-0.177+
		(0.081)		(0.090)		(0.110)		(0.080)
Some HS		-0.239*		-0.232*		0.015		-0.160+
		(0.061)		(0.058)		(0.065)		(0.068)
HS		-0.034		-0.049		0.042		-0.016
		(0.052)		(0.051)		(0.046)		(0.049)
Vocational training		0.015		-0.022		0.087		0.118
		(0.069)		(0.056)		(0.067)		(0.089)
Some university		-0.117~		-0.068		0.035		-0.005
		(0.062)		(0.052)		(0.061)		(0.062)
Unknown		-0.226*		-0.239*		0.006		-0.181+
		(0.057)		(0.056)		(0.077)		(0.071)
Father's education								
<=elem		-0.229*		-0.139~		-0.254+		-0.202+
		(0.073)		(0.080)		(0.106)		(0.084)
Some HS		-0.076		0.026		-0.060		-0.031
		(0.061)		(0.065)		(0.058)		(0.077)
HS		-0.106~		-0.131+		-0.041		-0.153+
		(0.061)		(0.058)		(0.050)		(0.063)
Vocational training		-0.061		-0.001		-0.025		-0.040
		(0.067)		(0.071)		(0.062)		(0.057)

... continued

TABLE 7
(Continued)

	Females		Males	
	Math	Science	Math	Science
Some university	-0.067	-0.068	0.018	-0.003
	(0.071)	(0.063)	(0.068)	(0.071)
Unknown	-0.158*	-0.015	-0.193+	-0.115
	(0.057)	(0.062)	(0.075)	(0.079)
Proportion in the school				
Immigrant	-0.241	-0.382	-0.496+	-0.519+
	(0.322)	(0.244)	(0.233)	(0.238)
Not home language	0.412	-0.296	0.198	-0.300
	(0.331)	(0.234)	(0.230)	(0.206)
Father has univ. degree	0.907*	0.634*	0.998*	0.696*
	(0.139)	(0.146)	(0.134)	(0.117)
R^2	0.143	0.228	0.054	0.148	0.091	0.159	0.051	0.138

Notes: Standard errors in parentheses: $p<0.10=\sim$, $p<.05=+$, $p<0.01=*$. N(females)= 6737; N(males)= 6906; N(Schools)= 345; N(Regions)= 7. Also included in the regression are six regional dummy indicators, four dummy variables indicating age 8, 10, 11, and 12, and an intercept. Indicator variables: YSM1, one if years since migration less than or equal to one; English, one if that language, as opposed to French, is the language of instruction.
Source: Author's compilation.

FIGURE 1
Comparison of Population 1 Immigrant Coefficients

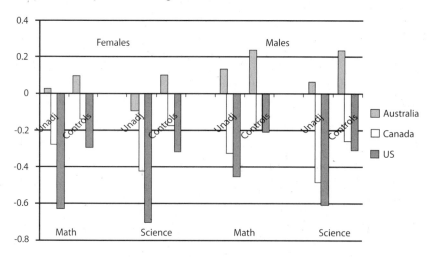

Source: Author's compilation.

TABLE 8
United States – Population 2: Male and Female Math and Science Regressions

	Females				Males			
	Math		Science		Math		Science	
Immigrant	0.117	0.223*	-0.195+	0.046	-0.153~	-0.084	-0.324*	-0.105
	(0.089)	(0.062)	(0.084)	(0.082)	(0.082)	(0.072)	(0.079)	(0.071)
YSM1	-0.532*	-0.670*	-0.232	-0.423+	-0.534*	-0.374+	-0.189	-0.119
	(0.201)	(0.209)	(0.202)	(0.211)	(0.194)	(0.172)	(0.232)	(0.239)
Lower grade	-0.366*	-0.325*	-0.338*	-0.311*	-0.484*	-0.457*	-0.347*	-0.334*
	(0.065)	(0.062)	(0.061)	(0.056)	(0.066)	(0.058)	(0.065)	(0.059)
Location								
Urban		0.006		-0.071		-0.025		-0.025
		(0.064)		(0.063)		(0.082)		(0.080)
Rural		0.217+		0.206+		0.092		0.195+
		(0.087)		(0.086)		(0.091)		(0.091)
Isolated		-0.145+		-0.241~		-0.316*		-0.297*
		(0.066)		(0.127)		(0.117)		(0.110)
Speaks instructional language at home								
Never		-0.243		-0.579+		-0.374*		-0.566*
		(0.207)		(0.243)		(0.134)		(0.188)
Some		-0.152+		-0.254*		-0.161+		-0.308*
		(0.066)		(0.059)		(0.073)		(0.076)
Mother's education								
<=elem		-0.342*		-0.097		-0.129		0.061
		(0.130)		(0.132)		(0.109)		(0.140)
Some HS		-0.222*		-0.301*		-0.076		-0.094
		(0.066)		(0.062)		(0.067)		(0.085)
HS		-0.152*		-0.128+		-0.048		-0.028
		(0.048)		(0.051)		(0.054)		(0.058)
Vocational training		-0.197*		-0.236*		-0.090		-0.103
		(0.056)		(0.067)		(0.060)		(0.071)
Some university		-0.060		-0.050		-0.054		-0.018
		(0.048)		(0.049)		(0.048)		(0.056)
Unknown		-0.091		-0.130		-0.184+		-0.117
		(0.078)		(0.081)		(0.092)		(0.086)
Father's education								
<=elem		-0.135		-0.290+		-0.341*		-0.365*
		(0.085)		(0.119)		(0.103)		(0.121)
Some HS		-0.166*		-0.171*		-0.234*		-0.283*
		(0.057)		(0.065)		(0.058)		(0.068)
HS		-0.150*		-0.138*		-0.102~		-0.102~
		(0.049)		(0.050)		(0.052)		(0.054)
Vocational training		-0.051		-0.038		-0.038		-0.051
		(0.057)		(0.066)		(0.058)		(0.059)
Some university		0.034		0.021		-0.011		0.051
		(0.044)		(0.051)		(0.054)		(0.064)

... continued

TABLE 8
(Continued)

		Females				Males		
		Math		Science		Math		Science
Unknown		-0.113~		-0.085		-0.043		-0.014
		(0.061)		(0.071)		(0.073)		(0.080)
Proportion in the school								
Immigrant		0.169		-0.361		0.473		-0.819
		(0.464)		(0.490)		(0.527)		(0.541)
Not home language		-0.174		-0.333		-0.361		0.017
		(0.384)		(0.373)		(0.429)		(0.430)
Father has univ. degree		1.911*		1.341*		2.058*		1.448*
		(0.218)		(0.183)		(0.278)		(0.225)
R^2	0.051	0.237	0.039	0.181	0.056	0.219	0.037	0.140

Notes: Standard errors in parentheses: $p<0.10$=~, $p<.05$=+, $p<0.01$=*. N(females)= 4480; N(males)= 4359; N(Schools)= 153; N(Regions)= 4. Also included in the regression are three regional dummy indicators, four dummy variables indicating age 8, 10, 11, and 12, and an intercept. Indicator variable, YSM1, is one if years since migration less than or equal to one.

Source: Author's compilation.

speak the language of instruction at home, tend to have lower test scores even after controlling for individual language usage. Of course, we do not understand how students select or are sorted into schools, so we do not know if this is a causal relationship, but it is suggestive of peer effects.

Population 2

In population 2, the story is much more optimistic than in population 1, and the immigrant coefficients, shown in Figure 2, are not as strongly negative. Many in the (smaller) regressions that control for fewer demographics have immigrant coefficients that are negative and statistically significant; however, they are not as large as in population 1. Those for science are more negative than those for math, especially in Canada and the United States. It is possible that the years between ages 9 and 13 are important in that children's educational outcomes during this period are increasingly determined by factors outside the home. Note that this is not an "assimilation" or integration effect, since there is no obvious test score profile across years in the host country except for the adjustment associated with the first year after entry. Further, for every regression sample, the immigrant indicator variable's coefficient becomes more positive when controls are added: either small and insignificantly negative, or positive (sometimes statistically significantly so).

FIGURE 2
Comparison of Population 2 Immigrant Coefficients

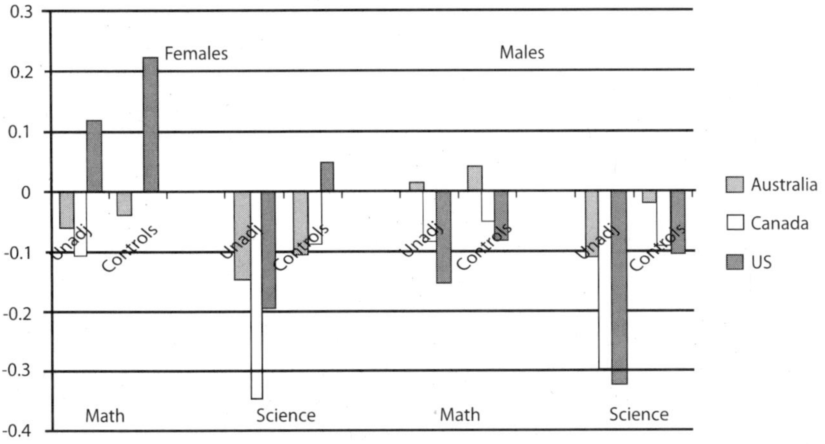

Source: Author's compilation.

Looking in detail at the smaller regressions that identify how well immigrants do without controlling for background and neighbourhood influences first, there is considerable heterogeneity in science across the three countries. Immigrant children in Canada and the United States, especially the males, appear to be at a sizeable disadvantage relative to the domestic born students in their age group. This is particularly striking since immigrant children are much more similar to the domestic born in Australia (although females have a negative and statistically significant coefficient in Australia, it is not nearly as large). For math, the only statistically significant negative coefficient is that for males in the United States, and the size of the coefficient is only half the size of the similar one in the United States for science. It seems plausible that more language skills are required for science than math, and that immigrant children have a deficit in this area.

Looking next at the regressions in the even-numbered columns that control for a variety of individual and neighbourhood characteristics, immigrant children appear to do as well as the domestic born. This result occurs because while immigrants, on average, are more likely to have some characteristics associated with higher test scores, such as parents who are more highly educated, many of the characteristics having negative coefficients, such as living in an urban area and speaking the language of instruction only sometimes or never at home, are also more common for immigrant than for domestic born children, and these latter score-reducing characteristics dominate.[10] It is remarkable that the measures in the dataset are sufficient to explain the gap. Looking more carefully at the individual language variables, the coefficients are always negative, and they are frequently large and statistically significant. In Canada and the United States, and for Australian males, the coefficients are much more negative for science than math, but this is not the case for females in Australia. These variables, as seen in Table 2, are defined for both immigrants and the domestic born, but immigrants are much more likely to not speak the dominant language (normally English, but sometimes French in Canada).

More on Neighbourhood Effects

The fraction of the pupils in each student's school who are immigrants and who do not speak the language of instruction regularly at home is highly collinear, and there are large changes in the coefficient estimates when they are entered singly into the regression, as reported in Table 9, compared to when they are both included in the regression, as in the even-numbered columns of Tables 3-8.[11] In both Canada and the United States, when these language variables are entered individually (as reported in Table 9), their coefficients are mostly negative, large, and statistically significant for the science test scores but more mixed for math. For Australia, the classroom language coefficient is similar for science, but it is not statistically significant. Once again, language seems to play a more important role in science than in math, and in North America than in Australia. One interesting observation is that in some cases both the fraction immigrant and the fraction not speaking the language of instruction at home regularly are negative when entered individually, but when they are included in the same regression, the fraction immigrant becomes positive. This suggests that, holding language skills constant, immigrants impose a positive externality on their classmates, and it is only language skills that are causing the low outcomes.

Whether specified alone, or with the other two neighbourhood variables, the neighbourhood effect is very similar in all countries: schools with a high fraction of children with parents with university degrees have substantially, and statistically significantly, higher outcomes in both subjects. Further, this occurs controlling for each child's parents' education. A very strong effect is captured by the neighbourhood parents' education variable.

DISCUSSION AND CONCLUSIONS

One of the advantages of a three-country international comparison of immigrant children's outcomes in elementary school is that it gives a better sense of the range of outcomes that are possible. Of course, the exercise is also much "messier" for exactly the same reason. While Canada and

TABLE 9
Neighbourhood Regression Coefficients

	Australia		Canada		United States	
	Math	Science	Math	Science	Math	Science
Population 1						
Males						
Immig.	-0.045	0.575	-0.065	-0.727+	-2.460*	-2.690*
Language	-0.505	-0.450	-0.913*	-1.178*	-1.306*	-1.518*
Females						
Immig.	0.237	0.122	-0.179	-0.791+	-2.448*	-2.944*
Language	-0.212	-0.490	-0.923*	-1.023*	-1.219*	-1.601*
Population 2						
Males						
Immig.	0.269	-0.121	-0.237	-0.669*	-0.082	-0.971~
Language	-0.429	-0.585~	-0.255	-0.721*	-0.790~	-0.895*
Father-univ.	2.113*	1.631*	-0.960*	0.695*	2.084*	1.464*
Females						
Immig.	0.161	-0.225	0.107	-0.573*	-0.455	-0.955+
Language	-0.463	-0.866*	0.152	-0.626*	-0.900*	-1.098*
Father-univ.	2.151*	1.639*	0.881*	0.641*	1.928*	1.407*

Notes: $p<0.10$=~, $p<.05$=+, $p<0.01$=*. Coefficients are from regressions similar to those in the even numbered columns in Tables 3 through 8, but (because they are collinear) with only the single neighbourhood variable shown included in each regression. Variables are the proportions of students in each school who: are immigrants, speak the language of instruction at home never or only sometimes, and have a father who has a university degree.
Source: Author's compilation.

the United States appear to have very similar patterns in the data, many results are quite different from those of Australia. To what extent these gaps arise from differences in the nature of the immigrants arriving in each country, as opposed to differences following from educational and immigrant settlement programs and/or social norms across the countries, cannot be completely determined in this data. Both Australia and Canada have points systems that screen immigrants on entry, while the United States does not; all three countries experience "waves" of immigrants from different source countries that may induce differences in language ability over time. Australia's system of language testing for adult skilled immigrants plausibly results in higher reported use of the language of instruction at home (and quite likely greater unmeasured English language skills), and this seems to be a particularly important issue to pursue.

An aging effect may be occurring whereby immigrant students' test scores accelerate positively as they gain language skills and maturity. As seen in Aydemir and Sweetman (2008), the 1.5 immigrant generation as adults (conceptually the same one looked at here) has educational attainment that exceeds that of the Canadian born, but the rate of return to education in the labour market is slightly lower. The acceleration seen here in test scores may translate into educational attainment. This is also consistent with the work of Finnie and Mueller (2010) and Schaafsma and Sweetman (2001) who observe remarkable educational attainment in the Canadian school system for immigrants who arrive as children.

In contrast to the heterogeneity, any regularities observed across countries can be taken to be quite robust. First among these is the implication for students of not regularly speaking the language of instruction at home, which is ubiquitous and has a very large negative effect. It appears that a strengthening of language instruction for these students would facilitate their education in sciences and, to a lesser extent, math. Neighbourhood or school (cohort) effects are also observed to be widespread and large. Controlling for a student's own language background and other demographics, having a higher fraction of those who do not speak the language of instruction at home regularly in a school is associated with reduced outcomes in that school. However, controlling for the fraction who do not speak the language of instruction at home, it appears that the fraction immigrant can have a positive impact, suggesting that once language is taken into account, immigrants exert an above-average and positive influence on the outcomes of students around them, both immigrant and non-immigrant. Of course, this paper does not look at causal mechanisms.

Overall, this study points to the importance and necessity of increasing language training for those whose home language is not the language of instruction. This characteristic is observed to have a large negative impact on student performance in math and science, and it is possible that this may well extend to other aspects of life.

Notes

Thanks to a SSHRC INE grant for funding and to Don Devoretz, Craig Riddell, David Robitaille, Chris Worswick, participants at the RIIM seminar series and the WRNET Summer Institute in Labour Economics for comments, and to Rob McPhee for excellent research assistance.

1. See Grant and Sweetman (2004) and Sweetman and Warman (2008) for introductions to the Canadian economics literature on immigration. Baker and Benjamin (1997) look at spousal labour supply and human capital investment post immigration. Borjas (1999) provides a more technical and comprehensive review of related economics research.
2. Bleakley and Chin (2004) look at adult labour market outcomes for child immigrants in the United States. They focus on the importance of relatively easy language acquisition for young immigrants and look at how this interacts with education.
3. Unlike in the school systems in most countries, each province in Canada has jurisdiction over education and operates a completely independent school system. A large sample was obtained since some provinces wanted a sufficient

sample size to permit province-level analysis. In contrast, in the United States, which also has a very decentralized school system, each state has considerable independence in operating its schools, but each must also meet federal standards. Related to regional issues, in Australia one of the provisions of the survey was that the individual regions would not be identified.

4. Using the sample from the three countries combined, the mean and standard deviation of the math and science scores are calculated. The mean is then subtracted from each individual's score, and this difference is divided by the standard deviation.

5. The data also identifies the region of the country in which the student lives, and there are differences in immigrant densities across regions, but we do not discuss that here.

6. Finnie, Laporte, and Sweetman (2010) compare parent and youth reports of parents' education in the Canadian Youth in Transition Survey (YITS), which asks the question to both youth and their parents when the youth are 15 years of age. While there is some evidence of measurement error in the youth reports, it is quite modest for levels of aggregation similar to that here.

7. The analysis was also conducted using the fraction who speak the language of instruction at home sometimes, and never, as separate variables. But these two variables are highly correlated, and the fraction reporting never is small enough so as to be poorly estimated in many schools. The sum of the two is therefore used to generate the school measure. In the regression analysis that follows, no appreciable difference in the results occurs as a result of using this specification. Note also that for Canada only the regressions contain an indicator for whether the language of instruction is English as opposed to French.

8. Specifications using mothers' education were also estimated, but those using fathers' education had slightly smaller sampling variances. The basic pattern does not change appreciably.

9. Recall that very recent immigrants without a sufficient mastery of the language of instruction were not tested. Examples of this type of analysis in the labour market literature include Baker and Benjamin (1994), Beggs and Chapman (1991), and Borjas (1995).

10. Of course, the individual language variables measure the same thing for both the domestic born and immigrants, and some domestic born children may speak a language other than the language of instruction at home much of the time.

11. These variables are always specified linearly. Versions of the models with quadratic specifications were also run, and the quadratic term was never statistically significant except for some of the Australian regressions. To facilitate comparability, only linear specifications are presented, but none of the substantive results would change, were quadratic specifications employed.

References

Aydemir, A., and A. Sweetman. 2008. "First and Second Generation Immigrant Educational Attainment and Labor Market Outcomes: A Comparison of the United States and Canada." *Research in Labor Economics* 27: 215-70.

Baker, M., and D. Benjamin. 1997. "The Role of the Family in Immigrants' Labor Market Activity: An Evaluation of Alternative Explanations." *American Economic Review* 87: 705-27.

Beggs, J.J., and B.J. Chapman. 1991. "Male Immigrant Wage and Unemployment Experience in Australia." In *Immigration, Trade and the Labor Market*, edited by J.M. Abowd and R. Freeman. Chicago: University of Chicago Press.

Bleakley, H., and A. Chin. 2004. "Language Skills and Earnings: Evidence from Childhood Immigrants." *Review of Economics and Statistics* 86: 481-96.

Böhlmark, A., 2008. Age at Immigration and School Performance: A Siblings Analysis Using Swedish Register Data. *Labour Economics* 15: 1366-87.

Borjas, G.J. 1995. "Assimilation and Changes in Cohort Quality Revisited: What Happened to Immigrant Earnings in the 1980s?" *Journal of Labor Economics* 13 (2): 201-45.

– 1999. "The Economic Impact of Immigration." In *Handbook of Labor Economics*, vol. 3A, edited by O. Ashenfelter and D. Card, 1697-1760. Amsterdam: North-Holland.

Chiswick, B.R., and N. DebBurman. 2004. "Educational Attainment: Analysis by Immigrant Generation." *Economics of Education Review* 23: 361-79.

Currie, J. 2009. "Healthy, Wealthy, and Wise: Socioeconomic Status, Poor Health and Childhood, and Human Capital Development." *Journal of Economic Literature* 47 (1): 87-122.

Currie, J., and D. Thomas. 2001. "Early Test Scores, Socioeconomic Status, School Quality and Future Outcomes." *Research in Labor Economics* 20: 103-32.

Finnie, R., C. Laporte, and A. Sweetman. 2010. "Dropping Out and Bouncing Back: New Evidence on High School Dynamics in Canada." In *Pursuing Higher Education in Canada: Economic, Social and Policy Dimensions*, edited by R. Finnie, M. Frenette, R.E. Mueller, and A. Sweetman. Montreal and Kingston: Queen's Policy Studies Series, McGill-Queen's University Press.

Finnie, R., and R.E. Mueller. 2010. "They Came, They Saw, They Enrolled: Access to Post-Secondary Education by the Children of Canadian Immigrants." In *Pursuing Higher Education in Canada: Economic, Social and Policy Dimensions*, edited by R. Finnie, M. Frenette, R.E. Mueller, and A. Sweetman. Montreal and Kingston: Queen's Policy Studies Series, McGill-Queen's University Press.

Gonzalez, A. 2003. "The Education and Wages of Immigrant Children: The Impact of Age at Arrival." *Economics of Education Review* 22: 203-12.

Gonzalez, E.J., and T.A. Smith. 1997. *User Guide for the TIMSS International Database: Primary and Middle School Years*. Chestnut Hill, MA: TIMSS International Study Center, Boston College.

Grant, H., and A. Sweetman. 2004. "Introduction to Economic and Urban Issues in Canadian Immigration Policy." *Canadian Journal of Urban Research* 13 (1): 1-24.

Gregg, P., and S. Machin. 2000. "Child Development and Success or Failure in the Youth Labour Market." In *Youth Employment and Joblessness in Advanced Countries*, edited by D.G. Blanchflower and R.B. Freeman, 247-88. Chicago: University of Chicago.

Robitaille, D.F., ed. 1997. *National Contexts for Mathematics and Science Education: An Encyclopedia of the Education Systems Participating in TIMSS*. Vancouver: Pacific Educational Press.

Schaafsma, J., and A. Sweetman. 2001. "Immigrant Earnings: Age at Immigration Matters." *Canadian Journal of Economics* 34 (4): 1066-99.

Sweetman, A., and C. Warman. 2008. "Integration, Impact, and Responsibility: An Economic Perspective on Canadian Immigration Policy." In *Immigration and Integration in Canada in the Twenty-First Century*, edited by J. Biles, M. Burstein, and J. Frideres, 19-44. Montreal and Kingston: Queen's Policy Studies Series, McGill-Queen's University Press.

Van Ours, J.C., and J. Veenman. 2006. "Age at Immigration and Educational Attainment of Young Immigrants." *Economics Letters* 90 (3): 310-16.

Worswick, C. 2004. "Adaptation and Inequality: Children of Immigrants in Canadian Schools." *Canadian Journal of Economics* 37: 53-77.

11

DIFFERENCES IN FERTILITY DECISIONS OF CANADIAN IMMIGRANT HOUSEHOLDS

ALICIA ADSERA AND ANA FERRER

Dans cet article, nous analysons les décisions en matière de fécondité chez les immigrants au Canada. Pour ce faire, nous utilisons les données portant sur les femmes de 16 à 45 ans de l'échantillon de 20 pourcent du Recensement de la population du Canada pour les années 1991, 1996, 2001 et 2006. Tout d'abord, nous étudions l'impact de l'âge au moment de l'immigration et la composition de la famille sur la fécondité. Les résultats montrent une relation non linéaire entre la fécondité et l'âge au moment de l'immigration; les femmes qui immigrent à l'approche de la vingtaine ont un taux de fécondité supérieur à celui des femmes du même âge nées Canada; et la composition de la famille a une influence particulière sur la fécondité chez la population immigrante. Ensuite, nous analysons le phénomène d'assimilation intergénérationnelle chez les immigrants. Nous observons que, si les immigrantes de la deuxième génération ont en moyenne un taux de fécondité semblable à celui des femmes nées au Canada, il y a des différences importantes lorsqu'on tient compte du pays d'origine des parents; par exemple, les femmes nées de parents asiatiques ont un taux de fécondité beaucoup moins élevé que celui des femmes nées de parents mexicains, européens et moyen-orientaux.

We explore the fertility decisions of Canadian immigrants using the 20 percent sample of the Canadian Census of Population for the years 1991, 1996, 2001, and 2006. Using women 16 to 45 years of age, we study the relevance of age at migration and family composition for fertility. We find a non-linear relationship between age of migration and immigrant fertility, with those migrating in their late teens having the highest fertility rates when compared to the Canadian born; moreover, family composition has a distinct influence on fertility among immigrants. We also investigate the intergenerational assimilation of immigrants. Using information on parental place of birth, we find that

Canadian Immigration: Economic Evidence for a Dynamic Policy Environment, ed. T. McDonald, E. Ruddick, A. Sweetman, and C. Worswick. Montreal and Kingston: Queen's Policy Studies Series, McGill-Queen's University Press.
© 2010 The School of Policy Studies, Queen's University at Kingston. All rights reserved.

although second generation Canadians have on average similar fertility rates to those of Canadian born, there are large differences in fertility by place of parental birth, with those of Asian descent having substantially lower fertility rates than those of Mexican, European, and Middle Eastern parentage.

INTRODUCTION

Canada has received continuous flows of immigrants throughout its history, although the intensity of migration and the source countries have fluctuated and changed over time. The immigrant population, as a percentage of total Canadian population, almost doubled between 1980 and 2006. Estimates from the 2006 Canadian Census indicate that 20 percent of Canada's population was foreign born and that another 13 percent were the children of foreign born parents or second generation Canadians. These estimates also report substantial changes in the composition of immigration. Whereas the majority of immigrants arriving before 1980 were from the United States or Europe (41 percent), only 19 percent of recent arrivals came from those places in 2006. The increase in immigration and the change in its composition have originated an extended literature documenting the economic performance of recent immigrants and how well they seem to assimilate in Canadian culture. In this paper we study fertility behaviour of both first and second generation Canadian women as compared to the childbearing patterns of women born in Canada of Canadian parents. Analyzing immigrant fertility differentials is important from a diverse array of reasons that include, among others, understanding the changing shape of family structure in this country and the socio-economic integration of immigrant women. In addition, this analysis is key to forecast the future demographic structure of the country and to assess the sustainability of generous welfare policies burdened by increasing age-dependency ratios and pressures on social services as the baby-boom generation retires (Belanger et al. 2005; Coleman 2006; United Nations 2000).

This paper looks into the fertility decisions of Canadian immigrants using the 20 Percent Sample of the Canadian Census of Population for the years 1991 to 2006 among women 16 to 45 years of age. We introduce measures of family composition and age at migration, which we find to have a distinctive influence on fertility. In particular, we find a non-linear relationship between age of migration and immigrant fertility. Those migrating as children or as adults show fertility rates only slightly higher than the Canadian born. Those migrating in their late teens, however, have substantially higher fertility rates. This finding points to some critical periods of immigration for smoother assimilation. We also look into the intergenerational assimilation of immigrants. The 2001 and 2006 Censuses provide information on parental place of birth that allows us to distinguish among immigrants by first, second, and second and a half generation. We use this information to study differences in fertility between the Canadian born children of immigrants and their immigrant parents.

The next section of the paper reviews recent findings on fertility behaviour and assimilation of immigrants that inform our analyses. We then describe the data employed and the empirical strategy followed, discuss the estimates of the fertility behaviour of Canadian immigrants as compared to the Canadian born, and show estimates on intergenerational fertility assimilation. We conclude with some general comments about the findings and future research.

BACKGROUND LITERATURE

Although Canada has traditionally been an immigrant receiving country, the nature and composition of immigration has changed significantly during the past 30 years. Before 1980, the majority of immigrants came from the United States or Europe (41 percent), while by 2006 only 19 percent of recent arrivals (that is, those arriving within the last five years) were coming from those places. Currently, immigration from Asia constitutes 58 percent of recent arrivals versus 34 percent of those who arrived before 1980, and twice as many recent newcomers are coming from Africa than did before 1980. The increase in immigration and the change in its composition have originated an extended literature documenting the economic performance of recent immigrants and how well they seem to assimilate in Canadian culture.[1]

Fertility behaviour likely plays an important role in many dimensions of immigrant well-being, as fertility rates shape the socio-economic assimilation and mobility of immigrant women. For instance, individual investments in human capital usually require postponement of fertility, and employment opportunities and career advancement tend to become too costly for women with a large number of children.[2] Therefore, high (and early) fertility may hinder the socio-economic integration of immigrant women, perpetuating more traditional gender roles within immigrant households. Improved economic opportunities in Canada compared to those in the country of origin and their interaction with the Canadian born may affect the fertility preferences of immigrants. Alternatively, even if childbearing preferences remain the same, the new environment that immigrants face in Canada, both in terms of opportunities and of costs, may alter their ultimate fertility decisions. Immigrant women may find better labour market opportunities than in their countries of origin and decide to reduce/postpone fertility in order to work. Alternatively, in the absence of informal child care provided by relatives, they may find formal daycare expensive. As a result, they may decide to either maintain the (generally higher) home country levels of fertility while staying at home or trade off children for work (Galor and Weil 1996). Further, given the trade-offs faced in terms of time and resources within households, the ultimate choice of more children over potentially more resources devoted to the rearing of each child may have repercussions on the well-being of the second generation of immigrants.[3] In this regard, Blau et al. (2008) find that in the United States second-generation women's schooling levels are negatively affected by the average fertility of immigrants of their parents' descent.

Different models of fertility adjustment try to explain the fertility experiences of immigrants. The *assimilation model* suggests that couples migrating from a country with higher fertility rates will initially follow their own country's fertility patterns and will only gradually adjust to the fertility rates of the host country. This assimilation process may take more than one generation to accomplish. Adaptation takes place as immigrants' expectations and cultural values change or as they gain knowledge of opportunity costs in the host country (Fernandez and Fogli 2006). In the short run, however, fertility may follow the *disruption model*, which postulates an initial drop in couples' fertility around the time of migration and a fertility rebound later on (Blau 1992; Kahn 1994). The two models can be combined, and it may be possible to observe an initial drop in fertility at the time of immigration, followed by a subsequent rise in fertility that gradually declines to converge to the host country levels. Economic theory builds on these ideas to incorporate the role that prices, opportunity costs, and fertility regulation play in fertility decisions. Changes from the source to the host country in female wages, household income, and fertility regulation will therefore affect couples' fertility.

In this regard, results from the empirical investigation of immigrant fertility are mixed. Blau's influential study (1992) seems to support the disruption model regarding short run fertility adjustments of immigrants in the United States. Current research is more focused on long run fertility adjustments. For instance, Parrado and Morgan (2008) find compelling empirical evidence of fertility assimilation for Hispanic women in the United States. In Canada, fertility studies show that up to 1980 Canadian immigrants had lower fertility rates than the Canadian born (Kalbach 1970), but the trend has since reversed (Belanger and Gilbert 2003). Ng and Nault (1997), and Ram and George (1990) find evidence of short lived fertility disruption upon immigration and quick convergence with domestic born fertility levels with socio-economic assimilation.

DATA AND EMPIRICAL APPROACH

The analysis of fertility behaviour can focus on the number of children women have and/or on the timing of childbearing over the fertile life of a woman. In this paper we focus on the total number of children born to women aged 15 to 45, conditional on their migration status as well as on a set of additional independent variables.

Because it can lead to negative predicted values, ordinary least squares is not the most appropriate model to explain variation in event count dependent variables such as fertility. Event count models measure how often an event – in this case, having a child – occurs over a given time interval. We estimate the model using the Poisson regression model in equation (1):

$$F_i = e^{\beta I i + \gamma X i} + \varepsilon_i \qquad (1)$$

where F is the measure of fertility of female i (in our case, total number of children), I is an immigrant indicator, X is a vector of individual charac-teristics that may influence fertility, including age, presence of additional members in the household, geographic location, socio-economic status of the household, and cultural/religious background, and ε is the error term. Since not all respondents, when observed, have experienced the same number of fertile years, we control for the exposure time (defined as age minus 15 years) in our models. In general, regression coefficients from non-linear models have no easy interpretation. For this reason we report in the tables the incident rate ratios (IRR). In the most parsimoni-ous model, we will be interested in comparing the predicted fertility rate (or fertility incidence) between two observations that differ only in that variable I_i takes on a value of 1 for immigrants and 0 for the Canadian born. The ratio of these two incidence rates is given by

$$IRR(I_i) = \frac{E(F_i|I_i = 1) = exp(\hat{\gamma}X + \hat{\beta}(1))}{E(F_i|I_i = 0) = exp(\hat{\gamma}X + \hat{\beta}(0))} = exp(\hat{\beta}) \qquad (2)$$

Equation (2) states the effect of a one unit change in the independent variable on the relative incidence rate of fertility. In the case of indicator variables such as our immigrant indicator I, the relative incidence rate can also be interpreted as the difference in fertility rate for immigrants relative to the Canadian born.[4]

We use the 20 percent sample of the Canadian Census of Population for the years 1991, 1996, 2001, and 2006 to analyze differences in fertil-ity between immigrant and domestic born women (including second generation Canadians), identifying some factors that underlie them. For each census, we linked all individuals belonging to the same household and selected all women between 16 and 45 years of age. We excluded aboriginal individuals. For each of the selected women we have infor-mation about age, education, marital status, number of children (in the 1991 Census), number of children living in the household, province of residence, immigrant status, and parental immigrant status (in the 2001 and 2006 Censuses). In addition, for immigrant women we have information about year of immigration, age at immigration, country of birth, and parental country of birth (in the 2001 and 2006 Censuses). To reduce computing time to a reasonable length, from each census we select all immigrant observations plus a 20 percent random sample of domestic born individuals. We weight observations accordingly. The four censuses are then pooled, resulting in approximately 1,800,000 observations.

In the absence of long panel data with sufficiently large samples of immigrants, immigrant studies typically use synthetic cohorts of immigrants from pooled cross-section surveys such as the census when a temporal perspective on the data is required. That way a researcher can follow groups of individuals with similar characteristics across time. By making use of the 1991 to 2006 Censuses, we are able to follow cohorts of immigrant women across time to look at patterns of fertility assimilation. Census data have the additional advantage of providing large samples necessary to perform robustness analysis of the estimates. The 20 Percent Sample of the Census not only provides a large number of observations but also allows access to more detailed information on individuals, as well as to a very rich categorization of relationships among members of the household. Using this detailed information, we are able to link individuals in the same household and to compute the number of children of each woman living in the household.

As we noted, the actual number of children a woman has had is only available in the 1991 Census. After 1991, the Census does not report a measure of total fertility for each individual but only the number of children living in the home. Although we use this variable as the measure of fertility in the analysis that follows, it imposes a limitation on our study since it introduces some amount of measurement error into the analysis.[5] To reduce this problem, we restrict our sample to relatively young women (up to 45 years of age) who are more likely to have children living at home. Still, the measure is subject to several caveats. It will miss all the children who are living only with their father; however, to the extent that young children are far more likely to live with their natural mothers, even after a disruption of the marriage, this should not be too important.[6] In addition, it may be difficult to properly capture the very early childbearing of older women in the sample as some of their children may have already left the home. That should be a concern particularly if children leave home in their late teens or early adulthood (e.g., attending college far from home, earlier marriage or cohabitation) at a differential rate between immigrant and Canadian born households.

To assess the importance of the potential bias introduced by our dependent variable, we undertake three types of robustness exercises. First, we use the actual total number of children available in the 1991 Census to re-estimate the models and compare them to estimates for the 1991 Census using our fertility measure. Second, we restrict the sample to women up to the age of 40. This reduces the likelihood that some children have already left home, but it misses late childbearing, which may in turn be differentially important among groups (e.g., according to education, country of origin, etc). In this regard, it is reassuring that Vezina and Turcotte (2009), after comparing data from the Canada Census and from the General Social Survey, note that there is no appreciable bias in the characteristics of the proportion of women aged 40 to 44 who have a child aged five or over based on whether some of the children live with them or not. Third, we re-estimate the models restricting the age of the children included into our fertility measure to those 18 and under. The overall pattern of the results and the estimated coefficients are quite robust across these different samples and are available upon request.

We have grouped the information on country of origin (both for the individuals and their parents) into 20 relatively homogenous groups. These are listed in Table A1 in the Appendix. In addition, we collected information on the generational status of the respondent. A woman in our sample can be classified as (a) Canadian, born to Canadian parents, what the immigration literature refers to as the third generation; (b) Canadian, born to two immigrant parents, or the second generation; (c) Canadian, born to one Canadian parent and one immigrant parent, or the 2.5 generation; and finally (d) foreign born respondents, or first generation. We will use this characterization to determine whether there is significant intergenerational assimilation in fertility.

Table A2 in the Appendix shows summary statistics of the main variables for the Canadian born and immigrants. The first two columns correspond to the whole sample over the 1991, 1996, 2001, and 2006 Censuses. In order to provide a sense of the temporal variation found in the data, we also present similar measures for the first and last year of the sample. On average, immigrants have more children than the Canadian born. For both groups, the average number of children observed in the sample diminished by approximately 15 percent between 1991 and 2006. Immigrants in the sample have higher levels of education and are generally older than the Canadian born. The latter characteristic may account for part of the gap in fertility observed between both groups. More immigrants are married or living together under common law (CL), whereas more Canadian born respondents remain single. Between 1991 and 2006, the percentage of married/CL individuals has fallen for both groups (around 9 points for Canadian born and 4 points for immigrants), while the fraction of single individuals has increased by a similar magnitude in each case. Finally, the fraction of households with additional family members other than the spouse is 3 percent among immigrants and 8 percent among the Canadian born. The average immigrant has been in Canada about 13.4 years and arrived at the age of 19.5. Yearly figures suggest that the fraction of recent immigrants over the whole pool has increased and that immigrants now arrive at a slightly older age than in the past. Immigrants are also increasingly arriving from countries in Asia and Africa rather than Europe. These trends are well documented in the Canadian literature of immigration and are likely to have an impact on fertility behaviour (Belanger and Gilbert 2003).

Table 1 shows the mean number of children by year and selected characteristics for women aged 16 to 45 in each census. As mentioned, fertility is higher among immigrants than among the Canadian born, although both groups reflect a similar diminishing trend over time. We show fertility by years since immigration for each census year to offer a rough idea of how fertility patterns evolve over time. In 1991, recent immigrants (less than five years in Canada) had on average less than one child. In 1996, the same cohort of immigrants, now having spent six to 10 years in Canada, had slightly over one child (1.06), and a slightly higher number of children in 2001, having now lived in Canada between 11 and 15 years. Previous cohorts of immigrants have a much higher fertility rate at any point in time, while immigrants who entered Canada later than 1991 show substantially lower fertility rates over time. The information in Table 1 is useful to show general trends and the source of variation in our data. However, changes in immigrant characteristics, such as source country or age at immigration from one census year to the next, will have important repercussions in the measure of fertility presented in this table. An increase in an arrival cohort's share of very young immigrants who may have not yet started a family will necessarily imply low initial fertility rates for that cohort, which will naturally rise as it ages.

Fertility rates among immigrants vary greatly by age at immigration. Those immigrating at a young age have low fertility rates, similar to or lower than those of Canadian born females, while those immigrating later in life show substantially higher fertility rates (Table 1). However, the fact that individuals who migrate as adults are observed at older ages constitutes a confounding factor. Country of origin is another important dimension to consider, as fertility behaviour is highly correlated with cultural norms regarding fertility in the source country (Blau et al. 2008; Fernandez and Fogli 2006; Ford 1990; Khan 1994).[7] High fertility rates can be observed among immigrants from the United States, UK/Ireland, Northern and Southern Europe, Mexico, Central America, Middle East, Southern Asia, and Africa (except Southern Africa). China, North East Asia, and Eastern Europe show the lowest fertility rates.

FIRST GENERATION IMMIGRANTS

Foreign Birth and Family Structure

The estimates that we report in this section correspond to relative fertility rates of immigrant females as compared to those of Canadian born

TABLE 1
Mean Number of Children for Women Aged 16-45 by Census Year and Selected Characteristics

	1991	*1996*	*2001*	*2006*
Non-immigrant	0.89	0.88	0.84	0.77
Immigrant	1.18	1.11	1.08	1.03
Years since migration				
0 to 5	0.88	0.84	0.88	0.85
6 to 10	1.11	1.06	1.00	1.00
11 to 15	1.22	1.18	1.08	1.02
16 to 20	1.26	1.25	1.23	1.08
More than 20	1.41	1.36	1.35	1.31
Age at immigration				
0 to 5 years old	0.77	0.77	0.72	0.68
6 to 11 years old	0.84	0.77	0.69	0.57
12 to 16 years old	0.91	0.78	0.71	0.62
17 to 19 years old	1.32	1.16	1.07	1.00
More than 19 years old	1.43	1.34	1.35	1.32
Country of origin				
US	1.13	1.20	1.23	1.12
Caribe	1.03	1.02	1.06	1.01
Mexico	1.63	1.72	1.52	1.42
Central America	1.39	1.33	1.25	1.18
South America	1.10	1.08	1.10	1.06
Northern Europe	1.24	1.16	1.16	1.21
UK/Ireland	1.09	1.10	1.14	1.16
Central Europe	1.25	1.15	1.11	1.06
Eastern Europe	1.09	1.04	0.92	0.86
Southern Europe	1.57	1.48	1.35	1.19
Middle East	1.34	1.30	1.21	1.11
China	1.02	0.85	0.78	0.74
North East Asia	1.06	0.91	0.84	0.76
South East Asia	1.03	0.89	0.94	0.95
Southern Asia	1.13	1.25	1.26	1.23
North Africa	1.37	1.39	1.31	1.23
Central Africa	1.15	1.14	1.21	1.21
West Africa	1.07	1.24	1.15	1.14
Southern Africa	0.97	0.98	1.00	0.94
Eastern Africa	0.99	1.01	1.19	1.19
Pacific	1.06	1.11	1.13	1.04
Observations	402,150	444,540	485,230	503,420

Source: Authors' compilation.

females, holding a number of factors constant. In particular, all models include controls for age of the woman, marital status (single, married, or divorced/separated), province of residence, and highest education level attained. These control variables consistently show the same effect on fertility across all specifications: fertility increases with age as women reach their late thirties, and then plateaus once we have controlled for the diminishing trend in fertility across census years; fertility rates are higher for married/CL and previously married/CL women and for the least educated. In order to control for the reported diminishing trend in fertility over the years, we include dummy indicators for census year. Although we do not report all of the control variables in the tables, to economize space, they are available upon request.

There is some controversy in the literature about whether or not it is appropriate to include controls for income in fertility analysis. Income measures are endogenous in that they reflect the respondents' former decisions to enter the labour force. Fertility and labour market decisions (which ultimately affect income) are so intertwined that it is not realistic to regard them as exogenous to one another. Females with strong preferences for career work may also have low preferences for child rearing, and this possibility introduces selection bias in estimates. The direction of the bias is not straightforward. To the extent that children are a normal good, females with more income may have more children, since they can afford to pay for the extra services involved in raising them. However, women may have higher incomes precisely because they reduced or postponed their fertility. Overall, considerations of joint labour market and fertility decisions require special modelling that is beyond the scope of this paper. For this reason we have decided not to include income controls in our analysis. Note, however, that education and marital status capture some important dimensions of economic well-being and to some extent help us to control for income.

Our initial set of estimates of immigrant fertility rates is reported in Table 2. The immigrant fertility rate summarizes the fertility rate of an immigrant over a domestic born Canadian, keeping constant other factors. Immigrants have significantly higher fertility rates than the Canadian born – around 1.083 times higher (column I, panel A), meaning that immigrants have, on average, 8 percent more children, after taking into account other factors affecting fertility such as education, marital status, geographic location, and year of survey. In panel B of Table 2 we show the predicted number of children for each group considered in panel A. Throughout the paper we present the average predicted number of children for married/CL females between 35 and 40 years of age in each group based on the corresponding regression estimates and with the remaining control variables (like education, province of residence, and census year) kept at the mean of each group. In that regard, between-group differences of the non-specified control variables will also be accounting for part of the gap of predicted fertilities across groups. Hence, the predicted average number of children has the advantage of being closer to the actual expected number of children in that particular group, but it has the shortcoming of confounding the ultimate impact of the variable of interest when looking at the gap of predictions.[8] Nonetheless, the fertility rates provided in panel A already present the deviations in fertility rates that are only attributed to that particular variable.

TABLE 2
Immigrant Fertility: The Relevance of Age at Immigration and Family Structure

	A. Relative Fertility Rate		
	(I)	*(II)*	*(III)*
Immigrant FR	1.083**	1.101**	--
Additional family member[a]	--	0.832**	--
Immigrant with additional family member	--	1.005	--
Age at immigration 0-5		--	1.005
Age at immigration 6-11	--	--	1.050**
Age at immigration 12-15	--	--	1.106**
Age at immigration 16-19	--	--	1.194**
Age at immigration 20-45	--	--	1.082**
	B. Predicted Number of Children		
	(I)	*(II)*	*(II)*
Domestic born	1.76		1.76
Nuclear family		1.78	--
Extended family	--	1.52	--
Immigrant	1.85		--
Nuclear family	--	1.90	--
Extended family	--	1.61	--
Immigrant at age 0-5		--	1.73
Immigrant at age 6-11	--	--	1.81
Immigrant at age 12-15	--	--	1.95
Immigrant at age 16-19	--	--	2.14
Immigrant at age 20-45	--	--	1.83
Observations		1,835,325	

Notes: Panel A shows estimates of the Poisson regression for number of children living at home for women 16 to 45 years old. The regression includes controls for age, marital status, province of residence, education and census year.
Panel B shows the average predicted number of children for married females between 35 and 40 years of age in each group based on the regressions in the same column in panel A and with the other control variables kept at the mean of each group.
[a] Additional family member is an indicator for a respondent with children living in a household with extended family.
** indicates significant at 1 percent; * indicates significant at 5 percent.
Source: Authors' compilation.

In column I, panel B, married/CL Canadian born women of 35 to 40 years of age are expected to have around 1.76 children as compared to 1.85 for immigrant women. This gap between migrant and domestic fertility is consistent with findings in Ng and Nault (1997) and Ram and George (1990). Both of those studies estimate that the fertility of foreign born women surpassed that of domestic born Canadian women in the early 1980s, after having been moderately lower for the previous decades. Belanger and Gilbert (2003) confirm that estimate with data from the 1981 to 2001 Censuses. Nonetheless, the wide dispersion across cohorts and ages at migration among immigrants in our sample and the shifting composition of countries of origin for recent arrivals demand a more detailed analysis of these dynamics.

In column II we introduce some basic information on family composition. Family structure may be an important determinant as well as consequence of fertility. On the one hand, additional family members present in the household may impose an added cost – in time or financial resources – that hinders fertility, particularly in the case of elderly parents. On the other hand, it may facilitate the care of children and reduce the costs involved in raising them. For immigrants, extended families may in addition create a stronger cultural pressure to maintain fertility patterns from the source country. To explore this possibility, we construct a variable indicating whether respondents with children live in extended families (that is, whether the household includes family members other than spouses/partners and children).[9] The variable is defined as an indicator and does not distinguish whether the additional members are grandparents or, say, aunts or uncles.

Further work should explore this area in more detail, since it would help to better interpret the implication of the estimated coefficient. Unfortunately census data lack any longitudinal information, so we are unable to determine whether the household already had this composition when the children were born or whether the additional individuals moved in as a result of childbirth (e.g., grandmothers to support their daughters) or some time after. Because of all of these restrictions, the coefficient is simply interpreted as an association. Estimates in Table 2, column II, panel A, show that individuals with children living in households with extended families have lower fertility rates than individuals with children living in nuclear families. Immigrants living in extended families have slightly higher fertility rates than the Canadian born living in extended families but still lower fertility rates than immigrants with children living in nuclear families (around 0.837 times lower).[10] In panel B, the predicted average number of children is 1.78 and 1.52 for the Canadian born living in nuclear and extended families, respectively, and, similarly, 1.90 and 1.61 for immigrants in nuclear and extended families. It is important to note that the prevalence of this type of household is higher among immigrant families (around 6 percent) than among Canadians (around 2 percent), as shown in Table A2 in the Appendix.

Age at Immigration

Age at migration has long been recognized as a decisive variable for understanding the process of assimilation of immigrants in many socio-economic dimensions. When observing any particular outcome of interest, age at migration should matter for two distinct reasons. First, the earlier the immigrant arrived in the country of destination, the more time she has already lived there and the more likely she is to understand the rules and institutions that govern its socio-economic life. In the earnings literature, years since migration are regularly used as a measure of time to assimilate or of exposure to the local labour market (Chiswick 1978). In general, for those arriving during childhood, school attendance provides an opportunity to become familiar with the culture and expectations of the country of destination.

Second, the age at migration by itself may matter even more than the time of exposure if there are critical ages at which an individual is able to learn particular behaviours or skills, such as the local language. For those whose mother tongue is not the same as that of the country of destination, arriving later in life may constitute a penalty. Recent work by Bleakley and Chin (2008) shows that immigrants to the United States who arrive before age nine (the critical period) become fluent in English regardless of the language of their country of origin, while those arriving later from non-English speaking countries tend to have worse proficiency. English proficiency, in turn, increases earnings, divorce rates, and intermarriage rates and decreases fertility rates among immigrants to the US (ibid.).

The average age at migration in our sample is 19.5 years of age among women, though it increases from 18.3 in the 1991 Census to 20 in the 2006 Census. The share of those who arrived before age 12 is 29 percent in 1991 as compared to just 26 percent for 2006. Around 50 percent of the individuals arrived in Canada as adults, past the age of upper secondary schooling. Figure 1 presents the distribution of ages at migration for the sample. After a small spike for toddlers, the fraction of entrants remains more or less flat until reaching its peak between the ages of 20 and 30.[11]

In column III of Table 2 we create a set of five dummy variables among first generation migrants for different ages of migration. Fertility significantly varies by age at immigration. Those immigrating as children (aged less than five at the time of immigration) have a similar propensity to have children as the Canadian born. All other immigrants have higher fertility rates than these groups. In particular, those immigrating between 16 and 19 years of age have significantly higher fertility rates than any other immigrant group (1.194 times higher). The same patterns show up in the predicted fertility in column III of panel B.[12]

FIGURE 1
Distribution of Immigrants by Age at Immigration, 1991-2006

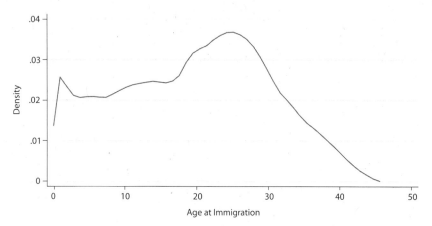

Notes: Kernel = epanechnikov; bandwidth = 0.6140
Source: Authors' compilation.

Discrepancies in assimilation between this particular group of immigrants and other age groups have been reported by Schaafsma and
Sweetman (2001), suggesting that those arriving at that age may find it
difficult to transition. In particular, this group has on average a lower
educational achievement, which in turn is associated with higher fertility. Interestingly, immigrants arriving under the age of six have a slightly
lower predicted fertility than Canadians, which may reflect their slightly
higher mean educational attainment in our sample.

Immigration Cohorts and Assimilation

As noted before, duration in destination has been a key factor in understanding the process of labour market adjustment of migrants to the local
market. Similarly, Ford (1990) notes for the United States that any analysis
of immigrant fertility that does not control for duration of residence in the
destination country is potentially misleading. Other studies have argued
accordingly (Hervitz 1985). Those who favour the "disruption" hypothesis argue that we should observe some decrease in fertility at the time
of migration, since the process itself is disruptive in many spheres of the
life of an individual, with a subsequent period of catch-up. Eventually,
migrant fertility can remain high (resembling that of the country of origin)
or slowly converge to that of the domestic born (as Ram and George (1990)
find from the 1960s to the mid-1980s). However, previous evidence for
Canada is mixed. Ng and Nault (1997) argue that the disruption happens
even before the individual migrates into Canada. Belanger and Gilbert's

(2003) results from more recent censuses are consistent with this story. Further, they find a monotonic reduction of the number of children under five by length of time since migration.

In addition, existing economic or social conditions in the country at the time of arrival may have eased or hardened the ability of a particular cohort to assimilate (Borjas 1999). Further, latest arrival cohorts will have on average been born more recently. If access to family planning, preferences on the number of children, and family structures of the Canadian born (and world) population have shifted over time, we should also observe some of those changes across immigrant arrival cohorts.

We extend our original equation to account for differences in fertility among different groups by time of arrival in Canada. For instance, we follow immigrants arriving in Canada between 1981 and 1985 (cohort 85) through the 1991, 1996, 2001, and 2006 Censuses when they have been in the country from six to 10 years, 11 to 15 years, 16 to 20, and so on. Note that immigrants arriving in Canada between 1986 and 1990 are observed through most of their assimilation process. Earlier cohorts are only observed after they have already been in Canada for some time; later cohorts may be observed only for a short period of time.

Table 3 shows our estimates of the evolution of fertility for different arrival cohorts of immigrants. Relative to the average domestic born Canadian in the sample, immigrants from cohorts who arrived before 1981 have higher relative fertility – almost 1.11 times higher.[13] The interest of these estimates, however, comes out in observing the evolution of particular arrival cohorts. Those arriving between 1981 and 1986 have higher fertility rates than the average Canadian born in the sample – almost 1.025 times higher, everything remaining constant. Note that this cohort of immigrants is observed for the first time once they have been living in Canada for at least six years. For cohorts that we observe from their arrival in Canada, we find evidence of the disruption hypothesis. Relative to the Canadian born, fertility rates are lower for the first five years after migration. After this period, fertility rates are higher on average. Note that these estimates are obtained holding constant the age of the immigrant. Column II in Table 3 presents the predicted average fertility for a married woman of 35 to 40 years of each subgroup. Overall, as expected, we observe a decrease in fertility by cohort and an increase of the number of children with increased years in the country.

Country of Origin

The observed fertility behaviour of a woman is the result of choices made under a set of constraints (e.g., economic, educational, and/or institutional) and with a collection of social attitudes toward fertility, contraceptive measures, gender preferences, and out of wedlock childbearing, among many others. Those attitudes constitute an important component of individuals' cultural background. Since many of those attitudes are linked to common norms and expectations of different societies, we try to account for them in part by looking at the woman's country of origin. Place of origin has already been shown to be relevant to explaining variation of fertility outcomes in different geographical and cultural contexts. Anderson (2004), for example, finds important differences in levels of childbearing propensities between women from different countries of origin among migrants to Sweden from the 1960s to the 1990s. More recently, Georgiadis and Manning (2009) analyze whether Muslims (Pakistanis and Bangladeshis) are not successfully assimilating to British society as compared to other migrant groups in different dimensions that include fertility. Similar research for the United States has been undertaken by Kahn (1994) and Parrado and Morgan (2008), among others. The bottom line of these studies is that even if on average fertility differentials between the second generation immigrants and the domestic born still look large, the trend is toward convergence.

TABLE 3
Fertility Behaviour of Immigrant Cohorts

	Relative Fertility Rate	*Predicted # of Children*
	(I)	*(II)*
Immigrants from previous cohorts	1.109**	1.97
1985 cohort: 6 to 10 yrs in Canada	1.025**	1.97
11 to 15 yrs in Canada	1.044**	2.05
16 to 20 yrs in Canada	1.049**	2.07
21 to 25 yrs in Canada	1.042**	1.96
1990 cohort: 1 to 5 yrs in Canada	0.911**	1.76
6 to 10 yrs in Canada	1.010*	1.96
11 to 15 yrs in Canada	1.030**	1.97
16 to 20 yrs in Canada	1.043**	2.01
1995 cohort: 1 to 5 yrs in Canada	0.876**	1.68
6 to 10 yrs in Canada	0.977**	1.82
11 to 15 yrs in Canada	1.010*	1.89
2000 cohort: 1 to 5 yrs in Canada	0.874**	1.55
6 to 10 yrs in Canada	0.982**	1.71
2005 cohort: 1 to 5 yrs in Canada	0.854**	1.46
Observations	1,835,325	

Notes: The dependent variable is the number of children living at home for women 16 to 45 years old. The Poisson regression includes controls for age, marital status, province of residence, education, and census year.

The second column shows the average predicted number of children for married females between 35 and 40 years of age in each group based on the regression in the first column and with the remaining control variables kept at the mean of each group.

** indicates significant at 1 percent; * indicates significant at 5 percent.

Source: Authors' compilation.

The speed at which newcomers adapt may be endogenous to the country's cultural expectations and policies toward immigrants. For example, multiculturalist movements that encourage cultural continuity of newcomers could potentially deter the assimilation to the receiving culture. In other instances, policies in the country of origin, either pro-natalistic (e.g., Ceceascu's regime) or restrictive (e.g., China's one child policy), may have shaped fertility of migrants before their arrival in such a decisive way that their behaviour in the country of destination reflects a readjustment of their preferences after breaking free of policy constraints.

To account for these influences, we expand equation (1) to include place of birth. Table 4 shows the relevance of the source country to immigrant fertility. The relative incidence rate of fertility across different places of birth conveys whether high fertility rates are common among all immigrants or whether they are restricted to certain ethnic or national groups.

As mentioned above, the composition of the immigrant population and, consequently, the continent of origin of young immigrant mothers have changed substantially over the last decades. Well until the 1981 Census, the majority of immigrant women with children under five were originally from Europe. However, Asian immigrant mothers overtook all other continents in the 1996 Census for this category. In our sample, and throughout the Census years, around one-fifth of the immigrants were born in the Americas (Table A2, Appendix), around 6 percent in the Middle East, and around 1 percent in Pacific countries. The share of Europeans moved down from 41 percent in the 1991 Census to only 23 percent in 2006. Conversely, the share of Asian and African countries moved up from 30 percent and 5 percent, respectively, in 1991 to 44 percent and 8 percent in 2006.

Estimates in Table 4 show that immigrants from North, Central, and South America (including the United States) portray substantially higher fertility rates than the Canadian born, particularly those from Mexico and Central America, with fertility rates around 1.5 times higher than those of Canadian born. Other immigrant groups with high fertility rates come from Africa, the Middle East, and South Asia. Northern and Eastern European immigrants as well as those from elsewhere in Asia have relatively low fertility rates in comparison. Chinese immigrants have the lowest fertility rates of all groups, 0.83 times that of the Canadian born. The implied fertility of the most prolific groups in column II is well above the level of replacement that stands at 2.1, while that for the whole population of immigrants in column I, panel B, of Table 2 is merely 1.85.

There is a caveat regarding these numbers, however, since our prediction portrays a married woman of 35-40 years of age originating from each of these source regions. Therefore, differences in the age at arrival and age distribution among groups from different countries may change this

TABLE 4
Country of Origin and Fertility Behaviour of Immigrants

	Relative Fertility Rate	Predicted # of Children
	(I)	(II)
Canadian born	--	1.76
Immigrant		
US	1.118**	1.88
Caribe	1.267**	2.23
Mexico	1.540**	2.71
Central America	1.467**	2.64
South America	1.087*	1.90
Northern Europe	0.982	1.68
Europe	1.027**	1.76
Eastern Europe	0.955**	1.57
UK / Ireland	1.000	1.74
Southern Europe	1.099**	2.02
Middle East	1.359**	2.31
China	0.824**	1.37
North East Asia	1.002	1.61
South East Asia	0.998	1.72
Southern Asia	1.166**	1.97
North Africa	1.270**	2.03
Central Africa	1.442**	2.38
West Africa	1.376**	2.34
Southern Africa	1.059**	1.76
Eastern Africa	1.275**	2.22
Pacific	1.046**	1.80
Observations	1,835,325	

Notes: The dependent variable is the number of children living at home for women 16 to 45 years old. The Poisson regression includes controls for age, marital status, education, province of residence, and census year.
The second column shows the average predicted number of children for married females between 35 and 40 years of age in each group based on the regression in the first column and with the remaining control variables kept at the mean of each group.
** indicates significant at 1 percent; * indicates significant at 5 percent.
Source: Authors' compilation.

picture in the near future. For instance, if most of the Western African immigrant women just arrived in Canada, the predicted number of children among married Western African women 35-40 years of age may be a very poor prediction of the fertility rates for younger Western African women immigrants when they reach that age five or 10 years on. Although this is generally the situation with all groups, as different cohorts may have different fertility preferences, it is likely to be exacerbated by changes in the composition of immigration.

SECOND GENERATION IMMIGRANTS: INTERGENERATIONAL ASSIMILATION

The importance of the socio-economic outcomes of the second generation for the future of a country has taken the centre stage in many academic and policy debates. In general, the ability of second-generation immigrants to assimilate should depend on the human capital of their parents as well as on the role of ethnicity for the group, either as a provider of cohesion and social capital or as a negative marker potentially associated with discrimination. Depending on the combination of those factors, the second generation will ultimately be more or less successful in assimilating. With regard to fertility, several recent studies have explored what role ancestry (or more generally, the cultural background in which the individual was brought up) has in the fertility outcomes of the second generation. Fernandez and Fogli (2006) examine the effect of culture on the fertility of second generation American women of different ancestry and find that it significantly explains differences in fertility. Blau et al. (2008) also find second generation women's fertility to be positively affected by the fertility of the first generation immigrants from their parents' country of origin.

In Tables 5 and 6 we add parental place of birth and generational status to our model to assess whether either fertility assimilation occurs within one generation or relatively high fertility rates can also be observed for the children of immigrants. This is an important point to address since the second generation constitutes approximately 20 percent of Canada's domestic born population. Hence, fertility rates of the children of immigrants, if different from the rest of Canadians, should have a role in determining future demographic projections. Information about parental immigration status is only available in the 2001 and 2006 Censuses of population; therefore our estimates refer only to these two years of data.

In Table 5 we use the whole sample and differentiate individuals by generational status: domestic born of Canadian parents; domestic born with both or one foreign born parents (second or 2.5 generation) and first generation immigrants (with foreign or domestic born parents). Results illustrate that second generation immigrants have lower fertility than both third generation Canadians and first generation migrants. The relative ratio is the lowest when either both parents are foreign born or when only the mother is. Those groups represent 12 percent and 4 percent of the domestic born population (Table A2, Appendix). However, the differences in fertility across the second and the 2.5 generation are small.

This result is consistent with Belanger and Gilbert (2003), who show that the gap in the number of children under five across groups shrinks substantially once demographic characteristics are included, and that, in particular, the gap between the second and the 2.5 generation is usually negligible.[14] The predicted number of children for a married/CL woman between 35 and 40 years of age (column II) in the second generation group is 1.63, whereas for a similar individual in the 2.5 generation the number is around 1.64. In contrast, immigrants from immigrant parents have 1.78 children, slightly above the predicted number of children for the domestic born (1.75). To properly interpret these differences in fertility, it is important to remember that a large share of second generation women in Canada have European ancestry as opposed to those in the first generation, who are mostly Asian. This compositional effect does play some role in producing this gap. Still, the model controls for major demographic characteristics that should matter.

TABLE 5
Fertility Rate by Generational Status, 2001, 2006

		RFR	Predicted # Children
		(I)	(II)
Third generation	Domestic born – Canadian parents	--	1.75
Second generation	Domestic born – immigrant parents	0.964**	1.63
2.5 generation	Domestic born – immigrant father	0.971**	1.65
	Domestic born – immigrant mother	0.962**	1.63
First generation	Immigrants – Canadian parents	1.063**	1.82
	Immigrants – immigrant parents	1.063**	1.78
	Immigrants – immigrant father	1.049**	1.74
	Immigrants – immigrant mother	1.111**	1.92
Observations		988,640	

Notes: The dependent variable is the number of children living at home for women 16 to 45 years old. The Poisson regression includes controls for marital status, province of residence, education, census year, and age.
The second column shows the average predicted number of children for married females between 35 and 40 years of age in each group based on the regression in the first column and with the remaining control variables kept at the mean of each group.
** indicates significant at 1 percent; * indicates significant at 5 percent.
Source: Authors' compilation.

Next we run these estimates on Canadian born individuals only to better assess the influence of parental background on the children of immigrants. Table 6 shows the fertility rate of second generation Canadians (Canadian born children of immigrant parents) relative to that of Canadian born to Canadian parents (usually referred to as third generation). We distinguish between the impact of having an immigrant father (column I) and an immigrant mother (column III).

Results indicate that the second generation has an overall lower fertility rate than the domestic born. This, however, requires some qualification, as the ancestry of Canadians seems to have a distinct influence on fertility. Controlling for age, individuals whose father was born in Mexico, central

TABLE 6
Fertility and Parental Place of Birth of Second Generation Canadians, 2001-06

	RFR	Predicted # Children	RFR	Predicted # Children
	(I)	(II)	(III)	(IV)
Parental place of birth	**Father**		**Mother**	
Canada	--	1.76	--	1.76
US	0.979	1.64	1.018	1.70
Caribe	0.940*	1.65	0.861**	1.51
Mexico	1.555**	2.69	1.387**	2.40
Central America	0.823	1.49	0.891	1.61
South America	0.926+	1.62	0.963	1.68
Northern Europe	0.949*	1.61	0.935*	1.58
Central Europe	1.101**	1.87	1.085**	1.84
Eastern Europe	0.965**	1.59	0.963**	1.58
UK / Ireland	0.941**	1.62	0.935**	1.61
Southern Europe	0.918**	1.62	0.927**	1.64
Middle East	1.094*	1.86	1.152**	1.97
China	0.683**	1.12	0.691**	1.13
North East Asia	0.497**	0.79	0.549**	0.87
South East Asia	0.641**	1.09	0.674**	1.15
Southern Asia	0.663**	1.12	0.694**	1.17
North Africa	0.900+	1.45	0.942	1.52
Central Africa	0.780+	1.30	0.716	1.20
West Africa	1.030	1.75	0.947	1.61
Southern Africa	0.928	1.53	0.801**	1.33
Eastern Africa	0.550**	0.96	0.548**	0.96
Pacific	0.784**	1.34	0.760**	1.30
Observations		495,275		

Notes: The dependent variable is the number of children living at home for women 16 to 45 years old. The Poisson regressions include controls for marital status, province of residence, education, census year, and age. In Column I, place of birth refers to father's place of birth. In column III, place of birth refers to mother's place of birth.
The second and fourth columns show the average predicted number of children for married females between 35 and 40 years of age in each group based on the regression in the first column and with the remaining control variables kept at the mean of each group.
** indicates significant at 1 percent; * indicates significant at 5 percent; + indicates significant at 10 percent.
Source: Authors' compilation.

Europe, or the Middle East have substantially higher fertility rates than
the reference group (1.5 and 1.1 and 1.09 times higher, respectively). All
other groups show lower fertility rates. These rates are particularly low
among Canadians born to Asian fathers. The effect of maternal place of
birth is similar. The main difference is for Canadian daughters of Middle
East mothers, who show a significantly higher fertility rate than those
with Canadian mothers (1.15 times higher).

CONCLUSIONS

About two-thirds of total population growth in Canada in 2006 was due
to international immigration. According to Statistics Canada's projections,
natural population growth will become negative at some point between
now and 2056, and international net migration will be the only source
of population growth. This is the result of sustained low fertility rates –
below the replacement level – for more than three decades (Belanger et al.
2005). Slow population growth together with the aging of the baby boom
generation implies a rising demographic dependency ratio: the number
of children (0 to 14) plus elderly persons (65 or more) per 100 persons of
working age (15 to 64) is currently around 44. Hence, the evolution of
Canadian demographic trends questions the ability of the current working age population to support the retirement of the postwar baby boom
and to provide social services and maintain economic growth in the near
future. Further, immigration appears to be the only source of population
growth that can mitigate this trend in the short run. Already immigration
is the main contributor to the Canadian labour force, with 70 percent of
labour force growth attributed to immigrants.

In this context, the interplay of fertility and immigration rates has a
central role in determining the future demographic trajectory of Canada.
If the fertility of immigrants is sufficiently higher than that of the domestic
born population, even constant immigration rates may help boost overall
fertility rates, particularly if fertility is transmitted intergenerationally.
Our study shows that immigrant fertility is higher than that of Canadian
born women, but not by much. This result, however, conceals substantial
heterogeneity in fertility rates among immigrants, particularly regarding
place of birth. Immigrants from Asia, China in particular, have the lowest
fertility rates among the immigrant population, whereas South Americans
and most immigrants from African regions have the highest. Most importantly, these trends seem to be transmitted to the second generation
of Canadians born to foreign parents. Second generation women have,
on average, fertility rates similar to the domestic born. However, fertility
rates vary by place of origin of parents, with those of Asian descent having
substantially lower fertility rates and those from Mexican, European, and
Middle East parentage having substantially higher rates than the rest.

These results have important implications for social policy. First, in the years to come, the composition of the immigrant population will probably affect the future population growth of Canada, shaping demands for social services. Second, ethnic and cultural diversity in Canada will increase by even more than already predicted by current immigration levels, since the groups that portray higher fertility rates and higher transmission of those rates to the second generation are mostly visible minorities. Finally, this chapter's results suggest that more research is needed in order to understand the interaction between fertility and labour market choices of immigrant women. High fertility rates resulting from poor labour market opportunities for immigrant women, or from costly child care alternatives that constrain individual choices, may affect the economic well-being of immigrant families and perpetuate traditional gender roles that impede the economic integration of foreign-born women.

NOTES

1.   See, for instance, Ferrer, Green, and Riddell (2006) among others.
2.   Adsera (2004) shows the connection between labour market institutions and fertility using evidence from Europe.
3.   The trade-off between quality and quantity of children is outlined in Becker (1981).
4.   Similarly, in the case of a continuous variable such as age, the IRR could be interpreted as the increase in fertility rate when age increases by one year.
5.   Vital statistics and the Census may report countries of birth differently, and country of birth may be missing in some birth certificates. Belanger and Gilbert (2003) use a similar method (the own children method) and note that despite the potential problem of missing data, it has advantages over the use of vital statistics to calculate differential fertility according to mother's place of birth. The authors show nonetheless that estimated fertility differentials for immigrants and domestic born individuals for the period 1996-2001 using both methods are not very sizeable – with a downward bias of the Census for women younger than 30 and an upward bias for those aged beyond 30.
6.   The Census questionnaire asks respondents to include children in joint custody who live most of the time in a household as household members. There are also some instances in which several women live in a household with children and we can not be certain of which one is the mother of the children. This happens, for example, when the children are reported as grandchildren of the head of the household and there is more than one daughter of the head of the household living in the household. Fortunately, this is not a common occurrence.
7.   Nonetheless, some migrants arriving in Canada will likely have better access to contraceptive methods during the remaining years of their fertile life than in their country of birth. That should affect their ultimate fertility, independently of their cultural heritage.
8.   The predicted number of children for domestic born married women aged 35 to 40 years of age, shown in panel B as 1.76, is not comparable with Canada's

fertility rate (recently estimated around 1.58). The latter corresponds to the total fertility rate (TFR), which represents the number of children a woman would have if she were subject to prevailing fertility rates at all ages from a single given year and survived throughout all her childbearing years. It is not surprising that our predicted number is somewhat higher than the TFR in Canada as shifts of childbearing to later ages can show up in reductions in the TFR larger than the ultimate changes in the fertility of a certain birth cohort.

9. The respondent lives in an extended family if the number of individuals in the economic family is greater than that of two adults plus reported children if married/CL or greater than that of one adult plus reported children if not married/CL. For the latter group, we consider the respondent to live in an extended family only if she reports children. The reason is that we want to avoid counting single, childless females still living at home with their parents as living in extended families.

10. This is calculated as the exponential of the coefficient for additional family member plus the coefficient for the interaction between additional family member and immigrant indicator

11. It is worth noting, however, that the distribution of ages at migration varies substantially by country of origin. If immigrants from Europe or the United States are removed from the sample, the distribution of immigrants by age at immigration resembles more a normal distribution centred at the early twenties.

12. We tried finer subdivisions for older ages at migration and found no indication that fertility rates change much for immigrating after age 20.

13. Previous studies indicated that immigrants arriving in Canada before 1980 had on average lower fertility rates than the Canadian born. Our result is still consistent with this observation. It simply reflects the changing fertility of the domestic born population, since our sample includes more Canadians born in Canada after 1940 – hence with lower fertility rates – than the samples in older studies.

14. We introduce a finer distinction between immigrants, depending on the immigrant status of their parents. Immigrants with a domestic born father and a foreign born mother (only 1 percent of the migrants) have the highest fertility.

References

Adsera, A. 2004. "Changing Fertility Rates in Developed Markets: The Impact of Labor Market Institutions." *Journal of Population Economics* 17: 17-43.

Anderson, G. 2004 "Childbearing after Migration: Fertility Patterns of Foreign-Born Women in Sweden." *International Migration Review* 38 (2): 747-74

Becker, G. 1981. *A Treatise on the Family.* Cambridge, MA: Harvard University Press.

Bélanger, A., and S. Gilbert. 2003. "The Fertility of Immigrant Women and Their Canadian-Born Daughters." *Report on the Demographic Situation in Canada 2002,* 91-209.

Bélanger, A., L. Martel, and É. Caron-Malenfant. 2005. "Population Projections for Canada, Provinces and Territories 2005-2031." Catalogue No. 91-520-XIE. Ottawa: Statistics Canada.

Blau, F.D. 1992. "The Fertility of Immigrant Women: Evidence from High Fertility Source Countries." In *Immigration and the Work Force: Economic Consequences for the United States and Source Areas*, edited by G.J. Borjas and R.B. Freeman, 93-133. Chicago: University of Chicago Press.

Blau, F.D., L . Kahn, A. Yung-Hsu Liu, and K.L. Papps. 2008. "The Transmission of Women's Fertility, Human Capital and Work Orientation across Immigrant Generations." NBER Working Paper no. 14388.

Bleakley, H., and A. Chin. 2008. "Age at Arrival, English Proficiency, and Social Assimilation among U.S. Immigrants." Mimeo, August.

Borjas, G. 1999. "The Economic Analysis of Immigration." In *Handbook of Labor Economics*, vol. 3A, edited by O. Ashenfelter and D. Card. North Holland: Elsevier.

Chiswick, B.R. 1978. "The Effect of Americanization on the Earnings of Foreign-Born Men." *Journal of Political Economy* 86 (5): 897-922.

Coleman, D. 2006. "Immigration and Ethnic Change in Low-Fertility Countries, Demographic Transition." *Population and Development Review* 32 (3): 401-46.

Fernandez, R., and A. Fogli. 2006. "Fertility: The Role of Culture and Family Experience." *Journal of the European Economic Association* 4 (2-3): 552-61.

Ferrer, A.M., D. Green, and W. C. Riddell. 2006. "The Effect of Literacy on Immigrant Earnings." *Journal of Human Resources* 41 (2): 380-410.

Ford, K. 1990. "Duration of Residence in the United States and the Fertility of U.S. Immigrants." *International Migration Review* 24 (1): 34-68.

Galor, O., and D. Weil. 1996. "The Gender Gap, Fertility and Growth." *American Economic Review* 86: 374-87.

Georgiadis, A., and A. Manning. 2009. "Change and Continuity among Minority Communities in Britain." *Journal of Population Economics.* Published online: DOI No. 10.1007/s00148-009-0288-x.

Hervitz, H.M. 1985. "Selectivity, Adaptation, or Disruption? A Comparison of Alternative Hypotheses on the Effects of Migration on Fertility: The Case of Brazil." *International Migration Review* 19: 293-317.

Kahn, J. 1994. "Immigrant and Native Fertility during the 1980s: Adaptation and Expectations for the Future." *International Migration Review* 28 (3): 501-19.

Kalbach, W. 1970. "The Impact of Immigration on Canada's Population." Ottawa: Queen's Printer.

Ng, E., and F. Nault. 1997. "Fertility among Recent Immigrant Women to Canada, 1991: An Examination of the Disruption Hypothesis." *International Migration* 35 (4): 559-80.

Parrado, E.A., and S.P. Morgan. 2008. "Intergenerational Fertility among Hispanic Women: New Evidence of Immigrant Assimilation." *Demography* 45 (3): 651-71.

Ram, B., and M.V. George. 1990. "Immigrant Fertility Patterns in Canada, 1961-1986." *International Migration* 28 (4): 413-26.

Schaafsma, J., and A. Sweetman. 2001. "Immigrant Earnings: Age at Immigration Matters." *Canadian Journal of Economics* 34 (4): 1066-99.

United Nations. 2000. *Replacement Migration: Is It a Solution to Declining and Ageing Population?* New York: United Nations Population Division.

Vezina, M., and M. Turcotte. 2009. "Forty-Year Old Mothers of Pre-School Children: A Profile." *Canadian Social Trends.* Ottawa: Statistics Canada.

APPENDIX

TABLE A1
Classification of Countries of Origin by Region

Caribe: Cuba, Dominican Republic, Haiti, Puerto Rico, Jamaica, Trinidad and Tobago, Guadeloupe, Martinique, Bahamas, Barbados, Netherlands Antilles, Saint Lucia, Saint Vincent and the Grenadines Virgin Islands, US Grenada , Antigua and Barbuda, Dominica, Cayman Islands, Aruba, Anguilla, Bermuda, Montserrat, Saint Kitts and Nevis Turks and Caicos Islands, British Virgin Islands

Central America: Belize, Costa Rica, El Salvador, Guatemala, Honduras, Nicaragua, Panama

South America: Argentina, Bolivia, Brazil, Chile, Colombia, Ecuador, Falkland Islands (Malvinas), French Guiana, Guyana, Paraguay, Peru, Suriname, Uruguay, Venezuela

Northern Europe: Greenland, Denmark, Finland, Iceland, Norway, Sweden

Central Europe: Austria, Belgium, Germany, Liechtenstein, Luxembourg, Monaco, Netherlands, Switzerland, France

Eastern Europe: Bulgaria, Czech Republic, Slovakia, Czechoslovakia, n.i.e., Hungary, Poland, Romania, Estonia, Latvia, Lithuania, Belarus, Moldova, Republic of Russian, Albania Federation, Ukraine, USSR., n.i.e., Bosnia and Herzegovina, Croatia, Slovenia, Yugoslavia

Southern Europe: Andorra, Gibraltar ,Greece, Italy, Malta, Portugal, San Marino, Spain, Vatican City State, Macedonia

UK/Ireland: Republic of Ireland (Eire), United Kingdom

Middle East: Afghanistan, Cyprus, Iran, Turkey, Armenia, Azerbaijan, Georgia, Kazakstan, Kyrgyzstan, Tajikistan, Turkmenistan, Uzbekistan, Bahrain, Iraq, Israel, Jordan, Kuwait, Lebanon, Oman, Qatar, Saudi Arabia, Syria, United Arab Emirates, Yemen, Palestine/West Bank/Gaza Strip

China: People's Republic of China, Hong Kong, Macao, Mongolia

North East Asia: Japan, Korea, North Korea, South Taiwan

South East Asia: Cambodia, Indonesia, Laos, Malaysia, Myanmar, Singapore, Thailand, Vietnam

Southern Asia: Philippines, Bangladesh, Bhutan, India, Maldives, Nepal, Pakistan, Sri Lanka

North Africa: Algeria, Egypt, Libya, Morocco, Tunisia, Sudan, Western Sahara

Central Africa: Cameroon, Central African Republic, Chad, Congo, Equatorial Guinea, Gabon, Sao Tome and Principe, Zambia, Zaire

West Africa: Benin, Burkina Faso, Côte d'Ivoire, Cape Verde, The Gambia, Ghana, Guinea, Guinea-Bissau, Liberia, Mali, Mauritania, Niger, Nigeria, Senegal, Sierra Leone, Togo

Southern Africa: Botswana, Lesotho, Namibia, Republic of South Africa, Swaziland

Eastern Africa: Eritrea, Uganda, Sudan, Kenya, Tanzania, Rwanda, Burundi, Somalia, Djibouti, Ethiopia, Comoros, Madagascar, Malawi, Mauritius, Mayotte, Mozambique, Reunion, Seychelles, Zimbawe

Pacific: American Samoa, Australia, Cook Islands, Fiji, Polynesia, New Caledonia, New Zealand

---

TABLE A2
Summary Statistics of Main Variables for Canadian Born and Immigrants

	All		1991		2006	
	CB	*IMM*	*CB*	*IMM*	*CB*	*IMM*
Number of children	0.84	1.10	0.89	1.18	0.77	1.03
Age	30.41	32.93	30.08	32.91	30.31	33.04
Education						
Less than HS	0.25	0.22	0.30	0.29	0.19	0.14
High school	0.28	0.26	0.30	0.28	0.27	0.24
Trades	0.09	0.08	0.09	0.08	0.11	0.08
Non-university post secondary	0.19	0.16	0.17	0.15	0.19	0.15
University-BA	0.16	0.23	0.12	0.16	0.20	0.31
Graduates	0.02	0.06	0.02	0.04	0.03	0.08
Marital status						
Divorced	0.04	0.04	0.04	0.04	0.03	0.04
Married (+ common law)	0.54	0.64	0.59	0.67	0.50	0.63
Separated	0.03	0.03	0.03	0.03	0.02	0.03
Never married	0.39	0.28	0.34	0.25	0.44	0.29
Widowed	0.00	0.01	0.00	0.01	0.00	0.01
Additional family in household	0.02	0.06	0.03	0.06	0.02	0.07
Years since migration	--	13.39	--	14.61	--	12.92
Arrived 0 to 5 years ago		0.27		0.25		0.28
Arrived 6 to 10 years ago		0.20		0.14		0.20
Arrived 11 to 15 years ago		0.17		0.16		0.20
Arrived 16 to 20 years ago		0.14		0.19		0.14
Arrived more than 20 years ago		0.23		0.27		0.19
Age at immigration	--	19.56	--	18.32	--	20.14
Between 0 and 5 years of age		0.13		0.16		0.12
Between 6 and 11 years of age		0.13		0.13		0.14
Between 12 and 16 years of age		0.12		0.11		0.12
Between 17 and 19 years of age		0.09		0.10		0.08
Between 20 and 45 years of age		0.53		0.50		0.55
Country of origin						
Canada	1.00	--	1.00	--	1.00	--
US		0.19		0.21		0.18
Europe		0.30		0.41		0.23
Middle East		0.06		0.06		0.07
Asia		0.38		0.30		0.44
Africa		0.06		0.05		0.08
Pacific		0.01		0.01		0.01
Generation status						
Canadian born – Canadian parents	0.79		0.80		0.78	
Canadian born – immigrant parents	0.12		0.11		0.12	
Canadian born – immigrant father	0.05		0.05		0.06	
Canadian born – immigrant mother	0.04		0.04		0.04	
Immigrant – immigrant parents		0.97		0.97		0.97
Immigrant – other		0.03		0.03		0.03
Observations	914,260	921,070	203,820	198,330	242,340	261,080

12

HEALTH STATUS AND SOCIAL CAPITAL OF RECENT IMMIGRANTS IN CANADA: EVIDENCE FROM THE LONGITUDINAL SURVEY OF IMMIGRANTS TO CANADA

JUN ZHAO, LI XUE, AND TARA GILKINSON

Étant donné que les immigrants comptent pour une importante proportion de la croissance de la population canadienne, leur état de santé présente un intérêt particulier pour les chercheurs, les décideurs politiques et les responsables de programmes qui les concernent. Toutefois, à cause des limites des données, peu de recherches ont été menées, jusqu'à maintenant, sur les disparités qui existent entre l'état de santé des immigrants de diverses catégories – catégorie de la famille, catégorie économique, catégorie des réfugiés. De plus, peu d'études quantitatives ont examiné l'impact du capital social sur l'état de santé des immigrants. C'est donc de ces questions que traite cet article, à l'aide d'analyses économétriques. À partir de données de l'Enquête longitudinale auprès des immigrants du Canada (ELIC), nous étudions l'évolution de l'état de santé des immigrants récents durant les quatre années qui suivent leur arrivée au pays, en mettant particulièrement l'accent sur les effets du capital social sur leur santé. Nos résultats descriptifs et ceux que nous avons obtenus à l'aide de régressions confirment l'existence d'un « effet de l'immigrant en bonne santé ». Toutefois, nos résultats indiquent que cet effet décroît avec le temps, et qu'il y a des disparités entre l'état de santé de différents sous-groupes d'immigrants. Par exemple, les immigrants acceptés en tant que travailleurs qualifiés sont généralement en meilleure santé, alors que les réfugiés ont plus tendance à évaluer leur état de santé comme étant « assez bon » ou « faible ». Quand nous observons l'effet de certaines variables associées au capital social, nos résultats confirment le lien entre les réseaux d'amis et l'état de santé des immigrants récents : l'importance et la diversité, sur le plan ethnique, des réseaux d'amis ont un effet positif sur la façon dont les immigrants évaluent leur état de santé global. Dans le cas des immigrants de la catégorie de la famille, ce sont les réseaux organisationnels qui ont cet effet. En général, les réseaux sociaux ont un effet plus important sur l'état de santé des immigrants de la catégorie de la famille que sur les immigrants des autres catégories.

Canadian Immigration: Economic Evidence for a Dynamic Policy Environment, ed. T. McDonald, E. Ruddick, A. Sweetman, and C. Worswick. Montreal and Kingston: Queen's Policy Studies Series, McGill-Queen's University Press.

Given that immigrants represent a large proportion of Canadian population growth, their health is of particular interest to researchers, policy-makers, and program officials. Due to data limitations, there is little Canadian research on the disparities of health status among immigration categories, i.e., family class immigrants, economic class immigrants, and refugees. As well, there are few studies that examine the impact of social capital on immigrant health status at the quantitative level. This paper addresses these gaps through econometric analyses. Using data from the Longitudinal Survey of Immigrants to Canada (LSIC), we look at the dynamic changes in the health status of recent immigrants in their initial four years in Canada, focusing particularly on the effect of social capital on immigrant health. Our descriptive and regression results provide support for the "healthy immigrant effect"; however, the results show that this effect diminishes over time. Our results also suggest health status disparities between recent immigrant sub-groups. Skilled worker principal applicants are more likely to be generally healthy, while refugees are more likely to rate their health as fair or poor. Looking at the effects of selected social capital variables, we confirm the connections between friendship networks and health status of recent immigrants. The density and ethnic diversity of friendship networks are positively associated with immigrants' self-rated overall health. For family class immigrants, the analysis reveals a positive association between organizational networks and self-rated health status. In general, social networks are found to have stronger effects on the health status of family class immigrants than for immigrants in other categories.

INTRODUCTION

Between 2001 and 2006, roughly 1.2 million immigrants landed in Canada. Given that immigrants represent a large proportion – two-thirds – of Canada's population growth (CIC 2007), immigrant health status is of particular interest to researchers, policy-makers and program officials. Lack of data has limited Canadian research on the disparities among immigration sub-groups such as family class immigrants, economic class immigrants, and refugees (Zhao 2007a). This paper addresses this gap through econometric analyses. Its purpose is to look at the dynamic changes in the health status of recent immigrants in the initial years in Canada, focusing particularly on the effect of social capital on immigrant health.

This paper undertakes to answer the following questions:

- Does the health status of recent immigrants in Canada change over the initial four years after landing?
- Is there any disparity of health status among different immigrant sub-groups?
- Are there main social factors associated with the health status of recent immigrants?

- To what extent does social capital, embedded in social networks, affect the health status of recent immigrants?

The paper proceeds as follows. After a literature review on the concept of social capital, the data sources and indicators used in the analysis are described. The next sections present the descriptive analysis, the econometric models, and the regression results, followed by discussion. The conclusion summarizes the main findings and discusses some policy implications of the research.

Literature Review

Defining Social Capital

The term "social capital" is a hybrid notion that "brings together the theoretical and empirical rationale for considering social ties as a potentially important ingredient of well-being and prosperity in society" (PRI 2005b, 37). It is a geographical, political, economic, and sociological concept, and although there is much debate surrounding its definition and conceptualization, it carries with it a "seductive simplicity" (Mohan and Mohan 2002, 191) in that it is "based on the premise that an interpersonal network provides value to its members by giving them access to the social resources available within the network" (Staber 2006, 190). As Putnam explains, "like tools (physical capital) and training (human capital), social networks have value" (2007, 137); "they have value for the people who are in them, and they have, at least in some instances, demonstrable externalities, so that there are both public and private faces of social capital" (2001, 41).

Table 1 identifies some of the various definitions of social capital found within the literature.

TABLE 1
Definitions of Social Capital

The characteristics of the social organization such as networks, norms and social trust that facilitate coordination and cooperation for mutual benefit.	Putnam 1995, 67
The sum of the resources, actual or virtual, that accrue to an individual or a group by virtue of possessing a durable network of more or less institutionalized relationships of mutual acquaintance and recognition.	Bourdieu and Wacquant 1992, 119
The ability of actors to secure benefits by virtue of membership in social networks or other social structures.	Portes 1998, 6

Social capital has been linked to positive externalities such as better health, higher employment rates, and increased social interaction (Mohan and Mohan 2002, 193). However, not all the effects of social capital may be positive: "just as the sources of social capital are plural so are its consequences" (Portes 1998, 9). Portes (1998) has identified several negative externalities of social capital including "exclusion of outsiders, excess claims on group members, restrictions on individual freedom and downward levelling norms" (15). As Putnam explains, "although networks can powerfully affect our ability to get things done, nothing guarantees that what gets done through networks will be socially beneficial" (2007, 138). Therefore, "understanding social capital demands an emphasis on the *nature* of interactions, the *meaning* of linkages and their potential to *enable change*, rather than the structural casing and visible connections themselves" (MacKian 2002, 208; italics in original).

Social Capital and Immigrant Integration

The concept of social capital has been found to be particularly relevant to the study of immigrant integration. Research on social capital has emphasized the significance of social networks (both homogenous and heterogeneous) to a variety of outcomes, including employment. Results from recent analyses of the General Social Survey (GSS) and the Longitudinal Survey of Immigrants to Canada (LSIC) support the importance of social capital to the integration of immigrants to Canada (van Kemenade et al. 2006; Xue 2008). Evidence from both surveys shows that social capital is a major determinant of immigrant health (Zhao 2007a; van Kemenade et al. 2006).

Social capital has been connected to immigrant educational attainments. Ooka and Wellman (2006) found that educational attainment is positively associated with being in heterogeneous friendship networks. The authors found that first generation immigrants with post-secondary education are more likely to be in a heterogeneous network than those with less education. Educational and employment outcomes of immigrants play a role in influencing immigrant health outcomes. Dunn and Dyck (1998) analyzed results from the National Population Health Survey (NPHS 1994-1995). The authors' findings showed that immigrants with high levels of education and high incomes were more likely to report their health status as very good or excellent.

Mechanisms Linking Social Capital and Health

Despite a recent "flourishing epidemiologic and public health interest in the investigation of the effects of social capital on physical health outcomes" (Kim et al. 2008, 186), the mechanisms that link social capital to health are not yet clearly understood (Kawachi et. al 1999, 1190): "At the individual level, it is not completely established whether good health is the result of social capital or whether social capital is the result of good health and / or other unmeasured personal characteristics that determine both health status and patterns of social engagement" (Kawachi 2006, 992). Despite this major challenge, several researchers including Kawachi et al. (1999), Putnam (2000), and Berkman and Glass (2000) have attempted to identify pathways and mechanisms through which social capital impacts community and individual health outcomes.

Within the literature it is suggested that social networks may influence health outcomes – by serving as a tool that rapidly diffuses health information, therefore improving access to health resources (Kawachi et al. 1999; Berkman and Glass 2000); through the provision of tangible assistance such as "money, convalescent care, and transportation, which reduces psychic and physical stress and provides a safety net" (Putnam 2000, 327); through the reinforcement of health norms (e.g., physical activity) and social influence (networks' values and norms) (Kawachi et al. 1999; Putnam 2000; Berkman and Glass 2000); and finally, by providing emotional support (Berkman and Glass 2000), which may serve as a "psychological triggering mechanism, stimulating people's immune systems to fight disease and buffer stress" (Putnam 2000, 327).

Social Capital and Health

Putnam (2000) states that "of all the domains in which I have traced the consequences of social capital, in none is the importance of social connectedness so well established as in the case of health and well-being" (326). The relationship between social capital and health outcomes has been explored in both empirical and theoretical research. Social capital has been connected to a variety of health outcomes such as access to health care, binge drinking, leisure time, physical inactivity, food security, child behaviour problems, walking activity, violent crime and homicide, life expectancy, tuberculosis case rates, life satisfaction, and suicide rates (Kawachi et al. 2004).

Ecological studies have found that social capital is associated with lower rates of suicide and higher levels of life satisfaction (Helliwell 2003). Fisher et al. (2004) found that cohesive communities rich in trust are characterized by increased levels of physical activity, and results from Hendryx et al. (2002) suggest that community social capital is associated with better access to health care. Research in this area has also concluded that for neighbourhoods with higher social capital, members report better individual and self-rated health (Wen et al. 2003).

Self-rated health status, increasingly used as a measure of overall health, has been found within the literature to be linked to a variety of individual level measures of social capital (Kim et al. 2008). For example, research has found that self-rated health status is linked to longevity and functional ability (Idler and Kasl 1995; Idler et al. 1999) and social trust (Lavis and Stoddart 1999), as well as involvement in formal and informal networks (Rose 2000).

Immigrant Social Capital and Health

There is limited research that looks directly at the ways in which social capital affects the health outcomes of immigrant populations. However, the work of Deri (2005), Newbold (2009), van Kemenade et al. (2006), and Zhao (2007a) provides some insight into this area.

Deri (2005) used data from the Canadian National Population Health Survey (CNPHS) to examine if and how social networks impact the health care utilization patterns of immigrants whose mother tongue is neither English nor French. Following Bertrand et al. (2000), she measured social networks by the extent of linguistic concentration in an area of Census subdivisions. Deri's findings suggest that social networks play an important role in influencing health care utilization behaviours. She found that "for high utilizing language groups, living in areas of high concentration of the language group increases access. Conversely, for low utilizing groups, living in areas of high concentration of the language group decreases access" (Deri 2005, 1079).

Newbold (2009) used the LSIC to estimate health transitions of recent immigrants. According to Newbold, recent immigrants "who noted monthly social interactions with family or friends (relative to less than monthly social interactions), were less likely to transition to poor health. Otherwise, the degree of social interaction was unimportant" (329-30). However, the author's findings also indicate that having family or friends in close proximity and involvement in a social group do not appear to have any impact on health transitions.

Using the General Social Survey (GSS), van Kemenade et al. (2006) found that "having access to close networks of people from the same cultural origin – as well as to programs that support these networks – is associated with the social and economic integration of immigrants in the host county and with their well being" (19). Results indicate that (1) "there is a positive association between the size of networks of strong ties and reported good health among immigrants"; (2) "there is also a positive association between the number of ties with organizations and immigrants' self-reported health. Immigrants with a high number of ties to organizations perceive their health to be good"; (3) "immigrant women who say they had at least one reciprocal support relationship within their social networks were more likely to say they are in good health than their peers without such a relationship"; and (4) "immigrant men who volunteered in the year preceding the survey are more than twice as likely to say they are in good health as their peers who had not participated in volunteer activity" (19).

Zhao (2007a) conducted a duration analysis of the LSIC in an attempt to gain further insight into the health outcomes and socio-economic determinants of health among Canada's recent immigrants. According to Zhao, immigrants who had frequent interaction with friends in Canada, who spoke at least one of the official languages, who were not in low income families, and who owned a home rather than rented had a decreased risk of a decline in health status. Zhao also found that "immigrants with a social network and social support were more likely to visit doctors" (42). This reflects that immigrants with a social network and social support had fewer problems accessing health care services but possibly had more health issues. However, social capital effects were not the main interests in Zhao (2007a). The main differences between that paper and the present work are: (1) we categorize social networks into three types, i.e., kinship, friendship, and organizational networks; (2) for each type of network, we also look at its size, diversity, and density, etc; and (3) we apply a panel data model to take into account unobserved individual characteristics, such as differences in genes, lifestyle, and attitudes toward physical activities.

Data and Definition

Data Sources

The main data source used in this paper is the Longitudinal Survey of Immigrants to Canada (LSIC), which was designed to study how newly arrived immigrants adapt to living in Canada during their first four years after arrival. The survey's target population was immigrants who arrived in Canada between October 2000 and September 2001, were 15 years of age or over at the time of landing, and landed from abroad.[1]

The survey addresses a number of issues including demographic and household characteristics of the longitudinal respondent, health, citizenship, social interactions, groups and organizations, language skills, housing, education, employment, values and attitudes, income, and perceptions of settlement.

The LSIC is longitudinal – that is, the same respondents were interviewed at six months (wave 1), two years (wave 2), and four years (wave 3) after landing in Canada, providing a dynamic picture of the integration experiences of these recent immigrants. Approximately 12,000 immigrants participated in the wave 1 interview, representing about 164,200 of the target population. The final survey (wave 3) sample of 7,700 immigrants represents 157,600 immigrants of the target population who still resided in Canada at the time of the last interview (Statistics Canada, 2007). Our study focuses on these 7,700 immigrants who participated in all three waves. The longitudinal weights designed by Statistics Canada are used to account for sample attrition.

The second data source is the Canadian Community Health Survey (CCHS), a cross-sectional survey of the Canadian population. We use the CCHS to obtain data on the health status of the Canadian born by age group for the comparison analysis. The first year of collection for the CCHS (Cycle 1.1) was between September 2000 and November 2001, coincident with the first wave interview of the LSIC. The CCHS operates on a two-year collection cycle, and the target population for the survey represents 98 percent of the Canadian population residing in Canada's 10 provinces (Statistics Canada 2006). The first three cycles – Cycle 1.1 (2000-01), Cycle 2.1 (2002-03), and Cycle 3.1 (2004-05) – are used in this paper. The sampling weights designed by Statistics Canada are used to compute statistical estimates in order to make possible inference at the population level.

Definitions

Health status indicator: In this paper, self-rated health is used as an indicator of immigrants' health status.[2] The self-rated health indicator measures individuals' perception of their overall health. It can reflect aspects of health not captured in other measures, such as incipient disease, disease severity, aspects of positive health status, physiological and psychological reserves, and social and mental function. Epidemiologists have demonstrated that self-rated health is an accurate reflection of a person's health and a valid predictor of incident mortality and chronic morbidity (see Bond 2006; Idler and Benyamini 1997; Huisman et al. 2007).

In all three waves of the LSIC, the respondents were asked: "In general, would you say your health is excellent, very good, good, fair, or poor?" Health status was then grouped into two categories according to the answer: healthy (excellent, very good, or good) and unhealthy (fair or poor). The health status variable is the dependent variable in our logit panel regression models.

Social capital indicators: To determine the extent to which social capital influences the health status of recent immigrants, we used information unique to the LSIC data on social interactions and group organization participation. We employed the social capital indicators developed by Xue (2008), which use a network-based approach to measure social capital. Unlike many social network measures in the literature that use ethnic, linguistic, or neighbourhood characteristics as a proxy for social capital (e.g., Deri 2005; Bertrand et al. 2000; Chiswick and Miller 1996), this network based approach emphasizes both the structure and content of individuals' networks, using direct measures of social networks.

The structure of individuals' networks includes different levels of social networks. Similar to Xue (2008), in this paper social networks are categorized into three types: kinship, friendship, and organizational networks.

The *kinship network* includes relationships with family members and relatives living in Canada. The *friendship network* consists of ties with friends. The *organizational network* is defined as the participation of immigrants in groups and organizations, such as community organizations, religious groups, ethnic or immigrant associations, etc.

Within each type of network, the content is defined by the amount of social involvement and social support such as size, diversity, frequency of contact, and network reciprocity. Social network size is defined as the number of people or units with whom immigrants maintain different types of relationships (family, friends, organizations). While the LSIC does not provide information on the absolute numbers of people in all networks, there are some good substitutes for network size. For example, based on information available from the LSIC, we can obtain an approximation of network size for family ties by counting the number of types of relatives in Canada, such as spouse, children, parents, grandparents, brothers and sisters, uncles and aunts, and cousins. For friends network, sources where immigrants met new friends, such as ethnic association or club, religious activity, through relatives or friends, sports, hobby or other club, spouse's work, ESL or FSL classes, other classes, etc., are counted to proximate the absolute size of the network. For organizational network, LSIC provides a direct measure of absolute number of groups or organizations that immigrants participated in.

Social network diversity represents the social and ethnic heterogeneity of network members, which is measured by the relative numbers of non co-ethnic members and co-ethnic ones in a person's networks.

Social network density is defined as the frequency of contact between network members. Using the information on the frequency of contact with people in the networks and information on the relative number of co-ethnic members among friend networks and organizational networks, we create both diversity and density indexes for each type of network, which range from 0 to 1. The higher the diversity index, the more diversified the social network is. The higher the density index, the more frequently individuals contact family members, relatives, or friends, and/or the more frequently they take part in group and organizational activities.

Social network reciprocity can be measured as help received from networks as well as contribution made to networks. We create several indicators to measure the different types of help that an immigrant received from a particular type of network.[3] We also use a variable to indicate the number of organizations or groups for which an immigrant volunteered time.

The main social capital variables are shown in Appendix Table A1.

Income indicator: Family income is an important factor that significantly affects individuals' health status (Zhao 2007a). In this paper we group immigrants into four groups by economic family income quartiles from the lowest to the highest: 0-25 percent, 25-50 percent, 50-75 percent, and 75-100 percent. "Economic family" refers to a group of two or more persons who live in the same dwelling and are related to each other by blood, marriage, common law, or adoption (Statistics Canada 2007).

Employment status is also significantly related to the health status of immigrants (Zhao 2007a). The employment status of a respondent is grouped into two categories: employed, and not employed. The employment status of a respondent's spouse is grouped into three categories which also capture marital status: no spouse, spouse currently employed, and spouse currently not employed.

Other socio-demographic variables: Other socio-demographic variables that have potential impacts on the health status of recent immigrants and are controlled for in our regression analysis include age, gender, immigrant category, source area, education level at landing, official language ability, and incidence of problems accessing Canadian health care system.

We group immigrants into five categories: (1) family class immigrants, (2) skilled workers – principal applicants, (3) skilled workers – spouses and dependants, (4) refugees, and (5) other immigrants.[4] The source countries of immigrants are grouped into five broad areas: North America, United Kingdom and Western Europe, Europe except UK and Western Europe, Asia and Pacific, Africa and Middle East, Caribbean and Guyana, and South and Central America. Education at landing is grouped into four categories: high school or less, trade certificate or college/some university, bachelor's degree, and master's degree or above.

To investigate age-specific health status, we separate the population into five age groups: 15-19, 20-34, 35-44, 45-64, and 65+ years. Place of residence is grouped into six categories by census metropolitan areas (CMAs): living in one of the top five CMAs and living in an area other than the five major CMAs.[5] Official language ability (self-assessed)[6] is captured by two dummy variables for English and French: speaking English (or French) well (i.e., speaking fairly well, well, and very well with English or French as the native language) or not (i.e., speaking poorly or not able to speak in English or French).

Accessibility to the Canadian health care system is grouped into two categories: having and not having problems accessing health care services. Problems identified include long waiting times, discrimination, problems finding a family doctor, transportation, and/or insurance covering prescription medication, etc.[7] Health care service access is important because it influences immigrants' health status and quality of life. Health status may deteriorate as individuals become more prone to chronic conditions due to barriers to health care access (Rivers and Patino 2006).

DESCRIPTIVE ANALYSIS

Evidence from the LSIC and CCHS indicates that in the initial period after arrival, the self-reported health status of immigrants is better than that of their Canadian born counterparts. This reflects the "healthy immigrant effect," which is possibly due to the health standards required by the immigrant selection program and verified by a pre-migration medical examination. According to section 38 of Canada's Immigration and Refugee Protection Act (IRPA) issued in 2002, "a foreign national is inadmissible on health grounds if their health condition (*a*) is likely to be a danger to public health; (*b*) is likely to be a danger to public safety; or (*c*) might reasonably be expected to cause excessive demand on health or social services." However, this "healthy immigrant effect" is found to diminish gradually with time spent in Canada.

The gap of incidence of a healthy population between immigrants and Canadians narrows at four years after landing, as shown in Figure 1. Our results are consistent with existing studies on health status of immigrants (e.g., McDonald and Kennedy 2004; Newbold and Danforth 2003; Zhao 2007a).

FIGURE 1
Share of Immigrants and Canadian Born Self-Reporting as Healthy

Percentage (%)

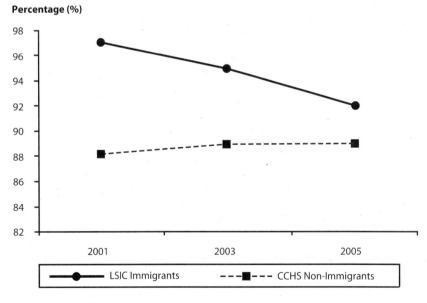

Note: The plots in Figure 1 are age standardized to represent a person of mean age in the Canadian population as measured by the CCHS.
Data source: LSIC (2005), CCHS (2000-2005).

The dynamic changes in health status of immigrants over the initial period after landing can be found in Tables 2 and 3. At the wave 1 interview, 97 percent of immigrants (152,908) report their health as good, very good, or excellent. Among these healthy immigrants, 5 percent and 7 percent report their health as fair or poor at waves 2 and 3, respectively, while 93 percent remain healthy at wave 3. In contrast, among the unhealthy immigrants at wave 1, 67 percent report their health as good, very good, or excellent at four years after landing. As shown in Table 3, 95 percent of immigrants (149,043) report their health as good, very good, or excellent at wave 2, while 6 percent of these healthy immigrants report their health as fair or poor at wave 3. Among the unhealthy immigrants at wave 2, 57 percent report their health as healthy at wave 3. Given all these changes, after four years in Canada 92 percent of the LSIC immigrants deem their health status as good, very good, or excellent.

TABLE 2
Immigrants' Health Status at Wave 1 Cross-Tabulated with Each of Waves 2 and 3
(Unweighted Sample Size N=7716)

Health Status, Wave 1		Health Status, Wave 2		Health Status, Wave 3	
		Not Healthy	Healthy	Not Healthy	Healthy
Not healthy (number)	4,706	1,590	3,116	1,533	3,174
(%)	100	34	66	33	67
Healthy (number)	152,908	6,959	145,927	11,121	141,787
(%)	100	5	95	7	93
Total (number)	157,615	8,550	149,043	12,654	144,961
(%)	100	5	95	8	92

Data source: LSIC (2005).

TABLE 3
Immigrants' Health Status at Wave 2 Cross-Tabulated with Wave 3
(Unweighted Sample Size N=7714)

Health Status, Wave 2		Health Status, Wave 3	
		Not Healthy	Healthy
Not healthy (number)	8,550	3,644	4,906
(%)	100	43	57
Healthy (number)	149,043	9,010	140,033
(%)	100	6	94
Total (number)	157,593	12,654	144,939
(%)	100	8	92

Data source: LSIC (2005).

As shown in Figure 2, when looking at the health status of immigrants by immigrant category, there are obvious disparities among immigrant sub-groups. In each wave, skilled workers have the largest share of healthy immigrants, followed by family class immigrants and refugees. Refugees are more likely to report their health as fair or poor initially because they often come from areas of conflict with poor public health infrastructure and are more likely to be at risk for malnutrition and infectious diseases.

FIGURE 2

Share of Immigrants Self-Reporting as "Healthy" by Immigration Category

Percentage (%)

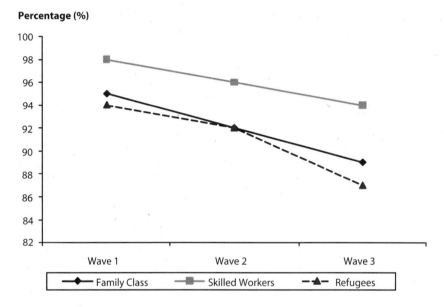

Data source: LSIC (2005).

Many refugees may have suffered physical or emotional trauma and unhealthy living conditions prior to migration. After arrival in Canada, most refugees are eligible for income support and other immediate and essential services from the Resettlement Assistance Program (RAP), which are offered for up to one year. Particularly under the Interim Federal Health Program (IFHP), resettled refugees are eligible for health benefits until their provincial health care coverage begins. Those with provincial/ territorial health coverage are provided with supplemental coverage for one year. The IFHP coverage can be extended up to 24 months for recipients identified with special needs. With the income support from the RAP along with other assistance, the LSIC refugees were able by the second wave of the LSIC to narrow the gap between proportions reporting being healthy as compared to other categories. However, after this initial period, refugees may have experienced more financial and cultural barriers, which had negative effects on their health outcomes, implied by the widened gap at four years after landing.

Friendship networks of recent immigrants in Canada represent an extremely important source of support and assistance (van Kemenade et al. 2006). Figure 3 presents the health status of recent immigrants by the presence of new friends. Immigrants who have made friends after their arrival in Canada are more likely to report a better health status in all three waves. This may be largely related to the ability of friendships to promote a sense of belonging and reduce loneliness. Sense of belonging can be considered a possible emotional outcome (Ueno 2004). Friendship networks also have potential impacts on immigrants' settlement outcomes and integration to Canadian society, such as housing, employment, education, and health care services usage (Xue 2008; Zhao 2007a; van Kemenade et al. 2006), which may affect both emotional and physical health as well.

FIGURE 3
Share of Immigrants Self-Reporting as "Healthy" by Having Made New Friends

Percentage (%)

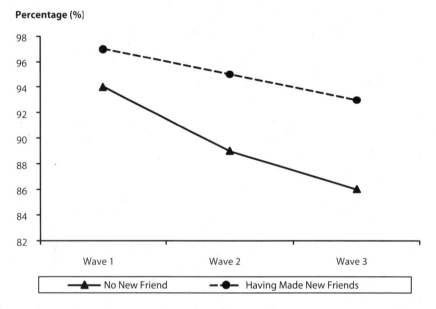

Data source: LSIC (2005).

Organizational networks such as community organizations, religious groups, and ethnic and immigration associations are important sources of assistance for recent immigrants. Findings from the LSIC indicate that the percentage of immigrants involved in group or organizational activities increases with time spent in Canada (Zhao 2007a). Good social integration generally makes for good social support (Franke 2006); this social support may also be beneficial for immigrant health outcomes. As shown in Figure 4, at six months after landing, there are almost no differences in the health status between immigrants involved in organizational or group activities and immigrants who are not involved in such activities. In contrast, two years after landing, the proportion of healthy immigrants among the immigrants involved in group or organizational activities is larger than those who are not involved. At four years after landing, the gap widens to 3 percentage points.

FIGURE 4
Share of Immigrants Self-Reporting as "Healthy" by Participation in Organizations

Percentage (%)

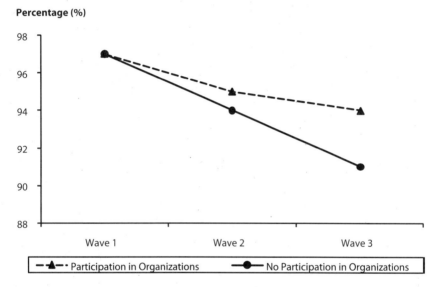

Data source: LSIC (2005).

ECONOMETRIC MODELS

As mentioned above, the LSIC data is longitudinal, consisting of very large cross-sectional micro-units – which include thousands of individuals and three time periods. In order to model the probability of reporting as healthy among immigrants while taking into consideration individual heterogeneity, panel data models are applied to our regression analysis by controlling for the individual stock of social capital and other socio-demographic variables. The fundamental advantage of a panel data model is that it allows modelling differences in behaviour across individuals. Panel data modelling techniques focus on heterogeneity across units rather than time series autocorrelations. The basic framework for the binary panel data models is a single equation model:

$$y_{it}^* = X'_{it}\beta + Z'_i\gamma + v'_i\alpha + \varepsilon_{it}, \quad i = 1,\ldots, n; \, t = 1,\ldots, T_i$$

$$y_{it} = \begin{cases} 1 & if \\ 0 & otherwise \end{cases} y_{it}^* > 0$$

where y^* is an unobserved latent variable of an immigrant's likelihood of reporting being healthy. X is a collection of k independent time varying variables denoted by the vector $x' = (x_1, x_2, \ldots, x_k)$. Z is a collection of m independent time invariant variables denoted by the vector $z' = (z_1, z_2, \ldots, z_m)$. Both X and Z are observable. The regressors also include a set of dummy variables for each wave of the panel in order to capture time effects. ε is an error term with mean zero and a standardized logistic distribution with variance $\pi^2/3$. Subscript i is an index for cross-section units and t is an index for time periods ($T = 3$). The unobserved individual effect $v'_i\alpha$ capturing the heterogeneity across individuals that determine the good health probability includes a set of individual specific factors which are unobservable, such as individual difference in personality or ability, group or family specific characteristics, and health behaviours. It is assumed that v_i and ε_{it} are uncorrelated with each other.

For the estimation of panel data model, the critical issue is whether the individual effects v_i are correlated with the observed regressors X and Z (Greene 2002; Jones 2007). Compared to the random-effects model, the generalized estimating equations (GEE) approach proposed by Liang and Zeger (1986) and Zeger, Liang, and Albert (1988) can be used to estimate population-average effects. The GEE model is an extension of the generalized linear model (GLM) approach to longitudinal data analysis using quasi-likelihood estimation. The GEE model has consistent and asymptotically normal solutions, even with mis-specification of the correlation structure, because the assumption of independence of the unobserved individual effects with the explanatory variables is not required in the model (Hu et al. 1998). The GEE approach relaxes the strict independence assumption of random effects estimation and takes the dependence among units into consideration. Furthermore, time invariant variables such as immigration category, ethnic group, and region of origin can be included in the regression as part of X, which is impossible in the fixed effects model. The GEE model is appropriate when inferences about the population average are the focus. In this paper, the average difference between groups with varied stock of social capital is of most importance, not the difference for any one immigrant. Thus we present our results from the GEE model framework in the current paper.[8]

REGRESSION RESULTS AND DISCUSSION

Table 4 presents the survey means and standard errors of the variables used in our empirical models for all immigrants. Time variant variables and time invariant variables are differentiated in the table. The regression results from the GEE models are reported in Table 5.

Let us first look at the regression results for all the LSIC immigrants (see Table 5).

Column 1 reports the regression results of the specification without social capital variables. The estimated effects of the demographic variables (e.g., age and gender) are consistent with the theoretical explanations and the findings from the existing empirical studies. Males are more likely to report good health than females. Immigrants in the older age groups are more likely to rate their health status as fair or poor. The marginal effects related to the 15-19 age group (reference group) decline as age increases. Immigrants in the oldest age group of 65 and over are less likely to rate their health status as healthy compared to those aged 15-19. However, region of birth does not have a significant effect on the health status of recent immigrants.

As discussed previously in the descriptive analysis, the health status varies across immigration categories. The regression results confirm that the health status is significantly different across immigration categories, controlled for other characteristics. Compared to family class immigrants, skilled worker principal applicants are more likely to report good health, while refugees are more likely to report poor health.

In terms of perceptions of official language ability variables, health status varies significantly across groups. Compared with no official language ability, being proficient in English is associated with a higher likelihood of reporting as healthy. However, the ability to speak French does not have a significant effect on health. The effect of level of education at landing is also not statistically significant during the initial four years after landing.

For the variables of accessibility to the Canadian health care system, immigrants who have had problems accessing health care services are more likely to rate their health as fair or poor. This may reflect the role of immigrants' ability to effectively identify and access health care services (including preventive care) in positive perceptions of health status.

Looking at family income quartiles, there are quite large differences in health status across groups. Immigrants in the lowest family income quartile are more likely to report poor health. Furthermore, the employment status of both respondents and their spouses is positively associated with immigrants' health.

When including time indicators in the regressions, we confirm the "healthy immigrant effect" – when compared with the situation in wave 1,

TABLE 4
Survey Means of Variables in the Final Specification Estimation, All Immigrants

	N=7656 *n=22320*	
	Weighted Mean	*Standard Error*
Healthy	0.946	0.002
Time invariant variables		
Immigration category		
Family class	0.266	0.003
Skilled worker principal applicants	0.349	0.004
Skilled worker spouses and dependants	0.257	0.003
Refugees	0.063	0.001
Other immigrants	0.066	0.002
Sex		
Male	0.497	0.004
Female	0.503	0.004
World region of birth		
Asia and Pacific	0.598	0.004
North America, the United Kingdom, and Western Europe	0.052	0.002
Caribbean and Guyana, South and Central America	0.059	0.002
Europe except UK and Western Europe	0.111	0.002
Africa and Middle East	0.181	0.003
Education at landing		
High school or less	0.250	0.003
Trade certificate or college, some university	0.199	0.003
University degree	0.361	0.004
Master's degree or above	0.190	0.003
Time variant variables		
Age group		
15-19	0.051	0.002
20-34	0.431	0.004
35-44	0.315	0.003
45-64	0.169	0.003
65+	0.035	0.001
Having problems accessing health care services	0.178	0.003
CMA of residence		
Toronto	0.439	0.004
Vancouver	0.147	0.002
Montreal	0.136	0.003
Calgary	0.052	0.001
Ottawa	0.033	0.001
Other cities	0.193	0.003
Self-assessed language ability		
English	0.832	0.003
No English ability	0.168	0.003
French	0.158	0.003
No French ability	0.842	0.003

... continued

TABLE 4
(Continued)

	N=7656 n−22320	
	Weighted Mean	*Standard Error*
Family income		
Income quartile 0-25%	0.251	0.003
Income quartile 25%-50%	0.252	0.003
Income quartile 50%-75%	0.248	0.003
Income quartile 75%-100%	0.250	0.003
Employment		
Employed	0.580	0.004
Not employed	0.420	0.004
No spouse	0.390	0.004
Spouse employed	0.325	0.003
Spouse not employed	0.286	0.003
Social capital variables		
Having relatives in Canada upon landing	0.547	0.004
Number of relatives in Canada	0.807	0.007
Frequency of contact with family sponsors	0.278	0.003
Having friends in Canada upon landing	0.574	0.004
Having made new friends	0.891	0.002
Number of sources meeting friends	2.629	0.012
Frequency of contact with friends	0.766	0.002
Ethnic diversity of friends	0.465	0.002
Number of organizations participated in	0.339	0.005
Ethnic diversity of organizational network	0.016	0.000
Frequency of activities with organizations	0.160	0.002
Numbers of organizations for which the respondent volunteered time	0.178	0.004
Time period		
Wave 1	0.336	0.003
Wave 2	0.331	0.003
Wave 3	0.333	0.003

Data source: LSIC (2005).

immigrants are less likely to report being in good health in wave 2 and wave 3 (the likelihoods are 3 percent points and 4.5 percent points, respectively, lower than that in wave 1).[9]

Columns 2 to 4 of Table 5 estimate models with social capital variables. As an initial step, column 2 only adds general indicators of the existing networks including relatives and friends in Canada upon landing, and development of new networks after landing captured by whether an immigrant made new friends in Canada. The addition of these indicators does not change other effects much. Also, making new friends in Canada shows a positive relationship with health status of immigrants. To further investigate which elements play a role among networks, column 3

TABLE 5

GEE Population-Averaged Estimations of Probability of Being Healthy for All Immigrants in the First Four Years in Canada

	1 No Social Capital Indicators	2 Social Capital (1)	3 Social Capital (2)	4 Social Capital (3)
	Marginal Effects (dy/dx)	Marginal Effects (dy/dx)	Marginal Effects (dy/dx)	Marginal Effects (dy/dx)
Immigration category				
[Family class]				
Skilled worker principal applicants	0.011**	0.008*	0.008	0.009**
Skilled worker spouses and dependants	0.003	0.000	0.000	0.002
Refugees	-0.015**	-0.018***	-0.018***	-0.016***
Other immigrants	0.013***	0.011**	0.011**	0.012***
Gender				
[Female]				
Male	0.016***	0.016***	0.015***	0.015***
Age group				
[15-19]				
20-34	-0.005	-0.004	-0.004	-0.003
35-44	-0.025**	-0.024**	-0.023**	-0.021**
45-64	-0.058***	-0.053***	-0.053***	-0.05***
65+	-0.094***	-0.085***	-0.082***	-0.078***
Region of birth				
[Asia and Pacific]				
North America, the United Kingdom, and Western Europe	0.017***	0.016***	0.014**	0.014**
Caribbean and Guyana, South and Central America	0.008	0.008	0.007	0.006
Europe except UK and Western Europe	0.001	0.001	-0.001	0.000
Africa and Middle East	0.003	0.004	0.003	0.002
Problems accessing health care services				
[Not having problems accessing health care services]				
Having problems accessing health care services	-0.039	-0.039***	-0.038***	-0.039***
Census Metropolitan Area (CMA) of residence				
[Other cities]				
Toronto	-0.005	-0.005	-0.004	-0.004
Vancouver	-0.019	-0.019***	-0.017***	-0.017***
Montreal	-0.002	-0.002	-0.002	-0.002
Calgary	-0.012	-0.011	-0.011	-0.011
Ottawa	0.003	0.003	0.004	0.004
Official languages				
[No English speaking ability]				
English	0.028***	0.027***	0.024***	0.024***
[No French speaking ability]				
French	0.007	0.007	0.007	0.006
Economic status				
[Income quartile 0%-25%]				
Income quartile 25%-50%	0.006**	0.006**	0.006**	0.006**
Income quartile 50%-75%	0.01***	0.01***	0.01***	0.01***
Income quartile 75%-100%	0.011***	0.011***	0.011***	0.012***

... continued

TABLE 5
(Continued)

	1 No Social Capital Indicators Marginal Effects (dy/dx)	2 Social Capital (1) Marginal Effects (dy/dx)	3 Social Capital (2) Marginal Effects (dy/dx)	4 Social Capital (3) Marginal Effects (dy/dx)
Employment status				
[Not employed]				
Employed	0.012***	0.012***	0.012***	0.011***
Employment status of spouse				
[No spouse]				
Spouse employed	0.007**	0.007**	0.007**	0.007**
Spouse not employed	0.004	0.004	0.004	0.004
Education level at landing				
[High school or less]				
Trade certificate or college, some university	0.000	0.000	0.000	0.000
University degree	0.004	0.004	0.004	0.004
Master's degree or above	0.003	0.002	0.003	0.002
Social capital				
Family and relatives				
Having relatives in Canada upon landing		-0.005*		
Number of relatives			-0.001	
Frequency of contact with family sponsors			-0.002	
Friends				
Having friends in Canada upon landing		-0.003		
Having made new friends		0.014***		
Number of friends		-0.003		
Having made new friends			0.000	
Frequency of contact with friends			0.015***	0.015***
Ethnic diversity of friends			0.013**	0.013***
Groups and organizational network				
Number of groups or organizations participated in			-0.003	
Frequency of activities with organizations			0.008	
Ethnic diversity of organizational networks			-0.001	
Number of organizations volunteered time for			0.002	
Time effect				
[Wave 1]				
Wave 2	-0.028***	-0.03***	-0.03***	-0.03***
Wave 3	-0.042***	-0.042***	-0.046***	-0.045***
No. of observations	22,377	22,375	22,049	22,320
No. of individuals	7,656	7,656	7,652	7,656

Notes: * p<0.1; ** p<0.05; *** p<0.01; marginal effects for dummy variables are for discrete change from 0 to 1; reference categories are in brackets.
Data source: LSIC (2005).

includes all network content indicators in the model. The results confirm what column 2 indicates – friendship networks matter, particularly frequency of contact and ethnic diversity of the networks. Column 4 presents the final specification with social capital effects.

In terms of social capital variables, our results indicate that friendship networks have a significant effect on the respondents' self-reported status of health. Both the frequency of contact with friends and the ethnic diversity of friends have significant and positive effects on immigrants' health.

Immigrants who have more diverse friendship networks and who are in contact with their friends more frequently are more likely to report being in good health. However, it is important to note that we do not find significant effects of family and relative networks or group and organization networks on health for all immigrants.

Regression Results for Family Class Immigrants

In order to investigate the different ways in which social capital affects the health status of immigrant sub-groups, we also present the regression results of our GEE model for the reference group of family class immigrants (see Table 6).

Noteworthy regression results indicate that family and relative networks, friendship networks, and group and organization networks all have significant effects on the health status of recent family class immigrants.

Unlike the results from the model for all immigrants, for each of the three networks the effects of frequency of contact with network members or units are all statistically significant. Compared to those who do not have contact with friends or take part in organizational activities regularly, family class immigrants who interact with friends or groups on a daily basis are more likely to report that they are healthy.

However, frequency of contact with family sponsors is associated with a lower likelihood of reporting a positive health status. This may be partly due to the fact that a large proportion of family class immigrants are sponsored parent and grandparent immigrants (PGPs), who tend to be much older than the average family class immigrant.[10] The LSIC shows that the majority of PGPs lived with their family sponsors during the initial years after landing, and elderly PGPs are more likely to live with their sponsors (Zhao 2007b). In addition, a significant number of PGPs (37 percent at six months after landing, and 34 percent at two years after landing) who live with their sponsors provide unpaid labour for their sponsors, such as maintaining a house and caring for family members, which might be a factor that negatively affects their health. Another possible explanation for this finding may rest in the negative potentiality of social capital. As indicated in the literature review, social capital is not inherently positive; it may be the case that the frequency of contact with family members is connected to increased demands for time, resources, and energy by these networks. These excessive demands may adversely affect the health of recent immigrants.

The regression results also indicate that social network size and social network diversity do not have any significant effect on family class immigrants' health.

TABLE 6
Social Capital Effects on Probability of Being Healthy in the Initial Four Years in Canada, Family Class Immigrants

	Marginal Effects (dy/dx)	Standard Error
Social capital		
Frequency of contact with family sponsors	-0.018**	0.008
Frequency of contact with friends	0.027***	0.009
Frequency of activities with organizations	0.031***	0.010
Time effect		
[Wave 1]		
Wave 2	-0.044***	0.009
Wave 3	-0.068***	0.013
No. of observations	5,621	
No. of individuals	1,985	

Notes: * p<0.1; ** p<0.05; *** p<0.01. Reference categories are in brackets; marginal effects for dummy variables are for discrete change from 0 to 1; GEE population-averaged regression is used. The regression also includes controls for sex, age group, area of birth, incidence of problems accessing Canadian health care system, CMA of residence, ability of official languages, family income, employment status of the respondent and the spouse, and education.
Data source: LSIC (2005).

CONCLUSION

Using all three waves of the LSIC, we investigated the changes in the health status of recent immigrants through both descriptive and regression analyses. Our descriptive analyses from the LSIC and the CCHS provide strong support for the existence of the "healthy immigrant effect," which suggests that the self-reported health status of immigrants during the initial four years after landing is better than that of the Canadian born population. However, both descriptive and regression results indicate that the proportion of immigrants reporting as healthy diminishes over time.

Our findings also suggest that there are disparities in health status among recent immigrant subgroups. Skilled worker principal applicants are more likely to be in excellent, very good, or good health, while refugees are more likely to rate their health status as fair or poor.

Looking at the effects of selected social capital variables, our study shows that friendship networks play a very important role in the health of recent immigrants. The density and ethnic diversity of friendship networks have significant and positive effects on immigrants' self-rated health status. For family class immigrants, aside from friendship networks, group and organization networks also have a significant and positive effect on health status during the initial four years after landing. Existing family ties in Canada at landing have a significantly larger positive relationship with the health status of family class immigrants than for other immigration categories.

Policy Implications

Evidence from the LSIC indicates that social capital plays an important role for immigrants in the maintenance of good health during the initial years after landing. Therefore, social capital research can be very useful in informing immigrant health policy. Government of Canada programs such as the Immigrant Settlement and Adaption Program (ISAP), the Language Instruction for Newcomers (LINC) program, and the Host program can play a significant part in increasing the social capital of immigrants and can in turn affect health outcomes. These existing programs can support and promote recent immigrants' settlement and integration into Canadian society by facilitating the building of bonding and bridging networks and community connections.

Evidence from this paper suggests that problems in accessing health care services, including language barriers, relate significantly to the health outcomes of immigrants. In order to overcome these problems and provide recent immigrants with the information they need to take charge of their health and that of their family, community based multicultural health events would be complementary to government programs. The Multicultural Health Fair (MHF), developed by the Affiliation of Multicultural Societies and Services Agencies (AMSSA) in 2005, is a free community event that brings together representatives and volunteers from ethnic communities across Vancouver to provide health care information to new immigrants (AMSSA 2008). Such events are beneficial because they provide a space where individuals can connect and share information, experience, and knowledge while also building community social capital.

Governments can also encourage policies and programs that facilitate linkages between organizations and agencies involved in immigrant population health. One example of a project that attempts to achieve this is British Columbia's Mapping Initiative. Mapping enables the identification of available services within the various communities, and also provides information for policy-makers and service providers on a wide range of health issues impacting diverse populations residing in the province. Furthermore, it encourages a community-based model for population health by connecting and linking various health organizations and community service agencies that are currently or may be potentially engaged in population health. These inter-institutional networks can "improve the effectiveness of programs and lead to the establishment of others" which can lead to an "increased circulation and sharing of tangible (money, materials, equipment) or intangible (information, expertise) resources" (PRI 2005a, 24).

Finally, further research on the effect of social capital on the health of immigrants is necessary in order to create a more robust evidence base to inform the development of policies and programs. Further analysis of datasets such as the GSS and the LSIC is an important first step. Looking forward, the development and funding of immigrant health-based datasets or the addition of a larger immigrant sample to currently existing health based datasets may also be beneficial.

NOTES

We wish to thank Health Canada and Citizenship and Immigration Canada for their support for this project. We would also like to thank Dr Charles D. Mallory from Health Canada and Martha Justus, Jessie-Lynn MacDonald, and Colleen Dempsey from Citizenship and Immigration Canada for their helpful comments and suggestions. This paper was presented at the 8th International Conference on Health Economics, Policy and Management in Athens, Greece, in June 2009. Thanks also go to Arthur Sweetman and the other anonymous referee for their insightful comments and suggestions. The views expressed in this chapter are those of the authors and do not necessarily represent those of the Health Canada and/or Citizenship and Immigration Canada. All errors are entirely the responsibility of the authors.

1. Individuals who applied and landed from within Canada are excluded from the survey. Refugees claiming asylum from within Canada are also excluded from the scope of the survey. For detailed information on sample selection of the LSIC and the survey design and frame, please consult *Longitudinal Survey of Immigrants to Canada, Wave 3 – Microdata User Guide*, Statistics Canada, 2007.
2. Self-reported health is a commonly used measure of health but has limitations. The data from survey that are self-reported and the degree to which they may be inaccurate because of reporting error is unknown (Perez 2002). One issue in particular is that the notion of what constitutes good health may well change not only with age but also with time in the new country. One of the weaknesses of the LSIC is its limited information on health, so we have few alternatives but to use self-reported health.
3. In the following regression analyses, not all indicators for network reciprocity are included. Because of low variability, the indicators for number of types of help received from a certain kind of network are not included.
4. Other immigrants include mostly business immigrants and a very small number of immigrants who landed under the categories not specified in aforementioned categories.

5.   The top five CMAs are Toronto, Vancouver, Montreal, Ottawa, and Calgary.
6.   It is important to note that since we are dealing with survey data, as with most other variables in the LSIC, knowledge of official language is self-assessed.
7.   Incidence of having problems accessing the Canadian health care system might be endogenously determined by social network variables, etc. To address this issue, we compare the GEE population averaged logit estimates with IV estimates, where incidence of barriers to the health care system is treated as endogenous, and education at landing is used as an instrument. We argue that education variables are correlated with incidence of reporting problems accessing health care services, but not with the health status of immigrants. The Wald test statistic of exogeneity from the IV results is not significant, suggesting that there is not sufficient information to reject the null that there is no endogeneity. With the thought that the instruments may not be adequate, we also ran a simultaneous bivariate probit regression of whether an immigrant reported as healthy and whether the immigrant reported having problems accessing health care services, based on the other covariates. The results of social capital effects on health are quite similar to what we report in Table 5. Both the IV results and the bivariate probit regression results are available on request from the authors.
8.   In this paper, we only present the results from the GEE models, while the results from random effects and fixed effects models are available upon request.
9.   To investigate the time effects, we control for two types of time variables: (1) number of weeks in Canada since landing (continuous variable), and (2) wave variables (dummy variables). Both methods provide us with similar regression results: the respondents' self-rated health status is significantly and negatively related to increased time in Canada. This is consistent with our findings in the descriptive analysis that the health of recent immigrants declines over time. In Table 5 we only report results from the models with wave indicators used.
10. In the LSIC, PGPs account for 34 percent of family class immigrants. In 2001, the average age at landing of family class immigrants was 34 years, while the average age at landing of PGPs was 52 years – calculations based on data extracts on 31 March 2009 from CIC's Permanent Resident Data System (PRDS).

REFERENCES

Affliation of Multicultural Societies and Services Agencies. 2008. "Promoting Healthy Living in Multicultural Communities: The Multicultural Health Fair." Vancouver: AMSSA.

Berkman, L., and T. Glass. 2000. "Social Integration, Social Networks, Social Support and Health." In *Social Epidemiology*, edited by L. Berkman and I. Kawachi. New York: Oxford University Press.

Bertrand, M., E. Luttmer, and S. Mullainathan. 2000. "Network Effects and Welfare Cultures." *Quarterly Journal of Economics* 115: 1019-55.

Bond, J. 2006. "Self-Rated Health Status as a Predictor of Death, Functional and Cognitive Impairment: A Longitudinal Cohort Study." *European Journal of Aging* 3: 193-206.

Bourdieu, P., and L.P.D. Wacquant. 1992. *An Invitation to Reflexive Sociology.* Chicago: University of Chicago Press

Chiswick, B.R., and P.W. Miller. 1996. "Ethnic Networks and Language Proficiency among Immigrants." *Journal of Population Economics* 9 (1): 19-35.

Citizenship and Immigration Canada. 2007. "Facts and Figures." Ottawa: CIC.

Deri, C. 2005. "Social Networks and Health Service Utilization." *Journal of Health Economics* 24: 1076-107.

Dunn, J., and I. Dyck. 1998. "Social Determinants of Health in Canada's Immigrant Population: Results from the National Population Health Survey." Research on Immigration and Integration in the Metropolis Working Paper Series No. 98-20. Burnaby, BC.

Fisher, K.J., F. Li, Y. Michael, and M. Cleveland. 2004. "Neighbourhood Influences on Physical Activity among Older Adults: A Multi-level Analysis." *Journal of Aging and Physical Activity* 11: 49-67

Franke, S. 2006. "What Is Social Capital and Why Is It Important to Health Research and Policy?" *Health Policy Research Bulletin* 2: 6-9.

Helliwell, J. 2003. "Well-Being and Social Capital: Does Suicide Pose a Puzzle?" NBER Working Papers from National Bureau of Economic Research Inc. http://econpapers.repec.org/paper/nbrnberwo/108896.htm (accessed 10 January 2009).

Hendryx, M., M. Ahern, N. Lovrich, and A. McCurdy. 2002. "Access to Health Care and Community Social Capital." *Health Services Research* 37 (1): 85-101.

Hu, F., J. Goldberg, D. Hedeker, B. Flay, and M.A. Pentz. 1998. "Comparison of Population-Averaged and Subject-Specific Approaches for Analyzing Repeated Binary Outcomes." *American Journal of Epidemiology* 147 (7): 694-703.

Huisman, M., F. van Lenthe, and J. Mackenbach. 2007. "The Predictive Ability of Self-Assessed Health for Mortality in Different Educational Groups." *International Journal of Epidemiology* 36 (6): 1207-13.

Idler, E.L., and Y. Benyamini. 1997. "Self-Rated Health and Mortality: A Review of Twenty-Seven Community Studies." *Journal of Health and Social Behaviour* 38 (1): 21-37.

Idler, E.L., and S. Kasl. 1995. "Self-Ratings of Health: Do They Also Predict Change in Functional Ability?" *Journal of Gerontology* 50B (6): S344-S353.

Idler, E., S. Hudson, and H. Leventhal. 1999. "The Meanings of Self-Ratings of Health: A Qualitative and Quantitative Approach." *Research on Aging* 21 (3): 458-76.

Jones, A. 2008. *Applied Econometrics for Health Economists.* Oxford: Radcliffe Publishing.

Kawachi, I. 2006. "Commentary: Social Capital and Health: Making the Connections One Step at a Time." *International Journal of Epidemiology* 35: 989-93.

Kawachi, I., B. Kennedy, and R. Glass. 1999. "Social Capital and Self-Rated Health: A Contextual Analysis." *American Journal of Public Health* 89 (8): 1187-93.

Kawachi I., D. Kim, A. Coutts, and S.V. Subramanian. 2004. "Commentary: Reconciling the Three Accounts of Social Capital." *International Journal of Epidemiology* 33 (4): 682-90.

Kim, D., S.V Subramanian, and I. Kawachi. 2008. "Social Capital and Physical Health: A Systematic Review of the Literature." In *Social Capital and Health*, edited by I. Kawachi, S. Subramanian, and D. Kim. New York: Springer.

Lavis, J., and G. Stoddart. 1999. "Social Cohesion and Health." CHEPA Working Papers Series 99-09. Hamilton, ON: McMaster University.

Liang, K., and S. Zeger. 1986. "Longitudinal Data Analysis Using Generalized Linear Models." *Biometrika* 73: 13-22.

MacKian S. 2002. "Complex Cultures: Rereading the Story about Health and Social Capital." *Critical Social Policy* 22 (2): 203-25.

McDonald, J.T., and S. Kennedy. 2004. "Insights into the Health Immigrant Effect: Health Incidence and Health Service Use of Immigrants to Canada." *Social Science and Medicine* 19 (8): 1613-27.

Mohan, G., and J. Mohan. 2002. "Placing Social Capital." *Progress of Human Geography* 26 (2): 191-210.

Newbold, B. 2009. "The Short-Term Health of Canada's New Immigrant Arrivals: Evidence from the LSIC." *Ethnicity and Health* 14 (3): 315-36.

Newbold, B., and J. Danforth. 2003. "Health Status and Canada's Immigrant Population." *Social Science and Medicine* 57: 1981-995.

Ooka, E., and B. Wellman. 2006. "Does Social Capital Pay Off More within or between Ethnic Groups? Analyzing Job Searches in Five Toronto Ethnic Groups." In *Inside the Mosaic*, edited by E. Fong, 199-226. Toronto: University of Toronto Press.

Perez, C. 2002. "Health Status and Health Behaviour among Immigrants." *Health Reports* 13: 89-100.

Portes, A. 1998. "Social Capital: Its Origins and Applications in Modern Sociology." *Annual Review of Sociology* 24: 1-24.

PRI. 2005a. "What Impact Does Social Capital Have on the Health of Canadians?" Policy Research Initiative Project: Social Capital as a Public Policy Tool. Ottawa: Government of Canada.

– 2005b. "Measurement of Social Capital: Reference Document for Public Policy Research, Development, and Evaluation," Policy Research Initiative. Ottawa: Government of Canada.

Putnam, R. 1995. "Bowling Alone: America's Declining Social Capital." *Journal of Democracy* 6: 65-78.

– 2000. *Bowling Alone: The Collapse and Revival of American Community*. New York: Simon & Schuster.

– 2001. "Social Capital: Measurement and Consequences." *Canadian Journal of Policy Research* 2 (1): 41-51.

– 2007. "E Pluribus Unum: Diversity and Community in the Twenty-First Century." *Scandinavian Political Studies* 30 (2): 137-74.

Rivers, P.A., and F.G. Patino. 2006. "Barriers to Health Care Access for Latino Immigrants in the USA." *International Journal of Social Economics* 33 (3): 207-20.

Rose, R. 2000. "How Much Does Social Capital Add to Individual Health? A Survey Study of Russians." *Social Science and Medicine* 51: 1421-35.

Staber, U. 2006. "Social Capital Processes in Cross Cultural Management." *International Journal of Cross Cultural Management* 6 (2): 189-202.

Statistics Canada. 2006. *Canadian Community Health Survey User Guide*. Ottawa: Statistics Canada.

– 2007. *Longitudinal Survey of Immigrants to Canada, Wave 3 – Microdata User Guide.* Ottawa: Statistics Canada.

Subramanian, S.V., and I. Kawachi. 2004. "Income Inequality and Health: What Have We Learned So Far?" *Epidemiologic Reviews* 26: 78-91.

Ueno, K. 2004. "Emotional Consequences of Racial Concordance in Friendship Network and School Context." Paper presented at the annual meeting of the American Sociological Association, 14 August.

van Kemenade, S., J. Roy, and L. Bouchard. 2006. "Social Networks and Vulnerable Populations: Findings from the GSS." *Health Policy Research Bulletin* 2: 16-20.

Wen, M., D. Browning, and K. Cagney. 2003. "Poverty, Affluence, and Income Inequality: Neighborhood Economic Structure and Its Implications for Health." *Social Science and Medicine* 57 (5): 843-60.

Wooldridge, J. 2005. "Simple Solutions to the Initial Conditions Problem in Dynamic, Nonlinear Panel Data Models with Unobserved Heterogeneity." *Journal of Applied Econometrics* 1: 39-54.

Xue, L. 2008. "Social Capital and Labour Market Outcomes of Recent Immigrants to Canada: Employment Entry, Wages and Duration of Access to the First Job in Intended Occupation." Ph.D. dissertation, University of Ottawa.

Zeger, S.L., K. Liang, and P.S. Albert. 1998. "Models of Longitudinal Data: A Generalized Estimating Equation Approach." *Biometrics* 44: 1049-60.

Zhao, J. 2007a. "Socio-Economic Determinants of Health and Health Care Utilization of Recent Immigrants in Canada." Prepared for Citizenship and Immigration Canada.

– 2007b. "Sponsored Parents and Grandparents: A Comprehensive Picture." Prepared for Citizenship and Immigration Canada.

APPENDIX

TABLE A1
Social Capital Variables

Family and relatives

Having relatives in Canada upon landing	1 if LR[1] had relatives in Canada upon landing, 0 otherwise.
Number of relatives in Canada	Number of types of relatives (spouse, children, parents, grandparents, brothers or sisters, etc.) in Canada, ranging from 0 to 11.
Frequency of contact with family sponsors	Frequency of contact with family sponsor (0~1): 0: No sponsor or having not seen or talked to sponsors since arriving; Between 0 and 1: Seeing or talking to sponsors in varied frequencies; the higher the index, the more frequently LR contacts with sponsors. 1: Seeing or talking to sponsors every day.

Friends

Having friends in Canada upon landing	1 if LR had friends in Canada upon landing, 0 otherwise.
Having made new friends	1 if LR had made new friends, 0 otherwise.
Number of sources meeting friends	Number of sources meeting new friends other than workplace, ranging from 0 to 14.
Ethnic diversity of friends	Ethnical diversity of friend network (0~1): 0: No friends or all friends belong to the same ethnic or cultural groups as LR; Between 0 and 1: Some friends belong to the same ethnic or cultural groups as LR; the higher the index, the more ethnically diversified is the friend network. 1: None of the friends belong to the same ethnic or cultural groups as LR.
Frequency of contact with friends	Frequency of contact with friends (0~1): 0: No friends or having not seen or talked to friends since arriving; Between 0 and 1: Seeing or talking to friends in varied frequencies; the higher the index, the more frequently LR contacts with friends. 1: Seeing or talking to friends every day.

Group and organizational network

Number of organizations participated in	Number of organizations or groups LR participated in. ranging from 0 to 13.
Ethnic diversity of organizational network	Ethnical diversity of organizational network (0~1): 0: Not participated in any organization or all the members of all organizations belong to the same ethnic or cultural groups as LR; Between 0 and 1: Some members of organizations belong to the same ethnic or cultural groups as LR; the higher the index, the more ethnically diversified the organizational network. 1: None of the members of organizations belong to the same ethnic or cultural groups as LR.
Frequency of activities with organizations	Frequency of activities with organizations (0~1): 0: Not participated in any organization; Between 0 and 1: Having taken part in organizational activities in varied frequencies; the higher the index, the more frequently LR takes part in activities. 1: Having taken part in activities every day.
Numbers of organizations for which LR volunteered time	Number of organizations or groups that LR volunteered time for organizations or groups, 0 otherwise.

[1] LR: Longitudinal Respondent.
Source: Xue (2008); LSIC (2005).

About the Authors

ALICIA ADSERA is an associate research scholar and lecturer in public and international affairs at Woodrow Wilson School (Princeton University). Previously she was an associate professor at the University of Illinois at Chicago and a research affiliate at the Population Research Center of the University of Chicago. Her research centres on the areas of economic demography and international political economy. Her latest work focuses on the relation between economic conditions, family dynamics, and fertility in OECD (and most recently Latin American) countries, with a particular focus on migrants. She has received fellowships from NICHD and the Alfred P. Sloan Foundation, among others. Her work has been published in journals including the *American Economic Review, P&P Journal of Population Economics, Population Studies, Journal of Law Economics and Organization*, and *International Organization*.

BARRY R. CHISWICK is distinguished professor in the Department of Economics at the University of Illinois at Chicago. He is also program director for Migration Studies at IZA (Institute for the Study of Labor) in Bonn, Germany. His research focuses on the economics of immigration, the economics of language, and the economics of religion/ethnicity. He received a PhD in economics from Columbia University and an honorary PhD from Lund University, Sweden.

ANA FERRER is an associate professor in economics at the University of Calgary. She obtained her PhD from Boston University in 1999 and developed her research career in Canada. She is a member of the Canadian Labour Market and Skills Research Network (CLSRN). She is associated with Metropolis, an international network on immigration, where she is the priority leader for the Economic and Labour Market Integration Domain for research centres in Canada. Her work focuses on the economics of education and training and its links with the economics of immigration. Her current research interests also include the economics of the household.

TARA GILKINSON is a research analyst at Citizenship and Immigration Canada's Research and Evaluation Branch and a teacher at Humber College. She holds a bachelor's degree in sociology and psychology and a master's degree in immigration and settlement studies. Her current research interests include the mental health and well-being outcomes of immigrants.

DAVID A. GREEN is a professor in the economics department at the University of British Columbia and a research fellow with the Institute for Fiscal Studies at University College London. He has received a UBC Killam Research Prize and twice won the Harry Johnson Prize for best article in the *Canadian Journal of Economics*. His recent research includes work with Paul Beaudry investigating the impact of technological change and policy shifts on labour markets. His current work focuses on links between redistributive policies and labour market outcomes. He is the current editor of the *Canadian Journal of Economics*.

MICHAEL HAAN received his PhD from the Department of Sociology at the University of Toronto and is currently an assistant professor in the Department of Sociology at the University of Alberta. His primary research interests are in the areas of immigration, housing, and the Canadian labour market, and his research has been funded by the Killam Fund, Metropolis, Social Science and Humanities Research Council of Canada, Citizenship and Immigration Canada, and Human Resources and Skills Development Canada. He has published in journals including *Housing Studies, International Migration Review, Urban Studies*, and *Population Research and Policy Review*.

TED MCDONALD is a professor of economics at the University of New Brunswick. He completed his PhD in economics at the University of Melbourne in 1996 and was a lecturer at the University of Tasmania prior to accepting his current appointment at UNB in 2001. He is also the co-domain leader of the Economic and Labour Market Integration Domain of the Atlantic Metropolis Centre and the academic director of the UNB Research Data Centre. His main areas of research include the labour market outcomes of immigrants, the health status and health services use of immigrants and minority populations, and the provision of health services in rural and remote areas of Canada. He has published his work in a broad range of academic journals including *Social Science and Medicine, Canadian Public Policy, Industrial and Labor Relations Review, Journal of Human Resources*, and *Canadian Journal on Aging*.

PAUL W. MILLER is a professor in the School of Economics and Finance at Curtin University of Technology in Perth, Australia, and is also a research fellow of the Institute for the Study of Labor (IZA) in Bonn, Germany. His primary research interest is labour market performance, particularly as it relates to educational attainment, gender, and ethnic and racial origin. He has published extensively in both Australian and overseas journals, including the *American Economic Review, Canadian Journal of Economics,* and *Economic Journal.* He is also the co-author of *The Economics of Language: International Analyses,* with Barry R. Chiswick (Routledge 2007).

ELIZABETH RUDDICK is director general of the Research and Evaluation Branch at Citizenship and Immigration Canada. Since joining the department in 1992, she has been responsible for a range of research and policy activities, development of new longitudinal databases to support research and evaluation of outcomes, policies for the skilled worker, and economic immigration programs, evaluation, and audit. In her current position she leads CIC's immigration and citizenship research program and heads the department's evaluation function. Prior to working in the immigration field, she held a senior position in macroeconomic forecasting and in energy economics, working in the public and private sectors in Canada. She began her career in 1973 at the Economic Council of Canada. She holds a bachelor's degree in commerce from McGill University and a master's degree in economics from the University of British Columbia.

HERBERT J. SCHUETZE is an associate professor in the Department of Economics at the University of Victoria. He earned a PhD in economics at McMaster University in 2000, and spent two years at Dartmouth College in New Hampshire before arriving at the University of Victoria. His primary area of expertise is applied micro-econometrics in the fields of public and labour economics. His research focuses on various aspects related to self-employment, including factors that influence the self-employment decision and the characteristics of self-employment ventures. His research is well recognized in the literature, with publications in general interest and field journals as well as keynote addresses at a number of international venues.

ARTHUR SWEETMAN is an economist and a professor in the School of Policy Studies at Queen's University. He is cross-appointed in the Department of Economics and the Department of Community Health and Epidemiology. His research interests are broad but primarily involve empirical issues in the areas of immigration, education, labour market, and health policy.

CASEY WARMAN received his PhD in economics from Carleton University in 2006. He teaches in the Economics Department at Queen's University. His research interests primarily involve empirical issues in the areas of immigration, gender differentials, labour market, and health economics.

CHRISTOPHER WORSWICK is an associate professor in the Department of Economics at Carleton University. Prior to moving to Ottawa, he was a faculty member for four years at the University of Melbourne. His main areas of research are labour economics and development economics. A particular focus of his research is in the area of the economics of immigration. In 2008-09, he was the priority leader for the Economic and Labour Market Integration priority area for the Metropolis network of research centres in Canada. He has twice won the John Vanderkamp Prize for best article in *Canadian Public Policy*.

Li Xue is a senior research analyst at the Research and Evaluation Branch of Citizenship and Immigration Canada (CIC). She holds a PhD in economics from the University of Ottawa. Her research interests include labour and health economics. Her current research focuses on labour market outcomes of immigrants, immigrant field of study, education-occupation match, and other related immigration issues.

Jun Zhao is currently an economist in the Applied Research and Analysis Directorate at Department of Health Canada. He has a PhD in economics from the University of Ottawa. His research interests include monetary economics, environmental economics, and health economics. His current research focuses on health care system efficiency.

Queen's Policy Studies
Recent Publications

The Queen's Policy Studies Series is dedicated to the exploration of major public policy issues that confront governments and society in Canada and other nations.

Manuscript submission. We are pleased to consider new book proposals and manuscripts. Preliminary enquiries are welcome. A subvention is normally required for the publication of an academic book. Please direct questions or proposals to the Publications Unit by email at spspress@queensu.ca, or visit our website at: www.queensu.ca/sps/books, or contact us by phone at (613) 533 - 2192.

Our books are available from good bookstores everywhere, including the Queen's University bookstore (http://www.campusbookstore.com/). McGill-Queen's University Press is the exclusive world representative and distributor of books in the series. A full catalogue and ordering information may be found on their web site (http://mqup.mcgill.ca/).

School of Policy Studies

Taking Stock: Research on Teaching and Learning in Higher Education, Julia Christensen Hughes and Joy Mighty (eds.), 2010, Paper 978-1-55339-271-2 Cloth 978-1-55339-272-9

Architects and Innovators: Building the Department of Foreign Affairs and International Trade, 1909–2009/Architectes et innovateurs : le développement du ministère des Affaires étrangères et du Commerce international,de 1909 à 2009, Greg Donaghy and Kim Richard Nossal (eds.), 2009, Paper 978-1-55339-269-9 Cloth 978-1-55339-270-5

Academic Transformation: The Forces Reshaping Higher Education in Ontario, Ian D. Clark, Greg Moran, Michael L. Skolnik, and David Trick, 2009, Paper 978-1-55339-238-5 Cloth 978-1-55339-265-1

The New Federal Policy Agenda and the Voluntary Sector: On the Cutting Edge, Rachel Laforest (ed.), 2009. Paper 978-1-55339-132-6

The Afghanistan Challenge: Hard Realities and Strategic Choices, Hans-Georg Ehrhart and Charles Pentland (eds.), 2009. Paper 978-1-55339-241-5

Measuring What Matters in Peace Operations and Crisis Management, Sarah Jane Meharg, 2009. Paper 978-1-55339-228-6 Cloth ISBN 978-1-55339-229-3

International Migration and the Governance of Religious Diversity, Paul Bramadat and Matthias Koenig (eds.), 2009. Paper 978-1-55339-266-8 Cloth ISBN 978-1-55339-267-5

Who Goes? Who Stays? What Matters? Accessing and Persisting in Post-Secondary Education in Canada, Ross Finnie, Richard E. Mueller, Arthur Sweetman, and Alex Usher (eds.), 2008. Paper 978-1-55339-221-7 Cloth ISBN 978-1-55339-222-4

Economic Transitions with Chinese Characteristics: Thirty Years of Reform and Opening Up, Arthur Sweetman and Jun Zhang (eds.), 2009. Paper 978-1-55339-225-5 Cloth ISBN 978-1-55339-226-2

Economic Transitions with Chinese Characteristics: Social Change During Thirty Years of Reform, Arthur Sweetman and Jun Zhang (eds.), 2009. Paper 978-1-55339-234-7 Cloth ISBN 978-1-55339-235-4

Dear Gladys: Letters from Over There, Gladys Osmond (Gilbert Penney ed.), 2009. Paper ISBN 978-1-55339-223-1

Immigration and Integration in Canada in the Twenty-first Century, John Biles, Meyer Burstein, and James Frideres (eds.), 2008. Paper ISBN 978-1-55339-216-3 Cloth ISBN 978-1-55339-217-0

Robert Stanfield's Canada, Richard Clippingdale, 2008. ISBN 978-1-55339-218-7

Exploring Social Insurance: Can a Dose of Europe Cure Canadian Health Care Finance?
Colleen Flood, Mark Stabile, and Carolyn Tuohy (eds.), 2008.
Paper ISBN 978-1-55339-136-4 Cloth ISBN 978-1-55339-213-2

Canada in NORAD, 1957–2007: A History, Joseph T. Jockel, 2007.
Paper ISBN 978-1-55339-134-0 Cloth ISBN 978-1-55339-135-7

Canadian Public-Sector Financial Management, Andrew Graham, 2007.
Paper ISBN 978-1-55339-120-3 Cloth ISBN 978-1-55339-121-0

Emerging Approaches to Chronic Disease Management in Primary Health Care,
John Dorland and Mary Ann McColl (eds.), 2007. Paper ISBN 978-1-55339-130-2
Cloth ISBN 978-1-55339-131-9

Fulfilling Potential, Creating Success: Perspectives on Human Capital Development,
Garnett Picot, Ron Saunders and Arthur Sweetman (eds.), 2007.
Paper ISBN 978-1-55339-127-2 Cloth ISBN 978-1-55339-128-9

Reinventing Canadian Defence Procurement: A View from the Inside, Alan S. Williams, 2006.
Paper ISBN 0-9781693-0-1 (Published in association with Breakout Educational Network)

SARS in Context: Memory, History, Policy, Jacalyn Duffin and Arthur Sweetman (eds.),
2006. Paper ISBN 978-0-7735-3194-9 Cloth ISBN 978-0-7735-3193-2
(Published in association with McGill-Queen's University Press)

Dreamland: How Canada's Pretend Foreign Policy has Undermined Sovereignty,
Roy Rempel, 2006. Paper ISBN 1-55339-118-7 Cloth ISBN 1-55339-119-5
(Published in association with Breakout Educational Network)

Canadian and Mexican Security in the New North America: Challenges and Prospects,
Jordi Díez (ed.), 2006. Paper ISBN 978-1-55339-123-4 Cloth ISBN 978-1-55339-122-7

*Global Networks and Local Linkages: The Paradox of Cluster Development in an Open
Economy*, David A. Wolfe and Matthew Lucas (eds.), 2005. Paper ISBN 1-55339-047-4
Cloth ISBN 1-55339-048-2

Choice of Force: Special Operations for Canada, David Last and Bernd Horn (eds.), 2005.
Paper ISBN 1-55339-044-X Cloth ISBN 1-55339-045-8

Force of Choice: Perspectives on Special Operations, Bernd Horn, J. Paul de B. Taillon, and
David Last (eds.), 2004. Paper ISBN 1-55339-042-3 Cloth 1-55339-043-1

New Missions, Old Problems, Douglas L. Bland, David Last, Franklin Pinch, and
Alan Okros (eds.), 2004. Paper ISBN 1-55339-034-2 Cloth 1-55339-035-0

*The North American Democratic Peace: Absence of War and Security Institution-Building in
Canada-US Relations*, 1867-1958, Stéphane Roussel, 2004.
Paper ISBN 0-88911-937-6 Cloth 0-88911-932-2

Implementing Primary Care Reform: Barriers and Facilitators, Ruth Wilson, S.E.D. Shortt,
and John Dorland (eds.), 2004. Paper ISBN 1-55339-040-7 Cloth 1-55339-041-5

Social and Cultural Change, David Last, Franklin Pinch, Douglas L. Bland, and
Alan Okros (eds.), 2004. Paper ISBN 1-55339-032-6 Cloth 1-55339-033-4

Clusters in a Cold Climate: Innovation Dynamics in a Diverse Economy, David A. Wolfe and
Matthew Lucas (eds.), 2004. Paper ISBN 1-55339-038-5 Cloth 1-55339-039-3

Canada Without Armed Forces? Douglas L. Bland (ed.), 2004.
Paper ISBN 1-55339-036-9 Cloth 1-55339-037-7

Campaigns for International Security: Canada's Defence Policy at the Turn of the Century,
Douglas L. Bland and Sean M. Maloney, 2004. Paper ISBN 0-88911-962-7
Cloth 0-88911-964-3

Understanding Innovation in Canadian Industry, Fred Gault (ed.), 2003.
Paper ISBN 1-55339-030-X Cloth 1-55339-031-8

Delicate Dances: Public Policy and the Nonprofit Sector, Kathy L. Brock (ed.), 2003. Paper ISBN 0-88911-953-8 Cloth 0-88911-955-4

Beyond the National Divide: Regional Dimensions of Industrial Relations, Mark Thompson, Joseph B. Rose, and Anthony E. Smith (eds.), 2003. Paper ISBN 0-88911-963-5 Cloth 0-88911-965-1

The Nonprofit Sector in Interesting Times: Case Studies in a Changing Sector, Kathy L. Brock and Keith G. Banting (eds.), 2003. Paper ISBN 0-88911-941-4 Cloth 0-88911-943-0

Clusters Old and New: The Transition to a Knowledge Economy in Canada's Regions, David A. Wolfe (ed.), 2003. Paper ISBN 0-88911-959-7 Cloth 0-88911-961-9

The e-Connected World: Risks and Opportunities, Stephen Coleman (ed.), 2003. Paper ISBN 0-88911-945-7 Cloth 0-88911-947-3

Centre for the Study of Democracy

The Authentic Voice of Canada: R.B. Bennett's Speeches in the House of Lords, 1941-1947, Christopher McCreery and Arthur Milnes (eds.), 2009. Paper 978-1-55339-275-0 Cloth ISBN 978-1-55339-276-7

Age of the Offered Hand: The Cross-Border Partnership Between President George H.W. Bush and Prime-Minister Brian Mulroney, A Documentary History, James McGrath and Arthur Milnes (eds.), 2009. Paper ISBN 978-1-55339-232-3 Cloth ISBN 978-1-55339-233-0

In Roosevelt's Bright Shadow: Presidential Addresses About Canada from Taft to Obama in Honour of FDR's 1938 Speech at Queen's University, Christopher McCreery and Arthur Milnes (eds.), 2009. Paper ISBN 978-1-55339-230-9 Cloth ISBN 978-1-55339-231-6

Politics of Purpose, 40th Anniversary Edition, The Right Honourable John N. Turner 17th Prime Minister of Canada, Elizabeth McIninch and Arthur Milnes (eds.), 2009. Paper ISBN 978-1-55339-227-9 Cloth ISBN 978-1-55339-224-8

Bridging the Divide: Religious Dialogue and Universal Ethics, Papers for The InterAction Council, Thomas S. Axworthy (ed.), 2008. Paper ISBN 978-1-55339-219-4 Cloth ISBN 978-1-55339-220-0

Institute of Intergovernmental Relations

The Democratic Dilemma: Reforming the Canadian Senate, Jennifer Smith (ed.), 2009. Paper 978-1-55339-190-6

Canada: The State of the Federation 2006/07, vol. 20, *Transitions – Fiscal and Political Federalism in an Era of Change,* John R. Allan, Thomas J. Courchene, and Christian Leuprecht (eds.), 2009. Paper ISBN 978-1-55339-189-0 Cloth ISBN 978-1-55339-191-3

Comparing Federal Systems, Third Edition, Ronald L. Watts, 2008. Paper ISBN 978-1-55339-188-3

Canada: The State of the Federation 2005, vol. 19, *Quebec and Canada in the New Century – New Dynamics, New Opportunities,* Michael Murphy (ed.), 2007. Paper ISBN 978-1-55339-018-3 Cloth ISBN 978-1-55339-017-6

Spheres of Governance: Comparative Studies of Cities in Multilevel Governance Systems, Harvey Lazar and Christian Leuprecht (eds.), 2007. Paper ISBN 978-1-55339-019-0 Cloth ISBN 978-1-55339-129-6

Canada: The State of the Federation 2004, vol. 18, *Municipal-Federal-Provincial Relations in Canada,* Robert Young and Christian Leuprecht (eds.), 2006. Paper ISBN 1-55339-015-6 Cloth ISBN 1-55339-016-4

Canadian Fiscal Arrangements: What Works, What Might Work Better, Harvey Lazar (ed.), 2005. Paper ISBN 1-55339-012-1 Cloth ISBN 1-55339-013-X

Canada: The State of the Federation 2003, vol. 17, *Reconfiguring Aboriginal-State Relations*, Michael Murphy (ed.), 2005. Paper ISBN 1-55339-010-5 Cloth ISBN 1-55339-011-3

Canada: The State of the Federation 2002, vol. 16, *Reconsidering the Institutions of Canadian Federalism*, J. Peter Meekison, Hamish Telford, and Harvey Lazar (eds.), 2004. Paper ISBN 1-55339-009-1 Cloth ISBN 1-55339-008-3

Federalism and Labour Market Policy: Comparing Different Governance and Employment Strategies, Alain Noël (ed.), 2004. Paper ISBN 1-55339-006-7 Cloth ISBN 1-55339-007-5

The Impact of Global and Regional Integration on Federal Systems: A Comparative Analysis, Harvey Lazar, Hamish Telford, and Ronald L. Watts (eds.), 2003. Paper ISBN 1-55339-002-4 Cloth ISBN 1-55339-003-2

John Deutsch Institute for the Study of Economic Policy

Discount Rates for the Evaluation of Public Private Partnerships, David F. Burgess and Glenn P. Jenkins (eds.), 2010. Paper ISBN 978-1-55339-163-0 Cloth ISBN 978-1-55339-164-7

Retirement Policy Issues in Canada, Michael G. Abbott, Charles M. Beach, Robin W. Boadway, and James G. MacKinnon (eds.), 2009. Paper ISBN 978-1-55339-161-6 Cloth ISBN 978-1-55339-162-3

The 2006 Federal Budget: Rethinking Fiscal Priorities, Charles M. Beach, Michael Smart, and Thomas A. Wilson (eds.), 2007. Paper ISBN 978-1-55339-125-8 Cloth ISBN 978-1-55339-126-6

Health Services Restructuring in Canada: New Evidence and New Directions, Charles M. Beach, Richard P. Chaykowksi, Sam Shortt, France St-Hilaire, and Arthur Sweetman (eds.), 2006. Paper ISBN 978-1-55339-076-3 Cloth ISBN 978-1-55339-075-6

A Challenge for Higher Education in Ontario, Charles M. Beach (ed.), 2005. Paper ISBN 1-55339-074-1 Cloth ISBN 1-55339-073-3

Current Directions in Financial Regulation, Frank Milne and Edwin H. Neave (eds.), Policy Forum Series no. 40, 2005. Paper ISBN 1-55339-072-5 Cloth ISBN 1-55339-071-7

Higher Education in Canada, Charles M. Beach, Robin W. Boadway, and R. Marvin McInnis (eds.), 2005. Paper ISBN 1-55339-070-9 Cloth ISBN 1-55339-069-5

Financial Services and Public Policy, Christopher Waddell (ed.), 2004. Paper ISBN 1-55339-068-7 Cloth ISBN 1-55339-067-9

The 2003 Federal Budget: Conflicting Tensions, Charles M. Beach and Thomas A. Wilson (eds.), Policy Forum Series no. 39, 2004. Paper ISBN 0-88911-958-9 Cloth ISBN 0-88911-956-2

Canadian Immigration Policy for the 21st Century, Charles M. Beach, Alan G. Green, and Jeffrey G. Reitz (eds.), 2003. Paper ISBN 0-88911-954-6 Cloth ISBN 0-88911-952-X

Framing Financial Structure in an Information Environment, Thomas J. Courchene and Edwin H. Neave (eds.), Policy Forum Series no. 38, 2003. Paper ISBN 0-88911-950-3 Cloth ISBN 0-88911-948-1

Our publications may be purchased at leading bookstores, including the Queen's University Bookstore (http://www.campusbookstore.com/) or can be ordered online from: McGill-Queen's University Press, at **http://mqup.mcgill.ca/ordering.php**

For more information about new and backlist titles from Queen's Policy Studies, visit http://www.queensu.ca/sps/books or visit the McGill-Queen's University Press web site at: **http://mqup.mcgill.ca/**